SS.00

REF
DV
266.4
.E17
2004

D1119871

TERRORISM

TERRORISM

A Guide to Events and Documents

Michael Kronenwetter

Greenwood Press
Westport, Connecticut • London

Library of Congress Cataloging-in-Publication Data

Kronenwetter, Michael.
 Terrorism : a guide to events and documents / Michael Kronenwetter.
  p. cm.
 Includes bibliographical references and index.
 ISBN 0–313–32578–2
  1. Terrorism. 2. Terrorism—United States. 3. Terrorists. I. Title.
 HV6431.K698 2004
 303.6´25—dc22   2004006619

British Library Cataloguing in Publication Data is available.

Library of Congress Catalog Card Number: 2004006619
ISBN: 0–313–32578–2

First published in 2004

Greenwood Press, 88 Post Road West, Westport, CT 06881
An imprint of Greenwood Publishing Group, Inc.
www.greenwood.com

Printed in the United States of America

The paper used in this book complies with the
Permanent Paper Standard issued by the National
Information Standards Organization (Z39.48–1984).

10 9 8 7 6 5 4 3 2 1

Copyright Acknowledgment

The author and the publisher gratefully acknowledge permission for use of the following
material:

"Open Letter from Osama Bin Laden" by Jason Burke, © 2002, has been reprinted with
permission by *The Observer*.

Contents

Introduction

Over the past century and a half, terrorism has been as common in the United States as in most other countries. Yet, before September 11, 2001, most Americans thought of terrorism as something foreign to the American experience. Terrorism was a terrible thing, we told ourselves, but it was something that happened in the Middle East. Or in Latin America. Or in Northern Ireland. Or on the mainland of Europe.

It didn't happen here.

Even when it undeniably *did* happen here—as when the Alfred P. Murrah building was destroyed by a truck bomb in 1995—we dismissed it as an aberration. We were shocked and appalled, but not overly worried, because it was unlikely to happen to us ever again.

We were vividly aware of the terrorist violence that took place in the United States, but we thought of it in other terms, and called it by other names.

We called it "resistance to Reconstruction" when the Ku Klux Klan terrorized freed slaves after the Civil War. We called it "labor troubles" when a bomb went off during a demonstration in Haymarket Square in Chicago in 1886. We called it "vigilantism" when black men were lynched in the first half of the twentieth century, and we called it "racism" when white men bombed black churches in the second half. We called it "madness" when the Unabomber started mailing bombs to scientists, academics, and businesspeople in 1985.

We called the homegrown American terrorists by other names as well. We called them "lone gunmen" when they shot our Presidents. We called them "racists" when they murdered black people. We called them "religious fanatics" when they killed abortion doctors. And we called them "right-wing crackpots" when they killed a Jewish radio talk-show host in Denver.

Some of these names were accurate enough, as far as they went, but they masked a broader reality. It was a classic example of the old cliché: we couldn't see the forest for the trees. We failed to notice that all these different things were really one thing.

Now, of course, we do.

The attacks of September 11 have thrust terrorism into the forefront of America's, and the world's, attention. The United States has responded to its new understanding of the terrorist threat by launching the so-called "War on Terrorism." In its first two years alone, that massive effort has overthrown the governments of two foreign countries, while drastically transforming both America's role in the world and America's view of itself.

Americans have stopped thinking of terrorist attacks as rare, isolated, and almost anarchic events, and come to regard them as incidents in an ongoing war. We have stopped seeing terrorists as unbalanced individuals and begun to see them as soldiers-without-uniforms in a powerful marauding army. In addition, we have gone from thinking of ourselves as immune to terrorism to thinking of ourselves as the primary victims of it. Most importantly, we have come to think of terrorism as a monolithic threat to our liberties, and even, perhaps, to our very survival.

In other words, we have gone from one extreme to the other—from all but ignoring the terrorist threat to being obsessed by it. In our shock and horror, we have, perhaps, invested the terrorists with more power than they actually possess. The reality is that terrorism is both a more ubiquitous phenomenon and a more limited threat than many Americans now believe.

This book attempts to explore the nature of that phenomenon, and to assess that threat, by approaching the subject of terrorism from a variety of different directions, and examining it in a variety of different, but complementary, ways.

The book begins by defining terrorism and exploring the ruthless philosophy that underlies it—a philosophy that regards individual human beings as victims to be sacrificed on the altar of some all-important cause. It goes on to provide both a narrative history and an extensive chronology of world terrorism.

Four historically important terrorist acts are examined in some detail: a 1906 lynching in Tennessee that resulted in the only trial ever held before the U.S. Supreme Court; a massive flaunting of power by the Ku Klux Klan some years later; Black September's attack on the Israeli athletes at the Munich Olympics in 1972; and, of course, the traumatizing events of September 11, 2001. Taken together, these examples illustrate the many forms of terrorism, the key strategies that terrorists employ, and the range of purposes that terrorism has been used to serve.

The United States Military Intelligence Center's list of known terrorist organizations is a graphic demonstration of the sheer range of the terrorist threat in the world. In addition, more detailed descriptions are provided of dozens of the most important groups, both past and present. Where possible, each description includes a brief account of the group's history and goals, an estimate of its size and influence, and a sampling of the outrages attributed to it.

Other sections of this book discuss the methods, tactics, and weapons used by terrorists—including the horrifying weapons of mass destruction that many experts fear may be the terrorists' weapons of choice in the future—and explore the attraction that terrorism holds for many individuals, groups, and movements.

Finally, this book includes a number of interesting and historically significant documents. These range from official government overviews of the terrorist threat, to international agreements related to terrorism, to presidential declarations on the subject, to statements issued by terrorists themselves in which they attempt to clarify their own motivations and intentions.

Taken together, the contents of this book provide the reader with a much-needed realistic perspective on this critical subject.

❶

The Philosophy of Terror

Of all the problems facing the world in the twenty-first century, few are more frightening, more immediate, or likely to menace us longer than terrorism. Although ancient in origin, terrorism has emerged as the weapon of choice for today's militants. It's not hard to see why. Terrorism is a weapon that can, at least temporarily, put a small number of determined fanatics on equal footing with the strongest military powers. Whole societies can be thrown into turmoil, and even chaos, by a relatively small group of ruthless and determined individuals.

Terrorism is a small weapon that has enormous range and firepower. In 1914, a single fanatic with a pistol set in motion the events that resulted in World War I. In 2001, fewer than 20 men brought down the World Trade Center, destroyed a large section of the Pentagon, and changed the United States' sense of itself forever. But terrorism is not a peculiarly American problem. It is a world problem. In fact, terrorism of one kind or another was a major problem for much of the rest of the world long before the United States awoke to the seriousness of the threat in September 2001.

Ordinary citizens all over the world mourn those close to them who have been lost to bombs, bullets, and other forms of terrorist violence, and are themselves at risk of falling victim to similar outrages at any time. Governments tremble. Whole societies live in fear, and not just in nations where terrorism occasionally becomes an immediate, omnipresent threat, as it has in Northern Ireland and Israel.

Terrorism has more than the ability to destroy the peace of nations; it has the power to unsettle the lives of millions of people, even those who are far removed from any military conflict and who have never been within hundreds of miles of any terrorist act. The perceived threat of terrorism infects the lives of millions of people like an insidious disease. In the present climate, we have all been contaminated by it to some degree. Everyone who travels by plane is subjected to delays and potential indignities because of the security prompted by terrorism. Anyone who attends a major sporting event is similarly inconvenienced. And who can ride an elevator to the upper floors of a skyscraper without reflecting with some trepidation on the fate of those who ascended to top of the World Trade Center on September 11, 2001?

Until that infamous date, most residents of the United States felt relatively safe from the worst dangers of the terrorism that plagued much of the rest of the world. When most North Americans thought about terrorism at all, they thought of it as an Old World and Third World phenomenon. They associated it with revolutions in the former colonies of European powers, or with the Israeli-Palestinian conflict, or with drug wars in places like Colombia. They did not, for the most part, associate it with their own communities, much less with their own lives.

The bombing of the Alfred P. Murrah Building in Oklahoma City rocked that complacency, but failed to destroy it. The Oklahoma City bombing felt like an aberration to most Americans. It was the rough equivalent of a bridge collapsing on a new highway: a freak event that was terribly unfortunate for those who happened to be there at the time, but was unlikely to be repeated. Even though Timothy McVeigh had help, he seemed to belong on the short list of deranged loners and criminal misfits to which American law enforcement had relegated the assassins, Lee Harvey Oswald, James Earl Ray, and Sirhan Sirhan—strange and twisted individuals who acted alone, or almost alone. They belonged to no large group. They were part of no ongoing conspiracy. Like those crackpot assassins, the crackpot Oklahoma City terrorists were part of no continuing pattern, no ongoing threat. You caught them. You executed them or put them away for life. Then you were safe.

People who believed otherwise were likely to be dismissed as cranks, or worse.

The attacks of September 11 shattered America's complacency for at least a generation. Since that date and for some time to come, the fear of terrorism has been and will be as deeply ingrained in Americans as it has long been in the residents of Israel and Northern Ireland.

The actual risk that any particular person will become a victim of terrorism remains small, but the awareness of that risk afflicts almost everyone. In countries like the United States, that awareness is constantly reinforced, not only by the graphic reminders disseminated by a sensationalistic and pervasive news media, but by the well-meant warnings of local, state, and national governments.

At one time, terrorism was considered virtually synonymous with anarchism. In the mid-twentieth century, it was identified largely with left-wing revolutionaries and right-wing reactionaries. At the moment, it is associated primarily with the Middle East—with the religious zealots of al-Qaeda and their Islamist brethren, and with the antagonists in the Palestinian-Israeli conflict. But terrorism was never limited to political fanatics, and it is certainly not limited to religious fanatics today.

Terrorism may be more compatible with some ideologies than with others, but it is a weapon that can be used by the advocates of virtually any cause. Because of this, terrorism is bound to remain a serious danger long after today's terrorists have disappeared. The threat of terrorism may increase or decrease, but it will not go away. The United States is starting to recognize this reality, but still doesn't know what to do about it.

For a long time, the government treated terrorism as a criminal matter. Now—with the so-called War on Terrorism—it seems determined to treat it as a military one. The criminal approach seems inadequate to deal with international networks of interconnected organizations bent on sowing death and chaos around the globe, some of which are suspected of getting their hands on weapons of mass destruction. On the other hand, the military approach seems wildly inappropriate to the threat presented by small groups of individuals, who are often unidentified, and who, in any event, operate in secret and use weapons like box cutters and the U.S. Postal Service to wreak havoc throughout entire societies.

Neither the criminal nor the military approach seems to be entirely relevant to the problem. Even together, they seem somehow beside the point. They are like some over-the-counter cold medicine that acts only on the symptoms of a cold. Even when they stop some particular terrorist group or operation, they leave the virulent infection of terrorism untouched. Unfortunately, there is not, as yet, any coherent alternative.

The first step in dealing with any problem is to see it clearly. In the case of terrorism, that is not easy. Shock and outrage cloud our view. Faced with a truly horrible terrorist act—a pretty young woman with a bomb strapped to her body walks into a crowd of happy teenagers waiting for a bus and blows herself and several other pretty young women into a bloody mass of gore—it is tempting to see terrorism as a manifestation of pure evil. After September 11, the terrorists of the American imagination have become a breed of demon: malevolent spirits that act out of irrational hatred toward all that is good and human.

But this is a fantasy, and it is a dangerous one. It grants terrorists a kind of unnatural power they do not, in fact, possess. Specific acts of terrorism may seem arbitrary and impossibly wanton, but they are rarely random and never pointless. Terrorism is not a tornado that strikes without reason and destroys without meaning. There is purpose behind even the most apparently senseless terrorist act. In this book, we will look at the goals and intentions of the terrorists, and at the methods and tactics they use to achieve them.

DEFINING TERRORISM

"A man with one clock always knows what time it is, but a man with many clocks never knows what time it is." That old saw has to do with the way we understand time. Something similar could be said about the way we understand terrorism.

We hear about terrorism every day. The news media are filled with coverage of terrorist incidents, and the subject is often discussed on radio and television talk shows. Politicians and government officials frequently remind us of the danger it presents. The United States is even fighting a so-called war against it. As a society, we are not only keenly aware of terrorism, we are almost obsessed by it. So, naturally, we assume that we know exactly what it is. And, in a sense, we do.

Why then is it so hard to come up with a definition that everyone can accept? Even within the U.S. government, as the U.S. State Department has pointed out, "No one definition of terrorism has gained universal acceptance" (U.S. Department of State 1999). A single book—*Political Terrorism*, by Alex P. Schmidt, Albert J. Yongman, and others—cites more than a hundred different definitions of the term. As with a variety of clocks, having so many definitions serves to obscure, rather than to clarify, the real meaning of the term.

One thing we know for sure: terrorism is wrong.

Since September 11, 2001, the word *terrorism* has taken the place that was once held by *Communism* and, before that, by *fascism*, in the American lexicon. It has become almost a synonym for both "evil" and "enemy." In the same way, the terrorist has become the great villain, the exemplar of the evildoer. Like *murder* or *rape*, *terrorism* and *terrorist* are words that carry the heavy weight of condemnation. They are not words you would ever use to describe something of which you approve.

Beyond that, most Americans use the term *terrorism* loosely, lumping together all kinds of violent activities under a blanket of opprobrium. We know that terrorism is a bad thing, and that is enough for us.

We talk about terrorism *in general*, as if every terrorist act were equivalent to every other. We speak as if there were two types of people in the world, the terrorists and the rest of us, and the dividing line were clear. More than that, we speak of terrorists and those who support terrorism as if they were one and the same, and anyone who falls into either category is equally guilty.

Because our condemnation of terrorism is so strong and so absolute, it is necessary for us to deny that we—in the sense of our country, our organizations, or anyone on our "side"—are guilty of it. This explains much of the problem governments have in coming up with a satisfactory definition. The difficulty is not finding a way to define what terrorism is; it is finding a way to define what it isn't. At least, by implication. We must be careful to leave our own actions out of it. We could hardly condemn terrorism so unequivocally if we were open to credible charges of terrorism ourselves.

A standard American dictionary has this definition: "The . . . use of force or threats to demoralize, intimidate, and subjugate, esp., such use as a political weapon or policy" (Guralnik 1980, 1469). It's not a bad definition, but it is extremely broad—so broad that it covers activities that most people would probably not regard as terrorism. It includes, for example, most forms of conventional warfare.

In his book, *The Lessons of Terror: A History of Warfare Against Civilians: Why It Has Always Failed and Why It Will Fail Again*, the popular author and historian Caleb Carr defines terrorism as: "[T]he deliberate military targeting of civilians as a method of affecting the political behavior of nations and leaders" (Carr 2002, 1). Unlike the previously quoted definition, Carr's is so narrow that it would exclude a wide range of acts that many people would argue do constitute terrorism. It would not include, for example, the terrorism inflicted by governments on their own citizens, nor the intimidation of ethnic minorities by groups like the Ku Klux Klan.

The U.S. government would not be satisfied with either of the above definitions. Nor with any other single definition. As we have already seen, the government finds terrorism so tricky to define that different departments are forced to use different definitions, at different times, and in different contexts. One section of the U.S. Code of Federal Regulations, for example, defines terrorism as "[T]he unlawful use of force and violence against persons or property to intimidate or coerce a government, the civilian population, or any segment thereof, in furtherance of political or social objectives." (28 C.F.R.) Since 1983, however, the State Department Office on Counterterrorism has used a definition from a different section of the Code: "The term 'terrorism' means premeditated, politically motivated violence perpetrated against noncombatant targets by subnational groups or clandestine agents, usually intended to influence an audience (Title 22 A.S.C.)."

When members of the Bush administration first began to talk about fighting a "war" on terrorism, they didn't spell out what they meant by the term, but they seemed to be talking primarily about attacks on American citizens and institutions by foreign individuals and nongovernmental groups. The massive omnibus bill known as the USA Patriot Act, passed hurriedly in the wake of September 11, amended the government's earlier definitions in a confusing variety of ways that are primarily designed to allow U.S. law enforcement agencies free rein to investigate terrorism and ferret out terrorists.

An essential difference can be seen between the definitions used by the government and those designed for lay readers. The latter attempt to capture the common understanding of the term, while the governmental definitions are essentially legalistic and self-serving.

The key word in the first governmental definition given above is *unlawful*, as if terrorism could be distinguished from other kinds of violence by the fact that there are laws against it. Terrorism is what the law says it is. By implication, nothing that is done under cover of the law can be regarded as terrorism.

Similarly, in the definition used by the State Department, terrorism is limited to the actions of "subnational groups or clandestine agents." This effectively exempts the actions of the uniformed military and most other government agencies from any charge of terrorism. At the same time, the State Department "interprets" the term *noncombatant* in this definition "to include military personnel who at the time of the incident are unarmed or not on duty . . . We also consider as acts of terrorism attacks on military installations or on armed military personnel when a state of military hostilities does not exist at the site, such as bombings against U.S. bases in Europe, the Philippines, or elsewhere" (U.S. Department of State 1999).

Such interpretations give the game away. Having ruled out the armed forces as potential perpetrators of terrorism, the State Department considers them potential victims of it. In this way, the government gerrymanders a definition of terrorism that can only be applied to its enemies, and not to itself.

The Federal Bureau of Investigation has a mandate to investigate and combat domestic terrorism, and the definition it uses is carefully crafted for that task. To the FBI, domestic terrorists are, "[g]roups or individuals operating entirely inside the United States, attempting to influence the U.S. government or population to effect political or social change by engaging in criminal activity" (FBI 2002). This is one of the few significant definitions of terrorism that excludes any reference, even by implication, to violence. Many laws prohibit nonviolent activities undertaken in support of terrorists or terrorist activities, but the FBI may be unique in maintaining that even groups and individuals that never participate in violence, or assist those who do, may be rightly designated as terrorist organizations. A group need only engage in "criminal activity" with the goal of achieving "political or social change." This formulation is so broad that it could be interpreted to include virtually every form of nonviolent civil disobedience, even blocking public sidewalks or parading without a permit. It is so broad that it comes perilously close to labeling political protest itself a form of terrorism.

Governments are not the only entities that try to define themselves out of any possibility of being labeled as terrorists. Many organizations accused of engaging in terrorism do the same, some in an effort to justify themselves to others, and others in an effort to justify their actions to themselves.

In February 2002, an op-ed piece by President Yasser Arafat of the Palestinian Authority appeared in *The New York Times*. Both Arafat and the Palestinian Authority have long been accused by Israel and others of supporting, planning, and carrying out terrorism. In his editorial, however, Arafat "condemn(ed) the attacks carried out by terrorist groups against Israeli civilians," and declared that, "[t]hese groups do not represent the Palestinian people or their legitimate aspirations for freedom. They are terrorist organizations, and I am determined to put an end to their activities" (Arafat 2002).

The Popular Front for the Liberation of Palestine (PFLP), which had carried out many of the attacks to which Arafat was referring, immediately issued a press release denying his charge that *it* was a terrorist organization. "The Popular Front for the Liberation of Palestine rejects the description of

George Habash, terrorist leader of the Popular Front for the Liberation of Palestine (PFLP) from 1968–2000. Courtesy of Israel Government Press Office.

our people's resistance as 'terrorism.' It is a cause for condemnation and astonishment that the Palestinian President would describe organizations of the legitimate, defensive Palestinian resistance against the occupation as 'terrorist' at a time when American imperialism and the Zionist entity strive intentionally to mix up terrorist acts with the legitimate resistance of subjugated peoples, first among whom are our Palestinian people, whose right to resist is guaranteed by international law and legality" (PFLP 2002). The indignant press release failed to explain precisely which international laws authorized the PFLP to slaughter innocent Israelis.

In their own eyes, when the PFLP detonates bombs on the streets of Israeli cities, killing at random anyone who happens to be there, they are not terrorists. Instead, they are "subjugated peoples" resisting an unjust occupation. (Typically, they refuse to acknowledge the obvious possibility that they could be both.) For them, the "Zionist entity" is the true terrorist organization. They are only "resisting" it.

The Israeli government takes a similar—but opposing—position. In its view, any attack on Israeli civilians is terrorism, while its own attacks on Palestinian cities populated largely by civilians are legitimate military operations. Retaliation for terrorism—even when it takes the form of violence directed against civilian areas, destruction of the property of family members of suspected terrorists, and outright assassinations of the suspected terrorists themselves—is not terrorism, but a kind of antiterrorism.

For the most part, both governments and insurgent groups define terrorism as something that the other side does. Terrorism, then, is often in the eye of the beholder. When our people are killed, that is terrorism. When we kill other people, that is not. Each side accuses the other of terrorism, while absolving itself of the charge for doing the same, or very similar, things. Abu Bakar Bashir, the Muslim cleric who reputedly heads the Jemaah Islamiyah group, is typical. When journalists questioned him about Jemaah's possible involvement in the October 2002 bombings of a foreign tourist area in Bali, he deflected them by declaring that, "The Americans and Jews are the terrorists" (Koch 2002), almost as though that absolved him and Jemaah Islamiyah of any possible guilt.

Indeed, most groups that others accuse of terrorism feel exonerated by the purity of their cause. If we are acting against terrorism, we are not committing it. If we are resisting oppression, we are not terrorists. If we are defending ourselves against a stronger enemy, we are not terrorists. If we are acting in the name of God, we are not terrorists. And so on.

The desire for absolution is understandable, but this kind of formulation makes the whole concept of terrorism meaningless.

The difficulty of defining terrorism is largely self-imposed. It is manufactured out of the need to justify certain violent actions, while condemning others. Once such national and political self-interest is put aside, terrorism becomes easy to recognize. For most of us, what U.S. Supreme Court Justice Potter Stewart said of pornography is equally true of terrorism. We may not be able to define it precisely, but we know it when we see it.

Most, if not all, terrorist acts are

1. malicious actions or threats,

2. directed against people who are regarded as innocent, or who are protected by the laws and conventions of modern warfare, and

3. designed (at least partly) to frighten, intimidate, or otherwise influence populations or governments.

Any action that meets all three of those criteria will be regarded as terrorism for the purposes of this book.

PROPAGANDA OF THE DEED

Since the French Revolution (which gave birth to the term) *terrorism* has often been associated with revolution, and, more often than not, with Socialist or left-wing revolution. In the late nineteenth century and the early years of the twentieth, terrorism was associated almost exclusively with the wave of *anarcho*-violence that took the lives of several heads of

Paul Newman as Armand in the 1965 film *Lady L*. Courtesy of Photofest.

state, high government officials, and others in Europe and North America. The anarchists, who saw the power of the state as tyranny, referred to such assassinations as "propaganda of the deed."

Some anarchists saw themselves as champions of the working class, and groups like Narodnaya Volya in Russia tried to link anarchist-style terrorism with revolutionary Socialism. Many doctrinaire Marxists, including both Trotsky and Lenin, the leaders of the revolution that would eventually overthrow the Czarist government of Russia, were wary of the anarchists and their methods. It was Trotsky who first pinpointed some of the great weaknesses of what he called "individual terrorism" as a weapon of Socialist revolution.

Among those weaknesses was the fact that individual or small-group violence tends to overshadow, and ultimately, to supersede all other elements of the revolution. "Everything that is outside the framework of terror is only the setting for the struggle; at best, an auxiliary means. In the blinding flash of exploding bombs, the contours of political parties and the dividing lines of the class struggle disappear without a trace" (Trotsky *Bankruptcy* 1909).

"Of course, the killing of 'tyrants' is almost as old as the institution of 'tyranny' itself, and poets of all centuries have composed more than a few hymns in honor of the liberating dagger. But, systematic terror, taking as its task the elimination of satrap after satrap, minister after minister, monarch after monarch—'Sashka after Sashka,' as an 1880s Narodnaya Volya-member familiarly formulated the programme for terror—this kind of terror, adjusting itself to absolutism's bureaucratic hierarchy and creating its own revolutionary bureaucracy, is the product of the unique creative powers of the Russian intelligentsia" (Trotsky *Bankruptcy* 1909). This kind of terror—dramatic and emotionally satisfying as it sometimes was—Trotsky opposed. He considered it antithetical to the revolution of the masses that he and his fellow Marxists advocated.

"Of course, one can easily collect a dozen odd quotations from Social Revolutionary literature stating that they pose terror not instead of the mass struggle but together with it," he admitted. "But these quotations bear witness only to the struggle the ideologists of terror have had to conduct against the Marxists—the theoreticians of mass struggle. But this does not change matters. By its very essence terrorist work demands such concentrated energy for 'the great moment,' such an overestimation of the significance of individual heroism, and finally, such a 'hermetic' conspiracy, that—if not logically, then psychologically it totally excludes agitational and organisational work among the masses" (Trotsky *Bankruptcy* 1909).

In Trotsky's view, the desire to kill the masters of oppression was perfectly understandable.

> Before it is elevated to the level of a method of political struggle, terrorism makes its appearance in the form of individual acts of revenge. So it was in Russia, the classic land of terrorism. The flogging of political prisoners impelled Vera Zasulich to give expression to the general feeling of indignation by an assassination attempt on General Trepov. Her example was imitated in the circles of the revolutionary intelligentsia, who lacked any mass support. What began as an act of unthinking revenge was developed into an entire system in 1879–81. The outbreaks of anarchist assassination in Western Europe and North America always come after some atrocity committed by the government—the shooting of strikers or executions of political opponents. The most important psychological source of terrorism is always the feeling of revenge in search of an outlet. (Trotsky *Why* 1909)

Not that revenge wasn't justified, and not that it didn't have its uses as a precursor to true revolution either.

> Whatever the eunuchs and Pharisees of morality may say, the feeling of revenge has its rights. It does the working class the greatest moral credit that it does not look with vacant indifference upon what is going on in this best of all possible worlds. Not to extinguish the proletariat's unfulfilled feeling of revenge, but on the contrary to stir it up again and again, to deepen it, and to direct it against the real causes of all injustice and human baseness—that is the task of the Social Democracy. If we oppose terrorist acts, it is only because individual revenge does not satisfy us. The account we have to settle with the capitalist system is too great to be presented to some functionary called a minister. To learn to see all the crimes against humanity, all the indignities to which the human body and spirit are subjected, as the twisted outgrowths and expressions of the existing social system, in order to direct all our energies into a collective struggle against this system—that is the direction in which

the burning desire for revenge can find its highest moral satisfaction. (Trotsky *Bankruptcy* 1909)

The trouble was that individual terrorism was just that: it was individual. It put the spotlight too brightly on the terrorist, and distracted, in many important ways, from the masses, and from the revolution itself.

> In our eyes, individual terror is inadmissible precisely because it belittles the role of the masses in their own consciousness, reconciles them to their powerlessness, and turns their eyes and hopes towards a great avenger and liberator who some day will come and accomplish his mission. The anarchist prophets of the 'propaganda of the deed' can argue all they want about the elevating and stimulating influence of terrorist acts on the masses. Theoretical considerations and political experience prove otherwise. The more 'effective' the terrorist acts, the greater their impact, the more they reduce the interest of the masses in self-organization and self-education. But the smoke from the confusion clears away, the panic disappears, the successor of the murdered minister makes his appearance, life again settles into the old rut, the wheel of capitalist exploitation turns as before; only the police repression grows more savage and brazen. And as a result, in place of the kindled hopes and artificially aroused excitement comes disillusionment and apathy. (Trotsky *Bankruptcy* 1909)

Besides, terrorism was playing on the government's court, if not by the government's rules. "[T]he anarchist 'propaganda of the deed' has shown every time that the state is much richer in the means of physical destruction and mechanical repression than are the terrorist groups" (Trotsky *Bankruptcy* 1909). Worse, the terrorists, or Combat Organization, made the revolution peculiarly vulnerable to the police—officials the Marxists regarded not as enforcers of the law but as enforcers of repressive state power. "[No] matter what sort of subordinate role terror is relegated to by the 'synthetic' theoreticians of the party, it always occupies a special place of honour in fact. And the Combat Organization, which the official party hierarchy places under the Central Committee, inevitably turns out to be above it, above the party and all its work—until cruel fate places it under the police department. And that is precisely why the collapse of the Combat Organization as a result of a police conspiracy inevitably means the political collapse of the party as well" (Trotsky *Bankruptcy* 1909).

But the greatest defect of "individual terrorism" was that, however psychologically beneficial it could be, it was ultimately ineffective. "[I]n order to murder a prominent official you need not have the organized masses behind you. The recipe for explosives is accessible to all, and a Browning can be obtained anywhere. In the [case of Socialist revolution] there is a social struggle, whose methods and means flow necessarily from the nature of the prevailing social order; and in the second, a purely mechanical reaction identical anywhere—in China as in France—very striking in its outward form (murder, explosions, and so forth) but absolutely harmless as far as the social system goes" (Trotsky *Why* 1909).

NONCOMBATANTS

Some terrorists try to escape the reality of their actions by effectively defining the concepts of *combatant* and *enemy* in ways that include civilians, the aged, and children of both sexes. The Popular Front for the Liberation of Palestine, for example, considers all Jewish settlers on the disputed West Bank to be part of an alien occupation. In the Palestinian organization's eyes, this makes all the settlers fair game for slaughter.

Islamist terrorists argue that everyone who votes or pays taxes in the United States (or who might vote or pay taxes in the future) is supporting the U.S. government, and is therefore responsible for U.S. actions around the world. This argument may sound spurious to modern Americans, but it is actually very much in line with an old American tradition.

In the American Old West, some Native Americans killed whites indiscriminately, regarding them all as invaders. In the same era, white settlers on the American frontier had a saying that, "The only good Indian is a dead Indian." When U.S. cavalry troops, led by Major John Chivington, raided the Indian village at Sand Creek, Colorado, in November 1864, most of the people they slaughtered were women, children, or old men. Following the massacre, Chivington was regarded as a hero by many whites on the frontier.

Only a few months before Sand Creek, the territorial governor of Colorado had called on "all citizens of Colorado, either individually, or in such parties as they may organize, to go in pursuit of all hostile Indians on the plains, scrupulously avoiding those who have responded to my call to rendezvous at the points indicated; also, to kill and destroy as enemies of the country, wherever they may be found, all such hostile Indians" (Klinkenborg 2000).

The U.S. Cavalry classified Indians as "hostiles" on much the same basis that the PFLP classifies Jewish settlers on the West Bank as "occupiers." Their mere presence on the land condemned them as enemies to be destroyed.

When Osama bin Laden and other Islamist leaders issued their *fatwah* against Americans in 1998, they made clear that they meant all Americans, not just those serving in the military or government. The Islamists claimed divine authority for this all-inclusive definition of their enemy: "The ruling to kill the Americans and their allies—civilians and military—is an individual duty for every Muslim who can do it in any country in which it is possible to do it . . . This is in accordance with the words of Almighty God, 'and fight the pagans all together as they fight you all together,' and 'fight them until there is no more tumult or oppression, and there prevail justice and faith in God' " (*Al-Quds al-'Arabi* 1998).

Most terrorists stop short of asserting divine sanction for their activities, but almost all claim an equivalent—an overriding cause that in their minds, justifies actions that ordinarily would be totally unacceptable.

Many terrorists refuse to acknowledge that their victims are individual human beings, or even human beings at all. A neo-Nazi addressing an Aryan Nations congress at Hayden Lake, Idaho in 1986 made a fundamental distinction between whites and virtually everyone else: "[I]f our race is left no choice . . . the White Youth of this nation will utilize every method . . . to neutralize and quite possibly engage in the wholesale extermination of all sub-human non-Aryans from the face of the North American continent: men, women and children, without exception, without appeals, who are of non-Aryan blood shall be terminated or expelled" (Center for Democratic Renewal n.d., 39).

White supremacy is hardly common among terrorists in general, but other forms of racism and ethnocentrism are. Also common among terrorists is the refusal to acknowledge a shared humanity with those they perceive as the enemy. This refusal shows a willful lack of imagination as well as of empathy. (It is a lack that is often shared by those they victimize. Each side is deeply conscious of its own grievances. Each is sincerely appalled by what it sees as the other's excessive and unjustified violence. Each finds it hard to understand how the enemy can do the things it does.)

For those who carry out terrorist attacks against noncombatants, and particularly women and children, it may be psychologically necessary to blind themselves to their victims' humanity. Even the most committed fanatics must find it hard to face the human reality of the horrors they perpetrate. Kim Hyun Hee, the woman who planted the explosives that destroyed Korean Flight 858 over the Indian Ocean, later wrote that, at the moment she activated the bomb, "I felt no guilt or remorse at what I was doing. I thought only of completing the mission and not letting my country down." She continued to show no remorse until she was confronted by several of her victims' relatives at her trial. It was only then that "I finally began to feel, deep down, the sheer horror of the atrocity I had committed" (Kim 1994, 104).

Most terrorists who survive the atrocities they commit probably never allow themselves such moments of human empathy. Certainly, few terrorist organizations ever acknowledge the depth of the suffering they cause. A notable exception is the Irish Republican Army (IRA), which issued a remarkable statement in 2002, on the 30th anniversary of one of their most deadly operations. While disingenuously denying that the IRA had actually targeted noncombatants, it admitted having killed and injured them. More than that, it acknowledged the suffering it had caused to the relatives of all those it had killed and maimed over the years, combatants and noncombatants alike.

"It is . . . appropriate on the anniversary of this tragic event, that we address all of the deaths and injuries of noncombatants caused by us. We offer our sincere apologies and condolences to their families. There have been fatalities amongst combatants on all sides. We also acknowledge the grief and pain of their relatives. The future will not be found in denying collective failures and mistakes, or closing minds and hearts to the plight of those who have been hurt. That includes all of the victims of the conflict, combatants and noncombatants." Nor would the future "be achieved by creating a hierarchy of victims in which some are deemed more or less worthy than others" ("IRA Statement of Apology" 2002).

By the time that statement was issued, the IRA was already involved in the difficult process of weaning itself away from terrorist activity. Until that time, the IRA, along with virtually every other terrorist group (or military force, for that matter), had its own "hierarchy of victims," some of whom were deemed more worthy than others. Without such a hierarchy, terrorism could not continue to exist.

MILITARY TARGETS

Not all forms of terrorism are directed against civilians. The U.S. State Department considers attacks on U.S. military installations in peacetime, as well as on off-duty military personnel at any time or place, as varieties of terrorism. This is an area in which the line between terrorism and guerrilla warfare becomes so thin that it is virtually invisible.

At the height of "the Troubles," the IRA and other rebels in Northern Ireland frequently attacked and often killed British soldiers whom they considered members of a foreign occupying force. Can wartime attacks on heads of state, other government officials, bureaucrats, or diplomats be reasonably considered terrorism? Or are they legitimate acts of war? What about the killing of an off-duty soldier stationed in a foreign country? The killing of a soldier on leave in his own country? What if there is no formal state of war but the terrorists have announced their enmity toward the country they attack?

The question of whether particular acts of violence are or are not also acts of terrorism is largely a legalistic one. What's more, the answers given by particular groups or governments are almost invariably self-serving. In the eyes of most governments, what one's enemies do is terrorism, what one does oneself is not.

TERRORISM AND CONVENTIONAL WARFARE

The nineteenth-century German military strategist Carl von Clausewitz famously described war as a continuation of politics with other means, and also as violence intended to force an opponent to one's will. Terrorism fits both descriptions.

President George W. Bush acknowledged this when he issued a proclamation referring to the attacks of September 11, 2001, as "despicable acts of war" (Bush 2001). Soon afterward, the Bush administration began talking about itself waging a "war" on terrorism. At that point, the president was not concerned with any distinctions between the two activities, although surely, if the issue had been raised, he would have justified the actions taken by the United States and its allies against terrorism as completely acceptable acts of self-defense, while condemning the "acts of war" committed by the terrorists as being entirely without legitimacy.

The similarities between terrorists and soldiers are obvious. Both are specialists in violence, whose function is to disrupt, to cause harm, to injure, and to kill. But vital distinctions can and should be made between terrorism and warfare. The first is that terrorist violence is usually (although not always) carried out by guerillas or other "clandestine" forces, rather than by the official armed forces of any nation; and two, as we have already emphasized, terrorism is directed primarily against noncombatants, while conventional warfare is directed primarily against the military forces and strategic capacity of the other side.

The targeting of civilians is central to the nature of terrorism, as well as to the special horror of it. But almost all modern warfare victimizes noncombatants. No matter how hard the military may try to minimize civilian casualties, women, children, and other noncombatants invariably perish whenever nations go to war.

In conventional warfare, however, noncombatant deaths are frequently incidental and often unintentional. They may result from a wide variety of factors. The military may be unaware of the civilians' presence in a given area; faulty intelligence may lead to an attack on the wrong target; bombs, artillery shells, or even bullets may go astray. Civilian casualties are not always inadvertent, however. In some cases, the military decides that their objective is worth a certain number of civilian deaths, and attack civilian-occupied areas knowing full well that they are killing innocent people along with enemy combatants. Even then, civilian casualties in all the above cases are considered "collateral damage," part of the unfortunate, but (or so it is widely believed) unavoidable destruction of modern warfare.

Terrorism, on the other hand, makes noncombatants the primary, and often the only, targets. The whole object of many terrorist actions is to kill civilians. As commonplace as noncombatant deaths have become, there is something especially terrible about the deliberate targeting of "innocent" people—people who are not actively involved in a conflict, and, in the case of the very young and the very old, people who *could not* be actively involved in it.

The section of Osama bin Laden's "Open Letter to America" in which he attempts to justify al Qaeda's attacks on American civilians is particularly interesting in this respect. (The entire "letter" is printed in chapter 9.) After complaining that America had long been attacking the Muslim world in a variety of ways, he goes on to anticipate America's response: "You may . . . dispute that all the above does not justify aggression against civilians, for crimes they did not commit and offenses in which they did not partake." That is, of course, exactly the argument that most Americans, including myself, would make. Bin Laden, however, rejects it, making a series of counterarguments, some of which resemble the kind of rationalizations a criminal might make to salve a guilty conscience:

> The American people are the ones who pay the taxes which fund the planes that bomb us in Afghanistan, the tanks that strike and destroy our homes in Palestine, the armies which occupy our lands in the Arabian Gulf, and the fleets which ensure the blockade of Iraq. These tax dollars are given to Israel for it to continue to attack us and penetrate our lands. So the American people are the ones who fund the attacks against us, and they are the ones who oversee the expenditure of these monies in the way they wish, through their elected candidates.
>
> Also the American army is part of the American people. It is this very same people who are shamelessly helping the Jews fight against us . . .
>
> The American people are the ones who employ both their men and their women in the American Forces which attack us.
>
> This is why the American people cannot be not innocent of all the crimes committed by the Americans and Jews against us.
>
> Allah, the Almighty, legislated the permission and the option to take revenge. Thus, if we are attacked, then we have the right to attack back. Whoever has destroyed our villages and towns, then we have the right to destroy their villages and towns. Whoever has stolen our wealth, then we have the right to destroy their economy. Whoever has killed our civilians, then we have the right to kill theirs. America does not understand the language of manners and principles, so we are addressing it using the language it understands.

The best (and worst) that can be said for such arguments is that they are in a language that we understand. They are depressingly familiar. They echo the self-justifications used by military and government officials around the world to justify their own military actions, which kill large numbers of civilians who are at least as innocent as any victims of terrorism. Citizens must pay the price for their leaders' actions.

On some level, those who conduct modern warfare prefer to believe that the enemy is not only evil but indivisible; that it speaks with one voice, and shares a single soul; that the women and children who will die on the other side are somehow as deserving of punishment as the tyrants who rule them. Those contentions may be false, but they are also eminently believable. Most citizens of countries at war accept them uncritically. Only when used by the enemy do they sound bogus.

However spurious and even far-fetched bin Laden's case may seem (for instance, the mere fact that Americans are required to pay taxes hardly makes them personally responsible for everything the taxes are spent on), one aspect of his argument does raise a real and uncomfortable issue. Using America's own rhetoric against it, he indicts the United States with its own political system and throws its most cherished platitudes back in its face. American citizens, bin Laden contends, are almost uniquely responsible for the actions of their government. Any attempt to deny this, he says, "contradicts your continuous repetition that America is the land of freedom . . . [T]he American people are the ones who choose their government by way of their own free will; a choice which stems from their agreement to its policies . . . The American people have the ability and choice to refuse the policies of their Government and even to change it if they want."

Is it not fair to hold the people in a representative democracy (or, as some would insist in the case of the United States, in a representative republic) uniquely responsible for what their government does? If they are not responsible, then who is? Certainly not all of the people approve of the government's actions, but that is the case in all countries at all times.

Most Americans who disapprove of what the government does—whether in the Middle East or elsewhere—take a kind of moral refuge in their own (presumed) insignificance. They adopt a passive, or at most a grumbling attitude toward the administration of which they disapprove, content to complain without ever making any serious effort to change, or even to influence it. Because they are not all-powerful, they convince themselves that they are powerless. And, because they cannot single-handedly *change* government policy, they hold themselves blameless for it.

It should be said that this is not an attitude with which terrorists—at least those with strong political or ideological bents—have much natural sympathy. They are activists. Far from taking refuge in their own powerlessness, they take on an awesome and even horrifying responsibility; often they do so knowing that that the action that they take is probably futile, at least in any foreseeable time frame, and may (in some cases, will certainly) result in their own deaths.

Who is more correct—the American people who hold themselves blameless for what their government does in their name, or the terrorists who hold them strictly accountable? Or, perhaps, does justice lie somewhere between? This book is not the place to try to answer that question, but the judgment is not as clear-cut as most people on all sides too often assume.

There is a true irony here. It is that Osama bin Laden—a terrorist, a religious bigot, and a fanatic zealot who hates America ("the worst civilization witnessed by the history of mankind"), and who has called on Muslims everywhere to kill Americans whenever and wherever they can—takes the American system of government more seriously than many Americans do.

THE MILITARY TARGETING OF CIVILIANS

For Caleb Carr, the defining characteristic of terrorism is the "deliberate military targeting of civilians." Such targeting can, of course, be done by the regular military as well as by guerilla forces and other clandestine actors. In some conflicts (Vietnam is probably the most widely discussed example), it can be difficult to tell the difference between civilians and enemy forces.

For a variety of reasons, the century just past saw many cases of regular armed forces, including those of the United States, deliberately targeting civilians: a practice that may be becoming more common, despite the fact that it is forbidden by the developing international law of warfare.

Although government officials would no doubt strongly deny the charge that the United States military engaged in terrorism during World War II, American bombers participated in the incendiary bombing of civilian populations, including the internationally protected city of Dresden, Germany. Both then and later, when it dropped atomic bombs on Japanese cities, the U.S. military's intentions were perilously close to those of the present-day terrorists who detonate bombs on crowded city streets hoping to demoralize populations and pressure governments.

Hiroshima contained military targets, but the atomic bomb was not directed primarily against them. The minutes of the Target Committee, which evaluated possible uses for the first atomic weapon, make clear that "psychological factors in the target selection were of great importance." The two main "psychological factors" the Committee considered were: "(1) obtaining the greatest psychological effect against Japan and (2) making the initial use sufficiently spectacular for the importance of the weapon to be internationally recognized when publicity on it is released" ("Minutes" 1945).

The committee decided, among other things, that Hiroshima had the particular "advantage of being such a size and with possible focusing from nearby mountains that a large fraction of the city may be destroyed" (Target Committee of the Manhattan Project 1945).

The publicly stated purpose of dropping the atomic bombs on heavily populated cities, rather than dropping them on purely military targets or making a demonstration of their power at some isolated spot where no one would be killed, was to horrify the Japanese into immediate surrender. Without such a surrender, American military forces would have had to invade the Japanese homeland—an operation that American military planners believed would lead to thousands, if not hundreds of thousands, of casualties on both sides. A key concern of American planners was to avoid, or at least minimize, American casualties. The fact that the new weapons would produce a similar, if not greater, number of casualties overall was recognized by those who made the decision. The immediate purpose of the attacks was to make them terrible enough to convince the Japanese government that there was no point to resistance, by demonstrating that the cost of resistance that would be borne by the Japanese people would be unacceptably high. A judgment was clearly made that it was better for Japanese civilians to die than for American military personnel.

Another purpose (one that was not announced publicly, but clearly understood within the U.S. government) was to demonstrate the massive destructive power of the United States' atomic weapons in order to discourage the Soviets from challenging the United States once the war was over.

This was why the Target Committee considered it necessary "to make the initial use sufficiently spectacular for the importance of the weapon to be internationally recognized" (Target Committee of the Manhattan Project 1945).

Hiroshima was chosen as the first target because, once all other factors had been taken into account, it was where the bomb was likely to do the most "spectacular" damage. And kill the most people—the vast majority of whom would be noncombatants. It was where an atomic explosion would produce the most sensational photographs to be spread around the world, and make the biggest possible impression, not only on the Japanese people and government, but on the Russian people and government as well.

The bombs dropped on Hiroshima and Nagasaki could be considered the most destructive terrorist acts in history. They are rarely thought of in that light, for a number of reasons. One is the fact that they were carried out by the conventional armed forces of the United States, while terrorist acts are usually associated with revolutionaries or other subnational groups. Perhaps more significantly, they occurred in the heat of a declared and incredibly destructive war. In many people's eyes, this gave them a legitimacy not shared by the actions of terrorists. The relevance of this difference is open to question, however. Many of today's terrorist groups announce in advance that they consider themselves at war with those they attack. Several Islamist organizations, for example, issued the equivalent of a declaration of war, in the form of a fatwah against the United States, three years before September 11, 2001. And since that date, the United States itself has announced that it is at war with terrorism wherever it exists. Doing so could be considered as lending a kind of false legitimacy to future terrorist actions against the United States.

A cynic might say that the real reason that the Hiroshima and Nagasaki bombings are not generally thought of as terrorist acts is that (as the saying goes) history is written by the winners. But it is more than that. It is also because the United States was so clearly on the "right" side in World War II. As we have seen, "terrorist" is a word we reserve for the bad guys. We are extremely reluctant to identify terrorism with righteous causes, or to acknowledge that "the good guys" could make use of it themselves.

To suggest that the tactical motivations of the Allies in bombing German and Japanese cities were similar to those of modern terrorists is not especially to condemn the Allied governments of the time. They did what most other governments, then and now, would do in the same circumstances. Nor is it to excuse the terrorists of today. Instead, it is simply to suggest that terrorism is not as different from conventional warfare as we like to assume, and that the ethical problems raised by the deliberate killing of noncombatants apply to both.

Also, although this book will focus primarily on terrorism as used by subnational groups attacking governments, it is important to recognize that similar tactics are frequently employed by both sides. It should always be remembered that the methods of repression employed by tyrannical governments are forms of terrorism as well. What's more—in places like Hitler's Germany, Idi Amin's Uganda, Pinochet's Chile, and Saddam Hussein's Iraq—they can be as cruel, and often more widespread and systematic, than the methods employed by the most ruthless terrorists.

REFERENCES

Al-Quds al-'Arabi (London). 1998. "International Islamic Front Fatwah for Jihad on the Jews and Crusaders," 23 February.

Arafat, Yasser. 2002. "The Palestinian Vision of Peace." *New York Times*, 3 February.

Bush, George W. Bush. 2001. Proclamation. "National Day of Prayer and Remembrance for the Victims of the Terrorist Attacks on September 11, 2001," proclamation 7462. *Federal Register* 66, no 179 (14 September): 47945–47948.

Carr, Caleb. 2002. *The Lessons of Terror: A History of Warfare Against Civilians: Why It Has Always Failed and Why It Will Fail Again.* New York: Random House.

Center for Democratic Renewal. n.d. "Aryan Youth Movement/White Students Union, Revolutionary Recruitment Issue," included in the Neo-Nazi Skinheads & Youth Information Packet. Atlanta, Ga.: Center for Democratic Renewal.

FBI Joint Terrorism Taskforce. 2002. Untitled pamphlet. October.

Guralnik, David B., ed. 1980. *Webster's New World Dictionary of the American Language*, 2d coll. ed. New York: Simon & Schuster.

"IRA Statement of Apology." 2002. Conflict Archive. http://cain.ulst.ac.uk/events/peace/docs/ira160702.htm (accessed 31 March 2004).

Kim, Hyun Lee. 1994. *The Tears of My Soul.* New York: Morrow.

Klinkenborg, Verlyn. 2000. "The Conscience of Place: Sand Creek," *Mother Jones*, November/December, 60–63.

Koch, Edward. 2002. "New Jersey's bigot laureate is no private citizen and his 'defenses' are idiotic." *Jewish World Review*, 23 October. http://www.jewishworldreview.com/1102/koch102302.asp (accessed 31 March 2004).

Office of the Coordinator for Counterterrorism. 1999. Washington, D.C.: U.S. Department of State.

Popular Front for the Liberation of Palestine (PFLP). 2002. Untitled press release. 5 February.

Schmidt, Alex P., and Albert J. Youngman. 1998. *Political Terrorism.* Amsterdam: SWIDOC.

Target Committee of the Manhattan Project. 1945. "Minutes of the Second Meeting of the Target Committee, Los Alamos, May 10–11, 1945," U.S. National Archives, Record Group 77, Records of the Office of the Chief of Engineers, Manhattan Engineer District, TS Manhattan Project File '42–'46, folder 5D, Selection of Targets. Title 22 U.S.C. Section 2656(f).

Trotsky, Leon. *The Bankruptcy of Individual Terrorism.* Trotsky Internet archive. http://www.marxists.org/archive/trotsky/works/1909/tia09.htm (accessed 25 March 2004).

Trotsky, Leon. *Why Marxists Oppose Terrorism*. Trotsky Internet archive. http://www.marxists.org/archive/trotsky/works/1909/tia09.htm (accessed 25 March 2004) 28 C.F.R. Section 0.85.

U.S. Department of State. 1999. *Patterns of Global Terrorism: 1998*. http://www. state.gov/www/global/terrorism/1998Report/1998index.html (accessed 31 March 2004).

A Short History of Terrorism

Terrorism is as old as war itself. The Greek historian Xenophon reports that the ancient Greeks used various tactics to spread terror among their enemies before engaging them in battle, and there is no reason to believe that they were the first to do so.

Terror is, of course, a part of the very essence of warfare. In any battle, each side hopes to make the other more afraid than they are themselves, and battles are often won when one side panics and flees the field; governments surrender when they become sufficiently afraid of the damage the enemy is doing or may do in the future. Armies have been known to summarily execute captured soldiers, or to treat them with daunting cruelty, in an effort to inspire their comrades to desert, or even to mutiny against their commanders rather than risk similar treatment.

The most elemental understanding of the use of terror as a weapon of war, and its origins, has been well expressed by, of all people, the folksinger Pete Seeger: "[F]or thousands of years our ancestors have been fighting each other in small bands—they have been trying to scare the other tribes into fleeing. If we can get them to run away, maybe we can take over their caves! So how do we scare them? Maybe throw some fire into their caves! And these scare tactics, of course, have been used by armies, and civilian populations have been murdered quite often just to make sure that civilians weren't contributing to war efforts. If a village is found to be supporting enemy soldiers in any way—Wipe The Village Out!" (Seeger 2001).

THE GARDEN OF TERROR

Although terrorism is a worldwide phenomenon, it was born in the deserts and mountains of the Middle East, and it retains its strongest roots there.

What might be considered the first real "terrorist group" appeared in that region in the first century A.D., when a Jewish sect called the Zealots used tactics that would today be recognized as terrorist in an attempt to precipitate rebellion against the Roman rulers of Judea. Zealot agents known as Sicarii—or *daggermen*—slipped secretly into Roman-controlled towns and stabbed or slit the throats of Roman soldiers and Jewish collaborators. The Zealots also used kidnapping-for-ransom and large-scale poisoning to promote their revolutionary cause.

More recently, the Middle East had been the birthplace of both Islamic extremism and Palestinian nationalism, the two movements that account for the lion's share of the terrorist atrocities that haunt the world today.

By any measure, Islam is one of the world's great religions. With more than a billion followers, it ranks second only to Christianity in the number of its adherents. Like Christianity, it is rent by one great division as well as many smaller ones, resulting in scores of sects that are fragmented by various combinations of history, ethnicity, and theological niceties.

The great split is between the main branch of Islam, known as the Sunni, and the Shiah, or Shi'ite, sect, which traces its tradition through Ali, the son-in-law of the prophet Mohammad. The Sunnis are the majority on the Arabian peninsula, in North Africa, and in the Mediterranean region. The Shiahs are the majority in Iran and Iraq, Azerbijan, Oman, and Bahrain, and have a strong presence in Pakistan, India, and Bangladesh as well (*Adherents* 1999).

The history of today's Middle Eastern terrorism is often traced back to a group of Isma'ilis (a minority sect of the Shi'ites), who became known as the Assassins—or, more accurately, the "Hashassins," so-named for the hashish they were believed, perhaps correctly, to smoke. From roughly the eleventh through the thirteenth centuries, this murderous cult attempted to keep Islam pure by killing prominent Sunnis whom they accused of defiling it.

The Assassins were founded in 1090 by Hassan-i-Sabbah, a shadowy figure who became infamous as the legendary Sheikh al-Jabal ("The Old Man of the Mountain"), so-called because of his fortress headquarters at Alamut, high in the almost inaccessible mountains of northern Persia (Iran), on the southern shore of the Caspian Sea. From there, he and his successors dispatched wave after wave of young fanatics, known as *Fedais*, to slaughter those they considered the enemies of true Islam. Their victims included not only several prominent Crusaders, but also Arab leaders who failed to uphold Sheikh al-Jabal's ideal of the Islamic faith. The Assassins' power eventually extended throughout western Asia and much of the Middle East, and even into Europe, where a *Fedai* was believed to have assassinated Duke Louis I of Bavaria in 1231 (Prawdin 1941, 305–307).

EUROPEAN ROOTS

In twelfth-to-fifteenth-century Italy, the Guelph and Ghibelline political sects often turned to terrorist tactics in their struggle for control of the Holy

Roman Empire. From the eleventh century until well into the seventeenth, a very different kind of terrorism was allegedly practiced by generations of "witches," in Europe and elsewhere, who used their supposed supernatural powers to cast spells and summon demons to bend the credulous to their will. The civil and religious authorities of the time used terrorism of another kind to seek out, try, and condemn the so-called witches. Those who were suspected of witchcraft were sometimes subjected to torture, and given a stark choice: they could maintain their innocence and be hanged, drowned, or burned at the stake unshriven, thus condemning themselves to hellfire for eternity, or they could confess their sins, thereby saving their immortal souls—and *then*, be hanged, drowned, or burned at the stake, anyway.

Both males and females were executed for witchcraft in Europe. The exact numbers are impossible to come by, but according to *The Encyclopedia of Witchcraft and Demonology,* the number was considerable, particularly during the period of the "witchcraft delusion" of 1450 to 1750: "If an approximation of those executed as witches be insisted on, the most reliable suggestion is that of George L. Burr, who estimated a *minimum* of 100,000 men, women, and children burned in Germany alone. One might double this figure for the whole of Europe" (Robbins 1959, 189).

Similar tactics to those of the witch-hunters were used by the infamous Spanish Inquisition of the Roman Catholic Church to uncover and eliminate heresies, and by Protestant groups to enforce their own theologies on various populations.

THE THUGS

A secret Hindu cult known as the Thuggee is said to have terrorized parts of India for several centuries. Founded sometime before the Muslim conquest in the twelfth century, the cult is said to have committed several thousands, if not hundreds of thousands, of murders before being destroyed by the British in the early nineteenth century.

Membership in the Thuggee was hereditary, and its members appeared to live perfectly ordinary lives when they were not actually engaging in their crimes. The Thugs (as members of the cult were known) became infamous for befriending travelers on the roads, winning their confidence, and then murdering them, taking their valuables, and burying their bodies in unmarked graves.

The Thugs have frequently been described as terrorists, and they certainly spread fear in the region in which they operated, but their motives seem to have little in common with the motives of those we define as terrorists today. Although they stole from their victims, economic gain didn't seem to play much of a role in their activities either. Instead, the Thugs worshipped the goddess Kali, and considered the ritualistic murders they carried out to be a kind of sacrament. It has also been suggested that they derived a sensual pleasure from their murders, which were traditionally committed by strangulation with a silk scarf (Roy 1996). It was said that they only murdered males, and that they deliberately refrained from attacking Englishmen.

"One contemporary journal, taking note of the phenomenon of [T]huggee as described in one work, said that 'the revelation of actual deeds done by these remorseless villains, so strikingly embodied by the author under the form of the confessions of a leader, are enough to freeze the blood in our veins.' Colonial officials gave a figure of 40,000 strangulations every year over the last three centuries" (Lal 1995, xxvii).

The British ended the Thuggees' murderous activities by either hanging or jailing more than 3,000 alleged cult members over a period of seven years in the 1830s.

THE ANARCHISTS

Although all the above forms of terrorism had already existed for a long time, the word "terrorism" does not seem to have been coined until nearly the end of the eighteenth century, when it was used to describe the "Reign of Terror" during the French Revolution, when the guillotine was used not only to destroy the enemies of the Revolution (real and imagined) but to cow anyone who might have been tempted to act or speak against the Jacobins (National 2001). The term, which not surprisingly comes from a French root, first appeared in English dictionaries around 1794.

From that time on, terrorism would be primarily identified with revolutionary movements, although similar tactics continued to be employed as means of repression by many governments as well.

In the nineteenth century, terrorism became closely associated with the anarchist and organized labor movements. The anarchists believed that the state was a fundamentally tyrannical institution, and they set out to disrupt it with acts of violence. Although they were portrayed as wild-eyed bomb throwers, their most favored weapon was not indiscriminate carnage but targeted assassination.

In the late-nineteenth and early-twentieth centuries, several heads of government and other high-ranking officials fell to the guns and bombs of anarchists and anarcho-Socialists. (Socialism is actually antithetical in theory to anarchism, but the two groups were often lumped together, perhaps because they were associated with similar kinds of violence.) The most notable victims were Czar Alexander II, who was killed by the anarcho-Communist Narodnaya Volya (or "People's Will") in 1881, and Crown Prince Franz Ferdinand of Austria, who was shot to death by a Serbian anarchist in 1914, thus precipitating the chain of events that culminated in World War I.

However mistakenly, the violence of the nineteenth century anarchists has come to symbolize the kind of terrorism that seems to be violence for the sake of violence itself—the irrational striking out, against some hated authority or group, that seems to have no tactical or strategic purpose beyond the pure expression of alienation, anger, and hatred.

GUERILLAS

The methods and tactics of unconventional warfare, used by weaker forces against stronger throughout history, have morphed almost seamlessly into the paramilitary and "urban guerilla" terrorism that plagues the world today. In his massive landmark study, *War in the Shadows: The Guerrilla in History*, the military historian Robert B. Asprey has traced the line of such tactics from the Scythians who fought Darius of Persia in the sixth century B.C. all through the Viet Cong and beyond (Asprey 1997).

Despite the antiterrorist stance it takes today, America played an important role in the history of guerilla terrorism itself. Ethan Allen and the Green Mountain Boys, who are hailed as heroes of the American Revolution, used the bullying tactics of violence and intimidation to hold onto the New Hampshire Grants for Vermont (rather than New York), before the Revolution ever started, then used similar tactics to fight the British. If the American Revolution were taking place today, Allen and his "Boys" would undoubtedly be condemned as terrorists—and not just by the British.

During the Civil War, civilians in the Confederacy used what would now be called terrorist tactics not only against the Union soldiers but also against one another. Union sympathizers in Maryland and elsewhere in the border areas lived in fear of their neighbors. In the deeper South, bands of Confederate outlaws, many of them ex-Confederate soldiers and deserters, roamed the countryside, stealing and marauding like many rebel paramilitaries today. On the Union side, the infamous scorched-earth campaign waged by General Sherman in his "march to the sea" was a form of terrorism directed against the civilian population of Georgia.

In the First World War, the legendary British colonel T. E. Lawrence organized and led a large contingent of Arab irregulars in a decisive guerilla campaign against the Ottoman Turks in Arabia that was sometimes as cruel and merciless as the Ottoman Turk forces themselves. In the Second World War, resistance movements in Nazi-occupied Europe used a variety of terrorist tactics, including assassination from ambush and bombings, to harass the Germans.

Fidel Castro's guerillas in Cuba established a model for rebels fighting to overthrow a ruthless dictator, and Castro's chief lieutenant, Che Guevara, set out to export that model to the rest of Latin America. Meanwhile, the United States was leading in the development of terrorist-like counterterrorism tactics, which it disseminated among the right-wing forces resisting the revolutionaries. On October 9, 1967, Che Guevara was executed by Bolivian forces that had been trained and otherwise assisted by the U.S. military and the CIA, although the CIA had wanted to keep Guevara alive (Kornbluth n.d.), thus becoming a martyr to generations of leftist- and would-be revolutionaries around the world. Many of the urban guerillas in Europe during the 1970s and 1980s (as well as many romanticizing college students in the United States and elsewhere) had posters of Che Guevara on their walls.

These are just examples, of course. During the twentieth century, the methods and tactics of guerilla warfare became more common than those of conventional war. At the same time, the line between guerilla warfare and terrorism—if it had ever existed—blurred to the point of irrelevance.

TERRORISM AS AN INSTRUMENT OF POWER

In the twentieth century, terrorism became increasingly identified with rebellions of both the right and left. It was a major factor in the struggles of many nations to throw off the bonds of colonialism, as well as in many revolutions, both successful and unsuccessful. And, as we have seen, the tactics of terror were also heavily employed by governments attempting to hold onto their power. Governments employed such measures not just to defeat revolutions but also to prevent them. A frightened citizenry is unlikely to find the courage to revolt.

Tyrants and dictators have always ruled, at least partly, by the fear they generated among their subjects. Some, however, are more notorious for their use of terror than others. The Roman Emperor, Caligula, for example, was unparalleled in his capriciousness—a quality that added an extra element of unpredictability to the unbridled cruelty of his reign. The rulers of the Aztec Empire in Mexico regularly killed thousands of their own people in ritual sacrifices.

The notorious fifteenth-century prince Vlad IV of Walachia (an area of what is now Romania) earned the nickname "the Impaler" for his practice of ramming the bodies of his enemies onto stakes and leaving them on display as gruesome lessons to others who would challenge his power. Impaling was not uncommon in that age, but Vlad carried it to unprecedented extremes. On one occasion, he is said to have displayed 20,000 Turkish prisoners on wooden stakes lined along the banks of the Danube like so many fence posts. While the majority of his roughly 100,000 victims were foreigners, about one-third of them were Vlad's own subjects who had displeased him in various ways (Medhurst 2000: lesson I, p. 4).

The twentieth century would see state terror raised to new levels. A preview of the horrors to come occurred in Africa around the turn of the century. In 1885, King Leopold II of Belgium convinced the Berlin Conference to award him title to a rubber-tree growing area of the continent along the Congo River. There, he established what amounted to a privately owned government administration, and presided over the region—ironically called the Congo Free State—as his own private rubber plantation.

Leopold, who may never have personally set foot in his African fiefdom, ruled the Congo from afar, establishing a regime of almost unprecedented ruthlessness and cruel indifference to the suffering of the people. It virtually enslaved the entire population. According to a report submitted by a British consul named Roger Casement in 1903, the people of the Congo Free State were forced, not only to farm rubber for the distant king, but to provide food and other provisions for his private government—a requirement that was so onerous that it resulted in severe deprivations for the people themselves. When a village failed to deliver its quota of food, its inhabitants were beaten or worse.

Leopold's entire enterprise was run on forced labor. His administration, called the Bula Matadi by the Africans, was both brutal and implacable. Government soldiers kidnapped family members of those who refused to work and held them hostage until the reluctant workers appeared on the job. Those who failed to work hard enough were beaten, tortured, or killed as examples to others. The country teemed with refugees who "endured such ill treatment at the hands of the government soldiers in their own [district] that life had become intolerable; that nothing remained for them at home but to be killed for failure to bring in a certain amount of rubber or to die from starvation or exposure in their attempts to satisfy the demands made on them" (Casement 1904).

The Bula Matadi terrorized the Congo for more than 20 years. Eventually, the atrocities of Leopold's African regime became so well known in Europe that they could not be ignored, and the Belgian monarch was forced to relinquish his title to the Congo Free State in 1908. The population of the Congo Free State had fallen from around 30 million to less than 10 million people during the 23 years of Leopold's rule. Some of that decline could be accounted for by the sleeping sickness that devastated the region during that time, but uncountable millions were either direct or indirect victims of Leopold's greed (*Encyclopedia Brittanica* 2000).

The Black Shirts in Italy and the Nazis in Germany both came to power at least partly by means of terror, and the governments of Adolph Hitler in Germany and Josef Stalin in the Soviet Union jointly put the seal of state terror on the history of the twentieth century. (Allegations of government terror on a similar scale have also been made, although with less clear evidence, against the government of China.)

While in the sheer numbers of their victims these regimes dwarfed those of other tyrannies, the degree of fear that they inspired in their populations was no greater than that inspired by dozens of lesser totalitarian regimes. From Pol Pot in Cambodia, to Idi Amin in Uganda, to Saddam Hussein in Iraq—there were many twentieth-century rulers whose atrocities were smaller in scale, but no less murderous in spirit, than Hitler's and Stalin's.

Compared to such state terrorism, the violence of even the most vicious and relentless subnational groups was relatively "small potatoes." But only relatively. In other respects, subnational terrorism was tragically widespread, destructive, and deadly in the twentieth century; perhaps more so than ever before in human history.

THE VERSATILITY OF TERRORISM IN THE TWENTIETH CENTURY

If nothing else, the twentieth century demonstrated the many uses of terror. During that century, terrorism was used by leftists, rightists, and ordinary criminals in nations around the world. It was used by revolutionaries, by death squads, and by drug dealers. It was used by resistance groups combating foreign occupations, and by foreign forces attempting to destroy the morale of indigenous peoples. It was used by minorities who wanted to assert their ethnic identities, and by majorities to assert their dominance. It was used by separatists to break nations apart, and by unionists to hold countries together. It was used to make ideological points, and to make financial profits.

Early in the century, terrorism was a long prelude to revolution in Russia. Later, it would be a key feature of the revolution in China. It would provide the means by which many of the smaller revolutions that swept through the colonial world were fought: the Viet Minh in Vietnam, the Mau Mau in Kenya, the National Liberation Front (FLN) in Algeria—all of these and many others employed the methods and tactics of terrorism to further their cause.

Genocide—a particularly abominable form of terrorism that had begun to come to the fore near the end of the nineteenth century with the pogroms against the Jews in Russia—became another of the key features of twentieth-century history.

Then, in the midst of the long, hot summer of 1968, an El-Al jetliner was hijacked en route from Rome to Tel Aviv by members of the Popular Front for the Liberation of Palestine (PFLP). It was flown to the Dar al-Bayda Airport in Algiers, where negotiations ultimately resulted in the release of the hijackers as well as the passengers and crew. Although no one was killed, and the incident pales in comparison with many of the terrorist events that would soon follow, the hijacking succeeded in gaining international attention for the hijackers' cause. According to a report disseminated by the Canadian Security Intelligence Service, this incident marked the beginning of "modern international terrorism." It "is widely regarded as a principal initiator of the deadly continuum of international terrorist attacks which have exerted significant political influence during the past three decades (*Report # 2001* 2000).

As terrorism expert Paul Medhurst has described: "During the 1960s up to the late 1980s, terrorism in Europe reached its zenith, under a variety of banners, many related to class and political perceptions (as in the case of the Red Brigades and the Baader-Meinhoff Gang or Red Army Faction). This terrorism emerged in some of the European countries that had very

Baader-Meinhof wanted poster, circa summer 1971. Courtesy of Collection of Richard Huffman / www.baader-meinhof.com.

rapidly and painfully exchanged totalitarianism for democracy following the conclusion of the Second World War, such as Italy and Germany. Japan was also subjected to this type of terrorism, which was characterized by the objective of anarchy and disintegration of the state. This was sought by violent terrorist action, carried out by fashionable young upper-middle class revolutionaries with a mixture of left-wing ideologies" (Medhurst 2000, 8).

In the United States, too, there were small groups of fashionable, young revolutionaries (some upper-middle class and some not), who dabbled in dangerous experiments combining left-wing ideologies and violence: groups like the Weathermen on one end of the social scale and the Symbionese Liberation Front on the other.

In Sicily throughout the century, the Mafia launched periodic terrorist campaigns against members of the press and the judicial system who challenged its power; and recently, Mafia-like organizations in Russia and other nations in Eastern Europe have started doing the same. Drug lords in Colombia and elsewhere have long managed to operate with relative impunity through a combination of terror and corruption.

INTERNATIONAL TERRORISM COMES TO THE UNITED STATES

For a long time, the United States seemed to be oddly exempt from large-scale terrorist attacks like those that rocked so much of the rest of the world. This apparent invulnerability was all the odder because of our country's extremely long and largely unpatrolled borders and its relatively lax security measures, and, most of all, because the United States was more hated by the international terrorist groups than any nation except Israel.

Of course, the United States was never as safe as it seemed. Its complacency was severely tested in the 1990s. First, in 1993 when a large e-bomb went off in a parking area of the World Trade Center in New York, and then again in 1995, when a truck loaded with an explosive mixture of fertilizers and chemicals destroyed the Alfred P. Murrah Building in Oklahoma City.

But, as shocking as they were, neither of those two events was widely recognized as presaging a future of terrorist calamities. "Only" six people were killed in the World Trade Center bombing (though as many as 1,000 were injured). It was horrible, but oddly limited; it hardly seemed an indication of devastation to come. And, although the bombing of the Murrah Building killed many more people and was widely perceived as more serious at the time, it, too, seemed to be an isolated event.

Timothy McVeigh and his friends were not only homegrown, they seemed almost stereotypically representative of young, white, middle-American manhood. The fact that such men would commit so terrible and fundamentally *anti-American* an atrocity at first suggested that something pathological might be growing beneath the outwardly healthy façade of our national life. But when, after closer investigation they turned out to be unconnected to any terrorist group, such fears were allayed. McVeigh was a maverick in the old American tradition of the crazed "lone gunman"—such as Lee Harvey Oswald, James Earl Ray, David Mark Chapman, John Hinckley—who periodically emerged from some deep psychological shadow to gun down an American (or, in the case of Chapman, an international) hero. True, McVeigh hadn't acted entirely alone, but then neither had John Wilkes Booth. And he hadn't acted against an individual, but against hundreds of innocent people going about their daily business. Still, the essential similarity seemed to hold. The Oklahoma City bombing, like the assassinations that occasionally marred American history, was an aberration. An anomaly. As such, it could be, if not actually dismissed, at least discounted as a threat for the future.

In fact, by the late-1990s, not only the United States but most of the world was less concerned about terrorism than it had been for decades. With a few notable exceptions—such as in the Middle East, where Palestinian groups continued their relentless campaign of violence against Israel, and in Turkey, where Kurdish groups kept up the pressure for independence—terrorism seemed to be on the wane almost everywhere.

There were still isolated atrocities, like a major spate of bombings in Bombay, and outbursts of violence in Colombia, the Philippines, and Chechnya. But most of the driving engines of twentieth-century terrorism seemed to have worn out or broken down. The revolutions in the once-colonial world had been won (and, all too often, corrupted), and even in Northern Ireland an uneasy peace accord had been reached. Hijacking planes was out of fashion, and so was blowing them up. The once-notorious left-wing terrorist groups in Europe and the United States had either vanished along with the Soviet Union or been seriously diminished by a combination of police action and ideological exhaustion.

In the United States, as in most other countries, "Domestic terrorism was a more widespread phenomenon than international terrorism" (Sheehan 1999), and more of a concern, as well. The U.S. State Department was receiving some 30,000 terrorist threats a year (Peterson 1998), but only a small fraction of them were serious, and the terrorist actions that did occur within the United States were relatively minor. They were hardly even noticeable in the yearly avalanche of national crime statistics.

Fears of major terrorist activity temporarily peaked in conjunction with the New Year's and millennial celebrations of 1999, simply because of the enormous symbolic significance attached to those events. When those fears proved largely unfounded—although one terrorist was caught attempting to smuggle explosives into the United States, presumably intending to use them to disrupt the celebrations—Americans began to feel safe again.

There was only one serious cloud on the terrorism horizon. The main concerns of antiterrorist agencies around the world were beginning to shift away from the politically motivated acts of politically motivated groups and onto the depredations of apparently less organized but potentially more destructive religious fanatics. This was worrisome because the behavior of religious fanatics is not only more difficult to predict than that of political terrorists, they are also more difficult to reason with; most of all, they are more likely to be apocalyptic.

Still, the more or less peaceful turn of the millennium seemed to promise a new age of relative safety from terrorism, and particularly of safety from international terrorism. Although there was some fluctuation in the annual statistics, the average number of terrorist attacks in the 1990s was considerably lower than the average had been in 1980s. And, even in 2001, when the attacks of September 11 shattered American complacency, there were actually 242 *fewer incidents* of international terrorism than there had been in the previous year.

What is more, even though there were more deaths from terrorism in 2001, that fact was entirely accounted for by the attacks of September 11. If those deaths were removed from the statistics, the total would have been over 2,000 *fewer* terrorist deaths than in 2001 (Zakis 2002).

REFERENCES

Adherents.com. 1999. http://adherents.com (accessed 31 March 2004).

Asprey, Robert B. 1997. *War in the Shadows: The Guerilla in History.* New York: Harper Collins.

Casement, Roger. 1993. "Report on My Recent Journey on the Upper Congo." United Kingdom. House of Parliament. 1904. *Parliamentary Papers*, 1904, LXII, Cd. 1933.

Encyclopedia Brittanica. 2000. CD-ROM edition. s.v. "Congo Free State."

Kornbluth, Peter, ed. n.d. *National Security Archive Electronic Briefing Book, No. 5, The Death of Che Guevera: Declassified.* George Washington University National Security Archive, http://www.gwu.edu/~nsarchiv/NSAEBB/NSAEBB5 (accessed 25 March 2004).

Lal, Vinay. 1995. "Criminality and Colonial Anthropology." Introduction to the reprint edition (1995) of *The History of Railway Thieves, with Illustrations and Hints on Detection*, by Rai Bahadur M. Pauparao Naidu. Gurgaon, Haryana: Vintage Press.

Medhurst, Paul. 2000. *Global Terrorism.* Denver, Colo.: United Nations Institute for Training and Research Programme of Correspondence Instruction.

Peterson, Scott. 1998. "Terrorism's Trend Lines." *Christian Science Monitor*, 10 August.

Prawdin, Michael. 1941. *The Mongol Empire Its Rise and Legacy.* Translated from the German by Eden Paul and Cedar Paul. London: George Allen & Unwin Ltd.

Report #2000/01, Trends in Terrorism. 2000. Ottawa: Canadian Security Intelligence Service.

Robbins, Rossell Hope. 1959. *The Encyclopedia of Witchcraft and Demonology.* New York: Crown Publishers.

Roy, Parama. 1996. *Indian Traffic: Identities in Question in Colonial and Postcolonial India*. Berkeley: University of California Press.

Seeger, Pete. 2001. "A Time to Mourn, A Time to Heal." *The Little Magazine* 2 (September–October): 8–14.

Sheehan, Michael A. 1999. "Introduction." In *Patterns of Global Terrorism: 1998*. Washington, D.C.: U.S. State Department. http://www.state.gov/www/ global/terrorism/1998Report/1998index.html (accessed 31 March 2004).

Zakis, Jeremy, ed. 2002. *Annual Report of International Terrorist Activity 2001*. Chicago: Emergency Response and Research Institute.

Turning to Terror

Virtually all definitions of terrorism, including those discussed in the previous chapter, turn to some degree on the intention of the terrorist. That is, not on his or her ultimate goal, but on the intent to use violence against noncombatants as a means of achieving that goal. This easily leads to the mistake of assuming that terrorists usually, if not invariably, act out of some kind of pathological hatred of the innocent.

In the wake of September 11, 2001, Americans repeatedly asked themselves and one another, "Why do the terrorists hate us?" President George W. Bush gave one answer to that question when he addressed a joint session of Congress on September 20 of that fateful year. "[Why] do they hate us? They hate what we see right here in this chamber—a democratically elected government. Their leaders are self-appointed. They hate our freedoms—our freedom of religion, our freedom of speech, our freedom to vote, and assemble, and disagree with each other" (Bush 2001).

This explanation was taken up by so many pundits and other opinion makers that it soon became politically correct—and, very nearly, politically required—for Americans to explain the terrorists' alleged hatred of America by such simple formulas as, "They hate us because of our freedoms," or alternatively, "They hate us because of our wealth and prosperity."

In the case of those responsible for the September 11 attacks, there was some truth to such explanations. The Islamists of al-Qaeda are radical Muslims who believe that American society and Western society, as a whole, is evil. Much of what we see as liberty, they see as libertinism. Much of what we proudly regard as freedom, they see as depraved license. More than that, they believe that the Western presence in the Middle East is not only desecrating and defiling their holy lands but corrupting their societies as well. Believing all that, they may indeed feel a kind of religiously inspired hatred for Americans and other Westerners. Others among the terrorists, who come from the poorer societies of the Middle East, and who regard Westerners as exploiters who are taking precious and nonrenewable resources out of the region to use them for their own benefit, also feel deep resentment and anger toward the West.

Such explanations (which seemed to imply that terrorism is a kind of emotional working-out) were comfortably self-serving. They reassured us that we were attacked, not because we were so *bad* that people hated us for it, but because we were so *good*.

By 2003, a Republican Congressman from Nevada named Jim Gibbons was crystallizing all such explanations somewhat differently. "The root of terrorism," he said, "is envy" (*Washington Journal* 2003). This explanation was even more comforting. In a sense, it transformed the terrorists' hatred into a form of flattery. The terrorists only attacked us because they wanted so much *to be like us*.

It never occurred to most Americans to question whether the terrorists actually *hated* us at all, or rather, to question whether it was necessary for the terrorists to hate us in order for them to attack us. That seemed obvious. If terrorists set out to destroy thousands of people, it must be because they hated those people, or, at the very least, were virulently angry at them. But, to accept hatred as a sufficient explanation of a terrorist attack is to drastically oversimplify the terrorists' motives. Terrorism is not primarily a personal or emotional act. Although terrorists, like regular soldiers, undoubtedly have individual reasons for doing what they do, it is no more necessary for them to personally hate their victims than it is for a soldier to hate his enemies on the battlefield.

Although there is a germ of truth in the naive observation that terrorists act out of envy and resentment, that observation is not very useful in explaining the phenomenon of terrorism itself. Terrorism is both a tactic and a strategy; in either case, it is a means to an end. It is employed for a purpose. Any effort to understand it must begin with an effort to understand both why some groups turn to it and also the goals they hope to accomplish by it. That is, to understand not merely the particular objectives of particular terrorist groups, but the overarching reasons that lead people to choose terrorism as a means of accomplishing their ends.

On the face of it, terrorism is manifestly ugly and cruel. No sane person would argue that slaughtering innocent people is a desirable thing in itself. And yet, terrorists not only do slaughter innocent people, they seem to do it without shame. As far as an observer can tell, most terrorists are not only unrepentant but proud of what they do. In this, as in other things, terrorists are similar to ordinary soldiers fighting a conventional war. They take pride in actions that, however terrible in themselves, are justified in their minds by the purposes for which they carry them out.

So, why do people turn to terror? Why do they choose to attack noncombatants, often in the most ruthless, brutal, and indiscriminate way possible? No doubt, terrorists, like everyone else, act out of a complex mix of motives, both personal and political. Hatred and revenge play their parts, but these alone are not enough to explain why people become terrorists, or why terrorists act as they do.

Among today's terrorists are thousands of people who identify themselves as Christians, Muslims, Hindis, or believers in other religions, all of which religions consider the killing of innocents to be wrong. And yet, many of these same terrorists feel morally justified. More than that, many of them claim to be driven by religious motives. When the devoted Islamist kills to drive Christians out of the sacred places of Islam, he believes he is acting in the name of Allah. When the devoted Christian kills to protect unborn children from being aborted, he believes he is acting in the name of Jesus Christ.

Whether their motives are religious or secular, terrorists feel that their cause is overwhelming enough, or urgent enough, to excuse actions that would otherwise be totally inexcusable. What is more, in the terrorists' calculus, there is no viable option open to them. They believe that terrorism provides them with opportunities and advantages that no other strategy can offer.

Leaving state terrorism as an instrument of war or repression aside, terrorism is often a weapon of the weak. It is typically chosen by those who have few other weapons available to them. The poor and relatively powerless minorities that spawn most terrorists, and whom most terrorists claim to represent, cannot afford to field the same elaborate armed forces, bristling with military hardware, that their oppressors often command. If such people are to resist, they have only two possible strategies: either passive resistance or some form of guerilla warfare on the cheap.

The first of these—nonviolent passive resistance, accompanied by civil disobedience—had some remarkable successes in the twentieth century. The *satyagraha* movement led by Mahatma Gandhi was chiefly responsible for achieving the independence of India in the first half of the twentieth century, and the American civil rights movement led by Dr. Martin Luther King in the United States in the 1950s and 1960s deserves the lion's share of the credit for ending legal segregation in this country. These examples, however, seem to lack attraction for most modern revolutionary movements.

It is hard for people who have been abused not to equate nonviolence with acceptance of that abuse. Those who have never themselves witnessed the power of nonviolent resistance find it hard to believe that such power exists. Consequently, they tend to equate the strategy with weakness, and even with inaction—a mistaken interpretation that Gandhi had to correct within his own movement.

"[N]onviolence," he insisted, "does not mean meek submission to the will of the evildoer, but it means pitting of one's whole soul against the will of the tyrant. Working under the laws of our being, it is possible for a single individual to deny the whole might of an unjust empire to save his honor, his religion, his soul, and lay the foundation for that empire's fall or its regeneration. And so I am not pleading for India to practice nonviolence because she is weak. I want her to practice nonviolence being conscious of her strength and power" (Mukherjee 1993, 99–100).

However, the instinct to return violence for violence is very strong, and the great majority of revolutionary movements and aggrieved peoples never get beyond it. As both Gandhi and King were well aware, people can only steel themselves to the sacrifices needed for sustained nonviolent resistance to succeed when they have a strong spiritual foundation for their pacifism.

It is very hard to establish a foundation firm enough to support a mass movement. Gandhi's movement appealed to many people around the world, but it was rooted in his own Hinduism, and that of many of his followers. King's movement was similarly rooted in a branch of southern Christianity. Both religions had long standing traditions that provided spiritual and philosophical frameworks for nonviolence.

ADVANTAGES

Most aggrieved ethnic and ideological minorities lack a strong shared framework for nonviolence, like the one Gandhi nurtured among his followers in India, or else they deliberately choose to emphasize a more militant tradition within whatever religious or philosophical traditions they share. Once having chosen violence, such groups are at an obvious disadvantage in combating the governments they oppose. Unable to field the large and sophisticated armed forces available to their enemies, they cast about for other means with which to fight.

Terrorism, in its myriad forms, offers certain obvious advantages.

Cost

Perhaps the most obvious advantage of terrorism is financial.

Terrorism is a remarkably inexpensive weapon relative to others that might do comparable damage to an enemy. This tends to make it the weapon of choice for revolutionaries and other subnational or nongovernmental groups who find themselves in conflict with governments. Such groups are at a huge disadvantage to their enemies, not least in terms of the financial and military resources available to them. For them, terrorism can be a way of redressing, or at least compensating for, that disadvantage. It provides more bang for the buck.

Some forms of terrorism are virtually free. It costs nothing, for instance, for members of a white supremacist group to waylay and beat a black man in an alley, and little more for a determined assassin to kill an unsuspecting target.

Not all terrorist operations come so cheaply, of course. In the months leading up to September 11, 2001, al-Qaeda spent enormous amounts of money (by terrorist standards) preparing its operatives to carry out the attacks on New York and Washington, D.C. It sent them traveling about the world, and even purchased professional flying lessons for them. Estimates of the total cost of these preparations range upwards of $100,000. Even if the actual costs ranged into the millions of dollars (which they probably did not) al-Qaeda must have considered the operation cheap at the price. September 11, 2001, shook the world, and it's shaking it still.

In any case, al-Qaeda—whose operation on several continents once included an elaborate training facility in the desert of Afghanistan, which was a kind of finishing school for terrorists from around the globe—is an exception among terrorists groups. Funded not only by the wealth of Osama bin Laden but by an elaborate system of "charities," it is (or at least used to be) known for the large amounts of time and resources it could afford to devote to its operations.

Most terrorist organizations are much less costly to organize and maintain than regular military forces. In fact, terrorists need little in the way of human or other resources to have a major impact. A handful of dedicated terrorists can kill large numbers of people, and cause an enormous amount of damage, both material and psychological.

All that is required initially to organize a terrorist cell is a cadre of like-minded people. Once they are brought together, a cell can be maintained over time with few expenses other than those necessary for communications between the members and whatever financing may be required for specific terrorist operations.

By their nature, terrorist units are much smaller than even the smallest army or other conventional armed force. What is more, while regular military personnel have to be fed, clothed, and sheltered by their organizations, terrorists often live what could be called ordinary lives and work at civilian jobs by which they feed, clothe, and shelter themselves.

Because they attack civilians and other noncombatants, they have no need to train and equip themselves for large-scale battles the way that conventional armed forces have to do. Most terrorist operations require little or no sophisticated weaponry. The weapons that are usually required tend to be simple and utilitarian. Guns and bombs. Usually, very rudimentary bombs.

The explosives used by terrorists rarely cost anywhere near as much as comparably destructive weapons used by regular military forces. The bomb that destroyed the Alfred P. Murrah Federal Building in Oklahoma City in 1995, for example, consisted of a homemade mixture of ammonia nitrate and fuel oil jammed into a rented (not even purchased) truck.

Another rented truck was used to hold the bomb that exploded in the garage of the north building of the World Trade Center in 1993. (Mohammed Salameh, one of the bombers, was arrested when he showed up at the rental company to demand his $400 deposit back.) Even the actual September 11, 2001, attacks were notoriously low tech—carried out with little more than box cutters.

Impact

Terrorism is a form of psychological warfare. In most cases, the terrorist is less concerned about the effect of his act on the immediate victims than he is about the much larger number of people who will hear about it.

The disproportionate impact of terrorism comes from a variety of factors and can be achieved in a variety of different ways.

The assassination of a political leader is a form of murder, but it has an obvious effect beyond the death of the individual man or woman who is killed. Often committed on the principle of "Remove the head and the body will die," an assassination can cripple a political movement, or even throw a whole society into chaos. Miscalculated, however, it can also have the opposite effect, creating a martyr and unifying a society against the terrorists.

Demonstrating the ability to strike at targets that have previously been assumed to be well protected, or even safe, can give a group credibility it never had before. When the Jewish Irgun bombed the King David Hotel in Jerusalem in 1946, the shock value of hitting the British military headquarters in Palestine was worth far more to the Zionists than any damage done to the building itself. The attack on the USS *Cole* in harbor at Aden, Yemen in 2002 derived much of its psychological effect from the revelation that a modern U.S. Navy destroyer could be disabled, and 17 U.S. sailors killed, by a small boat, probably manned by an inexperienced crew, and loaded with a homemade bomb.

The truck bomb that exploded in Oklahoma City in 1995 had another kind of profound psychological effect; it destroyed not only the Alfred P. Murrah Federal Building and 168 human lives, but Americans' naive assumption that the nation's heartland was safe from that kind of indiscriminate terrorist attack.

Even relatively small acts of terrorism, relentlessly repeated, can generate a feeling of vulnerability across an entire population. From the time the current campaign of violence began in 2000 until May 2003, more than 70 suicide-bomb attacks took place in Israel. Relatively few of those explosions killed more than a handful of people, and many of them killed no one at all beyond the suicide bomber him- or herself, and yet, taken together, they kept the population of Israel feeling under a constant state of siege.

One aspect of terrorism that is not widely recognized is the fact that terrorism can actually be a way of reducing the numbers of casualties in a conflict. Leaving so-called weapons of mass destruction aside, terrorist campaigns generally result in fewer casualties than conventional military campaigns, and may have as much, or more, of an effect on the enemy.

Eloquence

Most military operations are primarily functional. That is, they are designed to accomplish a practical objective, or to achieve a practical goal. A preemptive bombing raid on an airfield seeks to destroy the enemy's planes while they are on the ground and unable to escape. An artillery barrage attempts to weaken the enemy's fortifications. An army advances to seize territory, to capture an enemy city, or to defeat an enemy force.

The same is often true of terrorist operations. An assassination is carried out to remove a particular enemy leader from the scene. A wealthy businessman is kidnapped to extort ransom in order to obtain funds for a terrorist organization's other activities.

Often, however, terrorist operations have no such utilitarian purpose. Instead, they are designed not so much to *achieve* something as to *express* something: most often, anger, outrage, or pain.

What could have been more expressive than the attacks on the World Trade Center and the Pentagon on September 11, 2001? Another kind of eloquence was manifested by the Algerian Islamists on July 4, 2002. The Algerian Chief of Staff, General Mohammed Amari, chose that holiday (like the United States, Algeria celebrates its national independence on July 4) as the occasion to announce that the Algerian military had broken the Islamist insurgency and effectively defeated the terrorists who had plagued Algeria for a decade. Amari triumphantly proclaimed that the 27,000 Islamist militants who had once operated in Algeria had been reduced to fewer than a thousand.

Almost before the General was done declaring victory over the terrorists, three terrorist bombs were detonated at two different locations in Algeria. The largest explosion killed some 38 people in a crowded market in the town of Larba, south of Algiers. It was a cogent reminder to Amari, and to everyone else in Algeria, that the terrorists were still a force to be reckoned with.

Some terrorist actions are carried out for their lack of eloquence. Random attacks—in which the targets are chosen for their total lack of any symbolic (or, for that matter, practical) value—add an extra dimension of menace. When terrorists demonstrate a willingness to strike at any place, at any time, then there is no time or place in which anyone can feel safe.

Even failed terrorist attacks can have significant value for the terrorists. The mere fact that the terrorists have struck, whether or not the strike accomplishes its immediate purpose (assassinating an official, destroying a building, etc.) raises people's insecurity and reminds everyone of the terrorists' existence.

THE RATIONALE OF A REVOLUTIONARY TERRORIST

On the other end of the spectrum from government leaders like Hitler, Amin, Pinochet, and Hussein—who use terrorism to keep the citizenry under government control—are the revolutionary terrorists who use similar methods to undermine the governments.

The Concept [of the] Urban Guerilla, a pamphlet issued by the Red Army Faction (RAF) (better known as the Baader-Meinhof Gang) in the 1970s, offers some valuable insights into the way many revolutionary terrorists saw themselves and their mission. Although the day of the "urban guerilla" soon passed in Western Europe, some elements of that concept are common to revolutionary terrorists everywhere and of all ages. More important, certain aspects of the urban guerilla mindset apply equally well to terrorists of many stripes today (*Concept* n.d.).

The unsigned pamphlet was probably written by the notorious West German journalist and terrorist Ulrike Meinhof, the "Meinhof" of the Baader-Meinof Gang. The RAF was one of several European terrorist groups of the era that saw themselves as vanguards of an international Marxist-Leninist revolutionary movement. The concept of left-wing revolution was in the air in those days. In Asia, Africa, South America, and the Middle East, countries were violently emerging from colonialism. Even the former colonizers were being rocked by social turmoil.

The number of actual revolutionaries in the West was quite small in the 1960s and 1970s, but many university campuses were hotbeds of revolutionary thought and expectation. It was an age of protest, and the lines between peaceful and violent protest sometimes blurred. The reaction on the part of the authorities was often clumsy and sometimes brutal. Police battled students and workers in the streets of Paris in May 1968. In West Germany, an anti-war protest in Berlin was marred by the shooting death of a pacifist demonstrator by the police. In the United States, tens of thousands of people protested the American War in Vietnam and the denial of civil rights to black Americans. Four students were shot to death by National Guardsmen during a demonstration on the campus of Kent State University (Ohio).

The Concept [of the] Urban Guerilla was written for the handful of the rebellious young people who were willing to go beyond thought and expectation into the realm of violent action, those who were willing to become, in the words of its writer, "weapon(s) in the class war"; to become urban guerillas; to become—although the pamphlet didn't use the term—terrorists.

As envisioned by the RAF, the job of the urban guerilla (or terrorist) was not to fight in a revolution, but to prepare the way for one. The terrorist must start "by recognizing that there will be no Prussian order of march of the kind in which so many so-called revolutionaries would like to lead the people into battle." If all went well (from the terrorists' point of view) that would come later. In the meantime, the urban guerilla's job was, in essence, to soften up the enemy—"to attack the state's apparatus of control at certain points and put them out of action, to destroy the myth of the system's omnipresence and invulnerability" (*Concept* n.d.).

Using his own "illegal apparatus," made up of "apartments, weapons, ammunition, cars and papers," the pre-revolutionary terrorist forged ahead with his dark work, "recognizing that by the time the moment for armed struggle arrives, it will already be too late to start preparing for it" (*Concept* n.d.).

Marx had argued that the historical circumstances had to be ripe for a successful revolution against the capitalist class to take place in any particular country. Those circumstances would ripen at different times in different places. In the 1970s, however, the Red Army Faction, saw things somewhat differently. They saw the enemy as embodied in "American imperialism," a force whose presumed power extended around the globe. Since the enemy was worldwide, the revolution could be worldwide, too. Unlike doctrinaire, traditional Marxists, the RAF believed that revolution was possible anywhere. That is to say, it was possible *everywhere at once*.

"If we are correct in saying that American imperialism is a paper tiger, i.e. that it can be ultimately defeated . . . because the struggle against it is now being waged in all four corners of the earth, with the result that the forces of imperialism are fragmented, a fragmentation that makes them possible to defeat—if this is correct, then there is no reason to exclude or disqualify any particular country or any particular region from taking part in the anti-imperialist struggle because the forces of revolution are especially weak there, or the forces of reaction especially strong" (*Concept* n.d.).

Because the revolution—or the pre-revolution—was taking place "in all four corners of the earth," any blow against the enemy counted. Every blow helped to fragment, and thereby weaken, the worldwide forces of "imperialism." And that meant that anyone could take part. This was a key to the recruitment of new revolutionaries, and, more importantly, to the recruitment of new terrorists.

Such an argument could be expected to appeal to radical young men and women in Western Europe and the United States who felt alienated and adrift in the midst of a large postwar generation. They looked around the world and saw poverty, injustice, suffering, and struggle. Their own lives were comparatively easy, but also comparatively empty and pointless. They felt the need for a cause that would give them a sense of real purpose. Some few would find that cause in terrorist revolution.

This is one key to the mindset of not only the urban guerilla, but other terrorists as well. No matter how small or inadequate the individual terrorist feels (or fears) himself to be, the act of committing terrorist violence makes him feel important. More specifically, it gives him the feeling of *belonging to* something important.

Having lived a boring and aimless existence in which nothing that he did seemed to matter, he becomes part of something that matters very much. That something becomes an obsession. It comes to matter more than anything else is his life, more than anything else in the world. For members of the Red Army Faction in the 1970s, that something was the socialist revolution. For today's Hamas suicide bomber, it is the plight of the Palestinian people. For the Al Qaeda plotter, it is the jihad.

A terrorist act, like any other form of violence, gives the individual who commits it a sense of power. But terrorism has a separate and very different appeal from most other forms of violence—and particularly from other forms of criminal violence. It makes the terrorist feel *useful*. The terrorist feels that he not only *has* a cause, but he is helping to *further* that cause.

In that sense, the inclination toward terrorism has a lot in common with the more widespread inclination toward peaceful political activity. Both appeal to the participant's self-image, and also to his altruistic spirit. Each proceeds from the twin desires to feel useful and to feel fulfilled. Each makes him feel that he is doing something to further the common good. Each serves to justify his existence.

How do such basically positive desires get channeled into violence and destruction? Why do they drive some people to become terrorists and others to lick stamps for mainstream political candidates? These questions cannot be answered in general. The answers have everything to with the individual's psychology (and perhaps pathology), with his or her personal history and circumstances, and with the social and political climates in which he or she was raised.

A young man raised in a Palestinian refugee camp in Lebanon is more likely to choose terrorism over party politics. A young woman who is raised in a high-income American suburb and attends an exclusive private school is more likely to make the opposite choice. And yet, some people raised in poverty and oppression become peacemakers. Some children of privilege do become terrorists. For both of them, the desire to be useful in a worthy cause may be much the same.

Terrorism, the RAF pamphlet cautions, is not a pastime for dilettantes. It cannot be done as a hobby. "Those who have joined the revolutionary left just to be trendy had better be careful not to involve themselves in something from which there is no going back" (*Concept* n.d.). The life of an urban guerilla is likely to be a life commitment. Left unspoken is the implication that the life to which the urban guerilla commits is likely to be short.

The terrorist does not necessarily deny the value of conventional political activism, but he has to separate himself from it. "In our original concept, we planned to combine urban guerilla activity with grass-roots work. What we wanted was for each of us to work simultaneously within existing socialist groups at the work place and in local districts, helping to influence the discussion process, learning, gaining experience. It has become clear that this cannot be done." Trying to be conventional political activists, however, brought the RAF members to the attention of the authorities. "We have learned that individuals cannot combine legal and illegal activity" (*Concept* n.d.).

In other words, the terrorist has to lead a double life, or else go underground.

While the terrorist feels that he plays a useful role in a worthy struggle, he has to recognize that the struggle is being fought against overwhelming odds. "The concept of the 'urban guerilla' originated in Latin America," said the pamphlet. "Here [that is, in Western Europe] the urban guerilla can only be what he is there: the only method of revolutionary intervention available to what are on the whole weak revolutionary forces" (*Concept* n.d.).

THE "DOOMED MAN"

In October 2002, an unknown sniper began shooting people, one at a time and apparently at random, in the suburban area surrounding Washington, D.C. Both the media and law enforcement officials engaged in fevered speculation about the killer's motives. Some believed that the shooter was a common serial killer, driven by the demons of a diseased mind. Others believed that he or she was a terrorist.

The uncertainty was understandable.

Terrorist acts often resemble the crimes of serial killers and other "ordinary" mass murderers. They are frequently committed at random, by individuals, against victims who are unknown to them, and often in ways that are likely to result in the killer's own death or capture. Because of such similarities, and because of the horrific nature of most terrorist acts, we tend to equate terrorists with other violent criminals, particularly with those we think of as criminally insane.

We assume that only some personal pathology in the (often unidentified) terrorists can explain the viciousness and cruelty of their actions. We ask ourselves, What kind of monsters could do something like this? What's wrong with these people? That there is something wrong with them seems to go without saying. No mentally and emotionally healthy person could do such things.

Consciously or unconsciously, we assume that the people who could commit such savage actions must be particularly brutal or demented themselves. They must enjoy inflicting pain and derive a twisted pleasure out of their own cruelty. Walter Laqueur put it this way: "Terrorists are fanatics and fanaticism frequently makes for cruelty and sadism" (Laqueur 1977, 125).

It is probably true that most terrorists are damaged people. Certainly, many of them have been traumatized by what they have seen and experienced in their lives. But, while emotional trauma or mental defects may explain why some people make willing recruits for terrorist organizations, they do not account for terrorism itself. Nor is there any reason to assume that they account for the majority of terrorists.

To consider terrorism as a product of personal pathology is to misunderstand its nature. Worse, in an age when terrorism threatens the peace and stability of whole societies around the world, such misunderstandings interfere with our ability to deal rationally with the problem, either as a phenomenon or as a threat.

The methods and tactics of terrorism are designed to achieve certain ends, and they can only be understood in relation to those ends. Those methods and tactics may be terrible, vicious, murderous, cruel, and indiscriminately destructive, but so are many of the methods and tactics of ordinary warfare. In this sense, the terrorist who detonates a bomb on a crowded city street is not necessarily any more cruel or mentally unbalanced than the bombardier who reigns down indiscriminate death on a city from thousands of feet in the air.

It is a mistake to regard terrorism as a kind of special perversion, and terrorists as a variety of criminal psychopath. Individual terrorists may or may not be psychopathic, but terrorism is not irrational behavior, nor is it necessarily the product of some personality disorder in the terrorist. Nor is it even the product of some abnormal degree of anger or hostility toward the human race on his part. Such anger and hostility no doubt exist in many terrorists, but it is hardly a necessary element of the motivation for terrorist activities. Indeed, the decision to participate in such activities may even be undertaken with a great deal of reluctance.

In this respect, as in others, the psychology of a terrorist may be similar to the psychology of the ordinary soldier who is called upon to carry out actions that kill noncombatants. Both must turn off, or at least ignore, that part of themselves that recognizes the enemy as a fellow human being, the object of natural sympathy. Both must be willing to kill strangers who have done nothing to them personally, and, in the case of noncombatants, people who are in no position to do anything to them. And, they must be willing to do it when and how they are ordered to do it. What is more, both often act, not out of rage, hatred, or some other overpowering emotion, but because they are committed. That commitment may be to an organization, a country, or a cause. It may be voluntary or coerced.

Where the psychology of the terrorist and of the ordinary soldier is clearly different is in the social sanction given to their actions. In most nations, soldiers are members in good standing of their society. The people of that society respect, and may even highly honor, them. In times of crisis, the society looks to them for protection, and many people look up to them as heroes. They are warriors who are encouraged to wear their uniforms with pride.

Even the enemy may accord them a certain respect. If captured, their status as soldiers provides them with special rights and protections under international law, whether or not those rights are honored. Those who survive their time in the military are permitted to retire, often on a pension, and to peacefully pursue whatever other interests they may have.

A soldier who dies may be given a hero's funeral, regardless of whether he or she has personally performed any heroic acts. For the soldier, heroism is assumed. Not so for the terrorist, who is derided as a coward.

The terrorist is both an outlaw and an outcast. He is hounded throughout the world, and often within his own society most of all. He may be considered a hero by a small group of like-minded people, but everyone else condemns him. Even when he receives support and protection from a rogue government, its help is usually given secretly and publicly denied.

The terrorist is almost universally loathed. He is censured by UN resolutions. Law enforcement agencies around the world regard him as a criminal. Even those terrorists whose are successful enough to attain respectability in

Menahem Begin and Anwar Sadat greet each other at Camp David, September 6, 1978. Courtesy of Jimmy Carter Library.

their later lives can never feel entirely sure that they have escaped the consequences of their pasts.

Nor can terrorists confidently look forward to peaceful retirements. Their crimes have no statute of limitation.

Some terrorists do become respectable later in their careers. John Braithwaite of the Australian National University points out that "Most terrorism in the twentieth century . . . ended with the integration of some terrorist leaders into democratic power structures—whether it was Northern Ireland terrorism, Israeli terrorism, South African terrorism, East Timorese terrorism, the terrorism of the Italian Red Brigades, or that of the Baader-Meinhof gang in Germany. British Prime Minister Blair showed the wisdom of this option when he released IRA terrorists from prison in 1998 so they could speak and vote when their political party decided whether to end armed struggle and support power sharing in Northern Ireland" (Braithwaite 2003).

"Most" is overstating it, but the fact remains that some terrorist leaders do overcome their pasts, often using their terrorist activities as stepping-stones to positions of great and sometimes beneficial influence. Perhaps the most striking illustration of this ironic phenomenon would be a photograph of Prime Minister Menachem Begin of Israel and President Anwar Sadat of Egypt signing the Camp David Peace Accords between their countries on September 17, 1978. At that moment, Begin and Sadat earned a place in history as peacemakers. Indeed, they were later jointly awarded a Nobel Peace Prize for this unprecedented and dramatic leap toward reconciliation in the Middle East. And yet, both Begin and Sadat had first come to public attention as participants in activities that, by most modern standards, would be rightly regarded as terrorism.

Except for those whose acts have been committed in the service of successful revolutions, or who are eventually co-opted by the forces they once fought, most terrorists are condemned to lives as fugitives. Years after they have ceased to take part in terrorist activities, they may be hunted down and shot dead in the streets, and few will ever mourn them. Consider the fate of the three members of Black September who survived their attack on the Israeli athletes at the 1972 Summer Olympic Games in Munich. Two of them were later killed by Mossad agents and the third remains in hiding 30 years after the bloody events at Munich. Several other Black September members who were believed to have had a hand in planning or assisting the Munich operation have also been killed by the Israelis.

What the Russian anarchist Sergey Nechaev wrote about himself and his fellow revolutionaries in 1869 can be said of the mindset of many modern terrorists as well:

> The revolutionary is a doomed man. He has no personal interests, no business affairs, no emotions, no attachments, no property, and no name. Everything in him is wholly absorbed in the single thought and the single passion for revolution . . .
>
> The revolutionary knows that in the very depths of his being, not only in words but also in deeds, he has broken all the bonds which tie him to the social order and the civilized world with all its generally accepted conventions. He is their implacable enemy, and if he continues to live with them it is only in order to destroy them more speedily . . .
>
> He knows of only one science: the science of destruction. To this end, and this end alone, he will study mechanics, physics, chemistry, and perhaps medicine . . .
>
> He despises public opinion. He despises and abhors the existing social ethic in all its manifestations and expressions. For him, everything is moral which assists the triumph of revolution. Immoral and criminal is everything that stands in its way . . .
>
> The revolutionary is a dedicated man, merciless toward the state and toward the whole of educated and privileged society in general; and he must expect no mercy from them either. Between him and them there exists, declared or undeclared, an unceasing and irreconcilable war for life and death. (Nechaev 1869, 68–69)

Although it was written more than 130 years ago, much of the above could be applied to the self-doomed hijackers of September 11. They were not revolutionaries in the traditional sense, but they, too, had a cause that wholly absorbed them.

They, too, broke all ties with the generally accepted conventions of the civilized world the moment they boarded those planes with the intention of annihilating them.

They, too, studied science, learning the basics of aviation, only to destroy.

They, too, despised the social ethic of the world in which they lived, and of which they seemed to be a part.

They, too, believed in a twisted morality in which whatever assisted their cause was moral, and whatever hindered it was despicable and criminal.

They, too, were dedicated men.

They, too, were merciless toward the society they attacked—not because it was educated and privileged, but because it was corrupt and non-Islamic.

They, too, expected no mercy, and they certainly showed none.

And, between them and western society there clearly existed an unceasing and irreconcilable war for life and death.

The majority of terrorists come from the ranks of minorities, whether ethnic, social, political, religious, or ideological. The minorities that breed terrorists tend to be relatively poor, powerless, and often dispossessed. They feel, often correctly, that they are being oppressed, whether by the majority or by a foreign power. A disproportionate number of the foot-soldiers of terror—those who actually perform the assassinations, hijack the planes, and detonate the suicide bombs—were raised in imposed squalor in places like the Palestinian refugee camps of the Middle East or the slums of Belfast. Both as individuals and as members of their group, they feel embittered and angry.

As individuals, the futures they face are bleak. Their lives are blighted with poverty, powerlessness, and an oppression that seem to have no foreseeable end. As individuals, they may feel frustrated and on the verge of despair. Terrorism offers them both a way to break through their frustration and to fight their oppressors. More than that, it provides them an intense activity to occupy their minds and spirits, and give them a feeling of competence and value. They are no longer entirely helpless. They are taking action.

They become, as Nechayev put it, "wholly absorbed in the single thought and the single passion" of their cause. That cause gives a purpose to their lives, and a kind of hope that has nothing to do with their personal futures. In fact, many of them, who see nothing to look forward to but poverty and subservience, may be looking for a noble way of ending their own suffering. Whether consciously or subconsciously, they may be attracted to terrorism as a glorious form of suicide.

Some terrorists have a strong ideological commitment to their cause; others have personal reasons for their commitment. When the Black September commandos took Israeli athletes hostage in the Olympic Village at Munich in 1972, they had one major demand: the release of many of their fellows from Israeli and German prisons. The commander of the terrorists, who went by the nom de guerre "Issa," was motivated not only by Palestinian and left-wing politics, but by the fact that two of the prisoners being held by Israel were his own brothers (Reeve 2000, 61).

Although many of the foot soldiers of terror are bred in places like the slums of Belfast and the Palestinian refugee camps of the Middle East, not all terrorists have been deprived or oppressed. A very different breed comes from a relatively affluent and often even privileged background. The Vietnam War indirectly helped spawn a generation of terrorists who began their political activity as student activists at European and American universities during the 1960s and 1970s.

Before the 1990s, educated terrorists almost always came out of the liberal arts academies, having been trained in such disciplines as economics, history, or philosophy. Lately, however, more and more scientists and engineers have been showing up among the terrorist ranks, where they seem to be highly valued. Among those implicated in major terrorist actions in recent years have been biologists, chemists, computer experts, and physicists (Hudson 1999, 12).

Like the radicals who provided inspiration for the excesses of the French Revolution, and later for the failed revolutions of nineteenth-century Europe, the more affluent and educated terrorists tend to act as theoreticians, planners, organizers, and sometimes, the bankers of terror. They may or may not take an active part in the violence. They include the likes of Alexandros Giotopoulos, the alleged ideological mastermind of the November 17 assassins in Greece, and Osama bin Laden, the son of a wealthy Saudi Arabian family who used his money to help finance the Al Qaeda terrorist network. (Although bin Laden took an active part in the fighting during the Afghan war against the Soviets, he apparently took no direct part in Al Qaeda's terrorist attacks against the United States.)

Also included in ranks of the terrorists are the cohort of mercenaries who kill and maim innocent people for profit. The infamous Carlos the Jackel was one of these. The mercenaries are not to be confused with the terrorist organizations that fund their own operations by hiring out to perform terrorist operations for others, although in some cases, such as that of Abu Nidal, it can be hard to tell the difference. In addition, terrorist groups sometimes work out a kind of barter of blood, like the two men in the classic Alfred Hitchcock movie, *Strangers on a Train*, each of whom undertook to murder the other's wife.

CHEERING TERROR

Mao Zedong famously compared "the people" to water, and the revolutionary army to the fish that swim in it (Reuters 1976). Many terrorist groups could be compared to fish as well, swimming about in the water of the people who sympathize with them and/or their cause. For some terrorist groups (although by no means all) this can be a fairly large segment of the populations of the country (or region) in which they operate.

It was true, for example, of the Provisional Wing of the Irish Republic Army among the Catholics of Northern Ireland at the peak of the Troubles; it was true, perhaps to a lesser extent, of the Red Brigades who swam among leftists in Italy in the 1970s; and it is true today, perhaps to an even greater extent, of Hamas and the Palestine Liberation Front in much of the Islamic world. In such cases, only a relatively small number of people actively help the terrorists, but a significant proportion of the population accepts and tolerates them. Most terrorist groups could not operate, or could not operate nearly as well, without that tolerance.

The tolerance of terrorists, and terrorism itself, manifests in many ways. Residents of a neighborhood look the other way when men with guns move through their streets and backyards. People who suspect that their neighbor belongs to a terrorist organization do not pass on their suspicions to the police. Families take a kind of pride in the fact that one of their members occasionally vanishes for days to take part in terrorist activities. A woman hides a machine-gun for a boyfriend. A doctor secretly treats a wounded man. A young girl carries a message. A crowd openly celebrates news of a successful terrorist operation.

In many parts of the world, police and other antiterrorist forces are routinely met with a wall of silence and stubborn noncooperation from the public. Some of the reluctance to help the police combat terrorists that members of the public feel can be explained by fear. Terrorists are, after all, in the business of arousing terror. Informants may well be endangering not only themselves but their families. But fear can only explain so much. It cannot explain why so many people, even people who usually abhor violence, seem to take a perverse pleasure in the violence committed by terrorists.

Such pleasure can be hard for outsiders to understand, much less to sympathize with. How can ordinary people, who would ordinarily be expected to identify with the victims of terrorism, identify with the perpetrators instead? And even, in some cases, offer aid and comfort to them? How could peaceable Italian Communists look the other way when their ideological comrades gunned down university professors in the streets? How can Protestants in Northern Ireland be so bigoted as to support those who kill young men in Belfast simply because they are Catholics? How can Palestinians be so hateful as to mourn as a hero a suicide bomber who willfully blew up a crowd of shoppers innocently waiting for an Israeli bus?

All of which are just different ways of asking: How can ordinary men, women, and children approve of the murder of other ordinary men, women, and children?

How can human beings accept and even welcome the slaughter of people who in other circumstances could be, and in some cases are, their own fellow citizens, their neighbors, or even their friends?

These are good questions, but they reflect a narrow way of looking at the problem of terrorist violence. Some of the same questions might well be asked of the partisans in any civil war, or, for that matter, of the citizens of almost any embattled country in wartime. For, those people, too, cheer as their nation's troops attack the enemy, bomb its cities, and—inevitably, even when not intentionally—kill many of its people.

Merely asking such questions tends to prejudice the discussion. The questions imply that the populations involved are somehow exceptional—exceptionally callous or even cruel. Americans were outraged when pictures appeared on television that showed Palestinians dancing in the streets after hearing news of the September 11, 2001, attacks. Those images of celebration, repeated over and over again on American television, provoked a vast revulsion in many Americans—a visceral anger, not only at the perpetrators of the attacks but at the entire Arab and Islamic worlds. (And this despite the fact that the pictures showed a relatively small number of people in a single location.)

Reference to those images should not be made without acknowledging that they were not typical of the Palestinian reaction to the tragedy, much less of the reaction of the rest of the Arab world. Sandra Olewine, the United Methodist liaison in Jerusalem at the time, offered this corrective testimony only two days after the event: "Yes, there were some gatherings of people, particularly in Nablus, who were shown in the very early hours of the horrible attacks on the U.S. on the street, dancing and cheering, and passing out chocolate. But, these expressions were few and certainly did not represent the feelings or mood of the general population. The deep shock and horror of the Palestinian people, the real sorrow for all the dead and wounded, was, and continues to be, unseen by the world, particularly in the U.S.A. It is the story unheard" (Olewine 2001).

Nonetheless, the fact remains that some Palestinians *did* celebrate that day, and many more, then and since, have undoubtedly felt some degree of satisfaction at what the September 11 terrorists had done. Terrorists, even the worst of them, *do* generate a positive response in many people.

It is important to consider that response, to try to understand what it does, and does not, mean. Any attempt to do so, however, must necessarily be highly speculative. In making it, it is important to remember that human psychology is pretty much the same everywhere. The fact that one population applauds an act of terrorism, while another is shocked and appalled by it, has more to do with the circumstances that gave rise to the terrorism, and with people's differing relationships to those circumstances, than it does with any fundamental difference in the cultures or psychologies of the two populations.

Although the fact that terrorism is sometimes accepted, and even approved of, by many ordinary people around the world may be lamentable, it should hardly be shocking. Like terrorism, modern warfare invariably involves the deaths of ordinary citizens and other noncombatants. In a sense, then, it can be said that everyone who favors going to war and who applauds their country's military forces in that war, supports—or at least accepts—the slaughter of ordinary men, women, and children. It is only because terrorism is directed so deliberately, and often exclusively, at ordinary people that any approval of it seems so callous.

Even so, people's willingness to support terrorist movements can be hard to understand. Terrorists *do* direct their violence against ordinary people—

often, people who have no part in the conflict in which the terrorists are engaged, and sometimes people who may not even be aware of it. When a bomb goes off in an airliner, the passengers rarely have any rationally discernable connection to the cause their murderers claim to represent at all. You would think that other ordinary people would be far more sympathetic to the victims than to the victimizers. Why then do so many people identify with terrorists rather than with the terrorists' victims?

One factor may be simply the dashing images that some terrorists project. What terrorists actually do may be terrible, but the poses they strike can be both attractive and compelling. Images of masked men (or women) with deadly weapons in their hands have always had the power to both frighten and attract people. That power can be seen in the pictures in old comic books (*The Lone Ranger, The Durango Kid*), in countless movies, in the sword-wielding Ninja warriors of video games, in the media images of soldiers in battle, and even in the televised legions of the white-masked Feydaheen Saddam in the days before the fall of Baghdad.

Even people who have no particular stake in the terrorists' cause may be reluctant to take action against them. Partly this may stem from a general sympathy with the underdog, partly from a dislike of authority, and partly from a simple reluctance to get involved.

Something that can easily be overstated, but which should not be overlooked, is the attraction many people feel toward the drama inherent in terrorism, and in the figure of the terrorist himself. Terrorists are people who have committed themselves to a life of danger, and, in some cases, to the inevitability of an early and deliberate death. There is a romantic attraction in the figure of the rebel who believes in something so strongly that he is willing to sacrifice his life for it.

Terrorists have all the romantic appeal of outlaws. More, they have the special appeal of outlaws with a cause. That appeal must be especially strong when the cause is your own.

Terrorists typically claim to be acting on behalf of some much broader group or cause. In some cases, like that of the Provos and the Catholics in Northern Ireland, the cause may be an oppressed ethnic minority. In other cases, like that of the Ulster Freedom Fighters and other Protestant groups in the same country, it may be a beleaguered majority. In still other cases—like that of the urban guerillas in Europe in the 1970s, and the Islamists in many countries around the world today—the cause may be a shared principle or ideology.

Just as the terrorists identify with the group, the people who belong to that group may identify with them. Many of those people feel personally helpless to act against their enemies, and so are grateful, and even perversely proud, of those who claim to do so on their behalf. Others may abhor the terrorists' actions, but, however paradoxically, still not wish to see the terrorists captured, imprisoned, or executed. However wrong the terrorists' *actions* may be, at least the terrorists are *on the right side*.

People may not like the terrorists, much less admire them, but they are understandably reluctant to act against a force that champions their cause. Especially when the terrorists are the only ones who are championing their cause in a hostile or indifferent world.

Claiming to be paladins of the powerless, the terrorists strike out against the enemy, and the powerless cheer! What else could anyone expect?

It should be understood that for most people, whatever feeling of pleasure they may take in a terrorist's exploits, that pleasure is strictly vicarious. It does not mean that everyone who feels heartened when a terrorist act is committed necessarily fully approves of that act. It most certainly does not mean that he or she would do the same thing themselves.

To better understand this response to terrorism, it may be helpful to look away from foreign reactions to terrorism—whether the Palestinians' delight with September 11, or Irish support of Provo or UDA violence—and to focus on a similar phenomenon that occurred closer to home.

Consider the situation in the farm regions of the American Midwest during the Great Depression of the 1930s. At that time, American farmers were in serious trouble. Years of drought had ruined their crops. The banks were foreclosing on thousands of farms. Sheriffs were appearing at the doors of farmhouses across the Midwest, evicting families who had lived on the land for generations, and sending them onto the nation's highways in search of new places to live, new ways to put food on the table. Unfortunately, there were few jobs to be had anywhere in the country. The dispossessed roamed the countryside, while those who remained on the land lived in constant fear that they would soon be forced into joining those on the road.

In that atmosphere of fear and intimidation, a handful of desperate young people took to a life of crime. Specifically, they took to bank robbery, both as a way to provide for themselves and as a way to strike back at a society that had no place for them or their families. Why banks? Because, as the notorious bank robber Willie Sutton reportedly put it, "That's where the money is." It was practically the *only* place where money could be found in the region at that time.

But in a region full of people who felt themselves threatened by those banks, these dashing criminals became heroes of a kind. They were more popular, in a way, than movie stars. Millions of ordinary Americans thrilled to the newspaper and radio accounts of their exploits. John Dillinger, Bonnie and Clyde, Pretty Boy Floyd, Ma Barker's boys—they have passed into legend. Their names still resonate after more than six decades.

Some of these desperadoes could travel by car through the back roads and small towns of the American Midwest with relative impunity. Many who saw them recognized them from newspaper photographs, but few ever notified the authorities. Instead, they rooted for them to escape capture and continue their adventures for as long as possible.

Did this mean that more ordinary Depression-era Midwesterners approved of robbery and murder? That they had no respect for law and order?

That they had no sympathy for the innocent men and women who were gunned down by these ruthless sociopaths? Of course not. What it did mean was that people are complex beings. While one part of them may be repelled by something, another part may be attracted.

People who feel threatened by forces beyond their control will respond positively to anything that seems to challenge those forces. Farmers in the Depression-era Midwest saw their neighbors being swept away on waves of economic realities they could not even understand, much less control. They themselves felt helpless before the same implacable imperatives. Those imperatives might be incomprehensible, but they were symbolized by an institution that the Midwesterners could understand all too well—the local bank, an institution that must have seemed as heartless as the economic forces it embodied.

How could those timid, frightened people *not* admire those who dared to do what they could not do? Who dared to defy not only the power of the banks, but the power of the law enforcement agencies that did the banks' bidding?

Although only partially, and only momentarily, those people identified with the notorious criminals. On some level, they felt that when John Dillinger robbed a bank, he was robbing it for them. When Bonnie and Clyde shot it out with local law enforcement officials, they were getting even for all the poor farmers those officials had thrown off their farms. Rumors (perhaps true) circulated that fed these fantasies: it was said that when Dillinger robbed a bank, he destroyed the farm mortgages in the bank's vault.

But these *were* fantasies, and only fantasies. Feeling sympathy, and even admiration, for the criminals carried no real responsibility for their victims, and no real guilt for what happened to them. People regarded the real-life criminals they read about in the newspapers much the way they regarded the characters in a movie. The bank robbers were the heroes, the bankers were the villains. The fact that the real-life bankers, and the bank cashiers, tellers, and other employees who got caught up in the violence, were their own real-life neighbors did not enter into it. Certainly few, if any, of the people who inwardly cheered for the violent exploits of the bank robbers would have ever dreamed of shooting a bank teller or killing a policeman themselves.

The dispossessed Palestinians who celebrated on September 11 regarded the United States as an enemy—an enemy every bit as powerful, implacable, and unappeasable as dispossessed Midwestern farmers regarded the banks in the 1930s. It was hardly surprising that they were pleased to see such a mighty enemy struck down, if only for a brief historical moment.

In that moment, when the Palestinians watched in awe as the twin towers came crashing down, the people who suffered and died in those towers were not thought of as individual human beings. They were just more bloody victims in the endless parade of bloody victims that streams across the television screens of the world. But the symbolism of the great towers coming down—the might of the West collapsing before their eyes—that was something new and different. That was something that could be seen and felt as *real,* in a way that the people who died were not.

What the relatively few Palestinians who celebrated the destruction of the World Trade Center towers on September 11, 2001 felt toward the terrorists was perhaps not so very different from what many Depression-era Midwesterners felt toward John Dillinger.

REFERENCES

Braithwaite, John. 2003. "Pre-Empting Terrorism." Unpublished paper.

Bush, George W. 2001. "Address to a Joint Session of Congress and the American People." U.S. Capitol, Washington, D.C. 20 September.

Concept Urban Guerilla, The [sic]. n.d. Richard Huffman, This is Baader-Meinhof. http://www.baader-meinhoff.com (accessed 25 March 2004).

Gibbons, Jim. 2003. Interview. *Washington Journal.* C-SPAN Television, 19 March.

Hudson, Rex A. 1999. "The Sociology and Psychology of Terrorism: Who Becomes a Terrorist and Why?" Report. Washington, D.C.: Federal Research Division, Library of Congress. September.

Laqueur, Walter. 1977. *Terrorism.* Boston: Little Brown.

Mukherjee, Rudrangshu. 1993. *The Penguin Gandhi Reader.* New York: Penguin.

Nechaev, Sergey. 1869. "Catechism of the Revolutionist." Reprint., Walter Laqueur, ed. 1978. *The Terrorism Reader: A Historical Anthology.* New York: New American Library.

Olewine, Sandra. 2001. "The Sorrow Unseen, the Story Unheard," Study of Islam Section, American Academy of Religion. 13 September. http://www.mafhoum.com/press2/63C35.htm (accessed 25 March 2004).

Reeve, Simon. 2000. *One Day in September.* New York: Arcade.

Reuters. 1976. "Text of Announcement Issued by Peking Reporting Death of Chairman Mao." 10 September. http://www.hartford-hwp.com/archives/55/120.html (accessed 25 March 2004).

4

Varieties of Terror

We talk about terrorism in the way we talk about an ideology, and about terrorists in the ways we talk about adherents to an ideology. We say things like, "terrorists believe," and "terrorists want," and "for a terrorist, the most important thing is—," and so on. But terrorism is not an ideology; nor is it a movement, a cause, or even a principle.

Terrorism is better understood as a weapon, or as a tool that is used to accomplish something. Like other tools, it has no *necessary* relevance to the purpose for which it is employed. The same hammer can be used to build to a church or a gallows. The same gun can be used to hunt food for a family or to rob a liquor store. The difference is, of course, that the hammer and the gun are morally neutral. Terrorism is not.

The way one uses the tool varies from user to user, age to age, and circumstance to circumstance. At different times and in different places, terrorism has been employed as a military tactic, an expression of anger, a criminal methodology, a way of raising money, a means of enforcing the law, a tool of repression, a revolutionary statement; and in many other ways, besides. We have referred to terrorism as a tactic, but Israeli Prime Minister Ariel Sharon has said that he has "always seen terrorism as a strategic and not a tactical problem" (Glick 2002).

TERRORISM AS PART OF A LARGER EFFORT

A distinction can be made between terrorism that is carried out as an isolated activity by disaffected outlaws and that which is part of a larger organized effort. Some terrorist groups act solely on their own initiative, for their own motives; others act in conjunction with a broader movement, often as adjuncts to a more conventional paramilitary campaign, as when members of the French or Yugoslavian resistance sabotaged Nazi targets in occupied Europe, thereby weakening the Nazis in preparation for the Allied invasion of Europe.

In other cases, officially or unofficially, terrorists serve as the ersatz armed forces of a political movement. The Provos of the IRA (Irish Republican Army), for example, were widely considered the equivalent of a military arm of the Irish independence movement of which Sinn Féin was the political arm; Islamic Jihad serves as an adjunct to the political and other branches of Hezbollah in Lebanon.

Still other groups believe themselves to be part of a political movement without ever receiving the blessings—even the unofficial blessings—of that movement. They consider themselves being allied with a much larger ethnic, economic, or social group, and as furthering a cause beyond themselves. They may even consider themselves to be the vanguard of that cause. Their relation to that larger entity, however, may be only tangential at best. Often, in fact, those whose cause they claim to champion refuse to acknowledge the terrorists' assistance, and may even reject it. Many members of the larger group may be embarrassed and horrified by the terrorists' actions, and by their own presumed association with them.

DOMESTIC AND INTERNATIONAL GROUPS

Terrorist groups are categorized as either domestic or international. Domestic terrorists are those who act within a particular country, against people or institutions peculiar to that country, and for purposes related to that country. Most revolutionary or separatist terrorist groups fall into the domestic category, because they are usually concerned only with effecting change within a particular country or region, and so confine their violence to actions against a particular government. Likewise, groups that use terrorism to *combat* separatist or independence movements—such as the right-wing death squads in Latin America or the Ulster Freedom Fighters in Northern Ireland—are almost invariably local.

International terrorists, on the other hand, show little respect for borders or for the nationalities of their victims. They strike anywhere they can, against anyone whose death or deprivation might serve their cause. Most anti-American or anti-Western political terrorist groups fall into the international category, as do such religious terrorist groups as the Islamists. Ideas and beliefs know no borders.

When President George W. Bush declared the so-called War on Terrorism, the terrorism he was really talking about was of the international variety—or, as it is sometimes put, "terrorism with a global reach." As far as the United States is concerned, domestic terrorism remains primarily a local matter. International terrorism, however, is to be fought by a major international effort led by the United States.

Some groups are easy to categorize in this way. The Japanese Red Army and the Abu Nidal Organization were clearly international; the Ulster

Defense Association is clearly domestic. Others can be more difficult to categorize. Take a group like Abu Sayaaf. Although the focus of this Islamic separatist group is definitely domestic and the great majority of its crimes are committed within the watery borders of the Philippines, many of the group's victims (who are frequently held for ransom) are foreigners. The United States government clearly considers Abu Sayaaf to be in the international category, as it has sent military trainers and advisers to help the government of the Philippines combat the group.

Similarly, although the Provos of the IRA are concerned almost exclusively with Northern Ireland, and the vast majority of their outrages were committed inside that country (they are currently inactive), some of their attacks took place in England and elsewhere in the U.K.; and, even in Northern Ireland, many of their victims were British soldiers. In addition, the IRA raises money abroad and reportedly has connections with several foreign terrorist organizations.

During the Cold War—and before the War on Terrorism—American law enforcement agencies used a different standard to distinguish between domestic terrorists and those that represented an international, and therefore, it was thought, more serious threat. That standard was ideological, and under it, even a group like the Weathermen (or the Weather Underground [WUO]) was considered to be in the international category.

The Weathermen were a militant offshoot of the New Left, anti-Vietnam War student movement of the 1960s and 1970s, and specifically of the Students for a Democratic Society (SDS). They lived the lives of underground revolutionaries, built bombs, and committed several acts of violence against the American "power structure." They were American citizens who operated entirely within the United States against American targets. Yet, according to a report issued by the Chicago office of the FBI in 1976:

> Knowledgeable analysts who have followed the growth of . . . the Weather Underground (WUO) are well aware of the foreign influences on the collective thoughts and actions of these revolutionaries who have consistently carried out the Marxist-Leninist conception of armed struggle in the U.S. The WUO investigation is an excellent example of the native born American [sic] who adopts the faith of a foreign ideology and in behalf of his belief commits acts of armed violence, the purposes of which serve to acknowledge his revolutionary obligations to the international communist movement and at the same time create the conditions for revolution in the mother country. The revolutionary who has committed his destiny under the banner of Marxism-Leninism establishes his identity with a world center of revolution (in this case, Havana) . . . He ceases to be merely "domestic" when he adopts his international identity as a revolutionary. (Federal Bureau of Investigation 1976)

The report (which was classified "Top Secret" when it was written in 1976, but has since been made publicly available under the Freedom of Information Act) shows that, in those days, the FBI's focus was less on the terrorist *actions* of the Weather Underground than on the "foreign" ideology of the group. While the notion that an idea can be "alien," and therefore inherently dangerous, sounds quaint today, the idea that an international group presents a more serious threat is still very much current.

Despite this assumption, domestic terrorism, in the broadest sense of the word, which includes most incidents of genocide and ethnic cleansing, killed far more people than international terrorism in the twentieth century. Estimates run as high as 42 million (Medhurst 2000: I, 12).

STATE-SPONSORED TERRORISM

The overwhelming majority of the world's nations are signatories to at least one international agreement that condemns terrorism. It has become *de rigueur* for governments to publicly denounce terrorism and to take active police and military steps against it, and the showier and more dramatic those steps, the better. Yet, many of those very same governments support organizations that most of the world (although never the governments that support them) would agree are terrorist, and some of those governments commit acts that others (but again, not themselves) would consider terrorism, as well.

Terrorism may be less expensive than conventional warfare, but it is rarely free, particularly when it is committed on a large scale. A minority of terrorist groups are self-supporting, financing themselves by criminal activities such as drug trafficking, robbery, extortion, and kidnapping-for-ransom. Most terrorist groups, however, have to rely on support from outside the organization for at least some of their funding.

The Provos in Northern Ireland have traditionally received financial support from Irish-Americans who feel ties to their families' past and who are attracted by the IRA's romantic image. Some of this money may have been given inadvertently, in the form of contributions to "charities" that claimed to fight poverty, or to protect Catholic civil rights in Ireland. Likewise, some Arab-Americans have contributed, either wittingly or unwittingly, to "charities" that funnel money to Palestinian and Islamic terrorist groups. Among other groups that receive substantial support from those with ethnic bonds abroad include the PKK (Kurdish Workers Party), which receives funds from Kurds living in Western Europe, and the LTTE (Liberation Tigers of Tamil Elam), which is reportedly funded by Tamils living in Canada (Anderson n.d., 3).

But individuals and bogus charities pale in comparison to governments as sources of support for terrorism. Governments support terrorists in various ways. Some do it with money, some with arms, and some with ideological guidance or paramilitary training; others provide facilities for terrorists to train themselves. Still others provide terrorists with safe haven, or with diplomatic cover and other assistance. "This may include the provision of false identity documents in the form of a passport which is authentic but reflects [a] false identity. The cover used in the target country might include employment with an embassy under diplomatic cover or assistance from embassy-based security or intelligence officers who also function as the terrorist's support staff" (Medhurst 2000: VI, 10).

One of the stated reasons for the 2003 war on Iraq was Saddam Hussein's alleged support of international terrorism, and the United States righteously continues to accuse Syria, Iran, North Korea, and Cuba of supporting terrorist groups. But those are by no means the only governments known to give support to terrorists. In fact, the United States itself has frequently, and sometimes openly, given support, through the CIA and otherwise, to groups that practice terrorism, notably including the Contras who conducted a paramilitary insurgency against the left-wing Sandinista government of Nicaragua in the 1980s. The CIA also supported the Mujahadeen—the 10,000 Muslim fighters from more than 10 nations who went to Afghanistan to combat the Soviet occupation of that country in the 1980s—reportedly to the tune of $500 million. Ironically, many of those same Mujahadeen fighters, including Osama bin Laden, now form the core of the al-Qaeda terrorist network.

Governments support such groups for a variety of reasons. They may share a common ideology with the terrorists, as when the Soviet Union supported Marxist-Leninist insurgencies around the world during the Cold War. They may share a cause, as do the Arab governments that support groups like Hamas and Islamic Jihad in their efforts to destroy Israel. Sometimes governments offer help to terrorists in the hope that such assistance will lead the terrorists to concentrate their attacks elsewhere. This is probably a factor in the assistance some Arab governments allegedly give to al-Qaeda.

Governments frequently support groups whose activities they find helpful for geopolitical reasons. The United States helped both Iran and Iraq at different stages of the war between those two countries, even though it knew both of them to be guilty of sponsoring terrorism, not only against each other, but against Israel and Western interests, as well.

Throughout the Cold War, the Soviet Union and other Communist nations offered financial, logistical, and other support to left-wing paramilitaries and Marxist-Leninist terrorist groups in countries around the world. At the same time, the United States was giving assistance to the governments that were resisting such insurgencies, even those that did so using terrorist methods of their own. In that respect, it is poetic justice that the United States and the Soviet Union's successor, Russia, are two of the main targets of terrorism today.

THE TERRORISTS' FAVORITE WEAPON

Terrorism has even more manifestations than it has uses. The weapon of terrorism employs myriad weapons of its own.

For more than a century, the terrorists' favorite weapon has been the bomb. Bombs have certain obvious advantages for the terrorist. One, so obvious that it is sometimes overlooked, is the simple fact that bombs make a lot of noise—both literally and figuratively. This makes them uniquely useful for attracting attention, which is often the terrorists' first and most important objective.

Bombs are relatively simple (if dangerous) both to build and to transport. They are more destructive than knives, guns, or any of the other weapons readily available to terrorists. They are also spectacularly indiscriminate, which makes them ideal for spreading terror. What is even better, from some terrorists' point of view, bombs create their own monuments, in the form of the blasted ruins they leave behind them.

Bombs have been used for a variety of purposes, from assassinating individuals to decimating crowds, from destroying airplanes to blowing up large buildings. They come in all varieties, all levels of destructive power, and all degrees of sophistication. They range from incendiaries to bombs that kill by sheer concussive power; from "letter bombs" containing Semtex, to pipe bombs packed with nails; from Molotov cocktails to shapeable *plastique* set off by a complex timing device; from explosives tucked into suitcases to explosives jammed into trucks. The bomb that destroyed the Alfred P. Murrah Building was a sophisticated combination of unsophisticated materials: chiefly ammonium nitrate fertilizer and fuel oil.

Bombs can be delivered from virtually any distance, and by every conceivable means. They can be thrown by hand, launched as missiles, sent through the mail, left in bus-station lockers, or delivered to their targets in vehicles; there are bicycle bombs, and car bombs, and truck bombs. They can be detonated in any number of ways: mechanically, electrically, electronically, and chemically. They can be triggered by photoelectric cells, by clock mechanisms, by radio signals, by motion detectors, and by anything that makes or breaks an electrical connection. A bomb can be set off by another bomb or by a kitchen timer, by concussion, by contact between one chemical and another, and even by radiation. The possible delivery systems available to terrorists are as varied as the human imagination itself. In 1995, a Sri Lankan ferry worker was injured by a cigarette bomb that blew up in his face when he set a match to it (TamilNet 1997).

A NEW KIND OF BOMB

The most notable development in terrorism in recent years has been the proliferation of suicide attacks.

The hijackers who flew the planes into the World Trade Center and the Pentagon on September 11, 2001, obviously knew they were going to die fulfilling their mission. So did the nine terrorists who shot their way into the expatriate residential compounds in Riyadh, Saudi Arabia, in May,

2003, before detonating the explosives contained inside the two trucks they were driving, destroying themselves and more than 20 residents of the compound in the bargain. So did the 99 suicide bombers from Hamas and Hezbollah (or Hezbollah's affiliate, Islamic Jihad) who blew up themselves and more than 250 bystanders in Israel from the beginning of the Palestinian *intifada* in 2000 until June 1, 2003 (Daraghmeh 2003).

While acknowledging that suicide attacks of various kinds have occurred since ancient times, the counterterrorism researcher Yoram Schweitzer traces the current suicide-bombing phenomenon back to Hezbollah's attack on the American Embassy in Beirut, Lebanon, in April 1983, followed by the much more destructive attacks on the U.S. Marine barracks and the French Multinational Force in Lebanon six months later (Schweitzer 2000).

Despite Hamas' admitted role in the suicide-bombing campaign in Israel, the group considers the attacks a justified "exception" to its declared policy of not targeting civilians. "In recent times," says Dr. Azzam Tamimi,

> the Hamas military wing (Ezziddin Al-Qassam Brigades) planned and carried out a number of what Hamas calls *"amaliyyat Istish-hadiyah"* (martyrdom operations). These are usually described in the Western media as suicide operations. These operations, which target civilians, are considered an aberration from Hamas's fundamental position of hitting only military targets. Hamas officials insist that these operations represent an exception necessitated by the Israeli insistence on targeting Palestinian civilians and by Israel's refusal to agree to an understanding prohibiting the killing of civilians on both sides—an understanding comparable to the one reached between Israel and Hizbollah in southern Lebanon. The first *Istish-hadi* operation came in response to the massacre of Muslim worshippers as they kneeled in prayer in Al-Masjid al-Ibrahimi at dawn on the fifteenth day of the fasting holy month of Ramadan [25 February 1994]. Sheikh Yassin, who offered the Israelis a truce, explained that his movement does not endorse the killing of civilians, but that it is sometimes the only option it has if it is to respond to the murdering of Palestinian civilians. (Tamimi 1998)

The Liberation Tigers of Tamil Elam (LTTE)—a Hindu separatist group in Sri Lanka that killed an estimated 1,500 people in the decade of the 1990s alone—has no such scruples. Among the world's most expert practitioners of suicide bombing, the LTTE goes so far as to film some of its operations in order to use the films to inspire their surviving members to emulate the "martyrs" (Friedman 2002).

Although the overwhelming majority of suicide bombers are male, many LTTE bombers and a growing, but still relatively small, number of the Palestinian bombers are women.

It takes a deep commitment, or an equally profound despair, to make people willingly sacrifice their own lives in the process of killing others. (Although it is probably true that not all suicide bombers are willing participants in the process. Some have allegedly been forced into acting as human bomb-delivery systems by threats to their families, although this charge is difficult to prove.) Such cases, if they do in fact exist, are probably rare exceptions. Most suicide bombers believe in what they do—as attested by the videotapes several of them have made declaring their intentions.

Even so, terrorists bent on suicide act from a mix of motives. As John Braithwaite has pointed out, "Suicide bombers are often not only motivated by the embrace of their God in death as martyrs, but also by generous payments to the struggling families they leave behind" (Braithwaite 2003). Alleged payments to the families of suicide bombers by Saddam Hussein was one of the many charges the United States made against him in justifying the invasion of Iraq in 2003.

Like terrorism in general, suicide bombings help to "even the playing field" between small groups of impoverished guerillas and governments, which have massive manpower and arsenals of technologically sophisticated weapons at their disposal. For those who cannot afford the latest in technology, the suicide bomber provides a different kind of sophisticated weaponry. An Israeli military spokesman, Lieutenant-Colonel Olivier Rafowicz, put it this way: "You have a combatant with 20 to 30 pounds of TNT. Add a human brain, and you get a smart bomb. It's a new kind of battlefield" (Moore 2002).

ASSASSINATIONS

The politically motivated killing of a head-of-state or other public official is usually characterized as a form of terrorism, although the killing of a tyrant has historically been considered a justifiable or even a positively virtuous act. The great majority of Americans and Europeans during World War II would have applauded the assassination of Adolph Hitler and welcomed the assassin as a great hero.

In this area, as in so many others, the "terrorism" label can be tricky to apply, and where it is applied may depend on the political views of the applier.

The assassination of Abraham Lincoln clearly falls within most Americans' understanding of terrorism. The attempted assassination of Theodore Roosevelt in 1912, however, probably does not. John Wilkes Booth killed Lincoln for political reasons, both to avenge the vanquished Confederacy and to force a change of leaders which he no doubt hoped would change the national government's policy toward the South. But when John Schrank shot Roosevelt at a campaign rally in Milwaukee, Wisconsin, he was apparently driven by madness, not political purpose. (He claimed that he shot the presidential candidate at the behest of the ghost of William McKinley.) ("Appendix VII" 1964)

The United States government would vigorously deny that it ever engaged in or endorsed terrorism, and yet United States government agencies have, in fact, taken part in a number of assassinations and assassination attempts over the years. The United States made no less than eight separate attempts on the life of Fidel Castro under the aegis of Operation Mongoose, the notorious CIA-sponsored covert effort to remove the Cuban leader from power (Corson 1977, 3).

Other assassination attempts have been carried out by the U.S. military. These include the attack by American warplanes on the tent of Muammar Qaddafi in 1986—an attack that failed to hurt the Libyan leader, and succeeded only in killing his 15-month-old adopted daughter. (Ironically, Qaddafi was targeted for assassination in revenge for his sponsorship of terrorism around the world.)

Early in the war in Iraq there were news reports—never denied—that American special-assassination teams had infiltrated the country to assassinate key figures in the Iraqi leadership. The implication was that teams' chief target was Saddam Hussein himself. The assassination efforts in Iraq were presumably justified on the basis that the government officials, and even heads-of-state, are fair game in wartime—a principle that makes many Americans and others around the world extremely uncomfortable. The attempts on Castro lacked even that excuse.

Assassination is a clear, if covert, policy not only of many terrorist groups, but of many governments around the world, including our own. "Yet," as John Braithwaite of the Australian National University insists, "political assassination, even when it delivers a short-run benefit, has been repeatedly proven to be a long-run counterproductive strategy in the modern world" (Braithwaite 2003).

Even when the victim of the political assassination is himself a well-known terrorist, the results can often be very different, and more unfortunate, than the assassins intended. "There would likely be peace in Palestine today," opines Braithwaite, "if after the assassination of Prime Minister Rabin, the new Israeli Prime Minister Peres had not ordered the assassination of Yahya Ayyash, known as 'the bombmaker.' " His assassination was reciprocated with a devastating round of Hamas suicide bombings in February–March 1996 that killed more than 50 Israelis (Quandt 2001). "This allowed Benjamin Netanyahu to present himself as 'Mr. Security' and defeat Peres, who had—until his ill-conceived assassination plot—been way ahead in the polls. It was Netanyahu's provocations that then unraveled the peace process" (Braithwaite 2003).

ATTACKS ON AIRPLANES

When the Iron Curtain fell between Eastern and Western Europe after World War II, certain desperate people trapped in the East hit upon a way of getting out. They hijacked planes and forced the pilots to land in the West. As a means of escape, it had two great advantages: it was simple and it worked. True, the passengers and crews were put in danger, but the danger was not great, so long as everyone kept their heads. It was usually a short flight from East to West, and, although the Eastern European governments routinely gunned down individuals who tried to escape across the ideological borders, they were hardly likely to shoot a passenger airliner out of the sky.

Besides, it was a dangerous time. A war had just ended in which tens of millions of people had been slaughtered. The possibility that one planeload full of people should suffer an hour or so of worry was not overly alarming. Far from being outraged, the West welcomed the hijackers as refugees from tyranny, if not as heroes.

Almost two decades later, after the Castro Revolution in Cuba, there was a period of dueling hijackers between that nation and the United States. Right-wing Cubans seized Cuban planes to fly them to Miami, while leftists in the United States seized American planes to fly them to Havana. When Cuban planes landed in the United States, the U.S. government seized them, and "distributed" them "to companies and individuals owed money by Cuba" (Shoonakker 2001). It was only after Cuba began welcoming hijackers—in much the way the West had welcomed hijackers from Eastern Europe twenty years before—that the United States made air piracy a serious crime in 1961.

Such hijackings are usually classified as terrorist acts, and yet they do not really fit into most common definitions of the term. Crucially, although they made people nervous about flying on airliners in the regions where hijackings tended to occur, they were not intended to intimidate anyone. Presumably, if the hijackers had been able to simply buy a ticket to Havana or Miami, most of them would have done so.

It was not long, however, before commercial airliners became a favorite target for terrorists. Hijacking or blowing up an airplane in flight was relatively easy to do, and it was a great way to get international attention.

ETHNIC AND RACIAL HARASSMENT

Terrorism is usually thought of as a tool of outsiders, of the weak striking out at those who abuse their weakness, or of revolutionaries attempting to change an entrenched or oppressive system. However, the weapons of terrorism can also be used against such people, either by government authorities, or by essentially conservative elements of a society who feel that the authorities are not doing enough (or are unable) to protect the society's way of life.

This was the case with the practice of lynching in the American South during the days of Jim Crow, when groups of white citizens rose up periodically to abuse, hang, or otherwise kill black men whom they believed had violated the white-dominated social order. (The term "lynching" is some-

Lynched African American man hanging from tree.
Courtesy of Library of Congress.

times applied more broadly to include any more or less random murders of blacks by whites, carried out by any methods and for any reasons.)

Lynch mobs often saw themselves as vigilantes. They attacked those who had allegedly broken some serious law or social taboo: killers who had committed horrendous crimes, or black men who had had sexual relations with white women. In the American South from the mid-nineteenth to the mid-twentieth century, the second offense was considered, if anything, more serious than the first. Sexual contact between black men and white women was considered not only illegal and immoral, but unnatural. It didn't just violate the criminal laws of the place and time; it violated the very assumptions that underlaid those laws.

Black men were not the only ones lynched, however. A white man who committed a particularly atrocious crime—the murder of a child, say, or the rape of a particularly highly regarded woman—might be given a "necktie party" as well.

For a time in the 1880s, when federal troops withdrew from the South and the Ku Klux Klan and others set out to drive the white carpetbaggers from the region, whites were actually lynched more frequently than blacks. In 1884, for instance, 160 white people were reported lynched in the United States, compared to only 51 blacks; the following year, the numbers were 110 whites and 74 blacks. By 1886, however, more blacks were being lynched than whites, and by the early twentieth century, the lynching of whites had become a rarity (Tuskegee 2000).

Once Jim Crow was firmly established, the lynching of white men all but ended, while black men continued to be lynched in virtually the same numbers as they had before. In effect, 10 to 20 times as many black men became victims of vigilante "justice" as whites; sometimes even more. In 1912, for example, 62 black men are known to have been lynched in the United States, and only two whites (Tuskegee 2000).

The broader purpose of lynching—when used against black men, and particularly black men accused of violating (or merely failing to respect) white women—was to put fear into the hearts of *all* black men. It was a way of setting limits not only to black behavior but also to black social and sexual aspiration. Black men who failed to accept the white social structure they existed within, but were not a part of, knew that they could suffer the ultimate penalty. The punishment would be swift and sure, and would not depend on the rulings of courts of law or any kind of due process. Such offenders were not lynched primarily because they had broken the law (many white men did that and received lesser punishments, if any) but because they had violated something much deeper and more primitive.

The lynchings in the American South fell toward the middle of a spectrum of ethnic terrorism. At the most extreme end are the horrors of genocide: the pogroms against the Jews in Russia at the end of the nineteenth century, the slaughter of the Armenians by the Turks near the beginning of the twentieth century, the Holocaust of Jews in Europe, "ethnic cleansing" in Yugoslavia and elsewhere, and the massacres of Tutsis and moderate Hutus in Rwanda are all examples of this horrible phenomenon. The scale of these outrages put them beyond the scope of this book, but they, too, are symptoms of the same disease, only in its most extreme, virulent, and pernicious form.

At the other end of the spectrum of ethnic terrorism is the kind of harassment exemplified by "the swastika epidemic" that struck western Europe, the United States, and Latin America less than two decades after the end of the World War II.

> It started with the desecration of a synagogue in Cologne on December 25, 1959 by two young Germans who were promptly apprehended and severely punished. Some 685 incidents were recorded in Germany, and over 600 in the United States. All told, nearly 2,500 incidents were recorded in 400 localities throughout the world. Most of them occurred in January or February 1960, and consisted of cemetery and synagogue desecrations and graffiti.

Assault on a Jew in the presence of the military. Courtesy of North Wind Picture Archives.

Cases of a graver character, such as assaults on Jews and arson were rare, but some were also reported. (Epstein 1993)

The "swastika epidemic" was considered a right-wing phenomenon, a remnant of the fascist passions of the earlier part of the century. As such, it was a gasp of something dying, or even a kind of muscle twitch of something already dead. But now, in the new millennium, a new and very different kind of anti-Semitism seems to be breaking out. This is a left-wing anti-Semitism, exacerbated by Israeli policies and actions in the Middle East. Left-wing sympathy has long tended to be with the Palestinians in their struggle with Israel. In the past, that sympathy has tended to manifest itself largely in opposition to Israeli government policy. But now, not only in the Middle East but in Europe and to a growing extent in the United States as well, that sympathy is being tied to a growing hostility toward Jews in general.

A potentially much more serious wave of anti-Semitic harassment has recently broken out in France, ranging from protest demonstrations in which crowds chant "Kill the Jews!" to the teasing and physical abuse of Jewish schoolchildren, to beatings, to the burning of synagogues. There were hundreds of such attacks in 2002, and in the first three months of 2003, there were reportedly 326 incidents in Paris alone (Brenner 2003, 128).

Although these activities may fall outside the more restrictive definitions of terrorism, they clearly have a terrorist purpose. This is glaringly obvious when the incidents are taken together rather than as individual acts of vandalism, not merely as personal expressions of anti-Semitism, but as the expression of the hostility of a large segment of the non-Jewish population. What is more, such actions clearly have a terrorist result. The Jewish population in France and elsewhere where these episodes occur must inevitably feel less secure in their homes and communities than they would otherwise.

REFERENCES

Anderson, James H. n.d. "Modus Operandi." Paper. James Madison University, William R. Nelson Institute for Public Affairs, International Terrorism, and Crime: Trends and Linkages. http://www.jmu.edu/orgs/wrni/It5.html (accessed 25 March 2004).

"Appendix VII, A Brief History of Presidential Protection." 1964. Report of the President's Commission on the Assassination of President John F. Kennedy. Washington, D.C.: U.S. Government Printing Office.

Braithwaite, John. 2003. Pre-Empting Terrorism. Paper. Social Science Research Network. http://papers.ssrn.com/sol3/papers.cfm?abstract_id=330500 (accessed 25 March 2004).

Brenner, Marie. 2003. "France's Scarlet Letter." *Vanity Fair*, June.

Corson, William R. 1977. *The Armies of Ignorance*. New York: Dial Press/James Wade.

Daraghmeh, Mohammed. 2003. "Training Female Suicide Bombers." *Salt Lake City Tribune*, 1 June.

Epstein, Simon. 1993. "Cyclical Patterns in Antisemitism: The Dynamics of Anti-Jewish Violence in Western Countries since the 1950s." Research paper. Vidal Sassoon International Center for the Study of Antisemitism, the Hebrew University of Jerusalem.

Federal Bureau of Investigation (FBI). 1976. *Foreign Influence-Weather Underground Organization, Summary Dated 8/20/76, Part I, Comments of the Chicago Office*. Chicago: Federal Bureau of Investigation.

Friedman, Thomas L. 2002. "Lessons from Sri Lanka." *New York Times*, 7 August.

Glick, Caroline B. 2002. "Sharon: No Military Solution to the War with the Palestinians." *Jerusalem Post*, 26 September.

Medhurst, Paul. 2000. *Global Terrorism*. Denver, Colo.: United Nations Institute for Training and Research Programme of Correspondence Instruction.

Moore, Molly, and John Ward Anderson. 2002. "Suicide Bombers Give An Edge to Palestinians." *International Herald Tribune*, 19 August.

Quandt, William B. 2001. *Peace Process: American Diplomacy and the Arab-Israeli Conflict since 1967*. Berkeley: University of California Press.

Schweitzer, Yoram. 2000. "Suicide Terrorism: Development & Characteristics." Talk, delivered at the International Institute for Counter-Terrorism, Herzeliya, Israel, 21 February. ICT Web site. http://www.ict.org.il/articles/articledet/cfm?articleid=1997123003 (accessed 25 March 2004).

Shoonakker, Bonny. 2001. "The History of Hijacking." *Sunday Times* (South Africa), 12 September.

TamilNet. 1997. http://www.tamilnet.com/art.html?catid=13&rid=1997123003 (accessed March 25 2004).

Tamimi, Azzam. 1998. The Legitimacy of Palestinian Resistance: An Islamist Perspective. Paper, presented at 7th Annual Conference of the Centre for Policy Analysis on Palestine, 11 September, in Washington, D.C.

Tuskegee Institute Archives. "Lynching Statistics." Shipp Trial Web site, Famous American Trials. University of Missouri. http://www. umkc.edu/faculty/projects/ftrials/shipp/lynchingyear.html (accessed 25 March 2004).

❺

Weapons of Mass Destruction

The great specter that haunts every discussion of terrorism is the possibility that terrorists may have, or may soon acquire, weapons of mass destruction (WMD). These weapons have such awesome potential that the mere thought of them being used by terrorists is enough to throw a pall over the future.

"I believe we are facing a 'vertex of evil', " writes Senator Richard Lugar, "the intersection of WMD and terrorism" (Lugar 2002, 7).

Biological weapons have already been employed many times—by a range of people from foreign military leaders to the individual terrorists who sent letters containing anthrax spores to people in the United States in 2001. Chemical weapons were used in the trenches of World War I, and more recently by Saddam Hussein in Iraq and by Aum Shinrikyo terrorists in Tokyo. Al-Qaeda has even come close to playing the nuclear card, not by using a nuclear weapon as such, but with the ju-jitsu strategy they employed on September 11, 2001. Khaled al-Sheikh Mohammed, who was one of the men who planned those attacks, told an Al Jazeera reporter that the group was originally thinking of hitting nuclear installations, turning America's nuclear technology into a weapon against it. In the end, they refrained for fear the results might "get out of hand."

"It was decided to abandon nuclear targets for the moment," he told the reporter.

"I mean, for the moment," he added ominously (Tremlett 2002).

Al-Sheikh Mohammed was clearly indicating that al-Qaeda's rejection of nuclear targets on that occasion did not mean that it is rejecting the nuclear option for the future, much less that it was ruling out the use of any other WMD. A few years ago, al-Qaeda's leader, Osama bin Laden, and the "The International Islamic Front for Jihad on the Jews and Crusaders" released a statement entitled "The Nuclear Bomb of Islam," declaring that "it is the duty of Muslims to prepare as much force as possible to terrorize the enemies of God." And bin Laden and his associates have made clear that their threats are to be taken seriously (United States Department of State 1999).

And yet, so far, the terrorist threat represented by WMD has been largely theoretical—or, to put it another way, psychological. Paradoxically, that fact itself makes them peculiarly useful as a terrorist weapon.

The danger of a fatal vertex of WMD and terrorism clearly exists. But how real is it? And how serious? How close are terrorists to having, and using, such weapons? No one, it seems, can be quite sure.

> There is no reliable assessment of the quantity and quality of weapons, dual-use and related materials, devices and technologies the possession of groups and individuals associated with terrorism. It is clear, however, that as long as stockpiles of any kinds of weapons-related materials, devices or technologies exists, terrorists may seek to obtain them. Historical experience indicates that, in most cases, terrorists are more likely to continue to use conventional techniques that are technically undemanding and not dangerous for them to handle. Of course, the latter point does not apply to individuals and groups that are willing to risk or give their lives when carrying out terrorist attacks. In the light of the 11 September attacks on the United States, it has become tragically clear that the calculated use of civilian technologies, such as commercial airplanes, against civilian targets is a possible terrorist technique. Since 11 September, there is a greater probability of imitation and inventiveness in the planning and execution of terrorist attacks. (General Assembly 2002, 9)

When considering the terrible potential of WMDs, it should be remembered that, to some extent, the term "weapons of mass destruction" itself is misleading. Maybe deliberately so. It implies that the categories of weapons it describes—biological, chemical, and nuclear—are necessarily more destructive than other, merely "ordinary" weapons. So far, at least, that has only been demonstrated to be true of weapons in the nuclear category, which terrorists have never employed. Historically, there has only been one case in which biological or chemical weapons resulted in more deaths and injuries than conventional weapons might have accounted for—that was the siege of Kaffa, which is described below—and then was only because its effects did, in fact, "get out of hand."

When it comes to use by terrorists, conventional weapons are more than terrible enough themselves. Hundreds of people have been killed by a single terrorist bomb, and the horrors of September 11, 2001, were "accomplished" using no real weapons at all—only box cutters and presumably benign commercial airliners.

HISTORY OF WMD USE

Biological Weapons

Of the three broad categories of WMD, biological weapons have been most often employed in the past. As long ago as the sixth century B.C., the

Athenian-Archon poet Solon poisoned with skunk cabbage the water supply of a city he was besieging, and around the same time, the Assyrians contaminated enemy wells with rye ergot.

In 1346, the bubonic plague *(Yersinia pestis)* struck the Tartar army of Yanibeg Khan during their long siege of the Genoan-held walled city of Kaffa (modern day Theodosia) in the Crimea. Taking advantage of their own misfortune, the Tartars catapulted the diseased bodies of dead soldiers over the walls into Kaffa, thus infecting the Italians. Some historians have suggested that it was Genoans who escaped the Tartar army and fled back to Italy that brought the infamous Black Death to Europe. For the following decade, the Plague ravaged the continent, killing one-third of the defenseless population.

The historian, David Herlihy, quotes the Florentine chronicler Matteo Villani describing the Plague's hideous effects: "It . . . touched people of every condition, age and sex. They began to spit blood and then they died—some immediately, some in two or three days, and some in a longer time. And it happened that whoever cared for the sick caught the disease from them or, infected by the corrupt air, became rapidly ill and died in the same way. Most had swellings in the groin, and many had them in the left and right armpit and in other places; one could almost always find and unusual swelling somewhere on the victim's body" (Herlihy 1997, 25).

History provides many other examples. In the eighteenth century, for example, Napoleon tried to infect the city of Mantua with malaria, and British forces used smallpox-infested blankets as a way of decimating the enemy Indian population during the French and Indian War in America (Woods n.d.).

Most military uses of bioweapons were, not surprisingly, directed against enemy armies or populations. The first documented use of bioweapons in a neutral or noncombatant nation took place in the United States two years before it entered World War I. That attack was not directed against the human population, but against animals.

In 1915, a German-raised and -educated American physician named Anton Dilger set up a bio-laboratory in his Washington, D.C., basement. There, he cultured anthrax and glanders. He then gave test tubes containing the bacteria, suspended in liquid, to sympathetic (or mercenary) longshoremen, who surreptitiously stabbed cattle waiting at the docks for shipment to Allied countries, with needles dipped in the microbial soup. Altogether, some 3,000 cattle, horses, and mules were infected, and several hundred humans fell victim to the bacteria as well (Woods n.d.).

According to University of California microbiologist Mark Wheelis, all this was part of an ambitious German sabotage program: "Secret agents were sent to at least five countries (Romania, Spain, Norway, the United States and Argentina) with microbial cultures and instructions to infect shipments to the Allies of horses, mules, cattle and sheep. The bacteria that were used were those that cause anthrax and glanders" (Wheelis 1998). In Spain,

Argentina, and Norway, horses destined for France and other Allied countries were fed sugar cubes containing ampoules of the bacteria.

In 1925, the Geneva Protocol prohibited the use of biological weapons, but allowed them to be produced—an immense loophole, of which several nations would take advantage. In the middle half of the twentieth century, the United States, Great Britain, the Soviet Union, and South Africa were among the countries that developed extensive bioweapons programs, stockpiling a variety of organisms, both for research into defense against what was then commonly called "germ warfare," and for possible offensive use.

Among the countries that had major bioweapons programs in the years leading up to World War II was Japan, which was relatively brazen about its program, offering to buy yellow-fever agents from the United States only a few years before Pearl Harbor. (The United States refused to sell.) During the war, Japanese experiments with bioweapons killed hundreds, and perhaps thousands, of Chinese (Garrett 2000, 494).

The Soviets' bioweapons program began in 1928, and the United States launched its own program as part of the war effort in 1943 (Lord 2002, 4). Of these, the Soviets' program was the most ambitious, producing huge quantities of plague, anthrax, and smallpox bombs (Miller, Engelberg, and Broad 2001, 167). The Soviets also began experimenting with gene manipulation of smallpox bacteria, producing a so-called "supergerm" that is still of serious concern today (Lord 2000, 6).

The main products of the U.S. and British programs were anthrax bombs, capable of spreading spores of the highly communicable and deadly disease over wide areas. These bombs were never used in the war itself, but the British did test such bombs on the small island of Gruinard off the coast of Scotland in 1942. They expected the spores to dissipate to safe levels fairly quickly after the initial dispersal, but they failed to do so. Instead, the island remained infectious and therefore uninhabitable, not only for the duration of the war but for decades afterwards. The government of Great Britain didn't set to work decontaminating the island until 1986 (Woods n.d.).

Both the United States' and the Soviet Union's programs cultured and maintained significant quantities of anthrax, an organism they considered to have great potential for use as a weapon.

The development of antibiotics robbed bacterial diseases of a great deal of their potential effectiveness as weapons, and along with it much of their power to inflict fear. Both the Americans and the Soviets shifted their emphasis to viruses, for which there was, and still is, no "silver bullet" (Miller 2001, 43).

Declaring that "mankind already carries in its hands too many of the seeds of its own destruction," U.S. President Richard Nixon ordered the destruction of the U.S. offensive bioweapons program in 1969 (Lord 2002, 5). In 1972, an international negotiation produced the Convention on the Prohibition of the Development, Production and Stockpiling of Bacteriological (Biological) and Toxin Weapons and on Their Destruction, which prohibited research into, as well as the development and proliferation of, biological weapons. Eventually ratified by more than 140 nations, it went into effect in 1975.

Once again, however, there was a loophole. In fact, there were two. First, the Convention allowed work on defense *against* bioweapons to continue, and, in the field of weapons, the line between offensive and defensive can be difficult, if not impossible, to draw. Second, and even more serious, was the fact that it contained no effective means of verifying the signatory states' compliance with its provisions.

Chemical

There have been only a few instances of chemical weapons being used on a large scale. The most notorious of these were the use of mustard gas and Phosgene against troops in the trenches of World War I, the use of hydrogen cyanide in the Iran-Iraq War, and Saddam Hussein's use of a variety of gases to quash rebellions against his rule in the wake of the first Gulf War.

In the 1960s and 1970s, the Red Army Faction collected various ingredients for chemical attacks, but never used them (Purver 1995, 21). Other terrorist groups, including some in the United States, were found to possess similar materials, then and since, although they rarely have even tried to use them.

In 1968, there were several reports that the Yippies and the Weather Underground were planning to lace the Chicago city-water supply with the hallucinogenic chemical LSD (lysergic acid diethylamide), when the Democratic Convention came to town. Although the so-called conspiracy was highly publicized, and the authorities were apparently genuinely alarmed, such a thing was manifestly impossible. What's more, the involvement of the Yippies—a mischievous gaggle of fun-loving radicals—strongly suggests that it was never a serious scheme to begin with. (Among the Yippies' other Convention-related activities was the nomination of a photogenic pig named Pigasus for President.)

In 1986, the captured head of a radical right-ring terrorist group that called itself the Covenant, Sword, and Arm of the Lord (CSA) told federal authorities that the group had planned to use a large cache of deadly potassium cyanide found in a raid on CSA headquarters to poison the public water supplies of several American cities (Purver 1995).

The only terrorist group that has so far used chemical weapons on a significant scale has been the Aum Shinrikyo (Supreme Truth) cult, which used sarin gas in an attempted assassination attempt on a judge, which killed several people in the Kaichi Heights neighborhood of Matsumoto, Japan in 1994; they then used the same gas on a much larger scale in the Tokyo subway system the following year, injuring thousands of people, although only killing 12.

There have been scores of hoaxes involving chemical weapons, and several reports of planned chemical attacks, but relatively few incidents of chemical weapons actually being used, whether by terrorist groups or by individuals. The hoaxes have generally involved threats to commercial products—either as a way of striking at manufacturers whose practices displeased the hoaxers by hurting their sales, or as a means of extorting money from them. Animal-rights activists have been among the main perpetrators of the principled hoax, while individual criminals have been the main perpetrators of the mercenary kind.

As late as August 2001, several of the September 11 hijackers, including their operational leader, Mohammed Atta were making inquiries about the availability and capacity of crop-dusting airplanes (Australian 2001). This has led to much speculation that al-Qaeda may be in possession of chemical weapons inside the United States and looking for possible ways to disperse them over a wide area.

Serious international negotiations on banning chemical weapons began in 1980 and the Convention on the Prohibition of the Development, Production, Stockpiling and Use of Chemical Weapons and on Their Destruction was finally adopted by the Conference on Disarmament in Geneva, Switzerland, in 1992 and went into effect in 1997. According to the United Nations Department for Disarmament Affairs, the Chemical Weapons Convention is different from the earlier Convention banning biological weapons in that it's "mechanism for verifying compliance by States with the provisions of the Convention is unprecedented." What is more, "The CWC is the first disarmament agreement negotiated within a multilateral framework that provides for the elimination of an entire category of weapons of mass destruction under universally applied international control" (United Nations 2000).

Nuclear Weapons

The history of nuclear weapons can be summed up in two words: Hiroshima and Nagasaki. The devastation that the U.S. atomic bombs wreaked on those Japanese cities was so enormous that it has scarred human memory ever since. Such weapons have never been used again, although they have continued to be produced by a variety of countries, and their use has often been contemplated. While the governments that controlled them have so far shown restraint, however fragile, it is unlikely that terrorists who may come into possession of them will do the same.

So far, no terrorist has actually used a nuclear weapon, or even attempted to do so, but there have been many reports that terrorist organizations have attempted to acquire such weapons, or their essential components. The reliability of some of those reports may be questionable, but there have been so many of them that it would be remarkable if at least some of them were not true. Also, as we have seen, al-Qaeda has already considered attacks on nuclear installations, and it has to be assumed that other terrorists have done the same.

ADVANTAGES AND DISADVANTAGES OF CHEMICAL AND BIOLOGICAL WEAPONS

As far as terrorists are concerned, the chief advantage of WMDs, compared with conventional weapons, is that they *are* weapons of mass destruction. That is to say, that they are—by definition, and at least potentially—both more powerful and more devastating than other weapons that could be employed by terrorists.

Nuclear weapons, of course, are unquestionably the most destructive weapons known to mankind, the only ones that could destroy life as we know it. (Thankfully, quantities sufficient to wipe out life on the planet are far beyond the reach of even the most resourceful terrorists for the foreseeable future.)

Biological weapons, for example—as the Honorable John D. Holcum pointed out at the Fourth Review Conference of the Biological Weapons Convention at Geneva in 1996—are also "immensely destructive. [They] are truly loathsome instruments of war and terror. Anthrax, for instance, takes three excruciating days to destroy the membranes of the lungs and intestines. Botulinum toxin annihilates by slow asphyxiation, as the cells of the victim's breathing muscles die from within. Small wonder that the international community has placed such organisms out of bounds, even in combat. That was done in the 1972 Convention not only because these are weapons of mass destruction but because they are infinitely cruel—intrinsically weapons of terror" (Holcum 1996).

Chemical weapons "are at the lower end of the scale for weapons of mass destruction" (Purver 1995, 1)—but they are definitely *on* that scale, at least in terms of their potential killing power.

Each of the three categories of WMD has its own distinctive advantages and disadvantages, from the terrorists' point of view.

Chemical weapons, for instance, have the advantage of being more available, less difficult to produce, safer to handle, and easier to deliver than other weapons of mass destruction. Frank Barnaby, of the UK Oxford Research Group, predicts, "If terrorists manufacture weapons of mass destruction in the near future, they are likely to opt for chemical rather than biological or nuclear weapons" (Barnaby 1992, 85).

One reason is that chemical weapons are cheaper than bioweapons, and "[t]here can be no doubt . . . that the manufacture of chemical weapons would be much less expensive than the manufacture of nuclear weapons, for terrorists or for anyone else" (Purver 1995, 3).

Kurdish victims of an Iraqi poison gas attack lie where they were killed in March 1988, in the village of Halabja in Northern Iraq. The incident occurred on March 17, 1988, toward the end of Iraq's war with Iran. Courtesy of CNN/Getty Images.

Chemical weapons can be delivered in a variety of ways: they can be slipped into food and water supplies, or dispersed through the air, whether in gas or aerosol form.

Neither biological nor chemical weapons need to be directed against human beings to do significant damage. Such weapons can destroy crops and food supplies, seriously disrupting whole societies and causing enormous economic damage. Dr. David Franz has pointed out that one suckling pig infected with a contagious disease led to the destruction of 80 percent of all the hogs in Taiwan, costing that nation's pork industry some $15 billion (Picard 2002).

One of the greatest advantages of biological weapons is that small quantities of biological organisms, properly dispersed, are all that may be needed to kill large numbers of people. A study quoted by Douglass and Livingston claims that only 50 kilograms of anthrax spores could kill hundreds of thousands of people—as many as four tons of the nerve agent VX (Douglass and Livingstone 1987, 17).

However, it seems to be harder to disperse biological agents "properly" than terrorists might hope. While the anthrax that was sent to various addresses in the United States in 2001 was sufficient to kill large numbers of people in theory, there were "only" five deaths in fact.

Chemical weapons, too, may prove less deadly in reality than they are in theory. It is very probable that the Aum Shinrikyo terrorists expected the large quantities of sarin gas they released in the confined space of the Tokyo subway system to kill thousands of people. Instead, it merely sickened thousands, while killing "only" 12.

Some of the advantages of biological weapons are unique. Chief among them is that fact that, "In the right environment [they] can multiply and so self-perpetuate. And they can naturally mutate, frustrating protective measures. Chemical weapons, for all their horrors, become less lethal as they are dispersed and diluted. But even the tiniest quantities of disease organisms can be lethal. For example, botulinum toxin has been described as three million times more potent than the chemical nerve agent Sarin" (Holcum 1996).

Another unique advantage of bioweapons is the fact that, cleverly used, they could allow a terrorist to strike and be gone from the scene long before his victims are even aware that anything is amiss.

For the future, biological weapons hold out the possibility that they could be uniquely tailored to a particular target population. In May 2002, a South African scientist named Daan Goosen presented American intelligence officials with a toothpaste tube containing a sample of a DNA-altered bacterium.

"If U.S. officials liked what they saw," according to a report in the *Washington Post*, "Goosen said he was prepared to offer much more: an entire collection of pathogens developed by a secret South African bioweapons research program Goosen once headed" called Project Coast (Warrick and Mintz 2003).

Unlike the U.S. Cold War–era bioweapons program—which focused on ways that biological weapons might be delivered in wartime, over long distances, by means of missiles or other explosive devices—Project Coast was more of a boutique operation. Its weapons were intended for potential use against internal enemies, rebellious blacks or anti-apartheid activists, and consequently, the Project looked at more exotic organisms that could be delivered in highly targeted ways.

Pacific Coast even "explored—but never produced" biological agents that could target South Africa's black community while leaving the whites untouched" (Warrick and Mintz 2002). The mere fact that Project Coast seriously explored the possibility begs the question of whether bioweapons might one day be found to have a particular potential for use in race warfare. Although there is no evidence that any black group is currently doing so, might not some black terrorist organization be working even now on an organism that would specifically target whites?

Such racial/ethnic-specific weapons could be especially useful to certain categories of terrorists, such as white supremacists or religious fanatics whose religion is closely identified with one particular racial or ethnic group. At the moment, the development of designer-bioweapons requires levels of scientific skill, knowledge, resources, and sophistication available only to governments or major research institutions. Once such weapons have been developed, however, terrorists will be able to lay hands on them in the same ways they now lay hands on less sophisticated weapons. That is to say, they can buy them or steal them; or obtain them directly or indirectly from a government, either as a form of government sponsorship or as a gift from rogue elements with the government's military or intelligence services.

THE THREAT OF NUCLEAR TERRORISM

Nuclear weapons have two great advantages as terrorist weapons. First, they are unequaled in the sheer destructive power. A nuclear bomb can produce a larger blast and more widespread devastation than any conventional explosive weapon, and in addition, it is able to generate huge amounts of radiation that can have horrendous health consequences on people far away from the blast site.

Second, nuclear weapons have the uniquely terroristic attribute of being more frightening to more people than any other weapon. The image of the giant mushroom cloud haunts the imaginations of a generation that grew up ducking under school desks during nuclear disaster drills, as well as the generations that have followed them, watching the world on television, where the same image has been a regular feature of everything from commercials, to documentaries, to music videos—as well as going to movies set in a post-nuclear Apocalypse world.

Of course, terrorists would be unlikely to be able to obtain possession of the kinds of powerful nuclear weapons most people envision—much less to have access to the delivery systems that would be needed to use them.

> The Director-General of the International Atomic Energy Agency (IAEA) has stated that he considers the theft of a nuclear weapon and terrorists possessing the means and competence to manufacture and detonate a nuclear explosive relatively unlikely. The deliberate exposure to nuclear material leading to harmful effects on people, property and environment is a more plausible option. A "dirty bomb" scenario, in which radioactive material is dispersed by a conventional explosive, can be included as part of this option. Numerous difficulties remain, however, in defining the nuclear terrorist threat, given the hundreds of confirmed cases of nuclear smuggling (some involving small amounts of nuclear-usable materials), as well as significant uncertainties about the status of such materials in States that are known to possess nuclear weapons. (Policy Working Group 2002, 9)

Even that kind of radiation weapon would be inordinately difficult and dangerous for any terrorist to actually use. The first stumbling block might well be a major deterrent for any terrorist; the second might not. Many dedicated terrorists, belonging to al-Qaeda and other fanatical terrorist groups, have already proven their willingness to die for their cause. And their even greater willingness to kill.

An Islamist named Abu Shihab al-Qandahari published the following chilling call on a radical Islamist internet site, on the day after Christmas 2002. It was republished, in translation, by the International Policy Institute for Counter-Terrorism of the Interdisciplinary Center (ICT), Herzliya, on their Spotlight-News and Commentary website at ICT.com:

The Nuclear War Is the Solution for the Destruction of the United States

Yes, you did read the title correctly. It is the only way to kill the maximum number of Americans. This is the nuclear terror, which Americans have never feared. In the Second World War, the United States used this weapon twice in three days due to the successful Japanese attack in Pearl Harbor. These days the United States is using the most violent and modern weapons to bomb innocent civilians in Iraq and Afghanistan, and totally support the Russian war against the Chechens. Not out of love of the Russians but out of hatred of the Muslims.

The United States attacked Iraq using weapons that contaminated the lands and water by radiation for thousands of years. Furthermore, it used Uranium bombs to create maximum damage to the lands and human beings, so it could leave Muhammad's Peninsula after turning it into a forbidden area that no one would consider visiting. Yet, it seems that the beasts of the White House have forgotten one very important fact—and we are very proud to note it—[al-Qaeda].

This is the organization that terrorized the core of the infidel West, and made from several youngsters, who own nothing but love for Allah and his messenger, a means to punish the sons of the bitches. Moreover, these youngsters demonstrated the finest example of leaving the materialist life. They could enjoy the good life, yet they ran away from it, wishing only what Allah could give them. They sold their souls to Allah, and he accepted them.

Eye for eye and tooth for tooth. If the Americans have bombs that no one else owns, [al-Qaeda] is stronger. It owns "dirty bombs" and "lethal viruses bombs", which could cover the American cities with deadly diseases and turn this nation, which is "a professional in contempt for other nations," into a crowd of contaminated and sick people. The coming days would prove that Qa'idat al-Jihad is capable with Allah's help, of turning the United States into a lake of lethal radiation, that would seem as the last days of humanity. It would also prove that [al-Qaeda] is very popular all over the Islamic world.

Yes, the United States and its allies would be destroyed, as a result of the misuse of their power against the weak. Their end is closer now, by the arms of the uprising youngsters, who while riding their horses, never step down but victorious or martyrs. In both cases this is their victory.

Pray much for your victorious brothers and to Allah who is almighty.

This is an announcement to all people, to enlighten only the believers. As to the deviates we ask Allah either to direct them or hurry in gathering their souls. As to our enemy—Allah will help us to defeat them.

Allah is behind all intentions, and he is merciful.

REFERENCES

Australian Broadcasting Corporation. 2001. *Four Corners: A Mission to Die For.* 12 November. ABC.net.http://www.abc.net.au/4corners/atta/transcript.htm (accessed 30 March 2004).

Barnaby, Frank. 1992. *The Role and Control of Weapons in the 1990s.* London: Routledge.

Douglass, Joseph D., Jr., and Neil C. Livingstone. 1987. *America the Vulnerable: The Threat of Chemical and Biological Warfare.* Lexington, Mass.: Lexington Books.

Garrett, Laurie. 2000. *Betrayal of Trust: The Collapse of Global Health.* New York: Hyperion.

Herlihy, David. 1997. *The Black Death and the Transformation of the West.* Cambridge, Mass.: Harvard University Press.

Holcum, John D. 1996. "Remarks to the Fourth Review Conference of the Biological Weapons Convention" at Geneva, Switzerland. 26 November.

Lord, Alexandra M. 2002. "A Brief History of Biowarfare." Paper. Rockville, MD: Office of the Public Health Service Historian.

Lugar, Richard G. 2002. "Redefining NATO's Mission: Preventing WMD Terrorism," *Washington Quarterly,* Summer, 7–14.

Miller, Judith, Stephen Engelberg, and William Broad. 2001. *Germs: Biological Weapons and America's Secret War.* New York: Simon & Schuster.

Picard, Andr'e. 2002. "Bioterrorists Prey on Public Anxiety," *The Globe and Mail,* (Toronto) 18 February.

Policy Working Group on the United Nations and Terrorism. 2002. *Report of the Policy Working Group on the United Nations and Terrorism.* New York: United Nations Security Council.

Purver, Ron. 1995. *Chemical and Biological Terrorism: The Threat According to Open Literature.* Ottawa: Canadian Security Intelligence Service.

Tremlett, Giles. 2002. "Al-Qaida Leaders Say Nuclear Power Stations Were Original Targets: Reporter Meets Contender for Next Bin Laden," *The Guardian* (London), 9 September.

United Nations Department of Disarmament Affairs. 2000. The Chemical Weapons Convention. http://www.un.org/depts.dda/WMC/WC/ (accessed 26 March 2004).

United Nations General Assembly, Fifty-seventh Session. 2002. "Report of the Policy Working Group on the United Nations and Terrorism," 6 August. New York: United Nations.

U.S. Department of State. 1999. "Fact Sheet: The Charges Against International Terrorist Osama bin Laden" (15 December). Washington, D.C.: U.S. Department of State.

Warrick, Joby, and John Mintz. 2003. "Lethal Legacy: Bioweapons for Sale." *Washington Post*, 20 April.

Wheelis, Mark. 1998. "Correspondence: First Shots Fired in Biological Warfare." *Nature*, 17 September.

Woods, Michael. 2001. "History of Germ Warfare—Very Long, Very Deadly." Black News Alliance, 31 October. Rense.com. http://www.Rense.com/general16/thehistoryofgerm.htm (accessed April 28, 2004).

6

Their Name Is Legion—A Selection of Terrorist Groups

The bulk of this chapter is made up of short histories and descriptions of a variety of terrorist groups. A more comprehensive roster of such groups can be found in chapter 9, Documents.

For many reasons, it is impossible to come up with any definitive and completely noncontroversial dishonor roll of terrorist groups. One of those difficulties is summed up in the frequently repeated cliché that one man's terrorist is another man's freedom fighter—a cliché that doesn't really say anything about the terrorist (or the freedom fighter, for that matter), but only about other people's perceptions of them.

Those who attack us are obviously terrorists. Those who attack our enemies are obviously freedom fighters. When we disagree with a group's motives, it is easy to condemn the group as terrorist. When we approve of their motives, we do everything we can to find excuses for them. As hard as we try, it is almost impossible not to believe that, on some level, the end really does justify the means.

But, if the word "terrorist" is to have any real meaning—more than an epithet to hurl at our enemies—terrorists must be terrorists because of what they do, not because of which side they take, not because of the cause they claim to represent, however good that cause may be, and however legitimate their claim to represent it, and not because of the world they hope to bring about.

Some of the organizations described here acknowledge participating in terrorism, which they attempt to justify on a variety of grounds. Others deny terrorist activities altogether. Some admit to the activities of which they are accused but try to define these activities out of the category of terrorism using arguments like those discussed elsewhere in this book. All of these organizations, however, have been widely designated as terrorist groups by governments, nongovernmental organizations, and by the media. Such sources are as biased as any others, of course, but when writing for the general public about a subject of general concern, it is only reasonable to start with generally accepted designations.

Because there are literally hundreds of terrorist organizations in the world—and because they tend to come and go, grow and shrink, merge and split apart with bewildering frequency—not even the very long list in the back of this book can claim to be comprehensive. The selection of groups for discussion in this chapter has been fairly arbitrary, and a brief mention of the criteria for inclusion (and exclusion) is in order.

For the most part, the groups included in this chapter are either currently active or, although currently inactive, considered threats to resume terrorist activities at some time in the future. The handful of defunct organizations that appear here have been chosen for their special historical interest.

The overwhelming majority of these groups engage (or engaged) in cross-border or other international terrorist activities, although a few prominent American domestic groups have been included as well. Also included are some groups that, although they confine their activities to a single country, have attracted significant international attention, or who are known for targeting foreigners as victims.

When selecting foreign groups for inclusion here, preference has been given to those that are of special interest to Americans for one reason or another.

Among the organizations that have *not* been included here are the many governments and government agencies around the world that are credibly accused of using terror, either as a means of repression, as a way of eliminating their enemies, or intimidating their neighbors. Such organizations can and should be classified as "terrorist," but they can hardly be accurately defined as "groups."

THE QUESTION OF EQUIVALENCE

To put organizations on a list implies a certain equivalence. To put them on a list of terrorist organizations seems to imply a *moral* equivalence. This can be misleading. To the extent that these groups all kill civilians and other noncombatants as a part of their modus operandi, they are all equally guilty of being terrorists. But in other respects—including some that bear on morality—they may differ greatly.

All these organizations, as well as many others that could have been listed here, practice terrorism, but not all of them do it to the same extent or with the same degree of cruelty. Not all of them do it with an equal fervor, or, for that matter, with an equal regretfulness. A case can be made that there is a world of moral difference between the Molly Maguires (Irish American coal miners who specifically targeted mine owners and police officers for murder in nineteenth-century Pennsylvania) and Hamas, which sends suicide bombers to blow up anonymous noncombatants in Israel. Likewise, there is an obvious difference between November 17, which was known for gunning down politically and ideologically selected targets, and the Shankill Butchers, who seized randomly selected Catholics off the streets of Belfast, held them captive for a time, tortured them before killing them, and then dismembered their bodies to cause further distress for their families.

There is another kind of difference between groups like the Provos, who killed at the most a handful of people at a time, and al-Qaeda, which sets out to kill hundreds and even thousands. An argument can even be made that there is a significant moral difference between the Revolutionary Armed Forces of Colombia (FARC) and National Liberation Army (ELN), both of which are drug-dealing leftist terrorist groups in Colombia.

Classifying an organization as a "terrorist group" can be misleading in itself, no matter how accurate that classification may be. To designate an organization, or an individual, as "terrorist" is to make a tactic the defining thing about them. What is more, it seems to imply that terrorism is their essence: the core of their reality: terrorism is not just what they do, terrorism is what they *are*.

And yet, terrorism is only a part of the activities of many of these groups. The aforementioned FARC and ELN, for example, are both engaged in a long and ongoing civil war with the government of Colombia. Terrorism has been a large part of that war, but it is far from the only part. Those groups also engage in political activities, as well as in conventional combat against undeniably military targets, and, to varying degrees, they engage in the drug trade, as well. To call them terrorists is accurate, but it is not sufficient to explain them or their still-unfolding places in the histories of their country.

Overall, the effort has been to come up with a relatively short roster of terrorist groups that is representative of the full panoply of such organizations, and thereby, to help define the roles that terrorism plays in the world.

ABU NIDAL ORGANIZATION (ANO)

Hard-line Anti-Israel Palestinians. Also known as the Fatah Revolutionary Council, the Arab Revolutionary Council, the Arab Revolutionary Brigades, and the Revolutionary Organization of Socialist Muslims.

The Abu Nidal Organization, or the Fatah Revolutionary Council, was a more or less direct successor to Black September, which carried out the attack on the Munich Olympics in 1972. It rejected any possibility of peace with Israel from the beginning, acting to keep the Arab world focused on the armed struggle by striking not only Israel but any Arab organization, nation, or leader who showed a willingness to move toward peace. Fatah's enemies included the Palestine Liberation Organization (PLO), from which it split in 1974, and the PLO leader, Yassir Arafat, whom it apparently attempted to assassinate.

Formed soon after the dismantling of Black September in the early-1970s by Sabi al-Bana, who took the name Abu Nidal ("Father of the Struggle"), the ANO was originally headquartered in Baghdad, where the Iraqi regime was its principle sponsor. Iraq's war with Iran, which caused Iraq to move toward better relations with the West, put strain on the government's relations with Abu Nidal, who was forced out of Iraq and into Syria in the early-1980s. In 1985, Nidal and his organization moved again, this time to Libya. In 1998, with Libya trying to better its own relations with the West, the ANO reportedly moved back to Iraq, where it remained largely, if not entirely, inactive.

At the height of its strength, ANO probably consisted of no more than 500 people. It was, however, extremely well financed, acting both for its own purposes and as terrorists-for-hire on behalf of the Arab regimes that sponsored it.

The ANO committed some of the most infamous terrorist actions of the last quarter-century. Among them were the twin attacks on the Rome and Vienna airports in December 1985, an attack on the Neve Shalom synagogue in Istanbul, Turkey, in 1986, and the hijacking of a Pan Am airliner in Karahi, Pakistan, also in 1986. Altogether, it was accused of responsibility for the deaths of between 900 and 1,000 people in 20 countries.

Whatever his personal motives, said journalist Robert Hardy in an obituary report on Nidal for the BBC (British Broadcasting Corporation), "In the end, he was a mercenary" (Hardy 2002). That end reportedly came in an apartment in Baghdad, Iraq, in August 2002. Rumored to be in chronic bad health and wracked with addictions, his death was officially reported as a suicide, although there was speculation that he had been assassinated, either by his longtime enemies among the Palestinians or by his past friends, the Iraqis (Prendergast 2002).

ABU SAYAAF

Islamic separatists in the Philippines. Also known as Abu Sayaaf Group (ASG) and Abu Sayyaf.

Abu Sayaaf's declared goal is to carve an independent Islamic state out of the largely Muslim areas in and around the island of Mindanao in the Philippines. Cynical observers, however, point out that most of the group's operations are kidnappings and extortions, and seem to be designed less to foment revolution than to produce profits.

Several of the original members of Abu Sayaaf fought alongside the mujahadeen in Afghanistan, and the group may have ties of some sort with al-Qaeda or other Islamic extremists outside the Philippines. Most of the group's funding, however, comes from its own criminal activities.

Although most of its operations take place in the Basilan Province of the southern Philippines and in certain areas of the Sulu Archipelago—the area where it hopes to establish its independent nation—Abu Sayaaf has been known to travel far afield to find desirable victims (Federation of American Scientists 1998). In April 2000, for example, it kidnapped 21 people from a tourist resort in Malaysia; in that case, Libya eventually negotiated a large ransom from various European governments in return for their release. The following May, the group seized another large group of tourists, including three Americans, from a resort in the Philippines. Several of those hostages were later killed.

Although the U.S. State Department once labeled Abu Sayaaf the smallest of the Islamic separatist groups in the Philippines, it was also the most radical and violent (U.S. State Department 1999). Since then, its original ranks of 200 or so ideologically motivated members have reportedly been multiplied by opportunists who have joined the group in order to participate in the profits from its activities.

As part of the U.S. War on Terrorism after September 11, 2001, the United States began providing military trainers, advisors, maintenance, and support to the government of the Philippines, to help it deal with the threat from Abu Sayaaf.

AL-QAEDA (THE BASE)

The most extensive and notorious of the Jihadist terrorist groups. Also spelled Al-Qaida, Al-Qa'ida, Al-Qadr. Also known as the International Front for Jihad Against Jews and Crusaders, Islamic Salvation Foundation, the Islamic Army for the Liberation of the Holy Places.

Al-Qaeda is an umbrella organization, or network, made up of or connecting a variety of other organizations that it assists, advises, or directs. It opposes the secular rulers of the Middle East, and seeks to replace them with Islamic governments; in addition, it seeks the destruction of Israel and the elimination of what it sees as the corrupting and exploitative influence of the West in Muslim lands, and particularly the western military presence on the Arabian Peninsula.

Al-Qaeda was an outgrowth of the mujahadeen, a group of people who came from several countries to combat the Soviets and their puppet government in Afghanistan in the 1980s. One of the leaders of the mujahadeen was a wealthy Saudi Arabian named Osama bin Laden. Returning to his native country, he founded an organization known as the Mekhtab al Khidemat, or Service Office, for veterans of the mujahadeen. That organization had branches in several countries, including one at the Alkifah Refugee Center in Brooklyn, New York. The Mekhtab al Khidemat formed

Osama bin Laden. Courtesy of Federal Bureau of Investigation.

the foundation and original recruiting ground for al-Qaeda, which bin Laden founded sometime around 1989 or 1990.

When the Saudi government allowed U.S. military forces onto the Arabian Peninsula in response to the Iraqi invasion of Kuwait in 1990, bin Laden was outraged. He felt that the presence of western Christian forces defiled the country, which is the location of the holiest shrines in Islam. When the Saudi government expelled him for anti-government activities in 1991, bin Laden moved to Khartoum, in the Sudan, where he established headquarters for al-Qaeda. Bin Laden and his organization set up a variety of businesses that were reportedly run primarily to provide cover for purchasing explosives, chemicals, and other terrorist weapons, as well as to pay for al-Qaeda's activities.

Although its involvement, and even its existence, was not widely recognized at first, al-Qaeda burst on the world scene in spectacular fashion with the bombing of the World Trade Center on February 26, 1993. That blast, which occurred in the parking basement of one of the twin towers, killed six people and wounded nearly 1,000 others. As horrible as it was, this first World Trade Center attack was intended to be even more spectacular. It was apparently meant to be part of a larger operation, which was to include the crashing of a passenger jet into CIA headquarters in Langley, Virginia.

In that same year, al-Qaeda was actively training Somali tribesmen who were opposed to the U.N. and U.S. military presence in Somalia. That October, forces trained by al-Qaeda attacked American servicemen who were attempting to seize two warlords in Mogadishu and killed 18 of them

Destruction left from the 1993 World Trade Center bombing. Courtesy of Federal Bureau of Investigation.

in an incident that became known by the title of the book and movie that were made about it, *Black Hawk Down*.

Al-Qaeda is perhaps the most truly international of all terrorist groups. Although its roots and heart are in the Middle East, it recruits its members from Muslims around the world. What's more, it is the exemplar of a terrorist group with "global reach." Agents of al-Qaeda have conducted attacks on several continents, often planning and organizing an attack in countries far removed from the one in which it is to be carried out.

Egyptian Islamic Jihad—whose leader, Muhammad Atef, was a co-founder of al-Qaeda, along with Osama bin Laden—has been merged with al-Qaeda since the mid-1990s, if not before. Other groups that are believed to be either a part of or closely associated with al-Qaeda include the Islamic Army for the Liberation of the Holy Sites, which carried out the U.S. embassy attacks in Africa, and Jemaah Islamiyah (JI), which was allegedly responsible for the explosions that destroyed the Sari and Paddy's Pub nightclubs in Bali, Indonesia, killing 180 people and injuring hundreds more.

By far al-Qaeda's most spectacular and destructive operation was the four-pronged attack on New York City and Washington, D.C. that took place on September 11, 2001, and is described elsewhere in this book. Many commentators have credited that single operation with profoundly altering the course of world history.

Other operations carried out by al-Qaeda, or groups closely affiliated with it, include a massive bomb that roared through an apartment complex housing American, Saudi, and British military personnel in Dhahran, Saudi Arabia, in June 1996, leaving at least19 dead and more than 200 injured; the coordinated bombings of the U.S. embassies in Nairobi, Kenya, and Dar es Salaam, Tanzania, on August 7, 1998, in which a total of almost 300 people were killed and more than 4,000 injured; the bombing of the USS *Cole* at-anchor in the port of Aden at Yemen in October 2000, in which 17 American sailors were killed and nearly 40 injured; and a bomb detonated at a historic synagogue in Tunisia in April 2002 that killed 17 people, among whom were 11 German tourists.

The so-called "War on Terrorism" is primarily a war on al-Qaeda, and America's war in Afghanistan was undertaken with the declared purpose of destroying al-Qaeda and denying it safe haven. These events undoubtedly caused a great deal of tumult and disruption to al-Qaeda, although it remains to be seen whether it has been damaged in any fundamental way, much less destroyed. Because of the secret and diffuse nature of the organization, it is hard to determine al-Qaeda's actual size or membership.

AUM SHINRIKYO OR AUM

Japanese doomsday cultists. Also known as AELPH.

Founded in 1987 by Shoko Asahara, Aum Shinrikyo was at first recognized by the Japanese government as a legitimate religious and political organization. Its charismatic leader, who taught that the end of the world would be brought about by a war between the United States and Japan, was looked upon by group members as a kind of god.

Aum stockpiled hundreds of tons of chemicals, and was suspected in a number of chemical releases in Japan in the mid-1990s. In addition, it is believed that the group may have experimented unsuccessfully with biological weapons. In March 1995, several members of the group simultaneously released deadly sarin gas on several trains in the Tokyo subway system. Twelve people were killed and perhaps as many as 6,000 more were sickened by the attacks, which angered the Japanese government and alarmed many people around the world who were concerned about chemical weapons. In the wake of the attacks, Asahara and several other Aum leaders were arrested, and the Japanese government soon revoked the group's official status as a religion.

Fumihiro Joyu replaced the jailed Asahara as the group's leader. In January 2000, Aum renounced terrorism and renamed itself AELPH. The following year, however, Russian authorities uncovered what they claimed was a plot by Aum cultists in that country to institute a bombing attack in Moscow, as well as to free Asahara and take him to that country.

Prior to 1995, Aum claimed at least 9,000 members in Japan and roughly three times that many in other countries around the world. Since that time, widespread revulsion at the subway attacks, combined with Japanese government moves against the group, have reduced membership to perhaps 2,000 in Japan and an unknown number in Russia.

BASQUE FATHERLAND AND LIBERTY

Left-wing Basque separatists in Spain and France. Also known as Eusakadi Ta Askatasuna (ETA).

Together with its political wing, the Batasuna Party, Basque Fatherland and Liberty, or ETA, seeks to establish an independent Basque nation in the heavily Basque regions of northern Spain and southern France. ETA was founded in 1959 by young Basque radicals who resented the efforts to suppress the Basque culture and language introduced by Spain's dictatorial ruler Francisco Franco. The group's exact strength is unknown, but its active membership probably runs into the hundreds, and roughly half of the Basque population supports its goal, if not its methods.

Those methods include assassinations, bombings and other attacks on Spanish government officials, from local functionaries to the highest ranks of the Spanish government. Most ETA attacks occur in the Basque regions of Spain and France, but the group has also been known to strike internationally. In 1973, an ETA car bomb in Madrid killed Admiral Luis Carrero Blanco who was widely expected to be Franco's successor; in 1995, another car bomb narrowly missed killing the conservative Popular Party leader, Jose Maria Aznar, who was later elected president of Spain; and Spanish law enforcement officials claim to have disrupted a 1995 plot to assassinate Spain's King Juan Carlos. Altogether, ETA has been accused of having responsibility for some 800 deaths and several hundred serious injuries. Like many other terrorist groups, it carries out kidnappings, extortions, and other crimes to finance its activities.

In 1998, ETA announced a unilateral ceasefire, which it broke with a series of assassinations and bombings beginning in late 1999. Also in that year, a plan to explode a truck bomb at the Picasso Tower skyscraper in Madrid was uncovered by law enforcement authorities.

In the aftermath of September 11, 2001, ETA activities diminished, perhaps partly in reaction to that event, and partly as a result of a crackdown by the Aznar government. In October 2001, however, several ETA car bombs were detonated in major Spanish cities. The following month, the group was responsible for the murder of a judge and two police officers in Spain's Basque region.

It is believed that some ETA guerillas were trained in Algeria, Libya, Lebanon, and Nicaragua, and that ETA fugitives have received asylum in Cuba, although the group receives no financial support from these or any other countries. Neither does ETA receive any support from al-Qaeda or other international terrorist organizations, although it is believed to have close non-financial ties to the Irish Republican Army.

The base of ETA's support comes from Basque nationalists. In May 2003, 12 prominent international writers issued a statement condemning ETA violence. "Although citizens of the Basque Country are murdered for their ideas," it read in part, "and thousands have been mutilated or disturbed, the attacks take place and are celebrated in a sorry atmosphere of moral impunity created by nationalist institutions and the Basque Catholic hierarchy" (*New York Times* 2003).

Basque Fatherland and Liberty has long been classified as a terrorist group by the U.S. government. In the wake of the Iraq War, in which Spain was a staunch supporter of American policy, the United States added the Batasuna Party to its list of terrorist organizations.

BLACK SEPTEMBER

Elite force of the Popular Front for the Liberation of Palestine (PFLP) and, therefore, of the Palestinian Liberation Organization (PLO) in the 1970s.

Now defunct, Black September perpetrated of some of the most spectacular acts of international terrorism in the twentieth century. It took its name from the month in which the troops of King Hussein of Jordan drove the Palestinians out of that country, which had previously been their primary refuge. The group exploded onto the international scene with the assassination of Hussein's Premier Wasfi Tal, who had largely directed the Jordanian move against the Palestinians.

From the beginning, Black September acted on the international stage. Tal's assassination, which took place in Cairo, Egypt, was followed by the attempted assassination of another Jordanian official in London and attacks against utility installations, an oil refinery, and other targets in a variety of European countries. The group's most infamous action was the murder of several Israeli athletes at the Munich Olympics in 1972. Almost as spectacular was its takeover of the Saudi Embassy in Khartoum, Sudan the following March.

Unlike most of the Palestinian terrorists who would come later, Black September more often directed its violence against Arab governments that it believed had betrayed or deserted the Palestinians, and against the European supporters of Israel, than against Israel itself. Nonetheless, after Munich, Israeli hit squads began pursuing Black September members, killing several of the group's members, including at least three of its leaders ("Black September" n.d., 7).

One of the Black September guerillas who broke into the Munich Olympic Village, killed two members of the Israeli team, and took nine others. Courtesy of Getty Images.

Black September, and the PLO in general, received significant support from Syria. Yassir Arafat himself has been accused of directing at least some of Black September's activities, but there seems to be no conclusive evidence of this. Most likely, the organization's early activities were undertaken without either Arafat's support or his active opposition. After the Khartoum fiasco, however, Arafat turned against Black September and effectively closed it down.

The most notorious member of the group was Sari al-Bana, better known as Abu Nidal, who broke from the PLO in the early-1970s and went on to form the Fatah Revolutionary Council, or ANO.

CONTINUITY IRA (CIRA)

Dissident Republican organization primarily active in Northern Ireland.

The CIRA favors a united and independent Ireland, and rejects the peace process that was established in the late-1990s. British and Irish authorities believe the group to be associated with the so-called Republican Sinn Féin, a political party, which is itself a dissident offshoot of the actual Sinn Féin, and which shares the goals of the CIRA. The Republican Sinn Féin, however, denies the connection, and insists that it has no paramilitary arm.

Founded in the mid-1980s, the CIRA is believed to have as few as 20 members. Its most infamous act was a 1,200-pound bomb that destroyed the Killyhevlin Hotel at Enniskillen in 1996.

The CIRA has steadfastly refused to declare a cease-fire—even when virtually all the other Irish paramilitary groups did so in the late 1990s—and is still quite active. Shortly after key elements of power were transferred from Britain to Belfast, and with the process for disarming the IRA at a crucial point in February 2000, the CIRA detonated another bomb at a hotel in County Fermanagh. As recently as early 2003, the group admitted responsibility for a nail-bomb attack on police in Northern Ireland, and around that same time, it issued a joint threat with another militant organization that calls itself the Real IRA to launch a similar attack each week.

EAST TURKESTAN ISLAMIC GROUP

Ethnic Uighur separatists.

The East Turkestan Islamic Group seeks East Turkestani independence from China. Both the Chinese and U.S. governments identify it as a terrorist organization, although the accusations against it tend to be less than specific, and other Uighur groups play down these allegations. China also alleges that the East Turkestan Islamic Group has links to al-Qaeda and that several of its members trained in al-Qaeda camps in Afghanistan. Although the group is little known outside of China, it was added to the U.S. State Department's list of terrorist organizations in 2002.

EGYPTIAN ISLAMIC JIHAD (JAMAAT AL-ISLAMIYYA)

Islamists partnered with al-Qaeda.

Egyptian Islamic Jihad was founded in the late-1970s as a successor/offshoot of the Muslim Brotherhood. Its original goal was to overthrow the secular government of Egypt and establish an Islamic state. Although its activities originally centered in and around Cairo, it has been known to carry out operations in countries around the world, and currently refrains from any violence inside Egypt at all.

The group is estimated to have between 200 and 300 dedicated members. Its primary tactics have been assassination and car bombing. The group has carried out a number of attacks against high-level Egyptian government officials, as well as various Egyptian and U.S. government facilities. By far its most infamous attack inside Egypt was the assassination of President Anwar Sadat in 1981.

Some of the other actions for which it claimed responsibility were the attempted assassination, by a suicide bomber, of Egypt's Interior Ministry Hassan al-Alfi in August 1993, and the car-bomb attempt to kill Prime Minister Atef Sedky in November of the same year. It is also believed to be responsible for the bomb that exploded at the Egyptian Embassy in Islamabad, Pakistan, in 1995.

While it targeted U.S. government facilities both in Egypt and elsewhere for many years, it was never known to attack American tourists inside Egypt (although it may have carried out such attacks in other places). In fact, it ceased all attacks inside Egypt after 1993 (U.S. Department of State 2002). In March 1999 it agreed to a cease-fire with the Egyptian government.

None of this should suggest that Egyptian Islamic Jihad has renounced terrorism. In fact, it reportedly joined forces with, if not completely merged into, Osama bin Laden's al-Qaeda organization in the mid- or late-1990s. At that time two of Egyptian Islamic Jihad's members were welcomed into the leadership of al-Qaeda.

The two men, Ayman al-Zawahiri and Muhammad Atef, are believed to have had major roles in planning some of al-Qaeda's most spectacular and deadly attacks in the years since the merger, including the coordinated bombings of the U.S. embassies in Kenya and Tanzania in 1998, and even the events of September 11, 2001, in the United States. (Council, *Jamaat* 2003). Al-Zawahiri, in particular, has been identified by several governmental organizations as one of the most dangerous individual terrorists in the world.

Since ceasing its violent activities inside Egypt, Egyptian Islamic Jihad seems to have abandoned, at least temporarily, its goal of overthrowing the Egyptian government. Instead, it has changed its emphasis to attacking U.S. interests around the world. The shift of attention away from Egypt, which was its original focus, caused a serious split within Egyptian Islamic Jihad. Perhaps as few as 200 hardcore members joined al-Zawahiri's move to al-Qaeda. However, those few are believed to form the active heart of that organization (MacFarquhar 2001).

Not long after the bombings of the U.S. embassies in Kenya and Tanzania in 1998, a separate cell of Egyptian Islamic Jihad was thwarted in a plan to attack the U.S. embassy in Albania. One hundred and seven alleged members of the group have been tried (62 of them in absentia) by the Egyptian courts.

The Egyptian government has accused Iran of providing financial support to the Egyptian Islamic Jihad, which probably also received considerable financial support from Osama bin Laden even before the merger with al-Qaeda. The group also obtains funds from other sources, including a number of Islamic organizations as well as its own criminal activities.

GRAY WOLVES, *BOZKURTLER* (BKT)

The unofficial paramilitary wing of Turkey's Milliyetci Hareket Partisi (National Movement Party), or MHP.

The MHP and its terrorist supporters hope to bring together all the "Turkish peoples" in a so-called Great Turkish Empire. Their ideology seems to be a typical fascist-like mix of Turkish nationalism and racism.

The Gray Wolves take their name from the she-wolf that, according to legend, led the Turks of Central Agency to freedom. They are accused of being the main prosecutors of the so-called "dirty war" against leftists, Kurdish nationalists, and human rights activists in Turkey. Altogether, they have been accused of responsibility for hundreds and perhaps thousands of deaths, mostly of leftist Turks, ethnic Kurds, and Alevi-Muslims. They are believed to be associated both with right-wing elements of the Turkish government and with the Turkish Mafia, and are said to be heavily involved in drug trafficking. Memhet Ali Agca, who attempted to assassinate Pope John Paul II in 1981 was an agent of the Gray Wolves (Lee 1998).

GROUPÉMENT UNION DÉFENSE (GUD)

French right-wing, white supremacists. Also known as Groupuscule de Dieu (Party of God), the Waffen Assas, and the Union de Défense Assas (UDEA).

Founded in the late-1960s, in the wake of the breakup of the Occident movement, the GUD once consisted of perhaps a few hundred members, and was centered around the law faculty of the Assas branch of the University of Paris. Its present numbers are unknown.

In 1973, it founded the newspaper *Alternative* to promote its views.

It has competed in faculty elections at Assas, winning at least one seat on the Faculty Council in 1991. Four years later, however, following repeated acts of violence, GUD members were banned from serving in the future.

Over the past three decades GUD has had associations with a variety of other right-wing French groups. It is part of the coalition of French nationalist groups known as *Unité radicale*, and reputedly acts as a liaison between French neo-nazi, skinhead, and other militant, and often violent, groups. A member of GUD attempted to assassinate French President Jacques Chirac during the 2002 Bastille Day parade in Paris ("What is the GUD?" 2002).

GUATEMALA NATIONAL REVOLUTIONARY UNIT (UGRN)

Leftist guerillas in Guatemala.

In 1945, a reformist government came to power in Guatemala. Roughly a decade later, there was a CIA-assisted military coup, after which the government of Colonel Carlos Castillo Armas was duly elected. Three years later, Armas was assassinated, leading to nearly half-a-century of violent unrest in the country.

Starting in the early 1960s, a number of left-wing and rural-based guerilla groups were formed and began harassing a series of increasingly repressive, military-led governments backed by the United States. In 1982, the three most important of these groups—the Guerrilla Army of the Poor (EGP), the Revolutionary Organization of the People in Arms (ORPA), and the Rebel Armed Forces (FAR)—merged into the umbrella organization called National Revolutionary Unit. The three were later joined in UNRG by a section of the Communist Workers Party (PGT). At one point the UNRG had about 12,000 armed fighters in the field.

Officially, the civil war in Guatemala raged for 36 years, longer than any other civil conflict in the history of Latin America. An estimated 200,000 people were killed (about half of them in the 1980s), and a great many were injured and disabled.

On December 16, 1996, a historic peace agreement was signed between the UNRG and the government. The UNRG agreed to disarm in return for political and social reforms. As called for in that agreement, the UNRG began demobilizing under UN supervision the following March, and in June, the head of the UNRG, Ricardo Ramirez, and the newly elected president of Guatemala, Álvarez Árzu Irigoyen, were jointly awarded the UNESCO Houphouet-Boigny Peace Prize.

According to the Guatemalan magazine *Cronica*'s issue of August 8 through 14, the URNG had been responsible for 1,258 acts of terrorism during the long years of the war. They included "over 200 assassinations, 68 kidnappings, numerous bombings of buildings (including the National Palace in 1980), sabotages to the country's electrical grid, blowing up 62 bridges and massacres of entire villages." The magazine also described "purges the rebels carried out within their organization in which many members were liquidated" (quoted in *Guatemala* 1997).

Even so, Guatemala's Historical Clarification Commission concluded that the UNRG had been responsible for only about 3 percent of the atrocities committed during the war, while the Guatemalan army had been responsible for 93 percent. The URNG, which, unlike the army, acknowledged its crimes and apologized for them, is now a legal political party in Guatemala.

HAMAS

Palestinians seeking to replace Israel with an Islamic state. Also known as Islamic Resistance Movement.

Hamas—the name is an acronym for "Islamic Resistance Movement," which means *zeal* in Arabic—is virulently anti-Israel. It has consistently opposed all efforts by Palestinians to make peace with Israel.

Growing out of the Palestinian branch of the Muslim Brotherhood, the pan-Islamic organization founded by Hassan El Bana in the 1920s, Hamas was founded by Sheikh Ahmed Yasin during the early days of the *intifada* in late-1987. Sheikh Ahmed, who is an invalid, was arrested by Israel in 1989, and sentenced to life imprisonment for ordering kidnappings and murders, but was released several years later by Israeli President Benjamin Netanyahu.

Hamas is both a political organization and a terrorist group. It is believed to be loosely but elaborately structured with separate public, underground, and military wings. Most of the group's terrorist operations are carried out by the latter's "Qassim Battalions," small cells of desperate and committed young men who have grown up largely under "Israeli occupation."

Within the Palestinian community on the West Bank and Gaza, Hamas has been a rival and opponent of both the Palestine Liberation Organization and the Palestinian Authority, rejecting them for being secular and insufficiently devoted to the destruction of Israel. In the past, the rivalry with the PLO has led to armed confrontations between the two groups. Unlike the PLO, Hamas condemned Iraq's invasion of Kuwait in 1990.

Hamas is best known for its suicide-bombing attacks inside Israel, although it considers those attacks an exception to its previously declared policy of not striking civilians. It has also been accused, however, of striking Palestinians who oppose its policies, or who collaborate with the Israeli government. In addition to the suicide-bomb attacks, the Qassim Battalions' repertoire of terrorist tactics includes car bombs, targeted assassinations, drive-by shootings, and kidnappings. Other branches of the group organize demonstrations, strikes and other forms of protest, both peaceful and violent.

The size of Hamas' active membership is not known, although the group enjoys widespread support among the Palestinian population and in the Arab and Muslim worlds, in general. Most Hamas members are located in the West Bank and Gaza, and most of its terrorist activities are confined to that area, and, of course, to Israel.

Hamas representatives in various Arab capitals have come under increasing pressure. The group's headquarters in Amman, Jordan, were shut down by the Jordanian government in 1999. And, following the U.S./Iraq war in 2003, the group "froze" its activities in Syria, probably on orders from the Syrian government, which was itself under pressure from the United States.

Although Hamas has had a stormy relationship with the government of Iran, it is now believed to receive support from the Iranian government. Other financial support comes from individual Palestinians and other Arabs elsewhere in the Middle East. The group is also known to seek and receive help from sympathizers in Europe and America.

Hamas was outlawed by Israel in 1989. After Ariel Sharon was elected in Israel, his government adopted a policy of tracking down and assassinating Hamas leaders. Hamas has typically responded to each assassination with another suicide bombing, establishing yet another cycle-within-a-cycle of the seemingly endless pattern of retaliation-for-retaliation in Palestinian-Israeli conflict.

Although Hamas has not attacked American targets or interests, the U.S. government has officially designated it a Foreign Terrorist Organization.

HEZBOLLAH OR HIZBALLAH (PARTY OF GOD)

Anti-Israeli Shi'ites in Lebanon. Also known as Islamic Jihad.

One of the most hard-line, anti-Israel, and anti-Western political organizations in the entire Middle East, Hezbollah is also one of the region's most active terrorist groups. Formed in 1982 as a coalition of fundamentalist Lebanese Shi'ite groups (notably the Lebanese branch of the Da'wa Party and Islamic Amal), its declared aims are to combat what it sees as Western imperialism in Lebanon and Palestine, to reestablish Islamic rule in Jerusalem, and to reconstitute Lebanon as an Islamic republic on the Iranian model (Alexander 1994, 41).

Hezbollah's paramilitary played the major role in harassing the Israeli occupying forces in southern Lebanon until the Israeli forces finally withdrew from the country in 2000.

Claiming between 5,000 and 10,000 members inside Lebanon, the organization is believed to have terrorist cells or allied agents in a number of other countries as well. Hezbollah and affiliated organizations, including Islamic Jihad, have carried out several operations in Europe, Latin America, and Africa, as well as in Israel and elsewhere in the Middle East. They are believed to be responsible for the truck bombing that killed 241 Americans at the U.S. Marine barracks in Lebanon in 1983, as well as for the 1992 explosion that killed 29 people at the Israeli embassy in Buenos Aries, Argentina, and the bombing of a Jewish community center that killed almost 100 people in Buenos Aries two years later (Council, *Hezbollah* 2003). They have also been implicated in scores of other terrorist acts, large and small, ranging from kidnappings of American citizens, to airplane hijackings, to a wave of suicide bombings in Israel.

More than just a terrorist and paramilitary organization, Hezbollah is a significant force in Lebanese political and social life. It holds several seats in the Lebanese parliament and provides needed social services, including medical aid, to thousands of Lebanese Shi'ites. Not surprisingly, in light of the quasi-governmental roles it plays within the Shia community in Lebanon, Hezbollah is relatively complex organizationally. At the top are a Leadership Council, made up of Shi'ite clerics, and a Decision-making Council; under them are three Regional Councils that oversee the group's activities on the ground in Beirut, the Beka'a Valley, and in south Lebanon

(Council 2003: 42); and there are several lesser committees that help plan and carry out the group's myriad activities.

U.S. authorities believe that Hezbollah receives both inspiration and at least some political direction from the Shi'ite government of Iran, as well as money, weapons, and diplomatic assistance from both Iran and Syria.

HIZBALLAH KURDISH REVOLUTIONARY PARTY

Islamists seeking Kurdish independence from Turkey.

Made up primarily of separatist Muslim Kurds, the Hizballah Revolutionary Party initially opposed both Turkey's domination of the Kurds living in that country and the Kurdish Workers Party (PKK), which it considered a godless organization incompatible with Islam. The enmity between the two Kurdish groups was so strong that elements of the Hizballah Revolutionary Party launched a vicious campaign of murder and terror against PKK activists and sympathizers in Turkey in the early 1990s. In 1993, however, the two groups signed a "cooperation protocol," agreeing to act together against the Turkish state.

IRGUN ZVA'I LE'UMI (ETZEL)

Also known simply as the Irgun.

Founded in 1931 by several Haganah commanders who were unhappy with the charter adopted by the Jewish paramilitary defense force, the Irgun adopted a more militant and aggressive stance. The group's symbol, a raised fist holding aloft a rifle, and its motto, "Only thus," said it all.

At first, Etzel, or the Irgun, which numbered between 3,000 and 6,000 fighters, directed its violence primarily against Arab Palestinians, but later it broadened its range of targets to include officials and soldiers enforcing the British Mandate. In 1939, the Irgun itself splintered when perhaps 200 to 300 of its most rabid members, led by Abraham Stern, broke away to form an even more violent group which became known as the Stern Gang.

During World War II, the Irgun declared a truce with the British, while several of its members fought side-by-side with them in the war. On February 1, 1944, however, the group declared war on the British and demanded the establishment of an independent Jewish state. Over the next four years, the organization was responsible for several outrages, including the bombing of the Mandate headquarters at the King David Hotel in Jerusalem in 1946, and two bombs thrown into a crowd of Arab shoppers near the Damascus Gate. Also in 1946, the Irgun detonated two suitcase bombs at the British Embassy in Rome, Italy.

In May 1947, the Irgun retaliated for the execution of four of its members in the prison at Acre by breaking into the prison and freeing 41 inmates.

Rescue workers searching the ruins of the British Central government offices in Jerusalem's King David Hotel blown up by Etzel underground forces, July 22, 1946. Courtesy of Hugo Mendelson/ Israel Government Press Office.

When the British proceeded to execute three more group members two months later, the Irgun hanged two British soldiers and booby-trapped their bodies.

On April 9, 1948, a combined force of the Irgun and the Stern Gang attacked the peaceful Arab village of Deir Yassin, west of Jerusalem, killing hundreds of its residents and blowing up as many homes as they were able before they ran out of dynamite (Collins and LaPierre 1972, 285–291).

The Irgun disbanded after its primary goal had been achieved with the establishment of the state of Israel later in 1948. In 1977, Menachem Begin, who had been the head of the Irgun in the crucial period from 1944 to 1948, became the sixth prime minister of Israel. The following year, after a peace agreement had been reached with Egypt, Begin and the Egyptian President

Blood and scattered luggage at Lod Airport, Tel Aviv, after a terrorist attack. Japanese terrorists fired rifles and threw hand grenades into the terminal. Courtesy of Getty Images.

Anwar Sadat (another terrorist veteran) were jointly awarded the Nobel Prize for Peace.

JAPANESE RED ARMY (JRA)

Leftist Japanese revolutionaries.

The Japanese Red Army is strongly anti-capitalist, anti-United States, and anti-Israel. It seeks to foment an international Marxist revolution and to overthrow the Japanese monarchy. Never larger than perhaps 30 or 40 members, the JRA provides a vivid demonstration of the havoc that can be wrought by a relatively small group of ruthless and dedicated terrorists.

Founded by a young woman named Fusako Shingenobu, the JRA is an offshoot of the Japanese Communist League-Red Army Faction. It first seized international attention in March 1970, when nine of its members, wielding Samari swords, hijacked a Japan Airlines Boeing 727 enroute from Tokyo to Fukuoka, Japan, and forced it to fly to Pyongyang, North Korea. The incident was one of a series of hijackings, kidnappings, and murders that lasted for several years. In another attention-grabbing operation in

1974, the JRA invaded the French embassy at The Hague and held the Ambassador and 10 other people captive for five days.

For a time, the JRA took refuge in Lebanon, allying itself with Palestinian groups hostile to Israel. In May 1972, three JRA commandos armed with guns and grenades massacred 24 people and wounded 78 others in the terminal at Lod Airport in Israel. Recognizing that capture was imminent, two of the terrorists killed their companion, then one of the survivors succeeded in killing himself with a grenade; the third was arrested. This attack, the most spectacular in JRA's violent history, was carried out under the direction of the Popular Front for the Liberation of Palestine.

The group's visible activities lessened after the 1970s, but it seems to have stayed active underground. In April, 1988, it was suspected of carrying out the bombing of a USO (United Service Organizations) club in Naples, Italy that killed a U.S. servicewoman and four other people. Around the same time, a JRA commando was arrested with explosives in his possession in the United States.

Fusako Shingenobu herself was arrested in Tatasuki, Osaka, Japan, in November 2000. In captivity, she announced that, while she still sought the same goals, in the future she intended to cease terrorist activities and pursue those goals through peaceful political means.

JEMAAH ISLAMIYAH (JI)

Asian Jihadists, linked to al-Qaeda. Also known as the Islamic Group (IG).

One of the newer jihadist groups, Jemaah Islamiyah operates throughout Southeast Asia. It is based in Malaysia and is known to have units there and in Singapore and Indonesia, and may have them in other countries as well. The Malaysian unit, estimated at about 200 members, is believed to be the largest.

Jemaah Islamiyah's goal is to establish an Islamic pan-Asian state that would include at least parts of present-day Indonesia, Malaysia, and the Philippines. The group was inspired by the Darul Islam uprising that attempted to force the former Dutch colony of Indonesia to adopt Islamic law when it became an independent nation in the 1940s. Exactly when JI itself came into existence is not known. What is known is that its chief founder was Abu Bakar Bashir, an ex-Darul Islam member who had been imprisoned by Suharto's government in Indonesia along with several other Darul Islam veterans in the 1970s. It is believed that these veterans served as the nucleus of Jemaah Islamiyah.

Eventually surfacing in Malaysia, Bashir recruited a band of fighters to join their fellow Muslims waging war against the Soviets in Afghanistan. When the Suharto government that had once imprisoned him was replaced in 1998, Bashir returned to Indonesia. There, he established a *pesantren*, one of the Islamic seminaries, or boarding schools, that serve as rich recruiting grounds for Islamic terrorists.

Other major figures in Jemaah Islamiyah include Abu Jabril, who was once the group's second in command (he is now under arrest), and Nurjaman Riduan Ismuddin, better known simply as Hambali, who is said to lead the group's policy-making body and to direct many of JI's operations. Hambali is suspected of helping to plan an aborted attempt to blow up 11 American airliners over the Pacific Ocean in 1995.

In its early days, Jemaah Islamiyah directed most of its attacks against Christians. On Christmas Eve 2000, JI agents delivered bombs to many priests and churches around Indonesia. Fifteen of these bombs exploded, killing more than 13 people; 10 others failed to explode. A separate series of bombings killed more than 20 people in Manila, the Philippines, in the same month.

Most recently, Jemaah Islamiyah is suspected of being behind the car bombing that demolished two nightclubs in a tourist area of Bali in October 2002, killing 180 people and injuring some 300 more. Several of the dead were young Australians on vacation. Following that incident, both the U.S. State Department and the British government moved to officially declare the group a terrorist organization.

Officials in Singapore and elsewhere claim that Jemaah Islamiyah is linked to al-Qaeda. Bashir and other JI members have denied it. Whether or not there is a formal alliance between them, the two groups are clearly compatible in goals and ideology.

KACH AND KAHANE CHAI

Two branches of the same extreme right-wing Jewish movement.

The Kach seeks to restore the Biblical state of Israel, expanding the current borders, expelling Arabs from the country, and introducing the rule of Biblical law. The Israeli High Court of Justice has declared the movement's policies to be racist and banned Kach from participating in Knesset elections.

Kach, Kahane Chai, and groups associated with them have harassed Palestinians and other Arabs, as well as organized demonstrations and other activities to pressure the government of Israel to take action against them; and it has openly endorsed terrorist actions against Arabs in Israel and on the West Bank. Individuals and groups affiliated with the movement have been accused of making threats against both Arab and Israeli officials, and have claimed responsibility for a number of shooting incidents in the mid-1990s in which Palestinians were killed. When an American-born Kach supporter killed 29 Muslim worshippers in a mosque in Hebron in 1994, the group's leaders publicly hailed him as a "hero," although the organization itself was probably not involved in the atrocity.

The Kach movement was founded by the militant American rabbi, Meir Kahane, who had previously founded the Jewish Defense League (JDL) a group that advocated violence as a response to anti-Semitism in the United

States. Kahane left the United States for Israel in 1969. There, he almost immediately began campaigning for the expulsion of Arabs from the country. Kahane's movement became a political party that unsuccessfully stood for election to the Knesset in the 1970s and early-1980s.

In 1984, the Israeli government committee that vetted parties for inclusion on the ballot ruled Kach ineligible, but its judgment was overruled by the Israeli High Court of Justice. The controversy may have actually helped Kach because Meir Kahane finally won a Knesset seat in the next election. In 1988, however, the High Court ruled Kach candidates ineligible for election to the Israeli parliament based on a new law that made incitement to racism a bar to serving in the Knesset.

On a trip to New York City in 1990, Meir Kahane was assassinated by an Egyptian Islamist.

Two branches of the Kach movement survive. One, centered in Kiryat Arba in Hebron, continued under the original name. The other, led by Meir Kahane's son, Binyamin, and headquartered in the Israeli settlement of Tapuah, took the name Kahane Chai, or "Kahane Lives." Binyamin and his wife were killed in a random Palestinian terrorist attack in 2000. Some 20,000 sympathizers ran riot in the wake of their funeral.

In 1994, Kach and Kahane Chai were outlawed by the Israeli cabinet as terrorist organizations. In addition, the U.S. State Department has included both groups on its list of foreign terrorist organizations. Despite this, the Kach movement still has a number of sympathizers and supporters in the United States.

KU KLUX KLAN

White Supremacists in the United States. Also known as Invisible Empire of the Ku Klux Klan, and Knights of the Ku Klux Klan.

Through three major reincarnations, the Ku Klux Klan was synonymous with terror and bigotry in the United States for almost 150 years.

The original version of the Klan was founded by six young Confederate veterans on Christmas Eve night in 1865 in Pulsaki, Tennessee. The Klan began as a kind of secret fraternity, but it quickly evolved into the main means of combating Radical Reconstruction, and of preserving white power and authority in the postwar South.

The post–Civil War Klansmen dressed in robes and hoods to conceal their identities. They traveled in groups, often on horseback and usually at night, terrorizing ex-slaves who threatened to assert themselves. One black survivor of a visit from the nightriders described the event this way: "They had gowns on . . . and some would be red and some black, like a lady's dress . . . They said they wanted my [horse] for a charger to ride into Hell . . . They said they came from Hell and wanted to ride him back to Hell" (*Southern Exposure* 1980, 14).

John Brown in a reproduction of a 1850s photograph.
Courtesy of Library of Congress.

By 1868, the Invisible Empire, claimed 550,000 members, and freedmen and -women were no longer the Klan's only victims. In fact, the Klan's then-leader, renowned former Confederate General Nathan Forrest, denied that its primary object was to intimidate freedmen at all. "[S]ome foolish young men . . . put masks on their faces and rode over the country frightening negroes," Forrest told a Southern reporter, "but orders have been issued to stop that, and it has ceased. I have no powder to burn killing negroes, I intend to kill the radical [Republi-cans] . . . There is not a radical leader in [Memphis] but is a marked man, and if trouble should break out, none of them would be left alive" (*Report* 1872, 32–34). In fact, the Klan killed both "negroes" and whites. Most of the Invisible Empire's white victims were either carpetbaggers (Northerners who came South to profit from or to enforce Reconstruction) or scalawags (Southerners who cooperated with Reconstruction). But the vast majority of the Klan's victims were black. The toll of lives was enormous. According to evidence presented to a Con-

Oliver Brown, son of John Brown. Courtesy of
Library of Congress.

gressional committee, in the weeks leading up to the election of 1868 some
2,000 black people were killed in the state of Louisiana alone (*Hate* 1988,
76). Many, if not most, were killed by the Klan.

Klan members saw themselves as valiant defenders of the ante-bellum
Southern way of life. This meant, in the words of a declaration issued by a Klan
convention in 1867, the "maintenance of the White Race in this republic"
(*Hate* 1988, 75). The Klan "maintained" the White Race with arson, whippings, beatings, tortures, mutilations, and lynchings. Along with such similar
groups as the White Leagues, the Knights of the White Camella, and the Red
Shirts, the Invisible Empire spread fear throughout much of the South.

In 1871, Congress passed the Ku Klux Klan Act, mandating President
Ulysses S. Grant to take action against the group. Grant made an effort, but
it failed to seriously daunt the Invisible Empire. What finally ended the
Klan's reign of terror was success. Following the deadlocked federal election
of 1876, a compromise was struck in the Congress that ended Reconstruction in the South. The ante-bellum way of life in the South would never
return, but the dominance of the "White Race" would be maintained for
nearly another century.

The first resurgence of the Ku Klux Klan occurred in 1915, when a hard-
drinking ex-preacher and current insurance salesman named William Simmons took advantage of the enormous popularity of the D. W. Griffith
movie *The Birth of a Nation* to revive the organization for profit.

The new Klan was hostile to blacks, Catholics, Jews, organized labor, and immigrants. Although it routinely used violence, threats, and intimidation, it was considerably less violent than the original Klan had been. It emphasized "Americanism"—which it equated with small-town virtues and white Protestantism—allowing it to attract many members outside the South. At its height, it could credibly claim to have 5 million members. Sexual and financial scandals eventually destroyed the organization's reputation, and by 1930 it was bankrupt. Once again, the Klan disappeared for a time.

In 1954, the U.S. Supreme Court ruled that segregated schools were unconstitutional; in 1957, Congress passed the first federal Civil Rights Bill since Reconstruction. These things had little immediate effect, but the handwriting was on the wall: the Jim Crow laws that legally segregated blacks from whites in the South were in mortal danger. In response to that danger, die-hard segregationists revived the Klan in a desperate effort to preserve white dominance in the region.

Klan members committed many of the most notorious acts of race-related violence in the 1960s. These included the 1963 bombing of the Sixteenth Street Baptist Church in Birmingham, Alabama, in which one 11-year-old and three 14-year-old black girls were killed; the assassination of the black civil rights leader, Medgar Evers, also in 1963; and, the executions of three young civil rights workers (two white, one black) near Philadelphia, Missis-

Still from *Birth of a Nation* showing nightriders in action. Courtesy of Photofest.

sippi, in 1964. In addition, Klan members and sympathizers were responsible for the largest percentage of the estimated 1,000 race-related beatings, arsons, and murders that attended the Civil Rights struggle of the late-1950s and 1960s.

In 1965, President Lyndon Johnson called for an investigation of the Klan. Financial scandals uncovered by that investigation severely damaged the organization. Those, combined with the end of legal segregation, drastically reduced the Klan's activities, although isolated acts of Klan violence and intimidation continued to occur.

The Klan was loosely organized into so-called "klaverns," or cells, a fact that allowed the organization to deny responsibility for any atrocities committed by individual Klan members or local groups of Klansmen. In 1987, however, the mother of a young man lynched by members of a small klavern sued the parent organization for his death. The suit, taken up by Morris Dees and Joseph J. Levin of the Southern Poverty Law Center, effectively bankrupted the Klan, which has never recovered from the blow.

KURDISH WORKERS PARTY OR PARTIYA KARKEREN KURDISTAN (PKK)

Kurdish separatists in Turkey. Also known as Kadek, or Kurdish Freedom and Democracy Congress.

Founded in the 1970s, the PKK seeks to establish an independent Kurdish state in what is now southeastern Turkey, where Kurds make up the majority of the population. Ethnic Kurds also make up large parts of the populations of significant areas of northern Iraq and western Iran.

The PKK grew out of the leftwing-student ferment in Turkey the 1960s, and its activities have been primarily directed against that country. Led by Abdullah Ocalan, the group originally saw itself as part of a worldwide leftist revolution. For a time, it made its headquarters in the Syrian-controlled Beka'a Valley of Lebanon and allied itself with Palestinian groups combating the Israeli invasion of that country in 1982.

The PKK received support from the governments of Syria and Libya. In the 1980s, it conducted a series of brutal attacks against tribal chiefs and villages it saw as supporting the Turkish government. In 1984, the PKK declared war on Turkey from its headquarters in Syria.

Throughout the 1980s and 1990s, it was one of the most active and brutal of the world's terrorist groups, attacking security forces and foreign tourists within Turkey, as well as Turkish interests elsewhere in Europe. It was one of the relatively few groups to use suicide bombers, some of them women. By 1997, the Turkish government was accusing the PKK of responsibility for 31,837 deaths (Spotlight 2002, 10).

In 1990 it moved away from its Marxist roots, and established relationships with Islamic Kurds who also opposed the Turkish regime. As time went on, it attracted political and economic support from a widening base of the Kurdish population in several countries. In March, 1993, the PKK signed a "co-operation" agreement with its Islamic rival, the Hizbollah Kurdish Revolutionary Party. Following the Gulf War, the PKK established itself for a time in northern Iraq.

In 1994, the PKK initiated a new policy of seeking some sort of peaceful resolution with the Turkish government; it even declared its "intent" to abide by the humanitarian provisions of the Geneva Convention. At the same time, it declared that it would continue to consider members of the Turkish security, military, paramilitary, and police forces as fair targets for attack (Spotlight 2002, 5).

As the Executive Director, Europe & Central Asia Division of Human Rights Watch pointed out in a letter to the Italian Prime Minister, "At its Third National Conference in 1994, the PKK declared that, 'The struggle which the PKK carries out has left the stage of strategic defense . . . It is inevitable that we escalate our struggle in response to Turkey's declaration of all-out war. Consequently, all economic, political, military, social and cultural organizations, institutions, formations—and those who serve in them—have become targets. The entire country has become a battlefield.' " The PKK also announced its intention to "eliminate" political parties, as well as "imperialist" cultural and educational institutions, legislative and representative bodies, and "all local collaborators and agents working for the Republic of Turkey in Kurdistan" (Cartner 1998).

The new policy was a step toward moderation only in that it had previously directed its attacks not only against these enemies, but against the women and children of their families, and other civilians, as well.

In 1998, Abdullah Ocalan was forced to leave Syria when Turkey threatened to invade if that country continued to harbor him. In February 1999, Ocalan was arrested in Nairobi, Kenya. He was returned to Turkey and tried for treason. At his trial, he offered to serve as an intermediary between the Kurd separatists and the Turkish government. Nonetheless, he was convicted and sentenced to death. He was still on death row when Turkey abolished the death penalty in 2002.

In recent years, the PKK has stepped up its diplomatic activities, while its terrorist activities have been drastically reduced. In 2002 the group officially changed its name to the Kurdish Freedom and Democracy Congress (KADEK).

LASHKAR I JHANGVI

Militant Sunni Muslims in Pakistan.

Lashkar I Jhangvi was formed in 1996 with the objective of establishing an Islamic state in Pakistan along narrow sectarian lines. It is named after Maulana Haq Nawaz Jhangvi, the co-founder and head of the *Sipah-e-Sahaba*

Pakistan (The Pakistan Army of Mohamed's Companions), or SSP, a faction of Wahabi Sunni Muslims who had devoted themselves to a similar purpose.

After Jhangvi was assassinated, apparently by rival Shia Muslims, in 1990, his notorious bodyguard Riaz Basra rallied a number of SSP fanatics to launch a campaign of assassination and terror against Shias, who are both a minority in Pakistan and the majority in the neighboring nation of Iran. Eventually, they turned their wrath on rival Sunni factions as well.

Suspected of the assassination of an Iranian official in 1992, Basra was arrested but somehow escaped from custody. In 1996, Basra and his followers broke away from the SSP on the grounds that it was no longer sufficiently loyal to the ideals of the dead Jhangvi, and formed the *Lashkar I Jhangvi,* operating primarily out of Karachi, Pakistan.

Lashkar I Jhangvi was declared a foreign terrorist organization by the U.S. Department of State in January 2003. At that time, U.S. Secretary of State Colin Powell issued a press release describing the group as "a violent Sunni Muslim group located in Pakistan. It is responsible for numerous deadly attacks, and its involvement in the January 2002 kidnapping and killing of American journalist Daniel Pearl has been confirmed. The group has perpetrated bus and church bombings. It claimed responsibility for the 1997 killing of four American oil workers in Karachi. *Lashkar I Jhangvi* also attempted to assassinate then Pakistani Prime Minister Nawaz Sharif in 1999" (Powell, 2003).

While it was the group's involvement in the murder of Daniel Pearl that caught the attention of the American government, *Lashkar I Jhangvi* had already been proscribed as a terrorist organization by President Pervez Musharraf of Pakistan on August 14, 2001. It is believed to have been responsible for literally hundreds of murders, mostly of Iranians and of Pakistani members of rival Muslim factions, in the mid- to late-1990s. Its founder, Basra, was allegedly involved in some 300 terrorist incidents himself.

In 1999, with Pakistan under military control, Basra moved to Taliban-led Afghanistan, and the group became largely, if not entirely, inactive. After Afghanistan was attacked by U.S. forces, Basra returned to Pakistan, where he was arrested (Lashkar 2002). Several months later, while still allegedly in the custody of a Pakistani "secret agency," Basra participated in an armed attack on a Pakistani village official and was killed by police and villagers in an ensuing shootout. This mysterious event fueled previous speculation that Basra, and perhaps *Lashkar I Jhangvi* as well, may have been working under the direction of some elements within the military government of Pakistan (Jalal 2002).

LIBERATION TIGERS OF TAMIL ELAM (LTTE)

Tamil separatists in Sri Lanka. Also known as Tamil Tigers.

The Tamils are an ethnic and a religious (Hindu) minority in the largely Buddhist nation of Sri Lanka. The Liberation Tigers of Tamil Elam are one of three groups formed by the splintering of the Tamil Students Movement in the early-1970s. The Tigers want to carve an independent Tamil state out of the northern and eastern rims of Sri Lanka, where the Tamils are a majority and the LTTE controls much of the territory.

In 1983, the Tigers launched an armed insurrection against the government of Sri Lanka, a conflict that has been marked by widespread violence against civilians on both sides. The U.S. State Department estimates that the Tigers have some 10,000 armed combatants in Sri Lanka, about 3,000 to 6,000 of whom are trained fighters (U.S. Department of State 1997, 14). How many are also members of the Black Tigers, or otherwise participate in what would properly be called terrorist activities, as opposed to military activities, is not clear.

The Black Tigers branch of the LTTE became notorious for their extensive use of suicide-bombing attacks. In fact, the LTTE has probably carried out more suicide bombings than any other terrorist group. Some of these attacks were targeted assassinations, such as that of Sri Lankan President Ranasinghe Premadasa in 1993. Others, like the bomb at the Sri Lankan Central Bank in January 1996, were directed against the Sri Lanka economy. Many civilians have been killed or maimed by these explosions. In the 1990s alone, the suicide bombers of the LTTE killed an estimated 1,500 people. Some of these gruesome acts were filmed, and used by the group to inspire their surviving members (Friedman 2002).

The LTTE is also among the relatively few terrorist groups that have employed fertilizer (ammonium nitrate) truck bombs.

With economic support from expatriate Tamils living, working, and banking abroad, the LTTE has also conducted an elaborate guerilla campaign against the government. In addition to more ordinary guerilla activities, this campaign has included attacks against both Sri Lankan and foreign ships in Sri Lankan waters. The Tigers have generally refrained, however, from launching terrorist actions outside of Sri Lanka, presumably in order to prevent foreign governments from curtailing Tamil economic activities in their countries. The only major exception to this policy was the suicide bombing that killed the former prime minister of India, Rajiv Gandhi, in India, in 1991. Although the LTTE vehemently denied carrying out that attack, an Indian court found several of its members guilty of involvement in the assassination. Like many suicide bombers of the Black Tigers, Gandhi's assassin was a woman.

Members of the LTTE carry cyanide capsules with which they can kill themselves if they are danger of being caught. Of the 41 people the Indian authorities believed were involved in the assassination of Rajiv Gandhi, 12 committed suicide before they could be arrested or tried (CNN Interactive 1998).

In the wake of September 11, 2001, with the world focused on the problem of terrorism, both international support and funding for the Tigers began to dry up. Robbed of the sources of much of their funding, the Tamils "sued for peace" (Crossette 2002). A ceasefire was agreed to in December 2001. The ban the Sri Lankan government had imposed on the Tigers was lifted as of midnight on September 4, 2002, prior to formal negotiations between them, which were to take place in Thailand.

LORD'S RESISTANCE ARMY (LRA)

Religiously oriented Ugandan rebels.

The LRA was founded and is led by Major General Joseph Krony. A Christian religious visionary, Krony maintains he acts in the name of the Holy Spirit, with whom he claims to be in contact. Krony and his organization have been at war with the Ugandan government for over 15 years; during that time, they have received varying degrees of support and sanctuary from the Islamic government of neighboring Sudan. In the aftermath of September 11, 2001, however, the Sudanese government has been withdrawing its support in an effort to cooperate with the United States' antiterrorism efforts (Lacey 2002).

While it has been accused of a wide range of atrocities, including many kinds of terrorism, the LRA is most notorious for its practice of abducting children from Ugandan villages, impressing the boys into military service and the girls into various forms of slavery, including forcing them to serve as "wives" to LRA soldiers. Estimates of the number of children the group has seized range into the tens of thousands. Of that total, many have been killed, thousands have escaped, and thousands remain captive (Scars 1997).

MAU MAU

Anti-colonial revolutionaries in Kenya. Also known as the Land Freedom Army (LFA).

The Land Freedom Army was a notorious secret society, primarily but not exclusively made up mostly of Kikuyu tribesmen, that carried on a brutal terrorist insurgency against British rule in Kenya in the 1950s. (The name "Mau Mau," was never used by members of the society itself; it is used here simply because it is the name most likely to be familiar to readers.)

The British—who had confiscated almost all the fertile land in Kenya—ruled over the black population with a combination of arrogance and indifference. The Mau Mau came together after decades of African appeals to the British authorities, both inside the colony and back in England, had failed to produce more than empty promises. This, despite the fact that the Africans of Kenya had helped the British in World War II.

The Mau Mau were poor and, for the most part, uneducated. They had few modern weapons and relied mostly on clubs and machete-like pangas,

Jomo Kenyatta waving tasseled stick as he walks among supporters during victory celebrations following general elections in Kenya. Courtesy of Library of Congress.

along with a few rifles. Initiates in the group swore a secret blood oath to fight and kill the white colonialists and to take back the land the British had stolen. The oath was allegedly administered in an elaborate ceremony that included some of the trappings of African witchcraft. Kikuyus who refused to take the oath, or who showed loyalty to the British, were often killed. On March 26, 1953, Mau Mau warriors hacked 84 of their fellow Kikuyus to death as part of the fierce campaign of murder and intimidation by which the Mau Mau tried to force other Kikuyus to join them. Indeed, throughout the entire Mau Mau rebellion, the group's black victims consistently outnumbered the whites by a factor of several times.

For the most part, the Mau Mau's attacks against the British consisted of night raids on isolated farmhouses. There weren't many of these raids, but when they occurred, they were merciless. The white residents of the farmhouses were hacked and beaten to death. In one of the most notorious of the raids, a white female doctor, who ran a medical clinic for black Africans, was hacked to death along with her husband and their young son.

Early on, the English colonial government declared the taking of the Mau Mau oath illegal, and Jomo Kenyatta, a reputed member of the Mau Mau, and later the first president of post-colonial Kenya, was arrested and thrown in prison. Dedan Kimathi, another of the group's leaders, was captured, hanged, and thrown into a mass grave. In one month in 1953, 16,000 suspected rebels were rounded up in Nairobi. In October of the same year, the Mau Mau slaughtered 97 Kikuyu villagers whose chief had been accused of collaborating with the British in seizing African lands. Then, in 1954, the rebellion claimed its most prominent victim, when the body of famed archeologist, Dr. Gray Arundel Leackey, was discovered buried in a shallow grave. The body had been mutilated and perhaps partially cannibalized in such a way that it was believed to have been used in one of the more appalling Mau Mau oath ceremonies.

The British responded to the Mau Mau insurgency with overwhelming force, and only slightly less brutality than that of Mau Mau themselves. Altogether, some 10,557 Mau Mau or suspected Mau Mau were reportedly killed in the rebellion, while the Mau Mau killed "only" 2,484 people, all but a small percentage of whom were black (Paul 2000).

NARODNAYA VOLYA (PEOPLE'S WILL)

Nineteenth Century Russian anarcho-anarchists. Also known as National Will.

The Narodnaya Volya was a small, upper-class student movement, organized in 1879 by breakaway elements of Zemya I Volya, or the Land and Freedom Party. Led by Andrey I. Zhelyabov and Sofia L. Perovskaya, the daughter of the governor-general of St. Petersburg, the members of the new group despaired of fomenting revolution in Russia by the conventional means of organization and agitation, and concluded that more drastic and violent methods were necessary.

During its short, but historically important existence, Narodnaya Voyla devoted itself to the assassinations of high czarist officials, and particularly of Czar Alexander II himself. The group made several bomb attempts on his life, in which scores of people were killed, before finally succeeding on March 1, 1881. Roughly a month later, and despite appeals for clemency from Leo Tolstoy and others, Zehlyabov and Perovskaya were publicly hanged, along with three of their fellow conspirators.

Shortly before her trial, Perovskaya wrote an unrepentant revolutionary's letter to her mother, in which she urged her "not to grieve for me; for my fate does not afflict me in the least, and I shall meet it with complete tranquility, for I have long expected it, and known that sooner or later it must come. And I assure you, dear mama, that my fate is not such a very mournful one. I have lived as my convictions dictated, and it would have been impossible for me to have acted otherwise. I await my fate, therefore, with a tranquil conscience, whatever it may be (Stepaniak 1973, 131–132).

Alexander II, who had been relatively progressive, was followed by Alexander III, who cracked down on Russian revolutionaries in general and on Narodnaya Volya in particular. The group was quickly destroyed, but its example served as both a warning and an inspiration to younger Marxists like Vladimir I. Lenin and Leon Trotsky. Although both were children when Perovskaya and Zehlyabov were hanged, they learned from the legendary terrorists' mistakes, and used those lessons in organizing the revolution that overthrew Alexander III's son, Nicholas II, in 1917.

NOVEMBER 17

Leftists opposed to Western capitalist influence in Greece.

One of the best examples of a small, patient, and totally ruthless ideological terrorist group, November 17 was established in the wake of the 1973 student uprising that led to the overthrow of the military junta that had run the Greek government since 1967. Under the junta, right-wing thugs had been allowed, and perhaps actually encouraged, to harass, beat, and intimidate left-wing opponents of the regime. As the United States and Western European allies had supported the junta, November 17 determined to exact a price for that support. In addition, the Marxist group had strong ideological reasons for opposing western capitalist regimes.

Although the entire active November 17 membership probably never consisted of more than 13 individuals, the group managed to survive pretty much intact for a quarter-century. During that time, it assassinated at least 23 people, including U.S., British, and Turkish government and intelligence personnel.

Although November 17 struck both inside and outside Greece, the targets of its attacks were usually foreigners. In this way, it apparently avoided arousing the kind of outrage that might have been expected among the Greek population. In any event, the group and its members seemed to be strangely immune from capture, and rumors persisted of connections between it and Greek government officials (Carassava 2002).

The investigation into a bomb that exploded prematurely on June 29, 2002, resulted in the first arrest ever of a November 17 member some three weeks later. That arrest was soon followed by a series of others, and Greek authorities now believe that the group has been thoroughly dismantled (Davenport, 2002).

PALESTINIAN ISLAMIC JIHAD (PIJ)

Palestinian Jihadists. Also known as Harakat Al-Jihad Al-Islami Al-Filastini.

The Islamic Jihad ideology has spawned many terrorist groups, several of which are connected to some degree with the Palestinian cause. One of the most militant of all the anti-Israel terrorist groups is the Fathi Shqaqi faction of Palestinian Islamic Jihad, an organization that grew out of ferment among Palestinian students in Egypt who were associated with the Egyptian Islamic Jihad. Inspired by the Islamic revolution in Iran, the founders of PIJ believed that the destruction of Israel could be the key to unifying the Muslim world, and could provide a springboard to the establishment of a single, massive Islamic state.

Following the assassination of Egypt's president, Anwar Sadat, in 1981, militant Palestinian Islamists were expelled from Egypt and sent to Gaza. It was there that Palestinian Islamic Jihad began its violent activities in support of the Islamist cause. In 1988, the group's leaders were expelled from Gaza to Lebanon.

The American government believes PIJ to be connected to suicide bombings in Israel and the occupied territories that, as of early 2003, had killed more than 100 people, including two Americans. In the occupied territories, the group has been both a rival and an ally to Hamas, with whom it has sometimes carried out joint, or simultaneous, bombing operations. In the mid-1990s, PIJ carried out several deadly attacks inside Israel. Fathi Shqaqi, one of PIJ's founders and the most charismatic of its leaders, was killed, possibly by Israeli agents, in Malta, in October 1995.

Although PIJ operates almost exclusively in and around Israel, it has maintained offices in Beirut, Damascus, Tehran, and Khartoum. The U.S. government believes that the group has links with the governments of both Syria and Iran. It allegedly receives financial support from Palestinian sympathizers in other countries, including the United States. For a time, Dr. Ramadan Abdallah Shalah, Shqaqi's successor as leader of PIJ, lived in the state of Florida, in the United States.

In February, 2003, U.S. authorities set off a civil rights *cause célèbre* when they arrested several American residents and charged them with being active in support of the group. Among them was Sami al-Arian, a controversial university professor whom the government had long suspected of directing Palestinian Islamic Jihad's American fund-raising operation. Al-Arian had previously been suspended from his job at the University of South Florida because of his suspected involvement with PIJ.

PEOPLE'S MUJAHADEEN

Dissident Iranians. Also known as the Mujahedin-E Khalq Organization (MEK), the National Liberation Army of Iran, the National Council of Resistance, Organization of the People's Holy Warriors of Iran.

The People's Mujahadeen is the militant wing of MEK, an Islamic Marxist movement that began its existence opposing Western influence on the Shah's regime in Iran in the 1970s, and that opposes the clerical regime that is now in power in the country, as well. It is probably unique among terrorist groups in the Middle East—and among Islamic terrorist groups anywhere—in that it is currently led by a woman.

MEK grew out of the Iranian student movement of the 1960s. Its main purpose at the time was to overthrow the Shah of Iran, who was widely regarded as a puppet of the United States. In the 1970s, the People's Mujahadeen launched a number of attacks inside Iran in which several Americans were killed. After the fall of the Shah, the group supported the student invasion of the U.S. Embassy in Teheran, and the holding of American hostages that followed.

In 1981, an MEK bomb killed 70 Iranian government officials, including the president, the premier, and the attorney-general. Having aroused the displeasure of the new government in Teheran, the MEK leaders fled, first to France, and later to Iraq, where it helped the Iraqi government of Saddam Hussein put down the Kurdish and Shia uprisings that came in the aftermath of the Gulf War of 1991. From then until the American invasion of Iraq in 2003, the People's Mujahadeen performed internal security services for the Iraqi government. In return, it received financial support and permission to use Iraq as a base for attacks on Iran.

In April 1992, the People's Mujahadeen carried out attacks against Iranian Embassies in no less than 13 different countries. Over the next several years, members of the group assassinated several Iranian military personnel; the most prominent victim being the deputy chief of the Iranian Armed

Rebel Mujahadeen with a captured Soviet tank during the assault on Jalalabad, 1989. Courtesy of Robert Nickelberg/Getty Images.

Forces General Staff. In February 2000, MEK launched Operation Great Bahman, carrying out a dozen military operations against Iran; it has kept up small-scale raids and mortar attacks inside that country ever since.

After Iraq's capitulation to the Americans in 2003, the People's Mujahadeen agreed to a cease-fire with the U.S. military, in return for which it was allowed to keep much of its substantial arsenal of guns, tanks, mortars, and artillery, and perhaps its bases in Iraq, as well. At that time, there was some speculation as to why the United States, which was supposed to be waging a worldwide "War on Terrorism," would let such a notorious terrorist group escape virtually untouched. The best explanation seemed to be the United States would find the group's continued harassment of the government useful, and might even be looking forward to the group's assistance, should the United States itself choose to move against Iran in the future.

The People's Mujahadeen is estimated to have between 5,000 and 10,000 actual fighters. Until recently, it was financed largely by the Hussein government in Iraq and by donations from Iranian exiles in other countries.

PROVISIONAL WING OF THE IRISH REPUBLICAN ARMY

The best known of the so-called "Catholic" paramilitary groups active in the "Troubles" in Northern Ireland. Also known as the Provisionals, or Provos.

The Provisional Wing of the Irish Republican Army portrays itself as the champion of the struggle for Northern Ireland's independence from Britain. When the Provos were founded in 1969, they were called the Provisional Wing to distinguish them from the Official Wing of the Irish Republican Army, which functioned as an ordinary political party and denied any participation in violence. The Provos, on the other hand, used all manner of violence—including beatings, bombings, firebombings, killings, kneecappings, threats, and intimidation—to terrorize, not only the British but also Irish loyalists, the police, and even ordinary citizens who defied them.

Although they are usually identified with the Catholic minority in Northern Ireland, both the Provisionals and Sinn Féin seek to establish a secular and Socialist state throughout all of Ireland.

For some time now, the role the Official Wing once played has been taken over by the political party known as Sinn Féin. Many opponents of the IRA claim that the separation between the Provisionals and Sinn Féin was always largely artificial. They charge that it was only a handy subterfuge that allowed Sinn Féin to campaign politically and raise money openly, despite the fact that the Provisional Wing of the IRA was proscribed as a terrorist organization. Despite these claims, the British refrained from outlawing Sinn Féin itself. One British official explained their failure to do so by the fact that, despite the government's allegations, it had "no evidence of [Sinn Féin's] terrorist connections or actions" (Newhouse 1985, 12). In any event, the separation between the political and paramilitary wings of the Republican movement has proven useful for both sides in the conflict in Northern Ireland, if only because it facilitated negotiation between the British government and the Republicans.

Initially, some of the Provisionals' violence was random; car bombs were left in public places where the explosions would kill anyone who happened to be near. Later, however, the Provos renounced randomness, and claimed that they were directing their attacks exclusively against the British "occupiers" of Northern Ireland, and those Irishmen whom the Provos regarded as traitors for assisting them (Barich 1988, 108).

Among the many outrages committed by the Provos was a series of bombings that killed 13 people and wounded over 130 more in Belfast in 1972, and a bomb that destroyed the yacht of the British aristocrat and war hero Earl Louis Mountbatten, killing both the earl and his 14-year-old grandson. In 1984, a Provo bomb destroyed a section of a hotel in the British resort town of Brighton where Prime Minister Margaret Thatcher and other delegates to a Conservative Party convention were staying. By pure chance, the prime minister was absent at the time the bomb went off.

In addition to such headline-grabbing atrocities, the Provisionals are said to have virtually ruled some areas of Northern Irish cities by violence and intimidation, in much the same way that the Mafia once ruled some neighborhoods in American cities. Even so, and despite the fact that the Provisionals were known to be brutal and ruthless murderers, thousands of Catholics in both Irelands sympathized and supported them. The Catholics appreciated the Provisionals' willingness to take up arms against both the British and the Protestant majority in Northern Ireland, whom they regarded as oppressors.

The Provisionals also had a great many sympathizers and supporters among the Irish-American population in parts of the United States. To many American Catholics, they seemed romantic figures, classic underdogs engaged in a valiant struggle against a militarily superior enemy—the same enemy that Americans had fought to win their own independence two centuries earlier. Over the years, IRA sympathizers raised a great deal of American money for the cause of Irish independence, much of which, according to government officials on both sides of the Atlantic, made its way into the hands of the Provisionals.

The British sometimes fought the Provisionals with tactics that were, in some ways, similar to the Provos' own. In March 1988, British agents gunned down three unarmed Provos in cold blood on a street on the British island of Gibraltar. In May 2001, the European Court of Human Rights found that the British violated the rights of 10 other IRA men who had been shot to death by the security forces—not necessarily by killing them but in failing to investigate their cases properly (BBC News 2001).

The killings in Gibraltar were part of a wave of events that demonstrated the self-feeding nature of the violence in Northern Ireland. Thousands of Catholics turned out for the interment of the Gibraltar victims at a cemetery in Belfast. Three of the mourners were killed and 60 more injured when a Protestant gunman named Michael Stone opened fire on the gathering. During the large funeral procession for one of Stone's victims, two off-duty mem-

IRA in Whiterock. Courtesy of Pacemaker Press.

bers of the British Army inadvertently found their small car blocked by the crowd of mourners. Panicking, one of them showed a gun. When the crowd realized who, or what they were, it dragged them from their cars and beat them. Provos arrived, took the two men into an alley, and shot them to death.

The Provisionals called a cease-fire in 1997 and announced their support, first for the peace process and then for the Good Friday Peace Accords, which were signed by government of the United Kingdom and the government of Ireland the following year. As a part of the peace process, they began to disarm around the turn of the millennium.

Since the 1997 cease-fire, the Provisionals seem to have severely curtailed, if not entirely ceased, their activities against the British and Protestants in Northern Ireland. The violence that they have been accused of in recent years has been in the nature of revenge taken against those they believe had betrayed them in the past.

While the Provisional Wing of the Irish Republican Army has abandoned the armed struggle, dissident groups calling themselves the "Continuity IRA" and the "Real IRA" continue to carry out terrorist attacks in a continuing effort to scuttle the torturous peace process in Northern Ireland.

At times, the Provos have made common cause with other terrorist organizations. In his book, *The Informer: The Real-Life Story of One Man's Fight against Terrorism,* published in 1998, an ex-Provisional named Sean O'Callaghan alleged that the assassination of Lord Mountbatten was carried out in return for a payment of 2 million pounds from the government of Syria (O'Callaghan 1998). In August, 2001, three Irish nationals alleged to be Provisionals (or perhaps ex-Provisionals) were arrested in Colombia, leading to speculation in the U.S. Congress and elsewhere that the IRA had become part of a global terrorist network, and was training FARC rebels in Colombia.

REAL IRA (RIRA)

Die-hard Republicans in Northern Ireland.

When the Provisional Wing of the Irish Republican Army declared a cease-fire in Northern Ireland in 1997, some 100 to 200 republican dissidents, led by Michael "Mickey" McKevitt, elected to continue the campaign of violence against British rule in Northern Ireland under the name of the Real IRA.

Allied with the 32 County Sovereignty Movement, the RIRA proceeded to carry out a number of bombings in Northern Ireland, most of which were relatively minor. In fact, no deaths were attributed to the Real IRA until August 15, 1998, when a car bomb exploded in a shopping area of Omagh, killing 29 people and injuring some 220 others. It was the single worst act of terrorism in the entire history of the "Troubles" in Northern Ireland.

The large number of civilian deaths and injuries caused a wave of revulsion at a time when the movement toward peace in Northern Ireland seemed to be well underway. The Omagh bombing was roundly condemned by almost everyone, including Jerry Adams of Sinn Féin. The Real IRA itself claimed that the civilian casualties have been unintentional and in September 1998, declared its own cease-fire in the conflict with Britain. Two years later, however, it renounced the cease-fire and resumed attacks against British interests both in Northern Ireland and on the English mainland. Michael McKevitt and 40 other members of the organization were arrested over several months in 2001, but RIRA continued its operations.

Like the Provisionals, RIRA may receive funds from Irish-American sympathizers in the United States. The United States government formally declared the RIRA a foreign terrorist organization in May 2001, a designation that allows the government to freeze the assets of anyone tied to the organization in the United States.

RED BRIGADES, OR *BRIGATE ROSSE*

Would-be revolutionary cadre in Italy.

The Red Brigades was the most feared Italian terrorist group of the 1970s and 1980s. Its goals were to split Italy from the western alliance and, ultimately, to establish a leftist revolutionary state. It advocated "armed struggle," which it practiced in the forms of assassinations, fire-bombings, and kidnappings.

Founded in 1969 and growing out of the Metropolitan Political Collective in Milan, the Red Brigades was an extremely ideological organization. It considered itself a part of the *Autonomia Operaio* (Workers' Autonomy) movement, and its ideology was a mixture of traditional Marxist-Leninism and elements of the New Left thinking prevalent in the 1960s, with an eccentric brand of anarchism thrown in.

During its heyday, it was one of the most notorious terrorist organizations in Europe. Beginning with attacks on right-wing Italian industrialists and trade unionists, it progressed to killing policemen and Italian government officials. On one occasion, Brigadists machine-gunned three policemen to death. On another, they fired a bazooka at two police cars. In 1979, "urban guerillas" from the Red Brigades took control of a business school in Milan and held some 200 of the occupants hostage; 10 of the bound hostages were shot in the legs during the ordeal.

The Brigades were responsible for perhaps the most notorious terrorist act in Italian history. In 1978, they kidnapped the ex–prime minister of Italy, Alberto Moro, holding him for nearly two months before murdering him and leaving his body in the trunk of a car parked on a Roman street.

The group also claimed responsibility for the 1984 assassination of Leamon Hunt, the American chief of the Sinai Multinational Force and Observer Group. In another highly publicized operation against an American, the Brigades kidnapped a U.S. brigadier general assigned to NATO named James Dozier in 1981. The general was later rescued by Italian police.

The Red Brigades' ideology was appealing to many young people in Italy in the 1970s. One of them was Carlo Saronio, the son of a wealthy Italian family, who allowed himself to be kidnapped in order to extort money from his family to help the Brigades' cause. When the common criminals who conducted the operation murdered the idealistic Saronio, a Brigadist named Carlo Fiorono was arrested and convicted for involvement in the affair. After languishing for roughly five years in prison, Fiorono repented his terrorist past and turned informer (DePalma 1980). His information, combined with the Italian government's draconian crackdown on terrorism following the abduction and murder of Alberto Moro, led to the capture of many Brigadists.

Four of the group's imprisoned leaders signed an "open letter" in 1984 in which they renounced the armed struggle on the grounds that: "The international conditions that made this struggle possible no longer exist" (Karman 2002).

Elements of the group remained at-large and continued to function for some years afterwards, however. The assassination of a government adviser named Roberto Ruffilli by alleged Brigadists in 1988 is generally regarded as the last gasp of the original Red Brigades organization; and, in fact, the group has been inactive for more than a decade. The shadow of the Red Brigades continues to haunt Italy. The shooting of a government adviser named Massimo D'Antona in Rome in 1999 and the murder of a government economist named Marco Biagi in Bologna in 2003 were both attributed to reincarnations of the organization.

In the 1970s and 1980s, the Red Brigades was thought to have perhaps 500 to 600 hardcore members, with perhaps another 1,000 of what might be called active sympathizers. The strength, if any, of the so-called "new" Red Brigades is unknown.

RED HAND DEFENDERS (RHD)

Militant loyalists in Northern Ireland.

The name, Red Hand Defenders, has been used since 1998 by die-hard loyalist (or, unionist) terrorists in Northern Ireland. It is not clear whether it designates an autonomous terrorist organization, or is primarily a cover name adopted for certain operations by members, or ex-members, of old groups like the Ulster Defense Association (UDA) and Ulster Volunteer Force (UVF). According to the U.S. State Department, the RHD is made up "largely of Protestant hardliners from loyalist groups participating in a ceasefire" (U.S. Department of State 2001). If it is, in fact, a separate organization, it is believed to have no more than 20 active members, some of whom have extensive terrorist experience, and perhaps a few dozen other supporters. The group's favored weapons are pipe bombs, grenades, and guns.

According to the U.S. State Department, the RHD typically attacks civilian targets, hoping to provoke a response from the IRA or other elements of the Catholic community, and thereby to interrupt or scuttle progress toward peace in Northern Ireland.

Outrages committed by the group include several murders, starting with an explosion that killed a Royal Ulster Constabulary officer named Frankie O'Reilly in September 1998; the car bombing of Rosemary Nelson, a prominent human-rights lawyer, in 1999; and the shooting death of a 20-year-old postman named Danny MacColgan in north Belfast in early 2002, among others.

In September 2001, the RHD claimed a grisly first for itself when it took responsibility for the shooting death of Martin O'Hagan, the first journalist to be killed by paramilitaries of either side in the entire history of the Troubles.

In January 2002—along with three other loyalist groups (the Loyalist Volunteer Force, the Orange Volunteers, and the Ulster Defense Association), as well as the republican Continuity IRA—the Red Hand Defenders was designated an illegal organization by the United States State Department.

REVOLUTIONARY ARMED FORCES OF COLOMBIA—PEOPLE'S ARMY (*FUERZAS ARMADAS REVOLUCIONARIAS DE COLOMBIA*), OR FARC—EP

Leftist paramilitaries who seek to overthrow the government of Colombia.

FARC is the largest and most professional armed insurgent group in Colombia. Both a political and guerilla movement, it is ideologically leftist and class-oriented.

FARC traces its history to a vicious civil war between the Liberal and Conservative parties of Colombia that raged for nearly 10 years in the middle of the twentieth century. At that time, a group of surviving peasants, disillusioned and disgusted with both sides, withdrew to the remote region of Marquetalia in the Tolima Department. There, they came to be seen as a threat to the government that finally emerged out of the bloodbath of the civil war.

Then, according to the FARC Web site:

On May 27, 1964, the Armed Forces of Colombia, directly advised and oriented by the United States of America, initiated the largest military operation of encirclement and extermination known up to that time. The objective: to eradicate the subversive centre that was putting their "national security" and "Western democracy" in danger. . . . The Revolutionary Armed Forces of Colombia—People's Army, FARC—EP, arose in the course of the confrontation, with a revolutionary programme calling together all the citizens who dream of a Colombia for Colombians, with equality of opportunities and equitable distribution of wealth, and where among us all we can build peace with social equality and sovereignty. (Secretariat 2000)

For almost three decades, FARC has waged a violent war against the government of Colombia. It controls a large area of land in Colombia, from which it moves out to launch periodic attaches on the government and on other elements of what it calls the "ruling class." FARC engages in a wide range of violent activities. These range from armed clashes with Colombian military and police forces (as well as with right-wing paramilitaries like the United Self-Defense Forces of Colombia, or AUC), to targeted assassinations of the group's opponents, to such relatively indiscriminate terrorist activities as mortar attacks on inhabited areas and car bombings.

Like several other paramilitary groups in Latin America, of both the left and the right, FARC funds many of its activities through criminal enterprises, including bank robberies and narcotics trafficking. FARC profits from its military prowess by hiring out its services to protect the operations of Colombia's notorious drug cartels.

The group has made something of a specialty of kidnapping for ransom. Roughly 3,000 kidnappings a year take place in Colombia, and FARC is said to be responsible for more than half of them. The victims of these abductions include not only Colombians but many foreigners as well. Americans are favored, not least because the group is rabidly anti-American, blaming that country for helping to keep various repressive regimes in power in Colombia. And, in fact, the U.S. has provided successive Colombian governments with billions of dollars of assistance, including military training and resources, to help in their attempts to wipe out both FARC and a rival left-wing guerilla group known as the National Liberation Army (ELN).

FARC confines most of its violence to Colombia, although it has been known to conduct operations in a handful of other Latin American countries as well. It has roughly 6,000 to 7,000 members under arms, and many more supporters in Colombia.

The group has occasionally participated in normal political activities and has sometimes engaged in negotiations with the Colombian government. In 2002, Avaro Uribe was elected president of Colombia after a campaign in which he promised to subdue FARC and other leftist movements. FARC and other insurgents responded with a series of attacks on the day of Uribe's inauguration that killed 19 people, including 3 children, and injured some 70 others.

SHINING PATH, OR *SENDERO LUMINOSO* (SL)

Peruvian Maoists. Also known as the Communist Party of Peru for the Shining Path of Jose Mariategui.

The Shining Path was founded in the late-1960s by Professor Abimael Guzmán Reynoso after a trip to China, where he became a confirmed Maoist. Guzmán, who was known to his devoted, if not fanatic, followers as Comrade Gonzalo, believes that Peru's institutions must be thoroughly destroyed before a new Communist society can be built on their ruins. Beyond that, Shining Path seeks to reunite and rebuild the historic Inca Empire, which included modern-day Ecuador, Colombia, and Bolivia, as well as Peru.

The Shining Path took up arms against the Peruvian government, and Peruvian society, in 1980, and quickly earned a deserved reputation as one of the most ruthless terrorist groups in the world. Its uses all the tactics commonly used by other terrorist groups—including bombings, kidnappings, and robberies—but, reveling in its peasant identity, it is also known for hacking victims to death with machetes. Equally proud of its revolutionary and ideological purity, Shining Path spurns alliances with other terrorists, and has no ties with any government.

Together with its fellow leftists of the Tupac Amaru, the Shining Path spread traumatizing fear throughout Peru in 1980s. It has been estimated that at least 30,000 people died as a result of terrorist violence and the government's efforts to quell it in that bloody decade. Elected president of Peru in 1990, Alberto Fujimori vowed to end the two groups' reign of terror. In April, 1991, he seized emergency powers and dissolved the country's parliament and its courts, both of which he considered barriers to his effort to defeat the terrorists. The Fujimori government's counterterrorist campaign was as ruthless in its own way as the terrorists themselves. More than 2,500 alleged Shining Path members were tried and convicted under the system of "faceless judges" instituted by Fujimori. Among them was Comrade Gonzalo, who was taken into custody on September 12, 1992, and sentenced to life in prison.

Fujimori's draconian campaign effectively reduced the Shining Path from a powerful organization fielding thousands of armed guerillas to a small group of no more than a few hundred fighters at the most.

On March 7, 2003, a Peruvian court nullified the convictions of Shining Path members won during the Fujimori crackdown, and ordered all those convicted, including Guzmán, to be retried. His trial has been tentatively scheduled for 2004.

ULSTER DEFENSE ASSOCIATION (UDA)

Loyalist paramilitaries in Northern Ireland. Also known as the Ulster Freedom Fighters (UFF).

For more than three decades, the Ulster Defense Association has sought to assert and assure Protestant domination in Ulster. According to the Loyalist & Orange Information Service, the Ulster Freedom Fighters (UFF) is not a truly separate organization, but rather a "cover name" the UDA uses "to claim responsibility for the killing of Catholics" (Ulster Defence n.d.). In its heyday in the early 1970s, the UDA claimed 40,000 to 50,000 members. Current membership is probably less than 10,000, of whom a few hundred may be available for UFF activities.

Formed in 1971 by the melding of several previously autonomous Protestant vigilante groups, the UDA has been the largest paramilitary organization in Northern Ireland ever since. The group's founders believed that the UDA was needed to protect Protestants from the deprivations of the IRA. True to its working-class roots, the UDA set out to establish its control of the streets in Protestant neighborhoods of Northern Ireland. In response to the establishment of "no-go" areas by the IRA, the UDA set up "no-go" areas of its own.

The UDA opposed the British imposition of direct (or home) rule of Northern Ireland in 1972 as an attempt to undermine Protestant authority in Ulster. When the British tried to interfere with the UDA's plan to put up what amounted to roadblocks between two Protestant and Catholic neighborhoods of Belfast, the UDA brought 8,000 masked members onto the street to confront 250 British troops. The peaceful resolution of that confrontation demonstrated the UDA's power in Belfast, and seemed to confirm the Republicans' suspicion that Britain favored the Protestant side in the Troubles. And, in fact, after that initial confrontation the UDA tended to look upon Britain more as an ally than an opponent.

Over the past 30 years, the UDA and UFF have been accused of the responsibility for more than 400 deaths of Catholics and others in Northern Ireland.

In 2003, a British investigation, authorized by the Good Friday Peace Accords and headed by London Metropolitan Police Commissioner Sir John Stevens, concluded that British security forces in Ulster had colluded in some of the most extreme violence committed by the UDA/UFF (MacDonald 2003). One of the Stevens Investigation's most alarming revelations was that two members of the assassination squad that gunned down a Catholic Belfast solicitor named Pat Finucane while he was sharing Sunday dinner with his wife and children on February 12, 1989, were police double agents.

Much like the IRA, the UDA has historically funded its paramilitary activities by a combination of donations from sympathizers, profits from businesses—both legal and illegal (including drug trafficking), armed robberies, smuggling, extortion, and other criminal enterprises. The same month that Pat Finucane was murdered, the UDA commander for South Belfast was formally charged with forcing Belfast building companies to pay "protection" in return for the UDA's agreement not to disrupt their construction sites (Collins: May 18–19, 1989).

Although the UDA is not supported by any foreign governments, it has had arms dealings with at least one such government. In the mid-1980s, members of the UDA were arrested in Paris with a representative of the South African government. The men were there to negotiate an exchange of South African weapons for secrets about missiles partially manufactured by the Short Brothers electronics firm in Northern Ireland (Collins: May 4, 1989).

In the 1990s, the UDA cooperated closely with another violent Protestant group, the Ulster Volunteer Force, under the so-called Combined Loyalist Military Command, but this alliance fell apart in a violent conflict between the two in 2001.

Although the British government had previously outlawed the UFF, the UDA wasn't proscribed until August 10, 1992. The U.S. State Department designated both groups (as well as the Orange Volunteers and the Red Hand Defenders) as terrorist organizations in December 2001.

The UDA has taken an off-again, on-again stance toward the Good Friday Peace Agreements of 1998, and has alternately participated in and rejected ceasefires since they were signed. Most recently (as of the time this book was being written), the UDA declared a unilateral 12-month ceasefire in February 2003. At that time, it also apologized for its previous involvement in drug trafficking and racketeering.

UNITED SELF-DEFENSE FORCES OF COLOMBIA, OR *AUTODEFENSAS UNIDAS DO COLOMBIA*

Right-wing coalition of paramilitaries. Also known as the AUC.

The AUC was founded in 1997 by a merger of several of the vigilante groups, or private armies, that had long protected wealthy landowners and drug lords of Colombia from leftist groups like Revolutionary Armed Forces of Colombia (FARC) and National Liberation Army (ELN). Although these so-called self-defense groups had been outlawed in 1989, they had been neither militarily defeated nor disbanded; in fact, they continued to get unofficial help from the Colombian military, and the AUC may still be getting such help.

The Peasant Self-Defense Group of Córdoba and Urabá, known as the ACCU, forms the core of the AUC; among the other groups involved are the Cundinamarca Self-Defense Group, the Eastern Plains Self-Defense Group, the Cesar Self-Defense Group, the Middle Magdalena Self-Defense Group, the Santander and Southern Cesar Self-Defense Group, and the Casanara Self-Defense Group. The AUC finances its activities from the "tax" money it extorts from the drug lords and other wealthy Colombians it "protects"—"taxes" that are claimed to be as high as 60 percent of the profits taken in by the drug cartels (International Policy Institute for Counter-Terrorism 2003). In addition, the AUC itself is rumored to be engaged in processing cocaine.

Although FARC and ELN draw most of the counterterrorist fire in Colombia, the AUC may present a greater threat to the safety of the Colombian people. According to the testimony of the Executive Director of the America's Division of Human Rights Watch before a United States Senate subcommittee: "Paramilitaries associated with the AUC commit most human rights violations in Colombia today. These acts of terror include massacres, targeted killing and forced displacement. Like the FARC, the AUC kidnaps, threatens, and kills political leaders. It also exercises exclusive control over vast areas of Colombia, particularly in the north, where it polices civilians and taxes economic activity. It has shown no interest in relaxing its control as guerilla activity wanes. Also like the FARC, the AUC traffics in drugs. With its profits, it funds acts of terror" (U.S. Senate 2002).

The AUC claims to have 11,000 armed fighters. Although the true number may be closer to half of that, the group is known to be growing, both because of its close connection to the lucrative drug trade, and because it pays its guerillas a regular salary. The AUC is showing an increasing interest in accumulating political power, and has assassinated several of its political opponents, as well as many honest law enforcement officials, prosecutors, and judges. Other targets of the group include labor organizers and human-rights activists. One of the AUC's precursors was involved in the 1985 assault on the Supreme Court of Colombia building in which some 100 people were killed, including the chief justice.

The AUC is notorious for massacring residents of rural villages in coca-growing areas in order to terrorize any remaining villagers into fleeing and leaving the AUC in total control. The group was accused of killing at least 1,000 civilians in 2001 alone—more than five times the total attributed to the largest leftist paramilitary group in Colombia (ICT 2003). Recently, however, a spokesman announced that, in the hope of improving the AUC's public image, the group would limit its murders to three per attack in the future (Council, FARC 2003).

Although the AUC and its precursors had been widely known to be committing atrocities for decades, it was only on September 10, 2001, that AUC was designated a Foreign Terrorist Organization by the United States. In September 2002, the United States indicted three of the group's leaders (in absentia) for smuggling 17 tons of cocaine into the United States.

REFERENCES

Alexander, Yonah. 1994. *Middle East Terrorism: Selected Group Profiles*. Washington, D.C.: The Jewish Institute for National Security Affairs.

Barich, Bill. 1988. "Ulster Spring." *The New Yorker*, 21 November.

BBC News. 2001. "U.K. condemned over IRA deaths" 4 May. http://news.bbc.co.uk/1/hi/northern_Ireland/1311724.stm (accessed 29 March 2004).

"Black September and the Black September Terror Movement." n.d. *Cedarland*. http://www.geocitites.com/CapitolHill/Parliament/2587/black.html (accessed 29 March 2004).

Carassava, Anthee. 2002. "Greeks Claim Victory in Campaign against a Band of Political Assassination." *New York Times*, 18 July.

CNN Interactive. 1998. "26 Sentenced to Death in Rajiv Gandhi Assassination." *CNN Interactive, World New Story Page*, 28 January.http://www.CNN.com/WORLD/9801/28/india.gandhi/index.html (accessed 29 March 2004).

Collins, Larry, and Dominique LaPierre. 1972. *O Jerusalem!* New York: Simon and Schuster.

Collins, Tom. 1989a. Special Report. NINS (Northern Ireland News Service), 4 May.

———. 1989b. Special Report. NINS (Northern Ireland News Service), 18–19 May.

Council on Foreign Relations, in cooperation with the Markle Foundation. 2003a. *Terrorism Q&A: FARC, ELN, AUC*. Terrorismanswers.com. http://cfrterrorism.org/groups/fare.html (accessed 29 March 2004).

———. 2003b. *Terrorism Q&A: Hezbollah*. Terrorismanswers.com. http://cfr terrorism. org/groups/hezbollah (accessed 29 March 2004).

———. 2003c. *Terrorism Q&A: Jamaat al-Islamiyya, Egyptian Islamic Jihad*. Terrorism answers.com. http://cfrterrorism.org/groups/jamaat.html (accessed 29 March 2004).

Crossette, Barbara. 2002. "Sri Lankan Says U.S. Drive on Terror Helps Peace Effort." *New York Times*, 22 July.

Davenport, Coral M. 2002. "How 'November 17' Was Foiled," *Christian Science Monitor,* 22 July.

DePalma, Armando et. al. 1980. "Terror in Italy: An Exchange," *The New York Review of Books,* 17 April.

Federation of American Scientists (FAS). 1998. "Abu Sayaaf Group (ASG)," *1998 Global Terrorism: Background Information on Terrorist Groups.* http://www.fas.org/irp/threat/terror_98/appb.htm (accessed 29 March 2004).

Friedman, Thomas L. 2002. "Lessons from Sri Lanka." *New York Times,* 7 August.

Guatemala News Watch. 1997. August. http://www.quetzalnet.com/newswatch/GNW1997/edition12-8.html (accessed 29 March 2004).

Hardy, Robert. 2002. Nidal obituary. BBC World Service (radio). 19 August.

Hate Groups in America, A Record of Bigotry and Violence. 1988. New York: Anti-Defamation League of B'nai B'rith.

Holly Cartner to Prime Minister Massimo D'Alema of Italy. 21 November 1998. Letter asking him to turn down the asylum request of Abdullah Ocalan. Human Rights Watch. http://www.hrw.org/press98/nov/italy-ltr.htm (accessed 29 March 2004).

"In the Spotlight: PKK . . . " 2002. (21 May). Center of Defense Information Terrorism Project. Washington, D.C.: Center of Defense Information Terrorism Project. Jalal, Qasim. 2002. "Wahabi Terrorist Riaz Basra Killed in Shootout." ShiaNews.com, 15 May. http://www.shianews.com/urils/search.php (accessed 29 March 2004).

"Kurdistan Workers Party (PKK)." n.d. The International Policy Institute for Counter-Terrorism. http://www.ict.org.il/inter_ter/orgdot.cfm?orgid/=20 (accessed 29 March 2004).

Lacey, Marc. 2002. "Uganda's Terror Crackdown Multiplies the Suffering." *New York Times,* 4 August.

"Lashkar Chief Riaz Basra 'arrested.'" 2002. *Dawn: the Internet Edition,* 21 January. http://www.dawn.com/2002/01/22/nat10.htm (accessed 25 March 2004).

Lee, Martin A. 1998. "Turkish Dirty War Revealed, but Papal Shooting Still Unsolved." *Los Angeles Times,* 12 April.

MacDonald, Henry. 2002. "Stevens Fingers Special Branch." *Sunday Observer,* 20 October.

MacFarquhar, Neil. 2001. "Atef Had Been Leader in Egyptian Islamic Jihad." *Houston Chronicle,* 16 November.

Newhouse, John. 1985. "A Freemasonry of Terrorism." *The New Yorker,* 8 July.

New York Times. 2003. "E.T.A. Writers Sign Statement Denouncing Basque Nationalist Violence," 8 May.

O'Callaghan, Sean. 1998. *The Informer: The Real-Life Story of One Man's Fight Against Terrorism.* London: BCA.

Paul, James, and Martin Spirit. "The Struggle for Independence: The Mau Mau Movement." http://www.kenyaweb.com/history/struggle/index.html (accessed 29 March 2004).

Powell, Colin L. 2003. (30 January). (Press Release). U.S. Department of State. Washington, D.C.: U.S. Department of State.

Prendergast, Mark J. 2002. "Terror Leader Is Dead, Palestinian Reports Say." *New York Times,* 19 August.

"Red Brigades." 2002. The International Policy Institute for Counter-Terrorism (ICT). http://www.ict.org.il/inter_ter/orgdot.cfm?orgid/=36 (accessed 29 March 2004).

"Scars of Death: Children Abducted by the Lord's Resistance Army in Uganda, The." 1997. (A Human Rights Watch Report). New York: Human Rights Watch/Africa Human Rights Watch Children's Rights Project.

Secretariat of the Central General Staff. 2000. *36 Years for Peace and National Sovereignty*. May. Posted on the Revolutionary Army of Colombia Web site. http://www.farcep.org/pagina_ingles/ (accessed 2 April 2004).

Southern Exposure. 1980. ("Mark of the Beast," special edition). 3 (summer).

Stepniak, Sergei. 1973. *Underground Russia: Revolutionary Profiles and Sketches from Life*. Westport, Conn.: Hyperion Press.

"Ulster Defence Association." n.d. Loyalists & Orange Information Services. http://www.scottishloyalists.com/paramilitaries/uda.htm (accessed 29 March 2004).

"United Self-Defense Forces of Colombia." 2003. International Policy Institute for Counter-Terrorism (ICT), http://www.ict.org.il/inter_ter/orgdet.cfm?orgid/=91 (accessed 29 March 2004).

U.S. Congress. 1872. *Report of the Joint Select Committee to Inquire into the Condition of Affairs in the Late Insurrectionary States*. 42d Cong., 2d Sess., Doc. 426, XIII, 32–34.

U.S. Department of State. 1998. *Patterns of Global Terrorism: 1997*. http://www.state.gov/www/global/terrorism/1997Report/1997index.html (accessed 25 March 2004).

———. 1999. *Patterns of Global Terrorism: 1998*. http://www. state.gov/www/global/terrorism/1998Report/1998index.html (accessed 31 March 2004).

———. 2000. *Patterns of Global Terrorism, 1999*. http://www. state.gov/s/ct/rls/pgtrpt/99/pdf/ (accessed 31 March 2004).

———. 2002. *Patterns of Global Terrorism, 2001*. http://www. state.gov/s/ct/rls/pgtrpt/2001/pdf/ (accessed 31 March 2004).

———. 2003. *Patterns of Global Terrorism, 2002*. http://www. state.gov/s/ct/rls/pgtrpt/2002/html (accessed 31 March 2004).

U.S. Senate. 2002. Foreign Relations Committee's Subcommittee on Western Hemisphere, Peace Corps, and Narcotics Affairs. Testimony by José Miguel Vivanco. 24 April 2002. The Center for International Policy's Colombia Program. http://ciponline.org/colombia/02042406.htm (accessed 31 March 2004).

"What is the GUD?" 2002. *Le Figaro*, 14 July.

Four Aspects of Terror

In this chapter, we look at four examples of terrorism in some detail. The incidents described range from the most destructive terrorist operation of modern times to a nonviolent show of strength that many people would not recognize as terrorism at all. Each, however, helps to illustrate important aspects of the terrorist phenomenon.

THE POWER OF A LYNCH MOB—CHATTANOOGA, TENNESSEE, 1906

The overwhelming power of a lynch mob was vividly demonstrated by the death of a black man named Ed Johnson, in Chattanooga, Tennessee, in 1906. In this case, even the U.S. Supreme Court was helpless to stand in its way.

Johnson was accused of raping a white woman on a dark street at night. He protested his innocence and claimed that he had been at a local bar at the time of the rape. Several witnesses testified to that effect. But they were all black. The only real evidence against him was the equivocal testimony of the alleged victim, a 21-year-old blonde woman named Nevada Taylor. Under cross-examination, she said that she "wouldn't swear" that Johnson was the man who attacked her, but that she "believed" that he was (Linder 2000).

Feelings ran high in Chattanooga during the short trial. The black community sympathized with Johnson, while much of the white community called for his blood. There were two attempts to lynch the defendant even before the all-white jury found him guilty and he was sentenced to death—the standard penalty for a black man who raped a white woman in the South in those days.

Today, the appeal of a death sentence is automatic. Not so in 1906. Even at that time, however, it was customary to appeal that most drastic of sentences. This was particularly true when the prosecution's case had been as weak as the one against Johnson, and the trial had been conducted in such a highly charged atmosphere. The potential for an irrevocable miscarriage of justice was apparent. Amazingly, however, Johnson's white lawyers declined to appeal either the conviction or the death sentence. The lead lawyer in the case explained their decision in a remarkable letter to the *Chattanooga Times*:

> To the People of Chattanooga:
> I cannot leave my fellow-citizens ignorant of what occurred on yesterday. If any lawyer for a prisoner and any twelve jurors trying a prisoner should have the sympathy of the people, that sympathy should be freely given to the jurors and the defendant's attorneys' in this case. What we have suffered: the mental strain we have been under; the weight of the burden of the responsibility upon us cannot be told. The horror and awfulness of the last few days are things I hope never again to be called on to endure.
> When the jury brought in a verdict of guilty, we, as the attorneys had to settle the question whether the case would be appealed to the Supreme Court. I felt that we should not bear that responsibility alone, and I went to Judge McReynolds [who had presided at the trial] and asked him to appoint three other lawyers to meet with Judge Shepherd, Mr. Cameron and myself, and counsel and advise with us and help to share with us the responsibility. ("W.G.M. Thomas" 1906)

Altogether more than seven men, all attorneys and white, had met to consider the question.

> The case was reviewed; and our duty and the rights of the defendant were discussed. The most careful reflection was given to the horrible crime charged against the defendant, and the fact that a jury had, upon their oath, fixed that crime on the accused man. We discussed the recent mob uprising and the state of unrest in the community. It was the judgment of all present that the life of the defendant, even if the wrong man, could not be saved [and] that an appeal would so inflame the public that the jail would be attacked and perhaps other prisoners executed by violence. In the opinion of all of us a case was presented where the defendant, not that he had been convicted by a jury, must die by the judgment of the law, or else, if his case were appealed, he would die by the act of an uprising of the people. ("W.G.M. Thomas" 1906)

It was a remarkable defense of a cowardly action, but it was much more than that. It was a declaration by an attorney—an officer of the court—that he and several attorneys had concluded that the legal system was helpless before the power of the lynch mentality of the white community of Chattanooga, Tennessee. Even worse, it was a public acceptance of that helplessness, and a total concession to that power.

Ultimately, a few courageous black lawyers in Chattanooga refused to be cowed by the threat of mob violence and appealed the case ("S. L. Hutchins" 1906). A Tennessee federal judge granted a stay of Johnson's execution. When the local authorities in Chattanooga seemed determined to defy the federal order and proceed with the execution despite it, the governor of Tennessee agreed to halt the execution for 10 days, giving Johnson's attorneys a chance to take the case to the U.S. Supreme Court.

The U.S. Supreme Court agreed to hear the appeal, and, as customary in such circumstances, ordered all proceedings against the convicted man halted until it could make a ruling in the case.

On the very night the Supreme Court issued its order, a white mob in Chattanooga dragged Ed Johnson out of jail. He was severely beaten and taken to a bridge. A large crowd of white people gathered in a state of morbid excitement to watch what was happening. When the mob called on Johnson to confess, he insisted that he was innocent. He said that he knew he was going to die, but that he was not afraid. His last reported words were, "God bless you all. I am innocent" ("God Bless" 1906).

As the leaders of the group attempted to hang Johnson from a span of the bridge, several other members of the mob, all of whom seemed to have guns, decided that things were proceeding too slowly and began firing at the doomed man. One of the bullets severed the rope, and he collapsed onto the bridge. The gunmen gathered around and riddled the body with bullets. A doctor who examined the body later declared that it had been shot 50 times.

The U.S. Supreme Court was outraged that the local authorities had allowed the mob to kill Johnson in defiance of the Court's order. In an unprecedented action, the court took on itself the task of bringing the sheriff to trial on charges of contempt for not protecting his prisoner. After a trial conducted by the Supreme Court itself, Sheriff Joseph Shipp and two deputies were found guilty and sentenced to 60 days in jail (U.S. v. Shipp 1909). It was the first time that any law enforcement official had ever been held accountable for the lynching of anyone, prisoner or otherwise, in his jurisdiction, and it remains the only time in history that the U.S. Supreme Court actually conducted a trial (Gado 2000).

Even the anger of the Supreme Court was not enough to stop the practice of lynching, which continued to be widely practiced in the United States for decades afterwards. If anything, the Shipp case revealed the impotence of any authority before the raw power of the mob.

Statistically, certainly, the punishment of Sheriff Shipp and his deputies had no noticeable effect at all. According to figures compiled by the Tuskegee Institute Archives, Ed Johnson was one of 62 black men who were reported lynched in 1906, which was a typical year for lynchings in early-twentieth-century America. The number of lynchings dropped to 57 the following year, and then spiked up to 89 in 1908. The trial of Sheriff Shipp took place in 1909, a year in which there were 69 lynchings of blacks, followed by 67 in 1910, 60 in 1911, and 62 in 1912.

It wasn't until the 1920s that the number of lynchings began to decline significantly. By the 1930s, the annual average had fallen into the teens. By the 1940s, it was in the single digits, and, by the 1950s, lynchings had become rare (Tuskegee).

The terrorizing effect of lynching remained strong even after the numbers of actual lynchings began to decline. It was in 1939 that the great, black blues-singer Billie Holliday began singing the anti-lynching song *Strange Fruit*. Written by a white, Jewish New York schoolteacher named Abel Meeropol, the haunting anthem became famous as an indictment of the loathsome practice:

> Southern trees bear a strange fruit,
> Blood on the leaves,
> Blood at the root,
> Black body swinging in the Southern breeze,
> Strange fruit hanging from the poplar trees.

PAINTING ON THE MOUNTAINTOP—THE MUNICH OLYMPICS, 1972

The Summer Games of the Twentieth Olympiad were held at Munich, West Germany, in 1972. It was the first time the Olympics were held on German soil since 1936, when the Thirteenth Olympiad in Berlin had provided an international showcase for the Nazi regime of Adolph Hitler. Despite the standout performance of the black American track star Jesse Owens, those games had given Hitler an international stage on which to exhibit Nazi power, German modernity, and Aryan superiority. Since the end of World War II, however, Germany had looked back on those Games as a kind of grand embarrassment, while the rest of the world regarded them with grim distaste.

Now Germany had the Olympic stage again, and, with it, a chance to present a bright, new image to a worldwide television audience. As many as one billion people were expected to tune in to the Munich Games (Parrish 2002), and Germany planned to use the opportunity to show how far it had come since the Nazi era. Dubbing the Munich Olympics "The Games of Peace and Joy," the nation that had carried out the Holocaust was determined to serve as a gracious and generous host to athletes of all races and cultures.

For a while, it succeeded brilliantly. By the end of the first 10 days of competition, the Twentieth Olympiad was well on its way to becoming one of the greatest Olympics of modern times. The opening ceremonies had been spectacular, the events competitive and thrilling, and several of the athletes were not just setting records but capturing the hearts of tens of millions of viewers around the world. An American Jew named Mark Spitz electrified the world by setting seven new world records in seven different swimming events; the seven gold medals he won were themselves a new record for a single Olympics. Spitz was far from the only new athletic star. A 4 foot, 11 inch Belarusian girl named Olga Korbut charmed the world with her perky gymnastic performances and her dazzling smile. In perhaps the most remarkable single performance of the Games, the Finnish runner Lasse Viren had somehow won the 10,000-meter run despite falling down painfully in the middle of the event.

Things were going incredibly well when, at about 4 A.M. on the 11th day, the Games of Peace and Joy were forever transformed into the Games of Death and Terror. That was when a small group of determined terrorists seized the stage away from both the new Germany and the world's athletes, and commandeered it for their own purposes.

The event that would shock and appall the world began like a dormitory prank. Eight Palestinian men walked up to the fence surrounding the Olympic Village, the complex of buildings that had been specially constructed to house the roughly 10,000 athletes and coaches gathered for the Games. The men were wearing tracksuits to blend in with the athletic surroundings, and they carried athletic bags, partly as a similar form of camouflage and partly as a convenient way to transport the automatic rifles and grenades concealed within them.

At the fence, they met a group of Americans who had been out cruising Munich's historic beer halls. The Americans mistook the terrorists for athletic-team members like themselves, sneaking back into the Village after violating curfew. Members of the two groups helped each other scramble up and over the tall fence. Once on the other side, they chatted companionably for awhile, then went their separate ways: the Americans to their rooms to catch whatever sleep they could in the few hours that remained before the start of the day's events, and the terrorists to 31 Connollystrasse, where the Israeli Olympic team was housed (Reeve 2000, 1–2).

Most of the Israelis had been out earlier in the evening themselves, attending a performance of the popular American musical *Fiddler on the Roof*. "*Fiddler*" was a comedy-drama about Jewish peasants living in a rural Russian village early in the twentieth century. Much of the sentiment of the piece came from the fact that, unbeknownst to the characters, their simple way of life was doomed. Their village was about to be destroyed in a pogrom. As the Israelis enjoyed the show that night, they were unaware of a terrible irony. They were as blithely ignorant of their own impending doom as the fictional villagers were of theirs.

It took the intruders almost half an hour to change out of their tracksuits and reconnoiter in the building where the Israelis lay sleeping. They climbed some stairs and knocked on a door to Apartment 1, the temporary home of seven Israeli team members: four coaches, a trainer, a judge, and a wrestling referee.

The knocking woke the referee, who opened the door. When he saw the armed men in the hall, he screamed out a warning and tried to shut the door against them. It was to no use. The men burst into the room. Groggy from sleep, weaponless, and facing Kalishnokovs, most of the Israelis submitted at once. But not all. A wrestling coach named Moshe Weinberg resisted, bravely but foolishly attacking the leader of the terrorists with the only weapon he had, which was a grapefruit knife. Weinberg even managed to grab hold of the terrorist's gun before another terrorist shot him in the face (Reeve 2000, 5).

The only person to escape from Apartment 1 that morning was a weightlifting trainer named Tuvia Sokolovsky, who managed to break through a window and run away into the darkness with bullets nipping all around him (Reeve 2000, 8).

Several of the terrorists took the horribly injured Weinberg and proceeded to Apartment 3, where six Israeli athletes were still sleeping. It has been speculated that Weinberg may have led the terrorists to that apartment believing that the wrestlers and weightlifters who were housed there would have the best chance of overcoming the armed men. This speculation is borne out by the fact that the small party bypassed Apartment 2, where the more lightly built Israeli fencers were sleeping, unaware of what was happening in the hall outside their rooms.

The terrorists seized the residents of Apartment 3 and began herding them back to where their companions were waiting with the other hostages. On the way, one of the wrestlers, Gad Tsbari, ducked down a narrow staircase that led into the building's parking lot. One of the terrorists dashed after him, firing several bursts from his weapon at the fleeing Israeli. Hoping to make use of the distraction, the wounded Weinberg punched a nearby terrorist in the face, breaking his jaw, and made a grab for his gun. Another terrorist opened fire, killing Weinberg (Reeve 2000, 7–8).

A second Israeli was killed soon after the second group of hostages and their captors arrived at Apartment 1. Accounts of the death of Yossef Romano differ. One version has Romano, a large man who was on crutches as a result of an injury suffered in competition, grabbing hold of a terrorist's Kalishnokov and wrestling him for it; another has Romano grabbing a kitchen knife and stabbing one of the captors, wounding him in the forehead (Calahan 1995). Whatever Romano actually did, the terrorists responded by killing him on the spot.

The escaping Israelis raised the alarm. When the police arrived outside 31 Connollystrasse, one of the terrorists threw two sheets of paper down from a window. The papers identified the terrorists as members of the Black September group and contained their demands. Aside from specifying arrangements for their passage out of West Germany, the Palestinians demanded the release of more than 234 prisoners. The pages thrown from the window contained the names of all 234, 232 of whom were Arabs being held by Israel. Two, however, were Germans being held in West Germany. They were Ulrike Meinhof and Andreas Baader, the notorious guiding spirits behind the Marxist terrorist organization known as the Baader-Meinhof Gang.

The written demands were only the starting point for what became a series of negotiations, most of which were conducted on the closed-off street in front of 31 Connollystrasse. On the West German side, they were conducted by a variety of police, civic, and governmental officials. On the terrorist side most of the negotiating was done by the most visible of the terrorists, who was, in fact, Luttif Afif, but who went by the nom de guerre "Issa." This man, the apparent commander of the terrorists, made a striking figure for the long-distance TV cameras observing much of what followed. "Issa" wore a white hat and a light-colored safari jacket of the kind popular at that time, along with matching flared slacks. His clothing contrasted with his face, which was obscured by some kind of black paint or boot polish. When other terrorists would be glimpsed from time to time—peering out of widows, standing in doorways, or emerging briefly onto balconies— they were usually wearing balaclavas down over their faces.

The Israeli government gave the Germans permission to make any arrangements they saw fit with the terrorists, but the Germans had to understand that under no circumstances would Israel release any prisoners. Israel's prime minister Golda Meir was firm about that. "If we should give in," she said, "then no Israeli anywhere in the world can feel that his life is safe" (Reeve 2000, 61).

The first negotiating session took place between "Issa" and a veteran German female police officer around 8:15 A.M. on September 5. By that time, the first Olympic event of the day had already begun. Soon after that preliminary discussion, a larger and higher level delegation met with the terrorist leader. They told him that, even if the German and Israeli governments would decide to free the prisoners, it would be impossible to do so by the fast-approaching deadline set by the Palestinians. "Issa" agreed to extend the deadline.

The negotiations were conducted in an atmosphere of high tension. In a dramatic demonstration of their willingness to carry through with their threats, the terrorists dragged the body of Moshe Weinberg out of the door at 31 Connollystrasse and dumped it onto the street. To protect himself while he was exposed on the street, "Issa" pulled the pin from a hand grenade and gave it to one of his confederates to hold. Other terrorists kept guns trained on the Germans, and naturally assumed that the German snipers were also targeting them. Everyone was aware that it was not just the lives of the hostages that were in danger, but the lives of everyone involved in the negotiations.

Beyond that, the West German and Israeli governments, the Olympic Committee, and numerous other institutions were all vitally concerned with the outcome.

And yet, for Black September the negotiations were almost a sideshow.

The terrorists had had two main objectives when they climbed over the fence and entered the Olympic Village. Only the less important of the two (the demand for the freedom of the 234 Arab and German prisoners) was under negotiation. The second, and the one Black September considered by far the most important, had already been accomplished.

What the terrorists wanted most was to thrust the Palestinian cause onto the center of world stage provided by the Olympics. For a generation, Palestinians had languished in squalid refugee camps, ignored by a world that was hardly even aware that they were there. The terrorists had no illusions that seizing hostages and disrupting the Olympic Games would win them friends around the world, but they hoped that it would get the world's attention. Once the world was paying attention to the Palestinians, it would be forced to recognize the terrible conditions in the refugee camps, and to acknowledge the terrible wrongs the Palestinians felt were being done to them.

And now, the world was watching. There were no accurate worldwide ratings for the televised events at Munich, so the size of the audience can only be estimated. What is certain, however, is that it is among the largest international audiences ever. Somewhere between 800 million and one billion people had been expected to watch at least some of the Olympics. It is almost certain that the hostage crisis swelled that audience by hundreds of millions of new viewers attracted by the drama of the unfolding events, or by the potential for further violence.

The negotiations between "Issa" and the German authorities went on throughout the day and into the evening. The terrorists extended their deadline over and over again. They were clearly not eager to commence killing more of the hostages, but the Germans never doubted that they were prepared to do so if they thought it necessary.

At one point, the Germans moved several men with rifles into position for an assault on 31 Connollystrasse. Media reports described the men as "sharpshooters," but, in fact, they were simply amateur hunters with rifles, and the plan was eventually abandoned.

Gradually, it became clear to the terrorists that Israel was not going to release its prisoners while hostages were being held in Germany. At the same time, it became clear to the Germans that, so long as that remained true, the terrorists were not going to release the hostages either.

That evening, a deal was announced. The West Germans had promised to provide the terrorists with a Boeing 727 jetliner and crew to fly them and their captives to Egypt. There, either the hostages would be released or negotiations would be resumed in a setting more sympathetic to the Palestinian cause. Either way, the Germans and the Olympic Committee would be relieved of responsibility for whatever happened afterward. The Germans wanted the terrorists to believe that that was all they really cared about. In fact, however, the Germans had decided that they could not allow anyone to kidnap their foreign guests and remove them from the country. The plane would never leave the ground.

The Germans had hurriedly concocted a two-stage plan to rescue the hostages. According to the alleged deal, the terrorists and their captives would be taken to Furstenfeldbruck airfield in two helicopters. Not mentioned in the deal were five German snipers who would be lying in ambush when the terrorists arrived. The Boeing would be there waiting for the terrorists, supposedly all fueled up and ready to go, complete with a crew to fly the plane to Egypt. In reality, there would be no crew. Instead, there would be 17 German law enforcement volunteers, some dressed as Lufthansa personnel and others secreted inside the plane.

That was about as specific as the plan could get. There were too many uncertainties. The German police would have to look for an opportune moment. When it came, the volunteers inside the plane would seize or kill any terrorists who had gotten that far, while the snipers would take care of any remaining outside. With luck, the terrorists would be taken by surprise, and the thing could be done quickly, with no harm to the hostages.

The weaknesses of the plan were obvious. It was rife with opportunities for things to go horribly wrong, and it began to unravel before the helicopters ever got to Furstenfeldbruck. The volunteers had serious doubts about their part in the scheme. Discussing the situation among themselves inside the aircraft, they concluded that the operation was too poorly planned and that their own position was far too dangerous. They unanimously decided to abandon their mission, and left the plane before the terrorists and the hostages arrived.

Then, the helicopters landed some distance away from the spot where the snipers expected them to set down. The airfield was starkly lit, and the snipers discovered that they had poor visibility. They had poor sightlines, and found it hard to line up clear shots at the Palestinians. Nor could they get a clear view of the hostages inside the helicopters. The snipers had no walkie-talkies, no way of coordinating their actions, nor of contacting their superiors, nor of their superiors contacting them. Nor did they have any protective equipment. Worse, they were both outgunned and outnumbered by the terrorists. There turned out to be eight of them; the snipers had been told there were five.

Once the helicopters set down on the tarmac, "Issa" and a colleague walked to the 727 to check it out. Finding it empty, they were suspicious and began running back toward the helicopters. At that point, two of the snipers opened fire on them. The terrorists returned the fire, and all hell broke loose for a short time, with people shooting in all directions.

After a while, things quieted down.

What followed was a weirdly protracted shoot-out. Silence, then gun bursts, then silence again. Once the police had opened fire, apparently without much effect, they didn't know what else to do. Neither did the terrorists. According to Ulrich K. Wegener, then serving as aide-de-camp to the German Secretary of the Interior, and later to become the head of a crack German counterterrorism unit, there was a pause of roughly an hour during which no one did much of anything at all (Greenspan 2002).

Things came to a head around midnight, when four armored cars were moved into position on the airfield. This may have panicked the Palestinians, one of whom opened fire on the hostages in one of the helicopters. Wild firing broke out again, and one of the terrorists tossed a grenade into one of the helicopters, setting it on fire. Things were so chaotic—and the operation so poorly coordinated—that the guns of one of the German armored cars shot and wounded both a German helicopter pilot and one of the German snipers.

When it was over, all of the hostages were dead, along with five of the terrorists. One German policeman, who had been trying to back up the snipers with a machine gun, had been fatally shot in the first exchange of gunfire, and several other Germans were injured.

The three remaining terrorists were found cowering at various spots around the airfield. They were as terrified as the hostages must have been. At least one of the young Palestinians whimpered and pleaded for his life. One actually dropped to his knees. They were immensely relieved when they realized that they were not going to be summarily executed. "This was rather strange and unexpected for us," one of the German policemen said later. "We always had thought of terrorists as suicidal, but these three were completely happy that they hadn't been seriously injured" (Reeve 2000, 123).

It was a dramatic reminder that terrorists are human beings, with the same basic needs, emotions, and desires that other human beings have. Including their victims. Some have steeled themselves to death, and others may even seek it, but there are many who undertake their missions in the hope and expectation that they will survive. It is important to understand and acknowledge this, and not just because it is important to recognize our common humanity, as terrorists so often refuse to do. It is important for tactical reasons. A terrorist who hopes to survive can be dealt with in very different ways than one who does not.

The Black September men had come to the Olympic Village prepared for deadly violence, but not necessarily intending to commit it. As has already been mentioned, their operation had two main objectives: securing the release of 234 prisoners held in Israeli and German prisons, and drawing attention to the plight of the dispossessed Palestinians. Neither of these absolutely required the deaths of anyone involved.

The fact that the Black September terrorists were willing to kill was demonstrated early on by the murders of Moshe Weinberg and Yossef Romano. Even those murders, however, had not been inevitable. They would not have happened if the Israelis had not resisted. Even at the end, the Palestinians had been willing to move on to Egypt without further violence if they had been allowed to do so. Would they have eventually killed the hostages there if no prisoners had been released? There is no way to know.

What is sure is that the episode did not have to end as soon, and as tragically, as it did. Even at Furstenfeldbruck, the terrorists showed themselves less than eager to kill the hostages. In fact, they refrained from doing so even after the Germans ambushed them, and for more than an hour afterwards.

The rescue operation (if it deserves to be called that) was disastrously botched. Even worse, it was wrongheaded from the start. The Germans assumed that the terrorists were determined either to succeed or to die. The reaction of the survivors, however, casts serious doubt on that assumption. At the very least, it raises the possibility that some other approach—bottling up the terrorists in Connollystrasse 31, for example, or issuing a clear ultimatum that there would be an all-out attack on the building if the hostages were not released—might have brought about a less bloody end.

Even if the terrorists did have a succeed-or-die mindset, they still might have been more amenable to a peaceful solution than the Germans realized. After all, they had already succeeded in accomplishing their most important objective. As a Palestinian spokesman later rhapsodized: "A bomb in the White House, a mine in the Vatican . . . could not have echoed through the consciousness of every man in the world like the operation of Munich. . . . It was like painting the name of Palestine on the top of a mountain that can be seen from the four corners of the earth" (Hirst 2003, 439).

Years later, Abu Daoud, the man who planned the hostage-taking at Munich, told an American writer that he "would be against any operation like Munich ever again. At the time, it was the correct thing to do for our cause. . . . The operation brought the Palestinian issue into the homes of 500 million people who never previously cared about Palestinian victims at the hands of the Israelis." Today, however, the world is very much aware of the Palestinians' problems, and Abu Daoud believes that such an attack would only harm the Palestinian image (Wolff 2002, 65).

SYMBOLIC TERROR—THANKSGIVING EVE 1915 TO AUGUST 8, 1925

On the eighth of August, 1925, a huge parade of people marched down Pennsylvania Avenue in Washington, D.C. There were so many of them that the parade stretched as far down the Avenue as you could see, all the way from the U.S. Capitol at one end to the curve by the White House at the other, and even beyond.

There were no floats, or bands, or cheerleaders, only thousands upon thousands of marchers, all of whom looked very much alike. The front ranks of the parade carried American flags, and the rows and rows behind them kept to a strict marching order, so that the event had a military feel to it. The marchers might have been the members of a great army, except that the uniforms they wore were unlike those of any army in the world.

They wore immaculately white robes and conical white hoods that gave them the look of a cool white wave rolling down Pennsylvania Avenue in the steamy summer heat. Although the hoods of these strange uniforms had been adopted to conceal their identities, on this day the marchers wanted the spectators to see their faces. Some wore their hoods with open backs turned to the front, while others wore them pinned up in a way that revealed their faces to the world. On this day, of all days, they were proud of

A Ku Klux Klan group from Texas parading on a street with the dome of U.S. Capitol in the background, 1926. Courtesy of Library of Congress.

themselves and eager to show their affiliation with the organization the hoods represented.

Worn that way, however, the hoods looked a little like dunce caps. This gave the marchers a vaguely comic look, but it would have taken a brave man to laugh at them. For these were members of the dreaded Ku Klux Klan—40,000 strong—striding down the most famous street in the nation's capital as if they owned the place. As if they owned the nation itself.

This was the largest and most powerful terrorist group in American history, flaunting its power.

The dunce-cap hoods may have looked a little silly on the streets of the nation's capital in the broad light of day, but the sight of a hooded Klansman was far from comic by torchlight, in the dark of night, in the isolated rural backwoods of the rural South. In fact, the Klan was extraordinarily adept at using such images to inspire fear, and even a kind of awe.

No one knows exactly what the post–Civil War Klansmen were thinking when they first donned the robes and hoods that still identify the Klan today. The unique garb was probably meant both as a form of disguise (the hoods to conceal the Klansmen's faces, the robes to conceal their clothes) and as a kind of fancy-dress costume. The original Klan members were young men, bent on having fun. They were more interested in spreading mischief than in spreading terror (*Ku Klux Klan* 1988, 8). Many of the early Klan costumes were brightly colored, and the grotesque faces painted on some of the early hoods looked more comic than frightening.

The switch to white may have been a conscious effort at symbolism—a pure white costume to suggest a pure white cause—or, it may simply have been an effort to make the night riders more visible in the dark. One explanation that has been offered is that the outfits were an attempt to convince superstitious rural freedmen that the night riders were the ghosts of Confederate soldiers come up out of the grave to wreak revenge. But most of the terrorized black men and women were less afraid of ghosts than they were of the living, breathing white men inside those robes and hoods.

No matter. The Klan costume was a stroke of genius—instinctive genius, maybe, but genius nonetheless. The image of the white-robed and hooded Klansmen on horseback, galloping through the Southern night, caught the imaginations of both blacks and whites. Coupled with word of the Klan's violent exploits, that image spread terror throughout the black community, and a sense of misbegotten pride through much of the white. White Southern manhood was fighting back. Perhaps the South *would* rise again.

The original Klan's heyday ended with the end of Radical Reconstruction. Slavery was gone forever, but, thanks at least partly to the Klan, the white South had managed to outlast Reconstruction without allowing it to destroy the dominant relationship of whites over the freed slaves. Actual slavery was replaced by a sharecropper system that amounted to almost the same thing. Eventually, the legal institution of slavery was replaced by a legal system of segregation that used the majesty of the law to keep the descendants of slaves "in their place." From the white South's point of view, the "need" for the Klan was gone, and the organization disappeared. It would be almost 40 years before the "need" to resist Reconstruction was replaced by an ex-preacher's need to make money, and the Ku Klux Klan would be reborn.

The Klan members that marched down Pennsylvania Avenue on that hot summer day in 1925 did not belong to the Klan that fought a die-hard battle against Radical Reconstruction in the years after the Civil War. However, this Klan strove to look and act as much like the earlier Klan as possible, and most people, both in and out of the organization, probably assumed some kind of direct lineage. Like the original Klan, this Klan believed in white supremacy. All 40,000 faces in the parade were as "white," in one sense of the word, as the robes they wore were in another. Like the first Klan, this one used beatings, brandings, arsons, and lynchings to intimidate and terrorize. But this was the new, improved, go-getting, twentieth-century Ku Klux Klan. It upheld, not so much the virtues of the Old South, as the virtues of "Americanism" and "Christian Civilization." What's more, the new Klan wasn't just anti-black, it was also anti-Catholic, anti-Jew, and anti any religion that was not fundamentalist Christian. And the more fundamentalist, the better. It was also anti-immigrant and anti-organized labor, a movement it saw as alien to the American spirit of free-enterprise capitalism. A letter sent to prospective Klan members listed some of the group's "tenets" as, "The Christian Religion, White Supremacy, Protection of Our Pure American Womanhood, preventing unwarranted strikes by Foreign Labor Agitators, Upholding the Constitution of the United States of America, the Sovereignty of Our States Rights," and "the Promotion of Pure Americanism" (Gossett 1963, 340).

Along with the name Ku Klux Klan, the symbols and mystique of the earlier organization had been revived a decade before the parade by a man named William J. Simmons. Simmons was a hard-drinking ex-preacher who had taken up selling insurance after being kicked out of his pulpit for bad behavior. He envisioned his new Klan as a kind of drinking club, something "altogether . . . weird, mystical, and of a high class" (Wade 1987, 13). The Klan would turn out to be none of those things. But, for Simmons, it would be something even better. It would be immensely profitable.

Profit had been Simmons's main motive for reviving the Klan in the first place. His plan went something like this: You start an organization where men can get together and have a few drinks and a little fun; you get people to join it; then you sell them all the regalia they need to be part of the group, plus a little insurance on the side. It worked like the proverbial charm.

On Thanksgiving Day Eve in 1915, the enterprising Simmons herded his first 15 recruits into a bus and rode to the top of Stone Mountain, near Atlanta, Georgia. There, they burned a cross under the night sky to announce the rebirth of the Klan. Burning a cross on a high place was a way that ancient Scottish chieftains summoned members of their clan to battle. Although there is no evidence that the Reconstruction-era Klan ever burned a cross, the image of the burning cross had been used by Thomas Dixon in his 1905 novel, *The Clansman*. D. W. Griffith used that image even more powerfully when he put an actual fiery cross into the hands of a Klansman on horseback in, *The Birth of a Nation*, the enormously popular movie he made from Dixon's book (Adams 1993). That movie, which came out early in 1915, may have given Simmons the idea to use the burning cross as a symbol for the new Klan. (The movie's popularity certainly provided him the impetus—if not the idea—for his new organization.) The burning cross on Stone Mountain was a kind of advertisement, but the Klan soon turned the symbol into a fiery weapon with which to intimidate its victims.

Over the next several years, the burning cross became a familiar sight in many areas of the rural South. Residents of the region who had somehow angered or offended the Klan would awaken in the middle of the night to a strangely flickering light from outside their windows. Most would know immediately what it was—and what it meant. It was a message from the Ku

Robert Shelton, Imperial wizard of Ku Klux Klan, stands before a burning cross in Hemingway, South Carolina. Courtesy of Library of Congress.

Klux Klan—a warning that they had better stop whatever it was they were doing that the Klan didn't like, or else leave the county altogether. Those courageous souls who ignored the warning represented by the burning cross were apt to suffer from their bravery. If they were lucky, on the next visit the night riders might be satisfied with burning down the house. If they were unlucky, one or more of its occupants would be dragged outside and branded, or, if the Klan members were feeling especially bloodthirsty, hanged by their necks from a nearby tree.

Membership in the Klan was secret, but in many places, it was an open secret. Frequently, mayors, sheriffs, and other local officials willingly cooperated with the Klan. Often, they were members of the Klan themselves.

The local chapters, or klaverns, of the Klan operated independently. Some were relatively peaceful, remaining content with the fraternal activities that had been Simmons's first vision of his organization. Others expanded their range of targets to include, along with "uppity" blacks and their (rare) white allies, Catholics, Jews, and immigrants, anyone whom they regarded as immoral. In places, the Klan's victims included unfaithful wives, bootleggers, dope pushers, small businessmen who kept their stores open on Sundays (a day of rest for all good Christians), and even Christian ministers who dared to suggest from the pulpits that Klan membership was not reconcilable with true Christianity.

In 1921, a Congressional committee investigating the Klan revealed many of its violent activities. It was, said Simmons, who had been called as a witness, "the best advertising we ever got." (*Ku Klux Klan* 1988, 16) By the following year, the Klan was collecting $10 million in membership fees alone, not counting the profits from the robes, hoods, and other Klan paraphernalia. (Not counting insurance policies, either.) This was something new in the history of terrorism. It was widespread, large-scale terrorism for fun and profit.

The revived Klan spread, not only throughout the South but outside the South, as well. The Klan's racially bigoted, nativist message appealed not just to Southerners but to tens of thousands of Americans in the North, the Midwest and West as well. Traveling recruiters for the Klan fanned out around the country, signing up new members at an incredible rate. (Unlike its predecessor, the new Klan welcomed women as well as men; dues were dues.) The salesmen told people what they wanted to hear, tweaking the Klan's message to fit local prejudices. Having begun as a drinking club, the Klan was sold as a mortal enemy of Demon Rum in places where Prohibitionist sentiment ran particularly high.

By the time the Klan came marching down Pennsylvania Avenue in 1925, it credibly claimed some five million members. It may not have owned the United States of America, but it ruled over large portions of it. Although it had no real political ideology beyond hatred of all that was "alien," the Klan was one of the most politically powerful institutions in the country.

In the North, the Klan usually allied itself with Republicans. In the South, with Democrats. It is likely that at least three state governors and one U.S. senator belonged to the Klan, along with hundreds, perhaps thousands, of local officials. In much of the United States, even law enforcement officials rarely crossed the Klan. Those who were members could be counted on to do its bidding. Those who were not—even some who despised the Klan and all it stood for—would usually close their eyes, hold their nose, and look the other way when the Klan was around.

In other ways, too, the Klan's political power went far beyond its own membership. Outside the Deep South, where it was almost as dominant as it cared to be, the Klan was especially strong in Texas, Colorado, Arkansas, Oklahoma, Oregon, and Maine. David C. Stephenson, the Klan's "Grand Dragon" in Indiana, was the virtual dictator of that state.

The Klan's power was no longer merely regional. Only the year before the Washington march, it had had its way with the 1924 national convention of the Democratic Party in New York City, first by defeating a move by some northern delegates to condemn the Klan in the party's platform, then by helping to block the nomination of the hated Catholic Al Smith as the party's candidate for President.

Not long after the Washington march, however, "Grand Dragon" D. C. Stephenson would be convicted of the rape and murder of a young white woman in Indiana. Writhing under the pressure of the prosecutors, Stephenson talked, exposing many Klan secrets including its clandestine political involvements, as well as the cynicism and greed that drove the leaders of the organization. Many Klan members and supporters around the country were seriously disillusioned. The Klan's popularity quickly withered, and, once again, the Klan all but disappeared.

Even so, its symbols—the white robe, the hood, and most of all, the burning cross—remained vivid in the public imagination, and in another 40 years or so, they would be revived by yet another reincarnation of the Ku Klux Klan during the civil rights movement of the 1950s and 1960s.

Then, in 2003, the U.S. Supreme Court gave a backhanded tribute to the unique power of cross-burning, as it has been exercised by the Ku Klux Klan for three-quarters of a century, by upholding the constitutionality of a state law banning cross-burning in Virginia. Until the Court's landmark decision in *Virginia v. Black*, the legal consensus seemed to be that cross-burning was protected as a form of "symbolic speech," in the same way that the Court had ruled that burning an American flag was protected. Writing for the 6-to-3 majority, however, Justice Sandra Day O'Connor recognized that cross-burning was different because of that symbol's "long and pernicious history as a signal of impending violence." As paraphrased in an article by Jon Frank in a Virginia newspaper, the Court ruled that the burning-cross "symbolizes a 'reign of terror' in post–Civil War America that reverberates today with memories of KKK whippings, murders and threats of harm by such acts as lynchings and burnings at the stake" (Frank 2003).

TWENTY-FIRST-CENTURY TERROR—SEPTEMBER 11, 2001

The willingness to kill for a cause makes terrorists dangerous. The willingness to die for the same cause makes them formidable. When those two resolutions are joined with religious fanaticism—the absolute conviction that such deaths are blessed by a Power greater than oneself—terrorists become all but invincible.

The awesome potency of that combination was most clearly, and horribly, demonstrated in the attacks on New York and Washington, D.C., on September 11, 2001.

Those events traumatized the people of the United States. Their aftermath—which, as of this writing, includes two wars, the overthrow of two governments, an international counterterrorist campaign of unprecedented size and determination, and an upheaval in the relationships between the United States and its allies, large and small—has traumatized the world.

The remaining section of the World Trade Center on September 27, 2001, is surrounded by a mountain of rubble following the September 11 terrorist attacks in New York. Courtesy of Bri Rodriguez/FEMA News Photo.

What has become known simply as "September 11th" was the culmination of an unusually long, elaborate, and well-organized terrorist process: a process that took shape in several countries, over a period of nearly 10 years.

It was in 1992 that a 24-year-old Egyptian student named Mohamed Atta, who would be the operational leader of the attacks, received a visa to attend the Technical University of Hamburg-Harburg in Hamburg, Germany. Ironically, for someone who would become infamous for a massive act of destruction in the heart of a great city, he would be seeking a degree in urban planning.

Some reports have suggested that Atta was radicalized by people he met at the Al Quds mosque in Hamburg; but, according to Khaled al-Sheik Mohammed and Ramzi bin al-Shaibah, two of the men most responsible for planning September 11, he was already a terrorist-in-waiting by the time he arrived in Germany (Tremlett 2002). Indeed, al-Qaeda had sent him there as a sleeper agent. His true radicalization had probably taken place in Cairo, where he had studied engineering at the university and joined a professional association that was dominated by the Islamist Muslim Brotherhood, some of whose members had assassinated Egypt's President Anwar Sadat (Four Corners 2001).

In 1997, Atta vanished from Hamburg for more than a year, during which time he may have received training at one or more of Osama bin Laden's notorious camps in Afghanistan. Meanwhile, at least two more of the eventual hijackers, Marwan al-Shehhi and Ziad Jarrah, had moved to Hamburg as well, also on student visas, and like Atta, had traveled to Afghanistan around this time. Also like Atta, each of them would pilot one of the passenger jets on that fateful day in September 2001.

According to *Top Secret: The Road to September 11th,* a television report compiled by Yosri Fouda of the Arab television network Al Jazeera, when Atta returned to Hamburg near the end of 1998, he and Marwan al-Shehhi and Ziad Jarrah moved into an apartment in a building at 54 Marienstrasse in Hamburg, which became the center of an al-Qaeda terrorist cell established by Atta. The kitchen of that apartment was, in Fouda's term, "the kitchen" in which much of the September 11 plot would be cooked (Al Jazeera 2002).

The recipe for the plot would be formulated in a building known as the House of Gumad in Kandahar, Afghanistan, by two high-ranking al-Qaeda figures, Khaled al-Sheik Mohammed and Ramzi bin al-Shaibah. The building, which had once been a hangout for Saudi members of the Mujahadeen, was now the site of a meeting attended by Atta, al-Shehhi, Jarrah, and Nawaf al-Hazemi. The latter would be Atta's second-in-command on September 11, and would pilot the fourth plane (Tremlett 2002).

Toward the end of 1999, the three men from 54 Marienstrasse reported their passports stolen and received replacements. The new passports had no stamps showing that they had traveled to Afghanistan, or anywhere else that might arouse particular suspicions in U.S. immigration authorities. Then in the spring and early summer of 2000, the men arrived, separately and from different departure points, in the United States. Before long, they were in Florida, where they began taking flying lessons, paying nearly $40,000 for the training. Money, in fact, seemed to be no problem for the men from Hamburg, who received large sums from Dubai during this time (Chronology 2002).

Atta and al-Shehhi, who claimed to be cousins, attended the same flight school in Florida, but the other would-be pilots seem to have gone elsewhere. Unlike in Germany, the group does not seem to have hung out together in the United States, no doubt to avoid connections that might draw attention from the authorities. In the summer of 2001, however, at least five of the eventual hijackers—Atta, Salem Alhazmi and Hanu Hanjour, Al-Shehhi and Ziad Jarrah—were all in Las Vegas, presumably meeting to discuss the final plans for the attacks, which by then were little more than two months away.

The trip to Las Vegas came in the midst of a flurry of travel for Atta, who made at least three other trips between Florida, Boston, and New York in the days shortly before and after, and who then flew to Spain for 12 days in mid-July. He rented a car and drove more than 1,000 miles during his European stay, possibly stopping briefly in Switzerland before returning to the United States on July 19 (Four Corners 2001).

Things did not always go smoothly for the conspirators, but when things went wrong, both the men and their organization showed an impressive ability to adjust and improvise. When the operational leader Mohamed Atta was picked up for driving without a license, all the key members of the conspiracy, including Atta, quickly obtained driver's licenses (Smith 2002).

One of the men already in the United States tried to obtain a visa for Ramzi bin al-Shaibah, who had apparently intended to pilot another plane in the operation. Ramzi, however, came from Yemen, a place so identified with terrorism that it set off alarms in the U.S. Immigration Service, and his visa was denied four times. Before long, U.S. authorities now believe, al-Qaeda sent an Algerian named Zacarias Moussaoui to take Ramzi's place. Even when Moussaoui was arrested in Minnesota the month before the planned attack date, the operation kept on schedule.

Meanwhile, the remainder of what would turn out to be 19 hijackers had begun training in Afghanistan in the spring of 2001, after which they joined the others who were already in the United States (Tremlett 2002). The newcomers were mostly young Saudis who spoke little English. They knew they had been trained for a suicide operation, but not what that operation was going to be (Chronology 2002).

The final details of the mission, including the date and the flights that would be hijacked, were apparently left up to Atta and the others who would carry out the act. Three weeks before the attacks, the final targets were decided on and all the hijackers were told: they would be attacking the Pentagon, the U.S. Capitol building, and both twin towers of the World Trade Center. We have no record of their reactions to the news, but it is reasonable to imagine that they were overjoyed. They would be striking a devastating blow against four of the best-known symbols of American power and influence—military, political, and economic.

The hijackers communicated their plans to their friends in Germany in an almost light-hearted code. The Pentagon was referred to as "the Faculty of Fine Arts," the Capitol building was "the Faculty of Law," and, perhaps in honor of Atta's studies in Germany, one tower of the World Trade Center was "the Faculty of Urban Planning" (Al Jazeera 2002). In a late-night phone call, Atta gave bin Shaihab the date of the forthcoming attack in the form of a riddle: "Two sticks, a dash, and a cake with a stick down. What is it?" The answer, of course, was 11/9—September 11, in the month-day order common in much of the world.

One hijacker e-mailed bin Shaihab: "The first semester commences in three weeks . . . This summer will surely be hot . . . 19 certificates and four exams. Regards to the Professor. Goodbye" (Al Jazeera 2002). The "Professor" may have been Khaled Sheikh Mohammad, or it may have been Osama bin Laden. Soon after receiving these communications, the remaining members of the Hamburg cell hurriedly abandoned Germany. On September 6, bin Shaihab notified bin Laden of the final details of the plan, and those "in the know" settled down to wait for news.

When it came, that news was even better than the al-Qaeda leaders had hoped it would be. True, one of the planes failed to reach its target, but the three that did were wildly successful. In Washington, D.C., a large portion of the Pentagon—"the Faculty of Fine Arts," the beating heart of America's supposedly invincible military might—was destroyed. In New York, the destruction of the World Trade Center was not only complete, it was breathtakingly spectacular.

Roughly three months later, Al Jazeera television ran a videotape that was picked up and shown in the United States as well. In the tape, Osama bin Laden and some of his fellows were seen discussing where they were when they heard the news, much as others might discuss where they were on the moment when a man first walked on the moon.

"We were at (. . . *inaudible* . . .) when the event took place," bin Laden says, in a translation provided to television by the Department of State.

> We had notification since the previous Thursday that the event would take place that day. We had finished our work that day and had the radio on. It was 5:30 p.m. our time. I was sitting with Dr. Ahmad Abu-al-(Khair). Immediately, we heard the news that a plane had hit the World Trade Center. We turned the radio station to the news from Washington. The news continued and no mention of the attack until the end. At the end of the newscast, they reported that a plane just hit the World Trade Center . . . After a little while, they announced that another plane had hit the World Trade Center. The brothers who heard the news were overjoyed by it. (U.S. Department of Defense 2001)

When bin Laden's companion, who had known nothing about the attacks in advance, described his own reaction, he was almost babbling with religious fervor:

> I listened to the news and I was sitting. We didn't . . . we were not thinking about anything, and all of a sudden, Allah willing, we were talking about how come we didn't have anything, and all of a sudden the news came and everyone was overjoyed and everyone until the next day, in the morning, was talking about what was happening and we stayed until four o'clock, listening to the news every time a little bit different, everyone was very joyous and saying "Allah is great," "Allah is great," "We are thankful to Allah," "Praise Allah." And I was happy for the happiness of my brothers. That day the congratulations were coming on the phone non-stop. The mother was receiving phone calls continuously. Thank Allah. Allah is great, praise be to Allah. (U.S. Department of State 2001)

Bin Laden echoed the pious sentiments of his companion, and even credited the horrifying attacks with generating a new interest in Islam. "[I]n Holland, at one of the centers, the number of people who accepted Islam during the days that followed the operations were more than the people who accepted Islam in the last eleven years. I heard someone on Islamic radio who owns a school in America say: 'We don't have time to keep up with the demands of those who are asking about Islamic books to learn about Islam.' This event made people think *(about true Islam)* which benefited Islam greatly" (U.S. Department of Defense 2001).

It was clear from the conversation that both men were surprised and delighted by the sheer extent of the destruction. "We calculated in advance the number of casualties from the enemy who would be killed based on the position of the tower," marveled bin Laden. "We calculated that the floors that would be hit would be three or four floors. I was the most optimistic of them all. (. . . *Inaudible* . . .) Due to my experience in this field, I was thinking that the fire from the gas in the plane would melt the iron structure of the building and collapse the area where the plane hit and all the floors above it only. This is all that we had hoped" (U.S. Department of Defense 2001). Instead, both of the massive buildings—the tallest in the world when they were built three decades before—had collapsed into rubble.

Finally, bin Laden expressed immense admiration both for the men who had carried out the mission, and for the mission itself. "Those young men (. . . *inaudible* . . .) said in deeds, in New York and Washington—speeches that overshadowed all other speeches made everywhere else in the world. The speeches are understood by both Arabs and non-Arabs—even by Chinese" (U.S. Department of Defense 2001).

Bob Blitzer, who knew something about the dedication, persistence, and devotion of al-Qaeda from his time as the FBI chief of counterterrorism, expressed his own grudging and angry admiration to reporter Hedrick Smith: "When I saw those planes hit the World Trade Tower, I was not surprised. The first thought on my mind was, 'My God, they finished the job.' I knew it was these guys because they are so committed, they have so much hatred of the West. Incredible determination. Incredible people" (Smith 2002).

REFERENCES

Adams, Cecil. 1993. *The Straight Dope*. (Syndicated Column.) *Chicago Reader*. 18 June.

"Al Jazeera Offers Accounts of 9/11 Planning." 2002. CNN. CNN.com/WORLD, 12 September. http://www.CNN.com/2002/WORLD/meast/09/12/alqaeda.911.claim/ (accessed 30 March 2004).

Calahan, Alexander B. 1995. Countering Terrorism and the Israeli Response to the 1972 Munich Olympic Massacre and the Development of Independent Covert Action Teams. Thesis, submitted to faculty of the Marine Corps Command and Staff College. http://www.fas.org/irp/eprint/calahan.htm (accessed 30 March 2004).

"Chronology of the Sept. 11 Terror Plot." 2002. PBS. "Frontline: Inside the Terrorist Network," 17 January.

"*Four Corners: A Mission to Die For.*" 2001. Australian Broadcasting Corporation. ABC.net. 12 November.

Frank, Jon. 2003. "Supreme Court Upholds Va.'s Ban on Cross Burning." *Virginian-Pilot* (Norfolk), 8 April.

Gado, Mark. n.d. *Lynching in America: Carnival of Death*. The Crime Library. Court TV. http://www.crimelibrary.com/classics2/carnival/ (accessed 30 March 2004).

"God Bless You All—I Am Innocent." 1906. *Chattanooga Times*, 20 March.

Gossett, Thomas F. 1963. *Race: The History of an Idea in America*. Dallas: Southern Methodist University Press.

Greenspan, Bud. 2002. "1972 Munich Olympic Games: Bud Greenspan Remembers" (Showtime network). Cappy Productions.

Hirst, David. 2003. *The Gun and the Olive Branch: The Roots of Violence in the Middle East*. New York: Thunder's Mouth Press/Nateva Books.

Ku Klux Klan: A History of Racism and Violence. 1988. Montgomery, Ala.: Klanwatch.

Linder, Douglas. 2000. *The Shipp Trial: An Account*. University of Missouri Kansas City School of Law. http://www.law.unkc.edu/faculty/projects/ftrials/shipp/shipp.html (accessed 30 March 2004).

"On the Media: Black September," 2002. National Public Radio. 30 August.

Parrish, Paula. 2002. "Revisiting the Horror of Munich." Scripps Howard News Service, 4 September.

Reeve, Simon. 2000. *One Day in September*. New York: Arcade.

"S. L. Hutchins May Try to Save Ed Johnson." 1906. *Chattanooga Times*, 20 February.

Smith, Hedrick. 2002. "Reporter's Notebook." PBS, "Frontline: Inside the Terrorist Network," 17 January. http://www.pbs.org/wgbh/pagse/frontline/shows/notebook/html (accessed 30 March 2004).

Tremlett, Giles. 2002. "Al-Qaida Leaders Say Nuclear Power Stations Were Original Targets: Reporter Meets Contender for Next Bin Laden." *The Guardian*, 9 September.

Tuskegee Institute archives. Lynching figures available online at: http://www.law.umkc.edu/faculty/projects/ftrials/shipp/lynchingyear.html.

U.S. Department of Defense. 2001. Transcript (translation) of Osama bin Laden videotape shown on the Al-Jazeera Television Network, December. Available at CNN.com. http://www.CNN.com/2001/US/12/13/tape.transcript/ (accessed 30 March 2004).

U.S. v. Shipp, 214 U.S. 386, 15 November 1909.

Wade, Wyn Craig. 1987. *The Fiery Cross*. New York: Simon & Schuster. [Not to be confused with the Klan periodical of the same name.]

"W.G.M. Thomas Tells Why Case Will Not Be Appealed." 1906. *Chattanooga Times*, 10 February.

Wolff, Alexander. 2002. "The Mastermind: Thirty Years after He Helped Plan the Terror Strike, Abu Daoud Remains in Hiding—and Unrepentant." *Sports Illustrated*, 26 August.

Chronology

Thousands of terrorist incidents have occurred over the past century or so, sometimes hundreds of them in a single year. Since this chronology could not hope to be exhaustive, I have attempted to make it comprehensive instead.

The terrorist incidents recorded here range in scale from acts of relatively minor vandalism to mass slaughter. I have tried to include a large-enough sampling to reflect both the size and the complexity of the problem, and to give some sense of the ebb and flow of incidents over time. In addition, I have tried to make the list represent both the creativity and variety of terrorist acts, and their repetitiveness; also the numbing sameness of the results—the victims, counted and uncounted, the often unidentified human beings, dead, maimed, and bereaved.

This chronology has not been limited to any particular size or type of terrorist event, or even to events that can be attributed to identifiable groups or causes. In deciding which to include and which not, I have tried to reflect the changing nature and scope of terrorism, with particular (but not exclusive) attention to those varieties of terrorism that have had significant impact on history.

Although this chronology begins almost two centuries ago, emphasis has been given to the most recent decades, when contemporary patterns of terrorism have been evolving, and to those terrorist groups and actions that have most affected, whether directly or indirectly, the United States and its interests. This latter emphasis is not as ethnocentric as it may seem. There are three reasons for it: (1) it is reasonable to expect that most of this book's readers will be American; (2) much of the current wave of international terrorism has been directed against the United States; and (3) the United States has taken the international lead in combating terrorism by launching the so-called war against it.

One major exclusion: this chronology does not include the terrorism regularly inflicted by tyrannical governments on their own citizens, which tends to be too ongoing and systematic to lend itself to this kind of catalogue.

By their nature, terrorist acts are often anonymous. In many cases, both their purpose and the identity of those responsible can only be guessed at or assumed.

1831

August 22 Led by a black religious visionary named Nat Turner, eight slaves invade the house of a white family named Travis in Southampton County, Virginia, and slaughter all five white people they find there. Before they are stopped a day and a half later, Turner's band swells to as many as 60 or 70, and spreads fear throughout the state, killing 58 white men, women, and children in the vicinity of Jerusalem, Virginia.

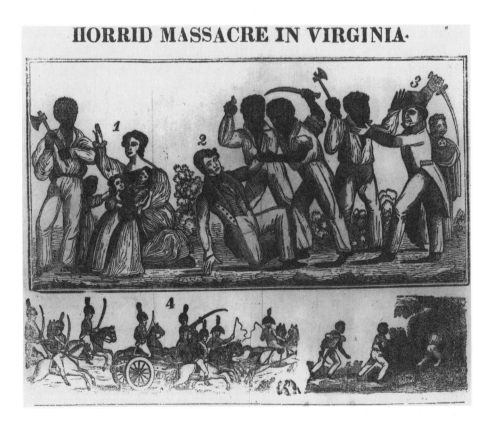

Composite of scenes of Nat Turner's rebellion. Illustrations from *Authentic and Impartial Narrative of the Tragical Scene Which Was Witnessed in Southampton County* (New York, 1831). Courtesy of Library of Congress.

1835

January 30   Attending a funeral at the U.S. Capitol, President Andrew Jackson is the victim of an attempted assassination. Although the would-be assassin, whose pistols misfire, is later found to be insane, the President suspects that the man is actually in the pay of his political enemies.

1865

April 14   U.S. President Abraham Lincoln is shot while attending a play at Ford's Theatre in Washington, D.C., by a young actor named John Wilkes Booth. He dies the next day. Lincoln's assassination is the only successful element of a pro-South plot intended to kill not only Lincoln but Vice President Andrew Johnson and Secretary of State William Seward, as well.

December 24   Six Confederate veterans of the Civil War establish the Ku Klux Klan at Pulaski, Tennessee. The organization, which begins as a social club, will become a tool for the intimidation and repression of freedmen in the South.

1866

April 16   Freedmen marching to celebrate the passage of the Civil Rights Act are attacked by a white mob in Norfolk, Virginia. In the resulting riot, five of the freedmen are killed.

July 30   Thirty-four blacks and four whites are killed, and some 150 people (mostly blacks) are injured, when a black suffrage meeting is attacked by a white mob.

1867

December   The Ku Klux Klan adopts a new tactic known as "night riding" as a mean of intimidating freedmen in Tennessee.

1880

February 17   A bomb, which has been painstakingly constructed by a workman in the basement of the Czar's Winter Palace in Moscow, explodes underneath the dining room at the time the Czar would normally be having his evening meal. Although the meal has been postponed and the Czar is not there, 67 other people are either killed or severely

The anarchist Haymarket riot in Chicago on May 4, 1886. A dynamite bomb exploding among the police. Illustration from *Harper's Weekly* 30 (1886 May 15). Courtesy of Library of Congress.

injured by the blast. The workman-assassin is a member of the notorious anarcho-Socialist group, Narodnaya Volya (People's Will).

1881

March 1   Two bombs are thrown at a carriage carrying Czar Alexander II of Russia through the streets of St. Petersburg. It is the fourth bomb attack on the Czar's life, and once again, he is unhurt although several bystanders are killed. When the Czar orders the carriage to stop and gets out to assist the wounded, another bomb is detonated. This time both the Czar and the bomber are killed. The assassins are members of Narodnaya Volya.

1886

May 4   A rally is held in Chicago's Haymarket Square to protest police violence against workers. When a large force of policemen moves in to disperse the crowd, someone, presumably an anarchist, throws a bomb into their ranks and one policeman is killed. The police response to the attack kills three workers.

1894

June 24	While attending an exposition in Lyon, French President Marie Francois Sadi Carnot is stabbed to death by Sante Caserio, an Italian anarchist.

1901

July 29	The king of Italy, Humbert I, is shot to death in Monza, Italy, by an Italian-American anarchist from New Jersey named Gaetano Bresci.
September 6	U.S. President William McKinley is shot at Buffalo, New York. (He will die several days later.) The assassin is Leon Czolgosz, a laborer who describes himself as a follower of the anarchist Emma Goldman.

1905

June 29	A large mob of robed and masked men takes nine black prisoners from the local jail at Watkinsville, Georgia. Marching them to the center of town, the mob beats the prisoners, ties them to a fence, and opens fire on them. Eight of the men die. One miraculously survives.

1906

March 19	When the Supreme Court agrees to hear the appeal of Ed Johnson, a black man convicted of raping a white woman in Chattanooga, Tennessee, a mob drags him out of jail, beats him, and hangs him from a bridge, riddling his body with bullets (see chapter 7).

1910

October 1	A bomb is detonated at the printing plant of the *Los Angeles Times*, a paper that is editorially hostile to labor unions. The explosion and the resulting fire kill 20 workers and injure several others. Two brothers, James and John McNamara, are tried and convicted of the bombing.

1914

June 28	A young Serbian nationalist named Gavrilo Princip sets off World War I when he shoots to death the Austrian archduke, Franz Ferdinand, and his wife, Sophia, in Sarajevo, the capital of Bosnia.

1915

November   Inspired by the popularity of the movie *The Birth of a Nation*, William J. Simmons gathers with a small group of men on the top of Stone Mountain, near Atlanta, Georgia, where they set fire to a cross. The event signals a reincarnation of the Ku Klux Klan, which will use a combination of terror and political influence to intimidate black people and maintain racial segregation in much of the United States (see chapter 7).

1920

September 16   A horse-drawn wagon loaded with dynamite explodes on the corner of Wall and Broad Streets in New York City's financial district. Forty passersby are killed. The explosion is blamed on anarchists.

1929

August 23   An anti-Jewish Arab mob riots in the town of Hebron, in Palestine, having heard false reports that a sacred Islamic mosque has been vandalized. Attacking a synagogue, the mob kills everyone it finds inside, then proceeds to a yeshiva (Jewish religious school), where it does the same. It then breaks into the house of a local rabbi, where most of the remaining Jews in the community have taken refuge and slaughters them all, male, female, young, and old alike. Altogether, 67 Jews die in the massacre.

1931

February 21   In the first recorded instance of the seizure of a commercial passenger airplane by force, a Panagra Ford Tri-Motor commercial airplane and its pilot, Byron Rickards, are taken captive by armed rebels in Arequipa, Peru, and held for two weeks until the revolutionaries have successfully taken over the Peruvian capital of Lima. At that point, Rickards, an American, is made to fly one of the paramilitaries to Lima, after which he is set free.

1932

May   A Russian anarchist assassinates President Paul Doumer, of France.

1933

February 15   An anarchist named Giuseppe Zangara attempts to shoot the U.S. president-elect, Franklin D. Roosevelt, with a pistol, in Miami, Florida. Zangara misses Roosevelt, but strikes Mayor Anton J. Cermak of Chicago, who later dies of his wounds.

1934

November 9   A Croatian gunman kills King Alexander of Yugoslavia and French Foreign Minister Louis Barthou in Marseilles, France.

1935

September 8   Louisiana's powerful Senator Huey P. Long, popularly known as "the Kingfish," is shot in Baton Rouge. The assassin, Dr. Carl A. Weiss, is immediately shot and killed by Long's bodyguards. Long dies two days later.

1936

August 24   The British assistant district commissioner in Jenin, Trans-Jordan (later, simply Jordan) is assassinated by a Palestinian gunman, AlthoTugh. The assassin is killed trying to escape; the event leads to massive British reprisals.

1938

January 6   Jewish forces attack the village of Atteel, killing several women and children. Survivors report that mosques were violated and copies of the Qur'an torn up.

November 9–10   Kristallnacht. In the wake of the assassination of a German diplomat by a Jew in Paris, gangs of Nazi thugs riot across Germany. Thousands of Jews are killed or beaten, an enormous amount of Jewish property is damaged or destroyed, and, ultimately, tens of thousands of Jews are taken into custody.

1945

October 31   The radical Zionists of the Irgun launch a terrorist campaign against the British mandate in Palestine. Four people are killed in the first wave of bombings.

November 27   The Irgun bombs a police station in Jerusalem, killing eight British soldiers.

1946

January 7   Nazi "Werewolf" terrorists set fire to a house in Passau, Germany, killing three American officials living there.

March 11   Members of the Iranian Fedayeen-e Eslam guerilla organization assassinate the Iranian author and scholar Ahmad Kasravi at Teheran.

July 22   Ninety people are killed and 45 more injured when a tremendous blast shatters the south wing of the King David Hotel in Jerusalem. Although the Zionist Irgun has targeted the hotel because it serves as the headquarters for the British military in Jerusalem, the dead and wounded include not only Britons, but Arabs and Jews as well.

September 30   An American soldier is killed in an ambush at Fort McKinley in the Philippines.

October 31   The Irgun shows its ability to strike outside of Palestine when two suitcase bombs devastate the British embassy in Rome.

1947

May   The Irgun engineers a jailbreak of 41 Jewish prisoners from the British fortress at Acre, a month after four members of the Irgun were hanged there.

July 12   Responding to the execution of three of their comrades, the Irgun hangs two British sergeants from a eucalyptus tree not far from Netanya, Palestine, the town from which they had been kidnapped more than two weeks before. The area around the tree is mined and the suspended bodies themselves are booby-trapped.

September 29   The Irgun bombs a police station in Haifa. Eight people, including four British and four Arab policemen, are killed.

December 3   Twenty people are killed when Communists derail a train near Arras, France.

December 12   Twenty-seven people, five of them Jews, are killed, and thirty more are injured in bus bombings by Jewish terrorists in Ramleh and Haifa.

December 13   Irgun commandos hurl grenades into a crowded cafe near the famous Damascus Gate in Jerusalem. Thirteen people are killed, including eleven Arabs and two British policemen.

December 18 or 19   The Haganah raids the village of Khisas, killing 10 Palestinian Arabs.

| December 19 or 20 | Five children are killed when the Haganah blows up the home of a prominent Arab in the village of Qazaza. |

1948

January 4–5	Agents of the Haganah detonate two suitcases filled with TNT in the Hotel Semiramis in the Katamon quarter of Jerusalem, which they believe is a headquarters for the defenders of Arab interests in Jerusalem. Twenty-six people die in the explosion, including a Spanish diplomat who had been living in the hotel and several members of the hotel owner's family.
January 30	At the dawn of India's independence, the man most responsible for that independence is gunned down on his way to evening prayers. After decades of leading a nonviolent campaign against the British raj, Mahatma Gandhi falls victim to the religious violence that plagues Indian society. The assassin is a fanatic Hindu named Nathuram Vinayak Godse.
March 7	The Viet Minh assassinate two American diplomats in the city of Saigon, in French Indochina.
March 11	A Christian Arab parks a car loaded with a quarter-ton of TNT in front of the Haganah office in the Jewish Agency compound at Jerusalem. When the bomb it contains explodes, 13 people are killed and 84 are injured.
April 9	Shortly before dawn, a commando force of the Irgun and the Stern Gang attack the Arab village of Deir Yassin, west of Jerusalem. Hundreds of village residents are slaughtered; some are gunned down, others beaten, still others killed by dynamite thrown indiscriminately into houses. In addition, the invaders reportedly rape many women of all ages.
May 8	Communist terrorists arrange to meet an American CBS correspondent on a boat in the harbor at Salonika, Greece. When he arrives, they murder him and throw his body into the ocean.
September 16	Four members of the Stern Gang, dressed in the uniform of the Israeli army, fire into the car of Count Folke Bernadotte while it travels through the streets of Jerusalem. Bernadotte, the well-respected United Nations mediator in Palestine, is killed.
December 28	Leaving his office in Cairo, the Egyptian prime minister, Mahmoud Nokrashy Pasha, is gunned down by a member of the Moslem Brotherhood. Nokrashy Pasha had outraged the Brotherhood by accepting a cease-fire with Israel.

1949

| December 3 | The British governor of Sarawak, Duncan George Stewart, is assassinated by knife-wielding Malaysians opposed to British rule. |

1950

November 1   Two Puerto Rican nationalists intent on assassinating U.S. President Harry Truman attempt to invade Blair House, in Washington, D.C., where the president has temporarily taken up residence while the White House is being renovated. Secret Service agents repel the attack. One of the agents and one of the would-be assassins are killed. The president, who was napping at the time, is not injured.

1951

July 20   King Abdullah, the founder and first ruler of the Hashemite Kingdom of Jordan, is shot to death entering the historic al-Aqsa Mosque in the Old City of Jerusalem, where he had gone to pray at his father's grave. The assassin, Mustafa Shukri Ashshua, is a Jerusalem tailor—one of the many Palestinian Arabs angered by Abdullah's willingness to accept the partition of Palestine, and to annex what remained of Arab Palestine into his kingdom.

September 11   A radical Afghan guns down Prime Minister Lisquat Ali Khan of Pakistan, while he is speaking to an audience in Rawalpindi, Pakistan.

October 6   The motorcade of Sir Henry Gurney, British high commissioner of Malaysia, is raked with machine-gun fire from Communist guerillas as it travels along the Gap Road through the Malaysian jungle. Sir Henry and 13 members of his British military escort are killed in the attack.

1952

The terrorist campaign known as the "Mau Mau Rebellion" begins in Kenya. Mau Mau is a secret society of guerrilla insurgents, most of whom belong to the Kikuyu tribe. In addition to attacking British colonists in Kenya, the Mau Mau launches a violent campaign of intimidation against their fellow Kikuyu, intending to frighten them into joining the rebellion.

October 20   In what becomes known as the Lari Massacre, 97 black Africans whom the Mau Mau believe to be collaborating with the English colonists are viciously slaughtered.

1953

January 14   The Mau Mau attacks a farmhouse in Kenya. The farmer, a man named Ruck, is hacked to death, along with his wife, a doctor who ran a clinic for black Africans, and their young son.

Victims of the conflict between the Mau Mau and Kenyan officials in 1952. Courtesy of Getty Images.

1954

March 1	Four Puerto Rican nationalists open fire in the chamber of the U.S. House of Representatives. Five U.S. congressmen are injured before the gunmen are subdued.
March 17	Bedouin nomads of the Negev Desert, angered at being driven from their traditional grazing lands by the state of Israel, ambush an Israeli bus in the Scorpion Pass, killing 11 passengers.
November	The body of Dr. Gray Arundel Leakey, head of the renowned Leakey family of archaeologists, is discovered buried in a shallow grave in Kenya. The body, which has been mutilated and perhaps partially cannibalized, is believed to have been used in secret Mau Mau ceremonies.

1955

April 1	A rash of bombings on the island of Cyprus marks the start of a campaign by the Greek Cypriot group EOKA for independence from British rule.

August 1	In a departure from its previous policy in its fight for Algerian independence from France, the Muslim rebel group FLN massacres 123 civilians, including women and children, in the Phillippeville area of Algiers. The outraged French authorities launch a massive campaign of retaliation against Algerian civilians.
August 27	A black 14-year-old boy named Emmett Till is dragged from the home of a relative in Money, Mississippi, and brutally murdered by two white men for the offense of being too familiar with a white woman.
October 17	Thirteen French citizens—five soldiers and eight civilians—are shot to death by Arab nationalists in Algeria.

1956

March 3	The EKOA destroys a British Hermes airplane on the ground at Cyprus's Nicosia Airport.
April 27	The EOKA destroys a second British plane at Nicosia Airport.
October 3	Agents of the EKOA gun down the wife of a British soldier on Cyprus, killing her.

1957

The British army barracks at Armagh, Northern Ireland, repels an attack by an armed force of the Irish Republican Army (IRA).

1958

February 24	Agents of the revolutionary 26th of July Movement kidnap the five-time World Champion Formula One racecar driver Juan Fangio and prevent him from participating in a highly publicized race in Cuba. The Movement hopes to embarrass the Baptista government and draw attention to the Cuban situation.
June 26–July 6	During this period, some 50 Americans and Canadians are taken hostage by Communist rebels led by Raul Castro in the Oriente Province of Cuba. They include 27 U.S. Marines captured while traveling unarmed on a bus. The hostages are relatively well treated and are eventually released.
July 18	The last of the U.S. Marines kidnapped by Communist Cubans is set free.
November 1	Pro-Castro rebels hijack an airliner over Cuba. It crashes when the hijackers force the pilot to attempt a landing at a small airport near Moa Bay. Of the 20 people on board, only three survive.

1960

March 4	At 9 A.M. there is an explosion aboard the French freighter *La Coubre* in the harbor at Havana, Cuba. The ship is loaded with munitions intended for the Cuban military, and the original explosion is followed by several others, which trap scores of firefighters and onlookers who have been drawn to the scene. Altogether, casualties are estimated at 100 killed and 200 wounded. Fidel Castro blames the United States, while the United States blames mishandling of the cargo by Cuban dockworkers. Others believe that anti-Castro Cuban rebels are responsible.
April 9	Attending the opening of an agricultural exhibition in Witwatersrand, South Africa, the prime minister and chief architect of the apartheid system Henrik Verwoerd is shot twice in the face by a white farmer. The would-be assassin, who is a well-known South African socialite, claims to be an opponent of apartheid, but the government declares him insane. Verwoerd survives.
August 29	A bomb in the foreign ministry building in Amman, Jordan kills 12 people, including the country's prime minister.

1961

February 23	The cruise ship *Santa Maria* and its 550 passengers are seized by Portuguese rebels who oppose the dictatorial regimes of António Salazar in Portugal and Francisco Franco in Spain. Eventually, the hijackers surrender under threat from U.S. and Brazilian warships.
May 1	For the first time, an American airliner is hijacked. The Puerto Rican national who seizes control of the plane forces the pilots to fly to Cuba, where he is granted political asylum.
May 25	Members of the Palestinian Al Fatah organization kill three Israelis in the Jewish settlement of Ramat Hakovash.
September 1	A British official of the Aden state council is killed by Arab nationalists in Aden City on the Arabian Peninsula.
September 8	As a car bearing French President Charles de Gaulle drives near the French village of Pont-sur-Seine, a would-be assassin presses a button and sets off an explosion that tears across the highway. De Gaulle is uninjured. The bomber and three accomplices are later captured. Although they claim ties to the French Algerian OAS (Organisation Armée Sécrete), that organization denies responsibility for the attack.
November 18	William Levy, the secretary general of the Socialist Party of Algiers, is shot to death on a street corner in Algiers by the terrorist branch of the outlawed OAS known as the Delta. Levy is well-known as an opponent of the OAS, which hopes to keep Algeria a French colony.

1962

April–May
The streets of Algiers are turned into a bloodbath as hundreds of Arabs are killed in a brutal series of shootings, stabbings, and stranglings, which are designed to frighten Muslims away from European neighborhoods. This mini-Reign of Terror has been ordered by the leadership of the OAS. Some of the killings are carried out by the Deltas, others by gangs of French Algerian teenagers, some of whom are as young as 13 and 14 years old.

May 15
On a day of incredible violence in Algiers, both the OAS and the FLN up the pace of their terrorist campaigns. Between them, on this day, they launch an attack every 15 minutes.

1963

November 22
U.S. President John F. Kennedy is shot to death while riding in a motorcade in Dallas, Texas. Lee Harvey Oswald, a leftist American with pro-Cuban sympathies, is arrested for the crime after killing a policeman who attempts to capture him. Oswald is later shot himself, before it can be conclusively ascertained whether he was acting alone.

1965

February 21
The Black Muslim leader Malcolm X (also known as El-Hajj Malik El-Shabazz), is shot to death in a New York City auditorium. A rival faction of the Nation of Islam is suspected, although the reason for the assassination is never conclusively established.

1966

August 4
Two Colombians and an American are killed in an explosion at the Binational Centre in Bogota, Colombia. Leftist rebels are believed responsible.

September 26
An Argentine airliner en route from Buenos Aires to the Falklands is hijacked by members of the nationalist El Condor organization seeking to draw attention to Argentina's claim to the Islands.

November 13
Israelis attack the Palestinian village of Al Samou' near Hebron, killing some 18 villagers and injuring more than 50 others.

1967

June 30
Katangan rebel Moise Tshombe is abducted when hijackers seize the plane on which he is travelling to Spain and force it to fly to Algeria where Tshombe is imprisoned.

| October 12 | A bomb planted on a British airliner explodes near the Greek island of Rhodes, killing 66 people. |

1968

February 21	For the first time since 1961, an American airliner is hijacked to Cuba, where the Castro government gives the hijacker political asylum.
March 18	Two adults are killed and nearly 30 children injured when an Israeli school bus drives over a mine planted by Al Fatah.
April 4	The black American civil rights leader, Reverend Martin Luther King, Jr., is assassinated from ambush in Memphis, Tennessee. A white man named James Earl Ray is alone convicted of the crime, although he later claims that he was only one part of a racist conspiracy to kill King.
June 5	U.S. presidential candidate Robert F. Kennedy is shot as he walks through the crowded kitchen area of the Ambassador Hotel in early-morning hours following his victory in the California Democratic primary. He dies the next day. Five other people are wounded in the attack. Kennedy's assassin, a young man named Sirhan Sirhan, who opposes Kennedy's position on Israel, is captured at the scene.
July 22	A Boeing 707 belonging to the Israeli national airline El Al is hijacked on a flight from Rome to Tel Aviv by three members of the Popular Front for the Liberation of Palestine (PFLP). The plane is diverted to Algiers where negotiations eventually result in the release of the crew and the 38 passengers.
August 28	A squad of the rebel Guatemalan National Revolutionary Unit (URNG) forces a car carrying U.S. Ambassador John Gordon Meir off a road in Guatemala City and riddles it with gunfire, killing Meir. It is the first assassination ever of a U.S. ambassador.
September 4	One Israeli is killed and 71 others wounded when three Palestinian bombs explode in Tel Aviv.
October 12	An American military adviser to the Brazilian army, whom leftist rebels accuse of committing war crimes in Vietnam, is killed at his home in Sao Paulo, Brazil.
November 22	A bomb detonated by Al Fatah kills 12 people and injures 52 others in the Mahaneh Yehuda market in Jerusalem.
December 2	In retaliation for the attack at the Athens airport three days earlier, Israeli agents storm the airport at Beirut, Lebanon, blowing up 13 airliners belonging to Arab airlines.
December 26	PFLP gunmen launch a multi-pronged attack on Israeli airliners at the Athens airport in Greece. One Israeli passenger is killed.

1969

February 18	An Israeli airliner is attacked by Palestinian gunmen on the ground at Zurich, Switzerland. The pilot and three passengers are killed, along with one terrorist, who is shot by an Israeli security officer.
February 21	Two people are killed and several more injured by a Palestinian bomb detonated in a Jerusalem supermarket.
August 14	A Catholic man named John Gallagher is shot to death by members of the Protestant group calling itself the Ulster Special Constabulary during a street engagement in Armagh, North Ireland.
August 15	A man named David Linton is shot to death by Republicans on a street in north Belfast, becoming the first Protestant victim of the Irish "Troubles." On the same day, a teenaged boy named Gerald McAuley is gunned down by Loyalists in Belfast, becoming the first IRA member to fall victim to "the Troubles."
August 29	PFLP hijackers take over a TWA airliner en route from Rome and force it to fly to Damascus, Syria.
September 3	The Marxist group MR-8 kidnaps the U.S. ambassador to Brazil, Charles Elbrick.
October 21	A bomber who is believed to be a member of the loyalist Protestant group known as the Ulster Volunteer Force (UVF) is killed when a bomb he is planting at a power station near Ballyshannon, Northern Ireland, explodes too soon.
October 22	Palestinian bombs tear through two apartments in Haifa, Israel, killing four people and injuring 20 others.
November 27	Several bystanders are killed in an attack on an El Al office in Athens, Greece.
December 12	Sixteen people are killed and 90 wounded when the Agricultural Bank in Milan, Italy, is devastated by a bomb. The authorities blame anarchists, but Italian leftists believe that the bomb was set by fascists who were hoping to the discredit them.

1970

February 10	Three Palestinian terrorists are thwarted in an attempt to hijack an El Al plane at the airport in Munich, Germany. One Israeli is killed and several others injured.
February 21	Shortly after it takes off from the runway at the airport in Zurich, Switzerland, a Swissair passenger jet is destroyed by a bomb planted by the PFLP. All aboard are killed.
June 26	Five people, including two members of the IRA, are killed by an IRA bomb that explodes prematurely in an IRA house in Derry, Northern Ireland.

August 10	The body of an adviser to the U.S. Agency for International Development (SAID), who had been kidnapped by Tupamaros guerillas 10 days before, is found in Uruguay.
August 24	A bomb explodes in the mathematics building of the University of Wisconsin, at Madison, Wisconsin. Although the bomb was set to go off in the middle of the night when no one would be present, it kills a student who happens to be working late. The university's mathematics department is known to be doing research for the U.S. Army.
September 6	The PLFP attempts to hijack four airliners bound to New York from different cities. One of the hijackings fails and the hijacker, a woman, is captured. One airliner is flown to Egypt, where the passengers are released and the plane blown up on the ground. The others are flown to Jordan.
October 5	Canada's "October Crisis" begins with the kidnapping of British Trade Minister James Cross in Montréal by the Liberation Cell of the *Fédération de Liberation du Québec* (FLQ), a separatist organization that demands independence for the French-speaking province of Quebec. Many days later, Cross will be released.
October 10	The Québec minister of labor, Pierre LaPorte, is kidnapped by members of the Chenier Cell of the FLQ. He will later be found dead.

1971

January 8	Tupamoros guerillas abduct the British ambassador to Uruguay, Sir George Jackson. They hold him for eight months.
February 6	A young soldier named Robert Curtis is gunned down by agents of the IRA while on foot patrol in North Belfast, Northern Ireland. He is the first British soldier to die in the "Troubles."
May 17	The Israeli consul-general in Istanbul is assassinated by a combined force of Palestinians and local anti-government terrorists.
November 28	In the first terrorist act claimed by Black September, Jordan Premier Wasfi Tal is gunned down while returning to his hotel in Cairo, following a meeting of the Arab League. One of the assassins reportedly kneels down in the street and licks Tal's blood.
December 4	A bomb detonated by the Protestant Ulster Volunteer Force (UVF) kills 15 people at McGurk's Bar in a Catholic neighborhood of Belfast.

1972

January 30	In an event that will become notorious as "Bloody Sunday," British troops open fire on an "illegal" Catholic civil rights march in the Bog-

side area of Derry, Northern Ireland. Fourteen unarmed marchers are killed in the incident.

February   The IRA intensifies its terrorist campaign against British rule in Northern Ireland. Two Irishmen serving in the British Army and two members of a loyalist terrorist group are murdered during the month, and an attempt is made on the life of a Protestant member of the Northern Ireland Parliament.

February 22   The IRA campaign of terror reaches into England when a car bomb explodes near the officer's mess of a British parachute regiment in Aldershot. The only British officer among the seven people killed is a Roman Catholic chaplain.

May 5   The left-wing Italian publisher Giangiancomo Feltrinelli is killed when a bomb he is attempting to place at an electricity facility near Florence, Italy, explodes prematurely.

May 8   Five soldiers, one passenger, and all four Black September hijackers are killed when Israeli forces storm a hijacked Belgian airliner at Israel's Ben Gurion Airport.

May 11   A Red Army Faction car bomb kills an officer and injures 13 other people at the U.S. Army headquarters at Frankfurt, Germany.

May 17   An ex-police chief of Milan, Italy, is gunned down in the street outside his house shortly before he was scheduled to go on trial for the alleged murder of an Italian anarcho-leftist.

May 30   Three men launch an indiscriminate attack with guns and grenades on passengers in the terminal at Lod Airport in Israel. Twenty-four travelers and bystanders are killed and 78 more injured. One of the terrorists is killed by his companions (presumably to save him from being captured), another blows himself up, and the third is captured. The terrorists are members of the Japanese Red Army, apparently acting under the sponsorship and direction of the Popular Front for the Liberation of Palestine.

July 21   Eleven people are killed and 130 injured when the Irish Republican Army (IRA) sets off 20 explosions, at 20 different locations in Belfast, within a single hour. The event becomes infamous as "Bloody Friday."

July 31   An IRA car bomb kills six people in Claudy, Northern Ireland.

September 5 Members of Black September descend on the Israeli section of the Olympic Village in Munch, West Germany, killing two Israeli athletes and taking nine others hostage. Daylong negotiations result in the transportation of the terrorists and their hostages to a nearby airfield, where the German authorities launch an ill-fated rescue attempt. All the Israeli hostages are killed, as are five of the terrorists and one West German police officer. The crisis is carried live on international television (see chapter 7).

October 29   Hijackers claiming to belong to a group called the "National Youth Group for the Liberation of Palestine," which is suspected of being a cover name for Al-Fatah, seize a Lufthansa plane en route from Beirut,

Lebanon, to Ankara, Turkey. They release the plane when the three surviving Black September terrorists who participated in the attack on Israeli athletes at the Munich Olympics are set free.

1973

February 4	Twelve people, including nine British soldiers, are killed in an IRA bomb attack on a bus on the M62 roadway in Yorkshire, England.
March 12	Black September kills an Israeli businessman on the island of Cyprus.
May 4	Members of the People's Revolutionary Armed Forces abduct the U.S. consul general in Guadalajara, Mexico.
May 17	Three bombs go off on three different streets in downtown Dublin, in the Republic of Ireland, killing 26 bystanders. Loyalist paramilitary groups are suspected.
	A Loyalist car bomb kills seven people in Monaghan, in the Republic of Ireland.
August 4	A bomb kills 12 people and injures 48 more on a train near Bologna, Italy. Neo-fascists are suspected.
August 5	Agents of Black September open fire with machine guns on passengers arriving at the airport in Athens, Greece, on a flight from Israel. Three people are killed and 55 wounded.
September 5	Fatah members take over the Saudi Arabian embassy in Paris, France, demanding the release of a fellow terrorist arrested in Jordan.
November 17	In Greece, a student uprising is met with massive force from riot police. Thirty-four people are killed and 800 injured in the resulting melee. What will become the most notorious terrorist organization in Greece takes its name from the date of this infamous event.
December 1	Members of the Abu Nidal Organization (ANO) attack the Pan Am facilities at Fiumicino Airport at Rome, Italy, killing some 32 passengers and injuring 50 others. Taking several policemen hostage, they hijack a nearby plane and force it to fly, first to Athens, Greece, and then to Kuwait.
December 20	A bomb kills Spanish Prime Minister Admiral Luis Carrero Blanco. A Basque separatist group calling itself the Basque Fatherland and Liberty (ETA) is responsible.

1974

February 4	A small African American group calling itself the Symbionese Liberation Army (SLA) kidnaps the white newspaper heiress Patricia Hearst from her apartment in Berkeley, California. She will later be forced, or otherwise persuaded, to take part in the group's activities.

February 22	A deranged small-businessman named Sam Byck takes over a Delta Airlines plane on the ground at the airport in Washington, D.C. He wants to fly it into the White House and assassinate President Richard M. Nixon. He shoots a security guard and both the plane's pilot and co-pilot, killing the latter. When his plan unravels, he turns his gun on himself.
March 1	A reception at the Saudi Arabian embassy in the Sudanese capital of Khartoum is invaded by Black September. The American *chargé d'affaires* Curtis Moore, who has been the guest of honor at the reception, is taken hostage along with the U.S. ambassador to Sudan and three others. The terrorists demand the release of the assassin of Robert Kennedy, Sirhan Sirhan, in exchange for their hostages. Eventually, both U.S. diplomats, as well as a diplomat from Belgium, are killed by their captors.
April 11	The Jewish settlement Qirayt Semmona is invaded by commandos from the PFLP. Eighteen of the Jewish villagers are killed when Israeli forces launch a rescue attempt.
May 15	Twenty-one people are killed and almost 80 injured when Israeli special forces attempt to rescue 90 children being held captive by the PFLP in a school in the Israeli town of Ma'alot.
May 17	A car bomb kills 20 people in Dublin, the Republic of Ireland.
June 13	A small PFLP force attacks a kibbutz in Israel. All the invaders are killed, along with several settlers.
November 21	The IRA bombs several bars in Birmingham, England. Twenty-one people are killed and many others wounded.
November 23	The Palestinian Rejectionist Front seizes a British airliner at Dubai in the United Arab Emirates. A German passenger is killed in the incident.

1975

January 19	Ten people are held hostage by armed Arabs at Orly Airport near Paris. The terrorists release the hostages after the French authorities are persuaded to provide the hostage-takers with a plane that flies them to Baghdad, Iraq.
January 21	A bomb detonated by members of the *Anang Marg* kills India's railway minister.
January 24	A bomb explodes in the historic Fraunces Tavern in New York City's financial district. Four diners are killed and scores are injured in the blast. The Puerto Rican nationalist group FALN is believed responsible.
January 27	A West German politician is abducted and held hostage by members of the June the Second Movement, in West Berlin. The hostage is released when five imprisoned terrorists are allowed to fly to South Yemen.

April 13　　Four Phalangists are killed in Beirut, Lebanon, by gunmen presumed to be Palestinians who are attempting to assassinate the founder of the Phalangist Party, Pierre Jumayyil. On the same day, Beiruti Phalangists attack a busload of Palestinians and kill 20 of the passengers.

April 24　　A floor of the German embassy in Stockholm, Sweden, is occupied by German terrorists from the Red Army Faction (Baader-Meinhof Gang). They threaten to kill one hostage an hour until all the Red Army Faction members being held by West Germany are released. Two hostages are killed before the occupation of the embassy is ended when explosives being handled by one of the terrorists go off accidentally, killing her and injuring several others.

September 5　　Lynette "Squeaky" Fromme, an erstwhile disciple of Charles Manson, attempts to shoot President Gerald Ford outside a Sacramento, California, hotel. Her pistol fails to fire.

September 22　　A middle-aged woman named Sara Jane Moore fires a pistol at President Gerald Ford in San Francisco, California. Although she is only a few steps away from the President, she is jostled by someone in the press of people at the very moment of the shot, and the bullet misses the president.

October 4　　Four Spanish policemen are killed by the First of October Anti-Fascist Resistance Group (GRAPO) in retaliation for the deaths of four members of the group in police custody.

November 27　　IRA assassins gun down British publisher Ross McWhirter in his London home, soon after he announces a reward for information leading to the apprehension of IRA bombers.

December 4　　The Indonesian embassy in Amsterdam, Holland, is taken over by South Moluccan terrorists.

December 21　　Led by the infamous Carlos "The Jackal," a PFLP force invades a meeting of the Organization of Petroleum Exporting Countries in Vienna, Austria. An OPEC employee, an Iraqi bodyguard, and an Austrian policeman are killed in the incident, and 70 people, including the oil ministers of 11 nations, are held hostage. They are released when OPEC pays a huge ransom, and the terrorists are allowed to fly to Algeria.

December 29　　A bomb goes off in a terminal at New York City's La Guardia Airport. Eleven people are killed and 80 injured. No one claims responsibility for the bombing, and no one is charged with any crime in relation to it.

1976

June 16　　The U.S. ambassador to Lebanon, Francis E. Meloy, is assassinated by agents of the PFLP in Beirut.

June 27　　A combined force of the Baader-Meinhof Gang and the PFLP hijack an Air France airliner and force the crew to fly to Entebbe, Uganda.

All 258 passengers are held hostage for a time before the non-Israelis among them are released.

July 4   An Israeli commando force storms the hijacked Air France airliner at Entebbe Airport in Uganda. All the hijackers, one of the raiders, and three passengers are killed in the assault. The rest of the passengers are freed.

July 12   The British ambassador to the Irish Republic is killed and his car destroyed by an IRA landmine near Dublin.

August 11   Working together, the Japanese Red Army and the PFLP kill four people and wound 20 more in the airport terminal at Istanbul, Turkey.

September 10   Croatian terrorists hijack an American airliner flying from New York to Paris, France. All of the passengers are released unharmed.

September 21   Exiled Chilean Foreign Minister Orlando Letelier is killed when his car explodes in Washington, D.C. Chilean secret service agents, perhaps working with the approval of an American intelligence agency, are believed to be responsible.

September 26   Supported by Iraq, the Abu Nidal Organization (ANO) takes over the Semiramis Hotel in Damascus, Syria.

October 10   The Cuban exile group El Condor blows up a Cuban Airlines jet as it leaves Barbados, killing 73 people.

October 11   The ANO launches twin attacks on the Syrian embassies in Islamabad, Pakistan, and Rome, Italy.

November 17   The ANO attacks the Intercontinental Hotel in Amman, Jordan.

December 13   The ANO attempts to take over the Syrian Embassy in Istanbul, Turkey, and to assassinate the Syrian foreign minister in Damascus, Syria. Both attempts fail.

1977

March 9   In an elaborate three-pronged attack, 12 Hanafi Muslims wielding shotguns and machetes seize hostages in three buildings in Washington, D.C. One hundred and twenty captives are taken at the B'nai B'rith Center, 15 at the District Building, and 12 at the Islamic Center. The terrorists' declared purpose is to end the public exhibition of a motion picture about Mohammad that they consider sacrilegious, and to force the American government to turn over to them five Black Muslims who have been convicted of killing Hanafis. During the siege, which goes on for 39 hours, a local radio reporter is shot to death, and dozens of other people (including the city's future mayor, Marion Barry) are injured, some of them devastatingly.

March 16   The Lebanese Druze leader Kamal Jumblatt is assassinated. Syrian Secret Service operatives are suspected.

| October 25 | ANO makes a second attempt to assassinate the foreign minister of Syria, this time in Abu Dhabi. The Syrian escapes, but the minister of state for foreign affairs of the United Arab Emirates is killed in the attack. |

1978

January 4	The PLO's representative in London is assassinated by the ANO.
February 18	The prominent Egyptian writer Youssef al-Seba'i is killed when the ANO attacks the conference of the Organization for Solidarity with the Peoples of Africa, Asia, and Latin America in Cyprus.
March 16	The Red Brigades kidnap ex-premier Aldo Moro of Italy. Fifty-five days later they kill him and dump his body in the middle of Rome.
March	Palestinian terrorists attack a bus on a highway near the Israeli capital of Tel Aviv. More than 30 Israelis are killed and twice that many injured.
May 25	A package with a Northwestern University return address is found in a parking lot at the University of Illinois-Chicago. Taken to the Northwestern campus in nearby Evanston, the package explodes. One person is injured, becoming the first victim of the so-called Unabomber.
June 15	The PLO representative in Kuwait is murdered by agents of the ANO.
June 28	The Lebanese villages of Ka'a, Ras Baalbeck, and Jdeidet El Fakaha are attacked by gunmen believed to be associated with a Syrian intelligence service. Several people are kidnapped, some of whom later are found dead. Others have never been found.
August 3	The PLO representative in Paris, France, and his assistant are murdered by agents of the ANO.
August 5	The ANO attacks the PLO offices in Islamabad, Pakistan.

1979

July 17	A Carabinieri colonel is assassinated by the Red Brigades in Rome.
August 27	The IRA kills 18 British soldiers with two remote-controlled bombs near Warrenpoint, Northern Ireland.
November 4	Outraged that the United States is harboring the hated ex-Shah of Iran, Iranian students take over the U.S. Embassy in Teheran, Iran. The Iranian government of Ayatollah Khomeini backs the students, who hold more than 50 Americans hostage for over a year.
November 20	Some 200 Islamic terrorists invade the Grand Mosque at Mecca, Saudi Arabia, effectively abducting hundreds of pilgrims worship-

ping there. Saudi and French forces eventually retake the shrine after a battle in which an estimated 250 people are killed and 600 injured.

December 12 The Red Brigades seize a business school in Turin, Italy, taking some 200 students and teachers captive. They tie up 10 of them and shoot them in the legs.

December 15 Three policemen are shot to death by members of the Red Brigades in Milan, Italy.

1980

January 26 The Red Brigades carry out a series of firebombings in Milan, Italy. Twelve different targets are struck in less than two hours, including a police barracks and the headquarters of the Christian Democratic Party.

February 1 Basque terrorists kill six Spanish policemen near Bilboa, Spain.

February 27 Colombian terrorists take over the Dominican Republic Embassy in Bogota, Colombia, holding 54 occupants of the embassy hostage.

March 14 Former U.S. Congressman Allard Lowenstein is shot and killed in his New York office by Dennis Sweeney, a former Lowenstein protégé and ally from the civil rights movement, who has come to see his mentor as a representative of the establishment.

March 24 Right-wing assassins gun down Archbishop Oscar Romero while he celebrates a mass in the cathedral in San Salvador, El Salvador.

April 14 A would-be assassin hurls a knife at India's Prime Minister Indira Gandhi in New Delhi.

April 30 Six anti-government Iranian terrorists seize the Iranian embassy in London, England. After six days, British troops storm the embassy. Five terrorists and two hostages are killed, and two other hostages injured in the rescue action.

May 29 One-time civil rights activist Vernon Jordan is shot in the back and seriously wounded, presumably by a white racist, in Fort Wayne, Indiana.

June 1 An African National Congress (ANC) bomb causes several million dollars worth of damage to a coal-to-liquid plant in South Africa.

July 17 In Paris, anti-Shah Iranians attempt to assassinate the ex–prime minister of Iran, Shahpour Bakhtiar. Two people are killed in the attack, but Bakhtiar escapes. Five terrorists are captured.

July 21 Lebanese Christian militiamen shoot down a hot-air balloon in which Palestinian terrorists are attempting to cross into Israeli territory.

July 22 The head of the Lebanese union of editors is assassinated. Syrian intelligence services are believed to be responsible.

August 1	A bomb kills 85 people and injures an estimated 300 more at a railway station in Bologna, Italy. Fascists, believed to be associated with elements in the Italian police or intelligence agencies, are believed to be responsible.
October 3	Palestinian terrorists bomb a synagogue in Paris, killing four people and injuring 12 others.
October 6	A mail bomb, sent by the American radical environmentalist known as the Unabomber, injures the president of the United Airlines Company.
October 13	Turkish security forces storm a hijacked Turkish Airlines plane on the ground in eastern Turkey. More than 150 hostages are freed in the rescue; four hijackers and one passenger are killed.
October 26	A young man with neo-Nazi ties detonates a bomb at the famous Octoberfest beer festival in Munich, West Germany. Thirteen people are killed and more than 70 wounded.

1981

January 21	The IRA guns down a former speaker of the Northern Ireland parliament and his son.
March 3	Olaf Palme, the highly respected prime minister of Sweden, is shot to death leaving a movie theater in Stockholm, Sweden.
April 16	A hot-air balloon carrying Palestinian terrorists is shot down by Israeli defense forces.
May 1	The president of the Austrian-Israeli Friendship Association is assassinated by the ANO in Vienna, Austria.
May 13	The supreme pontiff of the Roman Catholic Church, Pope John Paul II, is shot in the midriff and seriously injured in an assassination attempt in St. Peter's Square. The shooter, Memhet Ali Agca, is an agent of the Turkish terrorist organization, the Gray Wolves. He apparently has extensive connections both to Middle Eastern terrorists and to at least one eastern-bloc intelligence agency.
June 1	The PLO representative in Brussels, Belgium becomes the latest in a series of PLO representatives assassinated by the ANO.
August 29	The ANO attacks a synagogue in Vienna, Austria. Two Jewish worshippers are killed; 19 people, including two children and two Austrian policemen, are injured.
August 31	Twenty people are wounded by a Red Army Faction bomb detonated in a U.S. Air Force base parking lot at Ramstein, West Germany.
September 3	The French ambassador to Lebanon is assassinated, allegedly by agents of the Syrian government.

September 24	A small force of the Armenian Secret Army for the Liberation of Armenia (ASALA) seizes control of the Turkish Embassy in Paris and holds it for several days.
October 6	While reviewing a military parade at Cairo, President Anwar Sadat of Egypt, who had recently concluded a peace agreement with Israel, is gunned down by members of his own troops connected to the Egyptian Islamic Jihad. Seven others are also killed in the attack, and almost 30 wounded.
October 10	Two civilians are killed and 40 people injured by an IRA bomb near the Chelsea Army Barracks at London, England.
October 17	An IRA bomb injures British Lt.-Gen. Sir Steuart Pringle in London.
December 4	The bodies of three American nuns and a lay missionary are found near San Salvador, in El Salvador. They were murdered by a right-wing death squad.
December 5	Kamal Jemblatt, the Druze president-elect of Lebanon, is assassinated.

1982

June 3	The Israeli ambassador to England, Shlomo Argov, is wounded in a failed assassination attempt by ANO gunmen. The incident is used as the pretext for an Israeli invasion of Lebanon.
July 2	A University of California-Berkeley professor is injured by a letter bomb sent by the Unabomber.
July 20	The IRA detonates bombs in two London parks. Four soldiers and several Household Cavalry horses are killed by the explosion in Hyde Park, and seven more soldiers are killed by the bomb that goes off in Regent's Park two hours later. Several bystanders are wounded in the attacks.
August 22	Six people are killed in an Action Direct assault on the Goldengerg restaurant in Paris.
August 26	Two ANO assassination attempts—one on a United Arab Emirates consul in India and the other on a Kuwaiti diplomat in Karachi, Pakistan—fail.
September 14	Bashir Gemayel, the 34-year-old president-elect of Lebanon, is killed by a bomb that destroys the headquarters of the Christian Phalange in Beirut.
September 16	In revenge for the assassination of Bashir Gemayel, Christian Phalange militia move into two Palestinian camps near Beirut and massacre hundreds of residents while Israeli troops stand by and do nothing to stop them.

November 11	Seventy-five Israeli soldiers and 15 Palestinian and Lebanese prisoners are killed when a suicide bombers blows himself up at the Israeli military headquarters at Tyre, Lebanon.
December 6	An IRA bomb kills 17 people and injures 60 more at a bar in Ballykelly, Northern Ireland.
December 12	An anti-nuclear activist who has taken eight tourists hostage at the Washington Monument, in Washington, D.C., is shot to death by a police sniper.

1983

April 8	The Revolutionary Armed Forces of Colombia (FARC) kidnap a U.S. citizen and hold him for ransom.
April 18	Sixty-three people, including 17 Americans, are killed when a car bomb destroys the U.S. Embassy in Beirut, Lebanon. A Shiite Muslim group claims responsibility.
May 25	The left-wing Farabundo Marti National Liberation Front kills a U.S. Navy officer in El Salvador.
June 3	The ANO unsuccessfully attempts to assassinate the Israeli ambassador to the United Kingdom.
September 16	A Kuwaiti diplomat is murdered by the ANO in Madrid, Spain.
September 23	An Omani airliner is destroyed by a bomb en route from Karachi, Pakistan, to Abu Zabi in the United Arab Emirates. All 111 people on board are killed. Responsibility for the outrage is not clear.
October 8	Twenty-one people are killed and 48 wounded in a bomb attack on a delegation of South Koreans in Rangoon, Burma. Agents of the North Korean government are suspected.
October 23	Two hundred forty-one U.S. Marines are killed and more than 100 injured when a suicide bomber smashes through the main gate of the U.S. Marine headquarters in Beirut in a truck loaded with compressed-gas-enhanced explosives. A short time later on the same day, an explosion kills 58 soldiers at a French paratroop base in Beirut. The non-Lebanese Islamic Jihad claims responsibility.
November 15	A U.S. Navy officer is shot to death in his car in Athens, Greece. November 17 is suspected.
December 2	Basque terrorists bomb eight American facilities in Spain, in protest against U.S. involvement in Central America.
December 12	A truck bomb kills four people and inures more than 60 at the U.S. Embassy annex in Kuwait. Islamic Jihad claims responsibility.
December 16	Five people are killed and 91 are injured when the Provisional IRA bombs the famous Harrods Department store in London, England.

1984

March 16   A U.S. political officer named William Buckley is seized by agents of Islamic Jihad in Beirut, Lebanon. Buckley, who is in reality a CIA agent, is tortured and later killed.

April 12   A bomb explodes in a restaurant at the U.S. Air Force base near Torrejon, Spain, killing 18 U.S. servicemen and wounding 83 others. Hezbollah claims responsibility.

June 5   The Golden Temple at Amristar, India, is seized by Sikh terrorists. One hundred people are killed when Indian forces storm the sacred temple.

June 18   A Denver radio talk show host named Alan Berg is shot to death in his own driveway by members of a white supremacist group known as the Order, or the Silent Brotherhood. Acerbic and combative, Berg, who is himself a Jew, had often attacked the white supremacists for their anti-Semitism.

September 20   Twenty-three people are killed when an explosives-laden van explodes in the U.S. embassy compound in Beirut, Lebanon. Islamic Jihad claims responsibility, but Hezbollah is also suspected.

October 12   Two explosions rip through the Grand Hotel at Brighton, England, where British Prime Minister Margaret Thatcher and her cabinet members are staying during the annual Conservative Party conference. Although Thatcher and all of her ministers survive, five other people are killed.

October 31   Prime Minister Indira Gandhi, who has cracked down on Sikh insurgents in India, is gunned down by Sikh members of her own security guard.

December 4   A Kuwaiti airliner is hijacked en route to Pakistan and forced to fly to Teheran, Iran. The hijackers kill two airline officials and torture two passengers before the Iranian military storms the plane five days later.

1985

February 7   Narco-terrorists kidnap a U.S. Drug Enforcement Administration operative and his pilot in Mexico. The two captives are tortured and then killed.

February 28   An IRA mortar attack on a Royal Ulster Constabulary (police) base in Newry, Northern Ireland, kills nine RUC members.

March 8   An alleged CIA-sponsored attempt to kill a terrorist leader goes awry in Beirut, Lebanon. The car bomb kills 80 people and injures 200 others, but the target of the attack escapes.

April 12   A bomb explodes at a restaurant frequented by Americans in Madrid, Spain. Eighteen people, none of them Americans, are killed, and more than 80 others, only 15 of them Americans, are injured. Islamic Jihad claims responsibility.

June 6   Hezbollah hijackers seize a TWA airliner shortly after it takes off from Rome. The plane is forced to fly, first to Beirut, Lebanon, and then back and forth between Algiers and Lebanon. A U.S. Navy diver aboard the plane is killed by the hijackers before the remaining passengers are released in return for the release of more than 400 Palestinian and Lebanese prisoners.

June 19   A machine-gun attack on an outdoor cafe in San Salvador, El Salvador, kills 13 people, including six Americans.

August 8   Two people are killed and 20 injured when a Volkswagen car blows up at the U.S. Rhein-Main airbase at Frankfurt, West Germany. Both the Red Army Faction and the French Action Direct claim responsibility.

October 7   Four members of the PLO hijack the Italian cruise ship *Achille Lauro* in the Mediterranean Sea. They kill two of the passengers, one of whom is an elderly and disabled American of Jewish descent.

November 6   The Palace of Justice in Bogota, Colombia, is raided by guerillas of the April 19 Movement, or M-19. The Army lays siege to the building, and 100 people die in the resulting battle, including the president of the Supreme Court of Colombia and five other Justices, as well as all the M-19 guerillas involved in the operation.

November 23   An Egyptian airliner is hijacked and forced to land at Malta. The hijackers kill one American passenger, then, when Egyptian commandos rush the plane, the hijackers explode several hand grenades, killing 58 passengers and six crew members.

December 11   A computer-rental–store-owner named Hugh Scrutton, who is killed by a bomb outside his place of business in Sacramento, California, becomes the first fatality attributed to the so-called Unabomber.

December 27   The ANO launches twin attacks on Israeli airline counters at airports in Rome and Vienna. Sixteen people are killed and many more injured. On the same day, 22 people are killed at the Karachi airport in an ANO attempt to hijack a Pan-Am plane.

1986

April 2   A bomb explodes on a TWA plane en route from Rome to Athens, blowing a hole in the side of the aircraft through which four passengers are sucked out. A group calling itself the Arab Revolutionary Cell claims responsibility.

April 5   A bomb goes off in the La Belle discotheque in West Berlin, killing several customers, including two off-duty U.S. servicemen.

September 6   Twenty-three worshippers are killed when two members of ANO attack the Neve Shalom synagogue in Istanbul, Turkey.

September 14	A bomb kills five people and injures 29 more at Kimpo Airport in Seoul, South Korea. North Korean agents are believed to be responsible.

1987

April 24	A Greek Air Force bus transporting U.S. servicemen is damaged by a November 17 bomb near Athens, Greece. Sixteen of the Americans are injured in the attack.
November 29	A bomb, believed to have been placed by North Korean agents, downs a South Korean airliner over the Indian Ocean.

1988

February 17	A U.S. Marine lieutenant colonel serving with the United Nations Truce Supervisory Organization is kidnapped and later killed by the Hezbollah in Lebanon.
March 6	Two men and a woman belonging to the IRA are shot to death on a street in Gibraltar by a squad of British undercover agents. The British government claims that the victims were on their way to plant a car bomb.
April 14	An American sailor is killed by a car bomb outside a USO (United Service Organization) club in Naples. The Organization of Jihad Brigades claims responsibility.
June 28	A car bomb kills the defense attaché of the U.S. embassy in Athens, Greece.
December 21	A bomb destroys an airliner bound from London to New York as it flies over Lockerbie, Scotland. All 259 people aboard are killed, along with 11 on the ground. Libyan agents are suspected.

1989

April 12	A bomb kills one young woman and injures 30 bystanders near a Royal Ulster Constabulary building in the seaside town of Warrenpoint, Northern Ireland. The IRA, which admits planting the explosive, claims that it had intended to warn civilians to leave the area before the explosion, but that the bomb went off 15 minutes early.
April 21	An American colonel is assassinated by agents of the New People's Army (NPA) in Manila, the Philippines.
November 22	The president-elect of Lebanon, Rene Moawad, is killed by a bomb that explodes near his motorcade. Syrian agents are believed to be responsible.

November 24	Twenty-four civilians are killed when PKK forces attack a village in the Hakkari district of Turkey.
November 30	The chairman of the German National Bank is assassinated by the Red Army Faction in Frankfurt, Germany.

1991

January 15	The Tupac Amaru Revolutionary Movement bombs the U.S. embassy in Lima, Peru.
January 18–19	Bombs are discovered at the home of the U.S. ambassador to Indonesia and at the U.S. Information Service library in Manila, the Philippines. Iraqi government agents are suspected.
May 13	Two members of the U.S. Air Force are killed by NPA assassins near the Clark Air Force Base in the Philippines.
May 21	Ex–prime minister of India Rajiv Gandhi is killed by an LTTE bomb at an election rally in Madras, India.
June 8	Assassins slit the throat of ex-Iranian Prime Minister Shahpour Bakhtiar at his home near Paris. Bakhatiar's personal secretary is also killed in the attack.
November 5	The militant Jewish extremist Meir Kahane is assassinated in New York City by an Islamist follower of the "blind Sheik," Omar abdel Rahman.
December 25	Eleven people are killed and 18 injured by a PKK bomb at the Cetinkaya department store in Istanbul, Turkey.

1992

February 5	Five Catholics are killed in Northern Ireland by the unionist Ulster Defence Association.
March 17	The Israeli embassy in Buenos Aires, Argentina, is car bombed. Twenty-nine people are killed and more than 250 injured. Islamic Jihad claims responsibility.
June 22	PKK invaders kill seven children, an elderly woman, and two other residents in a village in Batman Province, Turkey.
June 29	Agents of the PKK gun down nine passengers of a minibus near the Turkish village of Yolbasti.
October 1	The PKK attacks the village of Cevizdali in Turkey, killing 40 residents and injuring 40 more.
October 11	PKK forces halt a minibus on a Turkish road and gun down the passengers, 19 of whom are killed, and six injured.

1993

January 25   Two Central Intelligence Agency employees are shot to death by an anti-American Pakistani outside the CIA's complex at Langley, Virginia.

January 31   Three American missionaries are kidnapped by FARC in Colombia.

February 26   Followers of Sheik Omar Abdel Rahman set off a large quantity of explosives in the parking basement at the World Trade Center in New York City. Six people are killed and roughly 1,000 others are injured.

March 13   Two hundred-fifty-seven people are killed and more than 1,000 injured by simultaneous explosions in Bombay, India. The carefully coordinated attacks are carried out by Islamic extremists in retaliation for the destruction of an historic mosque by fundamentalist Hindus the year before.

April 14   While on a trip to Kuwait, U.S. President George Bush is the target of a pre-empted assassination attempt, allegedly by agents of the Iraqi intelligence service.

May 24   PKK guerillas halt a bus carrying unarmed recruits for the Turkish army and kill all 36 recruits aboard.

June 16   Six people, four of them children, are murdered by PKK forces in a village in the province of Mardin, Turkey.

June 24   Eight Islamists of five different nationalities are arrested in New York City and charged with plotting a wide range of terrorist attacks, including the bombing of the United Nations headquarters, a U.S. federal office building, and two tunnels leading into New York from New Jersey, as well as assassinations of the U.N. secretary general, a senator, and the president of Egypt.

July 5   The PKK murders 30 people and burns 57 houses in the Erzincan province of Turkey.

August 4   The PKK halts six minibuses in the Mutki district of the Turkish province of Bitlis, killing 19 people and injuring 13 more. On the same day, the PKK raids the Konakbasi settlement in Bongol province, killing 11 people, eight of whom are children and another an elderly man.

September 17   PKK raiders kill six people at a teachers' club in Dayarbakir, Turkey.

October 12   Twenty-two women and children are killed in a PKK attack on a village in the Derince province of Turkey.

October 25   PKK forces kill 38 people in Erzurum, Turkey.

October 30   The Ulster Freedom Fighters (UFF) of the Ulster Defence Association kill six Catholics and one Protestant in Northern Ireland.

December 6   A mob of Hindu extremists destroys the Muslim mosque at Ayodhya in the Uttar Pradesh state of India, believed by Hindus to be the birthplace of the god Ram. The destruction sets off an extended wave of violence between Hindus and Muslims in which more than 1,000 Indians die.

| December 12 | Thirteen people are murdered by the PKK in Agackonak, Turkey. |

1994

January 1	PKK forces murder eight passengers of a minibus on the road from Diyarkakir to Elazig, Turkey.
January 10	A bomb is detonated near the NATO Defense College in Rome. The Combatant Communist Nuclei, apparently a division of the Red Brigades, claims responsibility.
January 14	An American family is kidnapped in Colombia. The kidnappers are believed to be members of the National Liberation Army (ELN).
January 22	Twenty people, including nine women and six children, are killed in PKK raids on two different villages in the Mardin province of Turkey.
January 29	A diplomat from Jordan is gunned down in Beirut, Lebanon.
February 2	A number of bombs go off in railway cars in the station at Baku, Azerbaizan. Five people are killed.
February 3	No one is killed, but a driver is badly wounded when a bomb goes off below the car of a Spanish military attaché in Rome.
	Half an hour after a warning phone call from the Revolutionary People's Struggle (ELA), a bomb explodes at a German culture center in Athens, Greece.
February 12	Terrorist Dominic ("Mad Dog") McGlinchey, Chief of Staff for the Irish National Liberation Army (INLA) an extreme left-wing offshoot of the IRA, is gunned down by three of his former associates from the INLA.
February 19	Islamic Group gunmen attack a train in Asyut, Egypt, wounding several foreign passengers and two Egyptians.
February 23	An explosion on a train at Asyut, Egypt, wounds six foreigners and five Egyptians. The Islamic Group claims responsibility.
February 26	Baruch Goldstein, a Jewish extremist and Kach supporter from the United States, machine-guns worshippers at a mosque in the West Bank town of Hebron. He kills 29 people and injures as many as 150 more.
February	A bomb at a Maronite Church in Zuq Mikha'il, Lebanon, kills 11 people and injures 59 others. Lebanese forces are believed responsible.
March 4	Members of the Islamic Group fire on a cruise ship in the Nile River, injuring a German passenger.

March 9–13	The Provisional Irish Republican Army (Provos) launches three mortar attacks on London's Heathrow Airport. The mortars fail to explode.
March 27	A bomb, set by the PKK, injures three foreign tourists on the grounds of the famous Saint Sophia Mosque and Museum at Istanbul, Turkey.
April 1	Members of the Revolutionary Armed Forces of Colombia (FARC) kidnap an American citizen in Colombia.
April 2	A bomb at the famed IC Bedesten bazaar in Istanbul, Turkey, kills two people and wounds 17. The PKK claims responsibility.
April 6	A Hamas car bomb explodes near an Israeli bus in the center of Afula, Israel, killing eight people.
April 13	A Hamas suicide bomber kills himself and four Israelis at the Hadera bus station.
April 27	Sixteen people, including a Russian diplomat, are injured by a car bomb at the Jan Smuts Airport in Johannesburg, South Africa. White separatists are suspected.
April	An off-duty flight engineer disables the crew of a freshly fuelled Federal Express cargo jet and attempts to fly it into the Memphis International Airport. The attempt is thwarted when the crew manage to overcome their injuries sufficiently to retake control of the plane.
May 8	Members of the Armed Islamic Group (GIA) gun down two French priests in the Casbah neighborhood of Algiers.
May 29	An Iranian dissident is shot to death in his car in Ghale-bieh, Iraq. No one claims responsibility.
June 18	Six people, including an 87-year-old man, are killed when the UVF (Ulster Volunteer Force) attacks a pub in Loughinisland, Ireland.
June 19	PKK forces slaughter the mother and five minor siblings of a former member of the Kurdish terrorist group.
June 21–22	Several bombs explode in tourist areas in Turkey, killing at least one foreign tourist and injuring several others. The PKK claims responsibility.
June 27	Seven people are killed and 150 injured when sarin nerve gas is released in an apparent assassination attempt on a judge by the Amu Shinrikyo (Supreme Truth) cult in the Kaichi Heights neighborhood of Matsumoto, Japan.
July 4	A branch of the November 17 group claims responsibility for the assassination of a Turkish diplomat gunned down in his car in Athens, Greece.
July 17	Five people are injured by a car bomb at a building used by several Jewish organizations in London.
July 18	A car bomb outside the Israeli-Argentine Mutual Association in Buenos Aires, Argentina, brings down a seven-story building, killing

at least 87 people and injuring more than 100. The Iranian government is suspected.

July 19   A commuter airliner is blown up in Panama, killing 21 people including three U.S. citizens. The source of the bomb is unknown.

July 20   PKK rebels stop vehicles along a Turkish road and kill 11 of the occupants.

July 26   A massive bomb at a Jewish cultural center in Argentina kills nearly 100 people. The Lebanese Hezbollah is believed responsible.

Fourteen people are injured when a car bomb explodes outside the Israeli embassy in London.

July 27   A car bomb explodes outside a building used by Jewish organizations in London. Five people are injured.

August 3   Armed Islamic Group (AIG) rebels attack a French compound in Algiers, Algeria, killing five French embassy employees and injuring another.

August 8   Kurdish separatist rebels abduct two Finns in the Kurdish region of Turkey, claiming that the foreigners have entered "Kudistan" without visas.

August 10   Eleven people, including three children, are killed when the PKK fires on a bus travelling along a Turkish road. Eight other civilians are injured.

August 12   A PKK bomb kills a Roumanian counselor official at the Topkapi Bus Terminal in Istanbul.

August 26   Four Portuguese nuns and a priest are abducted in Angola, apparently by members of the National Union for the Total Independence of Angola (UNITA).

August 27   The Moro Islamic Liberation Front (MILF) kidnaps 30 Filipinos and seven South Koreans in the Philippines.

October 18   AIG forces attack an oil base in Algeria, killing two European workers.

October 19   A suicide bombing attack kills 22 people in Tel Aviv, Israel. It is similar to recent attacks by Hamas.

November 2   Hani Abed, a Palestinian leader of Islamic Jihad, is killed by car bomb planted by Israeli Mossad agents.

November 11   In retaliation for the assassination of Hani Abed, a Palestinian suicide bomber on a bicycle kills three Israeli soldiers at the Netzarim Junction in the Gaza strip.

December 26   French antiterrorist forces storm an Air France airliner on the ground at Marseilles, France. The four AIG hijackers, who had killed three of their hostages since the plane was originally hijacked in Algeria two days before, are killed in the attack.

December 27   The AIG kill four Catholic priests in Algeria.

1995

January 1	The PKK kill 19 people, most of them women and children, in a village in Diyarbakir, Turkey.
January	The suicide car bombing of a police facility in Algiers, Algeria, kills more than 40 people, including the GIA terrorist.
January 12	Gunmen, believed to be members of the Islamic Group attack a passenger train in Egypt. Two Argentine tourists and four other passengers are injured.
January 15	Khmer Rouge guerillas open fire on a tourist convoy in Cambodia, killing a tour guide and a U.S. tourist.
January 22	Two Islamic Jihad bombs kill 18 Israeli soldiers and one civilian at a junction near Netanya, Israel.
January 25	The Revolutionary United Front takes 100 people captive at a mission in Sierra Leone.
February 28	An Egyptian citizen blows himself up at the consular department of Russian Embassy in Morocco. Moroccan investigators conclude that the man acted in protest against Russia's actions in Chechnya.
March 8	Gunmen fire on a U.S. Consulate van in Karachi, Pakistan. Two U.S. diplomats are killed and one wounded. No group claims responsibility.
March 20	Agents of the *Aum Shinrikyo* (Supreme Truth) cult release sarin nerve gas in a subway station in downtown Tokyo. Twelve people are killed and thousands sickened by the noxious gas.
April 9	A van carrying explosives plows into a bus in the Gaza strip, killing seven Israelis and one American and injuring 40 others. Responsibility is claimed by the Shaqaqi Faction of the Palestinian Islamic Jihad.
April 19	A rented truck bomb loaded with explosives destroys the Alfred P. Murrah Federal Building in Oklahoma City, killing 168 people and injuring more than 500.
April 2	One man is killed and a woman injured when a bomb goes off outside the Presidential Palace in Guatemala City. The bomb was apparently intended for U.N. Secretary-General Boutros Boutros-Ghali, who is visiting the city. No group claims responsibility, although the army blames the rebel Guatemalan National Revolutionary Unity (URNG) organization.
April 5	PKK forces slaughter seven people in a pasture in the Hatay province of Turkey.
April 19	A Colombian chauffer is killed and two Italian oil workers kidnapped by members of the National Liberation Army near Barrancabermeja, Colombia.
April 22	Two Turkish citizens are gunned down by Kurdish rebels in The Hague in Holland.

A scene of the devastation following the Oklahoma City bombing, April 26, 1995. Courtesy of FEMA News Photo.

April 24	The president of the California Forestry Association, Gilbert Murray, is killed when a package he is opening explodes at the headquarters of the Association. The Unabomber is assumed to be responsible.
April 29	Islamists kill a foreign businessman near Chisimayu, Somalia.
April	A car bomb set by Maoist Shining Path (Sendero Luminoso) guerillas explodes outside a luxury hotel in Lima, Peru. Four people are killed and scores are injured by the blast.
May 5	Five workers (two Frenchmen, a Briton, a Canadian, and a Tunisian) are killed when GIA commandos launch an attack on a gas pipeline in Algeria.
May 23	Three Lebanese businessmen are kidnapped by members of the Revolutionary United Front (RUF) in a heavily Lebanese area of Sierra Leone.
May 24	A Shining Path car bomb kills four people in front of hotel in suburb of Lima, Peru.
June 26	Visiting Addis Ababa for a meeting of the Organization of African States, Egypt's President Hosni Mubarak is the object of a failed assassination attempt by the Islamic Group (IG). Although Mubarak is unharmed, the Palestinian ambassador to Ethiopia is killed, along with two Ethiopian guards, and two of the attackers. It is the first time the IG is known to have acted outside the borders of Egypt.

June 19	Two U.S. missionaries are murdered by Revolutionary Armed Forces of Colombia (FARC) during a surprise confrontation with the Colombian army. The guerrillas had kidnapped the pair in January 1994.
July	Al-Faran rebels abduct two Europeans in Indian Kashmir.
July 11	A co-founder of the Algerian Islamic Salvation Front and his bodyguard are assassinated in a mosque in Paris, apparently by a member or members of another Algerian Islamist group.
July 25	Seven people are killed and 86 injured when a nail-filled bomb explodes aboard a train entering the St. Michel Metro station in Paris. The bombing is believed to be the work of the AIG.
August 21	A bomb attack on a bus in the Ramat Eshkol neighborhood of Jerusalem kills six people, including an American woman, and wounds more than a hundred passengers and passersby. Hamas claims responsibility.
September 1	A U.S. businessman and his Colombian partner are kidnapped for ransom in Cali, Colombia.
September 2	An Italian citizen is gunned down in Oran, Algiera. The GIA is suspected.
September 3	Two foreign nuns (one French, one Maltese) are shot to death in Algiers. The GIA is suspected.
September 5	Arsonists, presumed to be members of the PKK, set fire to a Turk-owned bistro in Luebeck, Germany, killing two people and wounding 20 more. A Turk-owned nightclub in Freital, Germany, is torched on the same day.
September 7	A freelance photographer is killed and two people are wounded when a parcel bomb explodes at the BBC office in Srinagar, Kashmir, India.
September 13	The U.S. embassy in Moscow, Russia, is hit by a rocket-launched grenade, fired by Serbs or Serb sympathizers.
October 20	A car bomb in Rijeka, Croatia, kills the driver and injures 29 Croatians. The IG claims that the bombing was carried out in retaliation for the Croatian government's arrest of one of their number.
October 26	Palestinian leader Dr. Fathi Shiqaqi is shot down on a street outside his hotel in Malta, presumably by agents of the Israeli Mossad.
October 27	Two people are killed and 32 abducted by the National Union for the Total Independence of Angola (UNITA) forces in Lunda Norte, Angola.
November 4	Israeli Prime Minister Yitzhak Rabin is assassinated while attending a peace rally in Tel Aviv. The assassin is an Israeli university student who belongs to the previously little-known EYAL (or Fighting Jewish Organization), which opposes Rabin's efforts to achieve peace with the Palestinians.
November 13	A bomb explodes in a vehicle parked outside the headquarters of an American military-operated Saudi Arabian National Guard office in

Riyadh, Saudi Arabia. The attack, which is motivated by opposition to the American presence in Saudi Arabia, kills seven people and injures 42 others. Five of the dead are Americans participating in a military training mission. The Islamic Movement of Change claims responsibility.

A representative of the Egyptian government is gunned down in Geneva, Switzerland. Responsibility for the killing is claimed by the International Justice Group.

November 19   A bomb-laden vehicle is driven into the compound of the Egyptian Embassy in Islamabad, Pakistan. The blast kills 16 people and injures 60 more, destroys the Egyptian Embassy, and causes damage to the Canadian High Commission, the Japanese and Indonesian Embassies, and other buildings, some as far as a quarter of a mile away. Several Islamic groups claim responsibility.

November 21   A bomb detonated near a restaurant in the Indian city of New Delhi, injures 22 people, including four foreigners. Both Kashmiri Islamic rebels and Sikh separatists claim responsibility.

November   Two trains frequented by tourists in northern Egypt are fired on by members of the IG in separate attacks. Two Europeans and 10 Egyptians are injured in the attacks, which are part of a long campaign of attacks on foreigners, intended primarily to damage Egypt's lucrative tourist industry.

Two suicide bombers belonging to the Liberation Tigers of Tamil Eelam (LTTE) blow themselves up at an army headquarters in Colombo, Sri Lanka. Three members of the security forces and 14 civilians are killed, and almost 60 are injured in the explosions.

December 16   Bombs set by the Basque Fatherland and Liberty (ETA) explode in different locations at a Valencia, Spain, department store, killing one and injuring eight others.

December 27   Abu Sayaaf rebels abduct 16 people, six of whom are U.S. citizens, at Lake Sebu, Mindanao, in the Philippines.

1996

January 8   Free Papua Movement (FPM) guerillas seize 26 people in a nature preserve in the Irian Jaya Province of Indonesia.

January 9   Chechen rebels take at least 2,000 hostages at a hospital in the town of Kizlyar in southern Russia. Most of the hostages are soon released, but the rebels flee Kizlyar with some 100 others. They are later trapped in another village, where Russian troops lay siege to them. At least 78 people are killed.

January 16   A Russia-bound ferry is hijacked by Chechen rebels at the Turkish port of Trezibond in the Black Sea. The hijackers threaten to kill the roughly two hundred passengers and crew members unless Russia abandons its pursuit of the Kizlyar rebels in Chechnya. The crisis ends peacefully four days later when the hijackers release the hostages unharmed.

January 31　A massive truck-bomb is crashed into the Central Bank in Colombo, Sri Lanka, killing 90 people and injuring 1,400. The LTTE claims responsibility.

February 9　An IRA bomb kills two people and injures over one hundred in London, England.

February 16　A U.S. citizen is kidnapped by the National Liberation Army (ELN) in Colombia.

February 23　A 69-year-old Palestinian teacher opens fire with a semi-automatic handgun on the observation deck of the Empire State Building, killing one tourist and injuring six others. The teacher, who leaves behind a letter accusing the United States of using Israel to persecute Palestinians, then turns the pistol on himself.

February 26　A suicide bomber kills 26 people, including three Americans, in Jerusalem.

March 4　A bombing near the Dizengoff Center, the largest shopping mall in Tel Aviv, Israel, kills 20 people and injures some 75 others. Both Hamas and the Palestine Islamic Jihad claim responsibility.

March 27　The GIA kidnaps seven French monks in Algeria, whom they later decapitate.

June 9　Two Israelis, one of whom has dual U.S. citizenship, are shot to death in a car near Zekharya, Israel. The PFLP is suspected.

June 15　A truck bomb explodes at a Manchester, England, shopping center, injuring 206 persons. The IRA claims responsibility.

June 22　Seven civilians are killed and 11 injured in a PKK attack on a Turkish tourist site.

June 25　A man parks a truck bomb near the U.S. Army housing compound at Al Khobar, Saudi Arabia. The detonation of the estimated 5,000 pounds of explosives kills 19 U.S. soldiers, and injures more than 500 other people, including a reported 240 Americans and 147 Saudis.

July 6　Agents of the Turkish nationalist group the Gray Wolves assassinate Kutlu Adali, a well-known Turkish Cypriot journalist who has been critical of the Turkish government and of Turkey's activities in Cyprus.

July 27　A woman is killed and 11 other people are injured when a pipe bomb explodes in Atlanta during the Olympics.

July 20　An ETA bomb injures 35 people at the Tarragona International Airport at Reus, Spain.

July　More than 70 people are killed and over 400 injured when two bombs explode on a train at the Dehiwala railroad station in Sri Lanka. The LTTE are believed to be responsible. On the same day, 25 people are killed and 50 injured when a female LTTE suicide bomber blows herself up near a convoy carrying a high official of the Sri Lankan government at the Stanley Road in Jaffna. Also on the same day, a force of more than 200 LTTE guerillas attack a Sri Lankan village, destroying several houses and hacking 14 villagers to death.

August 1   The French archbishop of Oran and his chauffeur are killed by a bomb at the archbishop's residence. The AIG is believed to be responsible.

August 17   Six missionaries—three Australians, an American, an Italian, and a Sudanese—are kidnapped by Sudan People's Liberation Army rebels in Mapourdit, Sudan.

August 18   Twelve people are killed and 60 injured by six gunmen at Dacota, near Kot Sher, in Pakistan. The terrorists are believed to be members of an extreme Wahabi Muslim sect.

August   Osama bin Laden issues a public "Declaration of Jihad" (usually defined as "holy war" or "struggle") "against the Americans occupying the land of the two holy mosques" in Saudi Arabia. The declaration calls on his "Muslim brothers in the whole world and especially in the Arabian Peninsula" to "expel the heretics from the Arabian Peninsula" (see chapter 9).

September 5   A federal court jury finds three Islamists guilty of plotting to blow up 12 airliners flying between Asia and the United States.

September 13   Four *Médécine sans frontiers* (Doctors Without Borders) workers, two Iraqis, and a Canadian official with the United Nations High Commissioner for Refugees (UNHCR) official are abducted by Patriotic Union of Kurdistan (PUK) guerillas.

September 30   The PKK kills four teachers in the village of Hantepe, Turkey.

October 1   A South Korean consul is murdered in Vladivostok, Russia. The South Koreans blame the North Korean government, which disclaims any responsibility.

October 26   Ali Boucetta, the mayor of Algiers, Algeria, is shot to death by Islamic militants.

November 12   A firebomb does an alleged $2 million worth of damage to a fur store in Bloomington, Minnesota. A group called the Coalition to Abolish the Fur Trade claims responsibility and says it took care to act when no one would be endangered.

November 19   An attack on the Egyptian Embassy in Islamabad, Pakistan, kills 17 people and injures 60 others. The attackers are suspected to have come from neighboring Afghanistan. Both the IG and the International Justice Group claim responsibility; some officials suspect that Osama bin Laden may be involved.

December 3   A bomb goes off in a car on the Paris Métro as the train arrives in the Port Royal station. Four people are killed, including a Canadian and a Moroccan. Algerian terrorists are suspected.

December 17   A party at the Japanese ambassador's residence in Lima, Peru, is invaded by more than 20 Tupac Amaru guerillas. Hundreds of people, including Peruvian government officials, Japanese businessmen, and American and other foreign diplomats, are taken hostage.

1997

January 4   Windows are shattered at 20 stores and restaurants in Salt Lake City. Animal-rights activists are suspected.

March 11   Almost $1 million of damage is done to the Fur Breeders Agricultural Cooperative in Utah by the explosions of five pipe bombs, spiked with screws and other pieces of metal. A 19-year-old–animal-rights activist is later convicted of the crime.

June 25   A bomb at a building on the U.S. airbase at Daharan, Saudi Arabia, kills 19 American soldiers and wounds 380. It believed to be the work of Islamist terrorists linked to Osama bin Laden and the al-Qaeda network.

July 30   Two Hamas suicide bombers kill 16 shoppers and injure more than 150 in a Jerusalem marketplace.

October 23   Two officials of the Organization of American States and a Colombian human rights official are kidnapped in an ELN effort to call attention to what they consider a flawed election in Colombia.

October   An LTTE truck bomb in the car park at the Galadari Hotel kills 12 people and injures more than 100 in Colombo, Sri Lanka.

November 17   A band of terrorists disguised as policemen go on a rampage in the 3,400 year old Temple of Hatshepsut at Luxor, Egypt, slaughtering at least 58 tourists and wounding 24 others. The casualties include men, women, and children from many countries, including Switzerland, Japan, Germany, and the United Kingdom. The massacre goes on for three-quarters of an hour before the terrorists are themselves killed by Egyptian police. Responsibility for the attack is taken by the IG, which, however, insists that the intention had been to take hostages to be bargained for the release of the IG spiritual leader Sheik Omar Abdel Rahman, who is being held in a federal prison hospital in Missouri after being convicted of masterminding the 1993 World Trade Center bombing.

December 11   Ten people are killed and four injured when a minibus hits a PKK mine in Dargecit, Turkey.

1998

January 25   Eight people are killed and more than 20 injured by an LTTE bomb in Kandy, Sri Lanka.

The bombing of the U.S. embassy in Kenya, August 7, 1998. Courtesy of Federal Bureau of Investigation.

February 24   Osama Bin Laden issues a fatwah approving attacks on U.S. citizens and interests anywhere at any time. Some Muslim experts say Bin Laden is not qualified to issue fatwahs.

March 5   Thirty-two people are killed and 252 wounded by a massive bus bomb at a junction on the Maradana Road in Sri Lanka. The LTTE is responsible.

April 24   A PKK attack on a cafeteria kills four people and injures six in Diyadin, Turkey.

July 10   A PKK bomb explodes at the Misir Carsisi bazaar in Istanbul, Turkey. Seven people are killed, and more than 100 wounded.

July 14   A PKK raid on the village of Cayozu, Turkey, kills four people and injures five.

August 7   In well coordinated attacks, the U.S. embassies in Dar es Salaam, Tanzania, and in Nairobi, Kenya, are bombed by Islamic terrorists.

The Kenya bombing, which takes place in Nairobi's busy downtown area, is especially destructive: more than 200 people, including 12 U.S. citizens, are killed, and a staggering total of 4,000 are injured. Ten people are killed and 77 injured in Dar es Salaam. The bombings are believed to be the work of the Islamic Army for the Liberation of the Holy Sites, a group connected to the Al-Qaeda network.

August 15   A bomb attack kills 29 people in the city centre of Omagh, Country Tyrone, in Northern Ireland. A splinter group that calls itself the "Real IRA," as distinguished from the official IRA, is suspected.

August 25   One person is killed and more than 20 injured by a bomb at a Planet Hollywood restaurant in Capetown, South Africa. No group claims responsibility.

October 18   Five buildings and four ski lifts are destroyed by fire at a resort in Vail, Colorado. Damage is estimated at $12 million. The environmental group Earth Liberation Front (ELF) claims responsibility.

December 28   Sixteen Westerners are kidnapped by the Islamic Army of Aden-Abyan in Yemen. Four of them are killed when the Yemeni authorities launch a rescue attempt.

1999

March 6   FARC claims responsibility for the deaths of three peace advocates found dead in Venezuela.

March 13   Three people are killed and six injured when a bomb explodes at a shopping center in Turkey. A Kurdish group calling itself the "Revenge Falcons of Apo" claims responsibility.

April 9   The November 17 group launches bomb and rocket attacks on several U.S. companies in Athens, Greece.

April 27   The Revolutionary Cells detonates a bomb in an Athens hotel in protest against NATO, of which Greece is a member.

May 20   The long-dormant Red Brigades claim responsibility for the killing of Massimo D'Antona, a labor union official, university professor, and senior adviser to the Italian government, gunned down by two young men outside his home in Rome, Italy.

August 13   Sixty-one people are killed in Colombia by right-wing paramilitary forces combating FARC.

September 4   Sixty-four people are killed by a massive bomb set off by Islamic Chechens at a Russian military barracks in Dagestan.

October 26   A British filmmaker who recently won an award for a TV documentary critical of the ALF, is kidnapped at gunpoint and taken to an unknown location where the letters "A," "L," and "F" are permanently burned into his back with a branding iron. The so-called Justice Department wing of ALF is suspected.

| November 22 | A black passerby is stabbed by attendees at the 30th anniversary celebrations for GUD, an extreme right-wing and white supremacist student organization based in Paris, France. |

2000

January 5	An LTTE suicide bomber kills 13 people and wounds 28 near the office of the prime minister of Sri Lanka.
January 21	In the first terrorist attacks for which the ETA takes responsibility since 1998, two car bombs explode in Madrid, Spain. A military officer is killed and a young girl wounded.
January 30	The presumed successor to the head of the South Lebanon Army is killed by a Hezbollah bomb.
February 2–4	Shining Path guerillas launch a four-day campaign of attacks on buses and trucks in the highlands of Peru.
February 6	An Afghan Ariana airliner is hijacked to London. The hijackers demand the release of an Afghan prisoner in Kabul, but eventually surrender to British authorities.
February 12	FARC and ELN begin a wave of attacks in Colombia, in which 12 people are killed and 16 kidnapped.
February 22	An ETA car bomb kills a popular politician and his bodyguard in Spain.
February 25	Bombs explode on two buses and a ferry in the Philippines, killing 49 and injuring 50. The MILF is blamed.
March 22	The ELN leaves a third of Colombia without electricity by destroying hundreds of pylons.
April 11	Bombs explode at four Mormon temples in Colombia. The ELN claims responsibility.
May 1	In Makeni, Sierra Leone, Revolutionary United Front (RUF) forces attack a facility of the United Nations Assistance Mission in Sierra Leone (UNAMSIL), killing five UN soldiers and abducting 20 mission members.
May 7	The ETA assassinates a journalist in Spain.
May 17	An LTTE bomb kills 29 people and injures 80 others at a Buddhist celebration in Sri Lanka.
June 12	Two Chechen suicide car bombs kill 10 Russian soldiers, and injure 6 others.
June 16	Thirteen people are killed and over 40 injured by a bomb at an Algerian market. The GIA is suspected.
July 18	Two people are killed when UNITA troops abduct 14 clergy members from the Dunge Catholic Mission in Benguela, Angola.

August 2	One hundred and two Hindus are killed in Indian Kashmir, presumably by Islamic militants.
September 28	A Palestinian police officer in the village of Kalkilya in the West Bank kills an Israeli counterpart while on a joint patrol.
October 12	The USS *Cole* is damaged by a bomb while it is in the process of refueling in the Yemeni harbor at Aden. Seventeen members of the crew are killed, and 42 are injured. The bomb is transported alongside the *Cole* in a small fiberglass boat by Islamists associated with Al Qaeda.
November 2	An Islamic Jihad car bomb kills two Israelis in a Jerusalem marketplace.
November 20	An Israeli school bus is bombed in the Gaza Strip, killing two adults and wounding nine.
November 22	A bomb on a bus in Hadera, Israel kills two people and injures more than 60 others.
December 9	A demonstration by expatriate Turks against the Turkish government's use of torture on political prisoners is attacked by a gang of Gray Wolves in Rotterdam, the Netherlands. One of the demonstrators is stabbed to death in the melee and another is badly beaten.
December 24	At least 15 bombs explode at or near various places of Christian worship around Indonesia. The sites include Pekanbaru in Sumatra; Batar island, Sukabumi, and Bandung in West Java; Mojokerto in East Java; and Mataram in West Nusatenggara. There are at least three explosions in the nation's capital of Jakarta, including one that goes off outside the Roman Catholic Cathedral just as the Christmas Eve service is about to start. More than 10 other bombs, some of which had been mailed to Christian clergymen, are found and defused before they can explode. Although no one claims responsibility for the coordinated bombing campaign that kills at least 13 people and injures as many as one hundred more, later evidence suggests that the bombings are the work of Jemaah Islamiyah.
December 28	A bus bomb injures more than 10 people in Tel Aviv.
December 30	Five almost-simultaneous explosions kill 22 people in metropolitan Manila, the Philippines. Jemaah Islamiyah is suspected.
December 31	Benyamin Kahane, the son of the assassinated Jewish extremist Meir Kahane, is shot to death, along with his wife Talia, while the couple rides in a car near the West Bank town of Ofra. The Palestinian attackers, members of the Martyrs of the Al-Aqsa Intifada, are apparently unaware of Kahane's identity.

2001

January 1	A Hamas car bomb injures more than 30 people in Netanya, Israel.
February 11	In the south of England, hundreds of animal-rights activists disperse from a rally called by the Stop Huntingdon Animal Cruelty organi-

zation and attack nine different facilities of the GlaxoSmithKline, Eli Lilly, Novartis, Roche, Bayer, and Pharmacia companies.

February 14	A Palestinian drives a bus into a crowd gathered at a bus stop in Azor, Israel. Seven Israeli soldiers and one civilian are killed.
March 4	Three people are killed and 60 injured by a suicide bomb in Netanya, Israel.
March 16	Saudi Arabian security forces storm a hijacked Russian airliner on the ground at Madinah. The plane had been seized by Chechen rebels at Istanbul and forced to fly to Saudi Arabia the day before. The majority of the 120 passengers being held aboard the plane had been previously freed. One Turkish passenger and a Russian flight attendant are killed.
May 27	Twenty tourists, three of them Americans, are kidnapped on Palawan Island by the Abu Sayyaf group. Over the next few weeks, some will be killed by the hijackers and others will escape. The rest are eventually freed after the payment of ransoms.
September 11	In the most elaborate and destructive act of terrorism in history, the Pentagon building in Washington, D.C., is severely damaged, and the massive twin towers of the World Trade Center in New York City are totally destroyed when they are struck by hijacked passenger airliners. As part of the highly coordinated attack, a fourth hijacked airliner, apparently en route for Washington, D.C., is brought down in a field in Pennsylvania when passengers attempt to overwhelm the hijackers (see chapter 7).
September 23	Two bombs go off in the Plaza Atrium Senen shopping mall in Jakarta, Indonesia.
September 27	Two bombs go off in the Gaza Strip near a convoy of Jewish settlers, marking the beginning of a new intifada against Israel.
November 2	An Islamic Jihad car bomb kills two Israelis in a Jerusalem marketplace.
November 20	Palestinian terrorists bomb an Israeli school bus; two people, both adults, are killed in the attack.
November 22	A bomb explodes on a bus in Hadera, killing two and injuring more than 60.
December 20	An American Airlines Boeing 767 en route from Paris to Miami is diverted to Florida after a passenger named Richard Reid is thwarted in an apparent attempt to light the fuse to an explosive hidden in his shoe. The son of a British mother and a Jamaican father, raised in London, Reid carries a British passport. He is believed to have links to the Al Qaeda organization.
December 28	A bus bomb injures several people in Tel Aviv.
	A terrorist bomb goes off alongside a road on the border between Israel and Gaza, killing two Israeli soldiers who are attempting to disarm it.

2002

January 1	Hamas claims responsibility for a car bomb that injures almost 40 people in the Israeli tourist and resort city of Netanya.
January 5	A 15-year-old American boy flies a small plane into an office building in Tampa Bay, Florida. A note found with his body expresses solidarity with the destruction of the World Trade Center.
January 21	Gunmen kill five members of the Indian security forces and wound 20 others at the American Center in Calcutta. No one claims responsibility for the attack.
January 23	The Hart Senate Office Building in Washington, D.C., reopens after being closed for more than three months after anthrax had been found in letters addressed to U.S. senators there.
	Daniel Pearl, an American reporter working for the *Wall Street Journal* is kidnapped when he attempts to attend a secret meeting with an Islamist leader in Kabul, Pakistan. His kidnappers, who identify themselves as the National Movement for the Restoration of Pakistani Sovereignty, threaten to kill the journalist if the United States does not immediately meet several demands,
February 21	The Pakistani government receives a videotape showing the beheading by his kidnappers of the American journalist Daniel Pearl, who has been missing since January 23.
February 27	A Muslim mob attacks Hindu activists on a train at Godhra, India, killing 58 people.
February 28–30	Hindu mobs respond to the massacre at Godhra by a wave of attacks on Muslims, killing hundreds of people, and rendering homeless tens of thousands of residents of the largely Muslim state of Gujarat. Muslims complain that Gujarat political and law enforcement authorities do little or nothing to protect them, and that, at least in some instances, they may be directly involved in the slaughter.
March 1	One Israeli is killed and nine are injured by a bomb concealed in a taxi in Wadi Ara.
March 4	A bomb detonated by a suicide bomber in the middle of a crowded rush hour in Netanya, Israel, kills three people and injures 60 more.
March 13	A grenade explodes in a church near the American embassy in Islamabad, Pakistan, killing at least five people and injuring some 40 others. Among the dead are two Americans.
March 16	Archbishop Isaias Duarte is gunned down leaving after a wedding ceremony in Cali, Colombia. Drug traffickers are suspected.
March 19	Two men on a motorcycle gun down Mario Biagi, an assistant to the Italian labor minister, outside his home in Bologna, Italy. The Combatant Communist Nucleii of the Red Brigades claims responsibility for the death in a 26-page statement released on the Internet.

March 21	A car bomb kills nine people and injures dozens of others outside the U.S. Embassy in Lima, Peru, just days before the U.S. president, George W. Bush, is due to arrive in the city.
March 27	On the eve of the Jewish feast of Passover, a suicide bomber enters the crowded dining room at the Park Hotel in the coastal city of Netanya and detonates an explosive device, killing 28 people and injuring 140. The majority of the dead, who were celebrating Seder when the bomb went off, are over 70 years old. The attack, for which Hamas claims responsibility, outrages the Israeli government, which responds by sending tanks into the main cities of the West Bank.
April 8	Four bystanders are killed when a bomb, apparently meant to kill Afghanistan's defense minister, Mohammed Fahim, explodes on a street in Jalalabad.
April 11	A truck bomb explodes at the Ghriba synagogue on the Tunisian island of Djerba. Nineteen people, 14 of them German tourists, are killed. The bombing was reportedly carried out by a member of the Islamic Army for the Liberation of the Holy Sites, a group connected with Al-Qaeda.
April 21	Three explosions kill 15 people and injure more than 40 others in and around the city of General Santos in the southern Philippines. The Abu Sayyaf Group is believed to be responsible.
April 26	Guerillas from the Lord's Resistance Army sweep down on a funeral in the southern Sudan. Sixty mourners are gunned down after reportedly being forced to cut up and eat the corpse that was being buried.
May 9	An explosion during a military parade commemorating the end of the Second World War kills 41 people, almost half of whom are children, in the small Russian town of Kaspiisk. The government blames Chechen rebels.
	Fourteen people, including 11 French engineers are killed when a suicide bomber blows himself up on a bus in Karachi, Pakistan. Islamic militants with links to al-Qaeda are suspected.
June 5	A suicide bomb kills 20 people and injures 50 more in Haifa, Israel. Palestinian Islamic Jihad is believed responsible.
June 7	An American missionary and a Filipina nurse who had been abducted and held for more than a year by Abu Sayyaf guerillas are killed in a gun battle when Philippine troops attempt to rescue them. The missionary's wife is wounded but survives.
June 14	Members of the Harkat ul-Mujahadeen al-Almi organization detonate a bomb outside the U.S. consulate in Karachi, Pakistan, killing 12 people and seriously injuring more than 20 others.
June 17–18	Twenty-six people are killed by two suicide bombings in Jerusalem.
July 4	The celebration of Algeria's 40th Independence Day is marred by three explosions, one in a crowded market, and the others at a

bathing beach and a cemetery. The most destructive of the bombs was concealed in a pile of garbage bags at the entrance to the marketplace in the town of Larba, south of Algiers. It killed close to 40 people and injured as many as 80 more. Although no group claims responsibility for the explosion, the Algerian government believes that the attack was carried out by Islamist rebels.

July 6   Vice-President of Afghanistan Haji Abdul Qadir is assassinated. No group claims responsibility.

July 14   A member of the extreme right-wing GUD fires a shot at French President Jacques Chirac during a Bastille Day parade in Paris.

July 16   With the 30th anniversary of Bloody Friday approaching, the IRA issues an apology for all the "noncombatants" it has killed and injured, and regret for all the death and suffering it has caused in its long campaign of violence against British rule in Northern Ireland.

July 26   Two Israeli cars are fired on by Palestinian gunmen on a road near the West Bank city of Hebron. Four Jewish settlers are killed and two others wounded.

July 30   The first suicide-bomb attack in Israel since June 18 kills the bomber and wounds four Israeli bystanders in Jerusalem.

July 31   A bomb left in a cafeteria at the Hebrew University in Jerusalem kills at least seven people and injures more than 80 others. Among the dead and wounded are several Americans and many Arabs, as well as Jews. Hamas claims responsibility, saying the attack came in response to an Israeli bombing in Gaza City that killed 15 people, including a Hamas leader and nine children.

August 4   A suicide bomber detonates his bomb on a bus at the Meron junction outside Safed in northern Israel. The bomber and nine Israelis are killed, and 50 other people are injured by the blast.

August 5   Six Pakistani defenders are killed by four gunmen who try but fail to force their way into the Murree Christian boarding school for the children of Christian missionaries. None of the 145 children cowering inside are injured.

August 7   A mortar shell fired into the El Cartucho district of Bogata, Colombia, during the inauguration of the recently elected president, Avaro Uribe, kills at least 11 people. Nearby, a second explosion kills another four people, three of them children. In these two attacks, and an attack on a nearly military base, at least 60 people are injured, two of whom later die. The incidents are believed to be the work of FARC, which was expected to disrupt the inauguration of Uribe, who promised that he would crack down on FARC during the campaign.

August 9   Three Islamic militants hurl grenades into a crowd of nurses leaving the chapel of a Christian hospital in Taxila, Pakistan. Three nurses are killed and 23 people are injured.

September 5   A bicycle bomb goes off in Kabul, Afghanistan. After a crowd gathers to gawk at the aftermath, a larger car bomb explodes, killing 25 of them and wounding many others. The authorities speculate that the blasts are either the work of warlords or of groups connected to al-Qaeda and the deposed Taliban.

A gunman opens fire on a car containing Afghan President Hamid Karzai in Kandahar, Afghanistan, missing Karzai but wounding the governor of Kandahar who was riding with him. U.S. Special Forces personnel who have been guarding Karzai kill the would-be assassin. An Afghan bodyguard is also killed in the shooting.

September 17	A bomb injures five Arab students at the Zif Elementary School in Yatta in the Hebron Hills of Israel. Jewish terrorists are suspected.
September 18	A suicide bomber blows himself up during the evening rush hour at a busy intersection of the Wadi Ara highway outside Umm el Fahm in northern Israel. One Israeli is killed and three others injured.
September 19	The explosion of a suicide bomb kills the bomber and five others on a bus in downtown Tel Aviv. Islamic Jihad claims responsibility.
September 23	A grenade explodes near the home of a U.S. diplomat in Jakarta, Indonesia.
September 24–25	Gunmen invade a large Hindu temple complex in Gujarat, India, and and open fire indiscriminately, killing 30 people, including several women and children, and wounding some 50 or 60 others. They proceed to hold a limited area of the complex for 14 hours before a squad of Indian commandos, flown to the scene to deal with the situation, storm the complex, killing at least two of the invaders. Although no one takes responsibility for the attack, Indian authorities blame Islamic militants, possibly linked to neighboring Pakistan.
October 2	A bomb explodes outside a military camp in the Philippines, killing four people and injuring 23 others. One of the dead is an American soldier.
October 6	An explosion and fire kills one seaman and injures 12 others aboard the French oil tanker *Limburg* in the Gulf of Aden. Evidence suggests that the tanker was the victim of an attack from a boat-bomb similar to the one that damaged the U.S. Navy ship *Cole* in-harbor at Yemen two years before. A Yemeni Islamist group calling itself the Aden-Abyan Islamic Army claims responsibility in communiqués, declaring that the French tanker was attacked because it was going to be used to supply the U.S. Fifth Fleet in an attack on Iraq.
October 8	Two Kuwaitis, who had reportedly fought with the Taliban in Afghanistan, open fire on American Marines who are taking a break from a training exercise in Kuwait. One Marine is killed and another injured. The attackers drive off and attack another group of Marines, who return fire, killing them both.
October 10	A would-be suicide bomber slips and falls as he attempts to leap aboard a bus in Tel Aviv, Israel. The bus driver and a passenger hold him down while the other passengers flee the scene. Shortly after they finally release him, the bomb explodes. The bomber and an elderly woman are killed, and several bystanders injured.

October 12	A massive car bomb goes off in a crowded club district in the Kuta Beach tourist district in Bali, Indonesia. At least 180 people are killed and more than 300 injured. Two nightspots, popular with foreign tourists, are destroyed in the blast. Many of the victims are young foreigners, primarily Australians, on vacation and out for a good time. No group claims responsibility, but suspicion falls on either Jemaah Islamiyah or the Abu Sayyaf.
October 17	Explosions in two department stores in the largely Christian city of Zamboanga, the Philippines, kill seven people and injure an estimated 150. The bombings are believed to be the work of either the Abu Sayyaf or the Moro Islamic Liberation Front (MILF).
October 18	A bomb on a bus in Manila, the Philippines, kills two people and injures 20.
October 20	A bicycle bomb explodes near a Roman Catholic church in Zamboanga, a largely Christian city in the Philippines. A young Filipino officer guarding the church is killed and 12 other people are injured.
October 21	A sport-utility vehicle carrying a powerful explosive plows into a bus at a stop at the Arkur Junction in Israel. At least 14 people are killed and 50 injured. Islamic Jihad claims responsibility.
October 23	Chechen Islamic rebels seize a Moscow theater during a sold-out performance and hold more than 700 occupants hostage. The terrorists demand that Russia withdraw from Chechnya or they will kill the hostages. On October 26, Russian antiterrorist forces storm the theater. Altogether, an estimated 50 Chechens and at least 128 hostages are killed in the incident.
October 27	Israeli soldiers open fire on a would-be suicide bomber at a gas station near the Jewish settlement of Ariel on the West Bank. The gunshots detonate the explosives, killing two people and injuring 20 others, including several soldiers.
November 25	The Raghunath Temple, a popular Hindu worship site in Indian-controlled Kashmir, is raided by Islamic extremists, who rake the inside with gunfire from semi-automatic rifles and toss in grenades. It is the second attack on the temple this year. The terrorists kill at least 11 people and injure as many as 50 more before they themselves are killed by security forces. The Lashkar-e-Taibu group takes responsibility for the attack.
December 8	At least 17 moviegoers are killed and hundreds of people are injured when four movie theaters are rocked by explosions in the Bangladesh town of Mymenshingh. The day is an Islamic holiday, and most of the casualties are Muslims. No group claims responsibility, but Islamic extremists, who oppose many forms of public entertainment, are suspected.
December 27	Two explosions tear through a government building in the Chechen capital city of Grozny. Some 80 people are killed and many others injured. Islamist Chechen rebels are suspected.

January 5	At least 20 people are killed and five times that number injured by two suicide bombings in a crowded area of downtown Tel Aviv, Israel.
January 26	The head of a special Nepalese antiterrorist paramilitary unit is gunned down from ambush, along with his wife and bodyguard, while walking near his home in Nepal. The assassins are believed to be members of the Maoist Communist Party of Nepal.
January 31	A bomb explodes on the Rambisi bridge near Kandahar in southern Afghanistan, destroying a passing bus and killing at least 18 people. The authorities, who blame remnants of the Taliban and al-Qaeda for the attack, speculate that the bus may have been hit by mistake; the bomb may have been intended for soldiers from a nearby military installation.
March 4	More than 20 people are killed when a rebel bomb tears through the airport at Davao City, in Chechnya.
March 5	More than 15 people, most of them off-duty soldiers, are killed by a bomb that destroys a city bus in Haifa, Israel.
March 12	The pro-Western and reformist prime minister of Serbia, Zoran Djindjic, is assassinated by a sniper in Belgrade. Djindjic had played an important role in seeing to it that the former Yugoslavian Prime Minister Slobodan Milosevich was brought to trial by an international war crimes tribunal.
March 13	An explosion rips through a Bombay, India, commuter train, killing at least 10 people and injuring 75 more. The bombing is believed to be part of the wave of terrorist attacks by Islamic extremists that have been taking place in Bombay.
March 18	Guerillas of the Moro Islamic Liberation Front stop a minibus on a highway in the southern Philippines, remove the male passengers, line them up by the side of the road, and fire on them. At least six are killed; several others survive.
April 25	An Islamist teenager, armed with a pistol loaded with blanks, hijacks a bus and its 19 passengers in Germany. He demands the release of suspected al-Qaeda prisoners, but, after being followed for 93 miles by German police, the hijacker eventually surrenders peacefully. No one is injured in the incident.
April 30	Three people are killed and more than 30 wounded when a suicide bomber blows himself up after a bouncer prevents him from entering a popular blues nightspot near the U.S. Embassy in Tel Aviv, Israel. Hamas and the Al-Aqsa Martyrs Brigades claim joint responsibility for the blast.
May 1	President George W. Bush declares the end of major combat in Iraq. Now begins a long period of bombings and other attacks on American

and coalition personnel in that country, which the coalition governments regard as terrorism, but which many Iraqis regard as patriotic resistance to occupation. A number of foreigners, some associated with al-Qaeda, are believed to be joining Iraqis in the attacks.

May 11

At least nine people are killed when a bomb explodes in a marketplace in the city of Koronadal in the Philippines. The Moro Islamic Liberation Front is suspected.

May 12

A suicide-truck-bomb kills more than 50 people and injures at least 300 in a government building and nearby apartments in Znamenskoye, Chechnya. The government building targeted in the attack houses the headquarters of the agency responsible for fighting terrorism in Chechnya.

In the Saudi Arabia capital city of Riyadh, three different, but obviously coordinated, suicide-truck-bombings are carried out at three residential compounds, populated largely by foreigners living and working in the country. The blasts kill at least 34 people, including nine bombers, and injure nearly 200 others. Among the dead are at least eight Americans, seven Saudis, two Jordanians, three Filipinos, a Lebanese, a Swiss, a Briton, an Irishman, and an Australian.

May 15

An untypical suicide bomber—a middle-aged woman—blows herself up in an apparent attempt to assassinate a pro-Moscow Chechen leader Akhman Kadyrov, while he is addressing a crowd made up of thousands of Muslims in the Chechen city of Ikaskhan-Yurt. Kadyrov is not injured, but 14 others, including the bomber, are killed, and at least 150 more are injured by the blast.

May 16

Five separate but apparently coordinated suicide-bomb attacks kill more than 40 people and injure over 60 others in Casablanca, Morocco; perhaps as many as one-fourth of the dead are the bombers themselves. The targets include a Spanish restaurant, a Jewish-owned restaurant, a hotel in Casablanca's famous old city, and a Jewish community center. Islamic militants are suspected.

May 17 to May 19

Over a period of roughly 48 hours, five separate suicide bombings in Hebron and Jerusalem, Israel claim a total of 17 lives, including the bombers.

In the last of these incidents, a 19-year-old Palestinian woman detonates a bomb in a shopping mall in Afula, Israel, killing four people, including herself. More than 50 other shoppers and mall personnel are injured. Islamic Jihad and the al-Aqsa Martyr's Brigade both claim responsibility.

June 11

Eighteen people are killed and almost 70 wounded in a suicide bomb attack in Jerusalem. Hamas claims responsibility.

July 22

Bombs explode at two tourist hotels in the resort towns of Alicante and Benidorm on Spain's Costa Blanca. Although anonymous phone calls had warned that the blasts were coming and the hotels are empty at the time, four people in a building near the Hotel Residencia Bahia in Alicante are injured by the explosion. The Basque separatist group ETA claims responsibility for the attacks, saying that the bombings were in retaliation for the Tour de France reneging on an agreement to promote Basque language during this year's marathon bicycle race and its failure to distribute an ETA communiqué during the event.

August 1	A truck bomb devastates a Russian military hospital in the sovereign Republic of North Ossetia, killing 50 people. Chechen rebels are blamed for the attack.
August 5	Ten people are killed and roughly 150 injured by a car bomb at the Marriott Hotel in Jakarta, Indonesia. Jemaah Islamiyah is suspected.
August 7	The Jordanian Embassy in Baghdad is the target of a car bomb attack that kills 19 people and injures over 60 more. Among the victims are several Iraqi police officers.
September 9	A suicide bomber kills 7 soldiers and wounds 14 others at a bus stop in Israel. One civilian is also injured in the attack.
	Six people are killed and 40 injured by a suicide bomber in a restaurant in Jerusalem. Hamas claims responsibility.
September 22	One guard is killed and nearly 20 people are injured when a suicide car bomb explodes outside the United Nations headquarters in Baghdad.
October 4	A female suicide bomber blows herself up in a restaurant in Haifa. Nineteen people are killed and more than 50 others wounded. Islamic Jihad claims responsibility.
October 15	Three private security guards are killed when a bomb goes off beneath a convoy carrying several American diplomats in the northern Gaza Strip. Most of the prominent Palestinian terrorist groups deny responsibility.
December 5	Forty-two people are killed and some 150 others injured by a suicide bomb attack on a Russian commuter train. Although Russian authorities suspect Chechen insurgents, a prominent Chechen leader denies that they have any involvement.
December 9	Six people are killed and 14 injured by an explosion outside the National Hotel in Moscow. Among the dead is the female suicide bomber responsible for the attack.
December 14	Suicide car bombers attack police stations in two Iraqi cities, killing 8 people and injuring 27 others.
December 24	A car bomb kills 5 people and injures at least 100 more outside the Kurdish Interior Ministry at Irbil, Iraq.
December 25	Two suicide bombers detonate their truck bombs in a joint attempt to assassinate President Pervez Musharraf of Pakistan who is passing nearby in a motorcade in Rawalpindi. Fourteen people are killed, but Musharraf escapes uninjured.

Four people are killed when a PFLP suicide bomber blows himself up at a bus stop near the town of Petah Tikva, Israel.

December 31   Eight people are killed and 35 injured when a car bomb explodes outside a restaurant in Baghdad. Among the injured are three reporters for the *Los Angeles Times*.

Documents

U.S. ARMY INTELLIGENCE CENTER LIST OF TERRORIST GROUPS

Terrorist groups come and go with such unsettling frequency that it's impossible to identify all that are active at any given time—or even to know how many there are. The following list has been made available to the public by the United States Army Intelligence Center, at Fort Huachuca, Arizona, with this explanation: "The organizations listed below have been identified as known terrorist organizations in the past. Many of these groups are still active and pose a threat." Because the groups on this list are arranged by their areas of operation, some names appear more than once. Nonetheless, the sheer length of the list dramatically suggests the size of the problem. So many terrorists, in so many places.

Latin America

Argentina

AAA *Alianza Anticommunista Argentina* (Anti-Communist Alliance

DP *Montoneros* ERP *Ejercito Revolucionario del Pueblo* (People's Revolutionary Army) (August 22 Movement)

ERP *Ejercito Revolucionario del Pueblo* (People's Revolutionary Army) (Communist)

MANO Argentina National Organization Movement TC *Tacuara* (Fascist)

Bolivia

EDM Death Squads

ELN *Ejercito de Liberacion Nacional* (National Liberation Army)

FSB Bolivian Socialist Phalange (Fascist)

MIR Revolutionary Movement of Bolivia

Brazil

AAB Anti-Communist Alliance of Brazil

EDM Death Squads

ELN Action for National Liberation

MR-8 Revolutionary Movement of the 8th

VAR *Vanguardia Armada Revolucionario* (Armed Revolutionary Vanguard)

Marighella)

VPR Popular Revolutionary Vanguard

Chile

EDM Death Squads

LP *Patria Libertad* (Right Wing)

MIR *Movimiento de la Izquierda Revolucionaria* (Revolutionary Movement of the Left)

NASAC Chilean National Socialist Alliance (Neo-Nazi)

PAG Proletarian Action Group

Columbia [sic]

ELN *Ejercito de Liberacion Nacional* (National Liberation Army)

EPL *Ejercito Popular de Liberacion* (Popular Liberation Army)

FARC *Fuerzas Armadas Revoluaionarias de Columbia* (Armed Revolutionary Forces of Columbia [sic])

M-19 *Movimiento 19 April* (April 19 Movement)

MAS Vigilante Group (Organized Crime)

MLFC Military Liberation Front of Columbia [sic]

Costa Rica

MRP People's Revolutionary Movement

RSC Revolutionary Solidarity Commands

RSRG Roberto Santucho Revolutionary Group

Dominican Republic

LB *La Banda* (Vigilante)

MPD *Movimiento Popular Dominico* (Dominican Popular Movement)

El Salvador

ERP *Ejercito Revolucionario del Pueblo* (People's Revolutionary Army)

FAPU *Frente de Accion Popular Unificado* (United Popular Action Front)

FARN *Fuerzas Armadas de Resistencia Nacional* (Armed Forces of National Resistance)

FDER Democratic Revolutionary Front

FPL *Fuerzas Populares de Liberacion Farabunda Marti* (*Farabundi Marti Popular Forces of Liberation*)

UGB *Union Guerrera Blanca* (White Fighting Union) (Right Wing Extremist)

WWU White Warrior Union (Right Wing)

Guatemala

EGP *Ejercito Guerrillero de los Pobres* (Guerrilla Army of the Poor)

FAA Armed Action Army (Right Wing)

MLN National Liberation Movement

MPR People's Revolutionary Movement

MR-13 *Movimiento Revolucionario Alejandro de Leon 13 Noviembre* (Revolutionary Movement Alejandro de Leon November 13)

NCG Guatemala National Commando

OPO WG Eye for Eye White Brotherhood (Right Wing)

Z Group Z (Fascist)

Haiti

CNLB Coalition of [N]ational Liberation Brigades

Honduras

MAR Armed Revolutionary Movement

MPL *Movimiento de Liberacion Popular* (Popular Liberation Movement)

MPLC *Movimiento de Liberacio Popular Cinchonero* (Cinchonero Popular Liberation Movement)

VEN *Venceremos Organization* (Terrorist Support)

Mexico

ACNR *Associacion Civica Nacional Revolucionaria* (National Revolutionary Civic Association)

BB *Brigade Blanca* (Right Wing)

ELP People's Revolutionary Army

ERPM Mexican People's Revolutionary Army

FRAP *Fuerzas Revolucionarias Armadas del Pueblo* (People's Revolutionary Armed Forces)

LCA *Liga Comunista Armada* (Armed Comm[u]nist League)

LCS-23 *Liga Comunista 23 Septiembre* (23rd September Communist League)

OLC Lucio Cabanas Organization

Nicaragua

ARD Democratic Revolutionary Alliance

SC Sandinistas (Contras)

Panama

IU *Indio Uno*

Paraguay

Movement Popular Colorado Movement (Armed Faction)
DEP Military Political Organization (Right Wing)

Peru

AAP Peruvian Anti-Communist Alliance
CO Condor
MANO Armed Nationalist Movement Organization
MIR *Movimiento de la Izquierda Revolucionaria* (Movement of the Revolutionary Left)
SL *Sendero Luminosa* (Shining Path)

Uruguay

AMS Militant Socialist Group
GAU United Action Group
MLN *Movimiento de Liberacion Nacional* (National Liberation Movement) (Tupamaros)
OPR-23 Popular Revolutionary Organization 23

Venezuela

GAS American Silva Group
GL Red Flag Group

Europe

Belgium

CCC Communist Combatant Cells
JLB Julian Lahout Brigade

Federal Republic of Germany

RAF *Rote Armee Fraktion* (Red Army Faction) (Formerly known as the Ba[a]der/Meinhoff Group)
RZ *Revolutionare Zallon* (Revolutionary Cells)
Wehrspotgruppe Hoffman (Defense Sports Group Hoffman) (Neo-Nazi)

France

AD *Action Directe* (Direct Action Group)
LARF Lebanese Armed Revolutionary Faction
NO New Order (Extreme Right Wing)
RSB Raul Sandic Brigade

Greece

ELA *Epanastatikos Laikos Agonas* (People's Revolutionary Struggle)
RA Revolutionary Action
N-17 November 17th Revolutionary Organization (Left-wing [*sic*])
DEV-SOL (Left-Wing [*sic*])

Italy

ACN Armed Communist Nuclei
AO Autonomous Workers
BR *Brigate Rosse* (Red Brigades)
NAR *Nuclei Armati Rivoluzionari* (Armed Revolutionary Nuclei) (Neo-Fascist)
ON *Ordine Nero* (Black Order) (Fascist)

Netherlands

RH *Rode Hulp* (Red Help)
RMS South Moluccan Freedom Federation

Portugal

CDEC Commando for the Defense of Civilians (Neo-Fascist)
ELP *Exercito de Liberacao Portugues* (Portuguese Liberation Army)
FP-25 *Forcas Populares do 25 Abril* (Popular Forces 25 April) (Trotskyite)
PACM Portuguese Anticommunist Movement (Counterterror)

Spain

ETA *Euskadi ta Askatasuna* (Freedom for the Basque Homeland)
FN *Fuerza Nueva* (New Force) (Neo-Fascist)
FRAP *Frente Revolucionario Antifascista y Patriotico* (Anti-Fascist and Patriotic Revolutionary Front)
GRAPO *Grupo de Resistencia Anifascista de Primero de Octubre* (1st of October Anti-Fascist Resistance Group)
NIG Nationalist Intervention Group (Right Wing)

Switzerland

JCAG Justice Commando of the Armenian Genocide LBJ *Les Beliers De Jura* (Marxist)
PKC Petra Klaus Commando (International)

Turkey

BKT *Bozkurtler* (Grey Wolves) (Right Wing)
DEV GENC Revolutionary Youth Federation

DEV SOL Revolutionary Left

DEV YOL Revolutionary Army

MLAPU Marksist Leninist Propaganda *Silahli Birligi* (Marxist-Leninist Armed Propaganda unit)

TIC Turkish Idealist Club (Right Wing)

TLPA *Turk Halk Kurtulus Ordusu* (Turkish People's Liberation Army)

United Kingdom

AB The Angry Brigade

AG Army of the Gael (Right Wing)

C88 Column 88 (Neo-Fascist)

INLA Irish National Liberation Army (Marxist)

IRA Irish Republican Army

IRA(P) Provisional Irish Republican Army

UDA Ulster Defen[c]e Association (Right Wing)

UDR Ulster Defen[c]e Regiment (Right Wing)

Middle East/Africa

Afghanistan

AIS Afghan Islamic Society (Religious Fundamentalists)

ANLF Afghan National Liberation Front

IALA Islamic Allegiance for Liberation of Afghanistan

Algeria

OPR Organization of Popular Resistance (Right Wing)

ULFNA United Liberation Front of the New Algeria

Angola

NUTLA National Union for Total Liberation of Angola

MPLA *Movimento Popular para a L'bertacao de Angola* (Popular Movement for Liberation of Angola)

Egypt

AJ-AJ Al *Jiahd-Al Jiahd* (Radical Islamic)

ATWH *Altakfir Waal Hijra* (Moslem Brotherhood Faction)

Ethiopia

ELF Eritrean Liberation Front (Separatist)

KLF Kurdish Liberation Front

MEK *Mujahdin El Khalk* (People's Strugglers)

OLF Oromo Liberation Front (Somali[-]backed)

PLF Popular Liberation Forces (Monarchist)

TPLF *Tigre* People's Liberation Front Iraq

Iraq

IMIA Iraqi Movement for Islamic Action

KRP Kirdish Revolutionary Organization

ALF Arab Liberation Front

Israel

PLO Palestine Liberation Organization (Arab)

WOG Wrath of God (Counterterrorist terrorist)

Jordan

JNLM Jordanian National Liberation Movement

Lebanon

AJM *Al Jihad Mugadis* AMAL Shiite Movement

PH Phalange

Libya

NFSL National Front for the Salvation of Libya

PCLS People's Committee for Libyan Students

Mozambique

COREMO *Comite Revolucionario de Mocambique* (Revolutionary Commit[t]ee of Mozambique)

FRELIMO *Frente de Libertacao de Mocambique* (Mozambique Liberation Front)

Palestinians

AF Al Fatah (Palestinian National Liberation Movement)

AS *Al Sa'iga* (Syrian Sponsored)

BSO Black September Organization

EPR Eagles of Palestinian Revolution

MBC Muhammed Boudia Commando (AKA Carlos Group)

OANY Organization of Arab Nationalist Youth

PFPL Popular Front for Liberation of Palestine (*Jabhat al-Shaabiya li Tahrir Falistin*)

PFLP-GC Popular Front for Liberation of Palestine General Command (*Jabhat al-Shaabiya li Tahrir Falistin al-Quiyadat al-Ama*)

PDFLP Popular Democratic Front for Liberation of Palestine

PLA Palestine Liberation Army

PLO Palestine Liberation Organization

RCF Revolutionary Council of Fatah (Abu Nidal Faction)

Somalia

SDSF Somali Democratic Salvation Front

SLF Somali Liberation Front

South Africa

ANC African National Congress (Marxist)

PAC Pan African Congress (Marxist)

SWAPO Southwest African People's Organization

Sudan

NFS National Front of Sudan (Right Wing)

SPF Sudanese Progressive Front

SSLF Southern Sudan Liberation Front

Tunisia

TARF Tunsian Armed Resistance Front

Yemen (North)

ENU Eagles of National Unity

FLOSY Front for the Liberation of Occupied South Yemen (*Jabhat al-tahrir al-Janubu al-Yemen*)

Asia

Bangladesh

JSD *Jatyo Samajtantrik Dal* (Nationalist Socialist Party) (Right Wing)

KIO Kachin Independence Organization

NUP National Unity Party Burma

NDF National Democratic Front (Right Wing)

Campuchea (Cambodia)

KPNLF Khmer People's National Liberation Front

India

AM *Anand Marg* (Path of Bliss)

KLF Kasmirir Liberation Front

UPRF Universal Proutist Liberation Front

Indonesia

DIHWC Darul Islam Holy War Command

PKI *Partal Komunis Indonesia* (Communist Party of Indonesia) (Maoist)

RMS Free Molucan Movement

Japan

CH Nucleous Faction

Chukaku-Ha—(Extreme Left-Wing [*sic*])

Middle Core

Nucleous Faction

Zenchin (Group's Periodical)

GT

Gijin To (Martyr's Party)

JRA/UJRA Japanese Red Army, United JRA

MAR *Maruseido* (Marxist Youth)

MCRA Middle Core Revolutionary Army

SGK Sokagakkai

URLG Unified Revolutionary Liberty Group (New Left)

Zengakuren (National Union of Autonomous Committees of Japanese Students)

Korea (ROK)

MD Masked Dance (Marxist Youth)

RPRK Revolutionary Party for Reunification of Korea

Malaysia

MNLA Malaysian National Liberation Army

PGRS Sarawak People's Guerrilla Force

SK Communist Party Organization

Pakistan

AZ *Al Zulfikar*

NAP National Awami Party (Maoist)

PPP Pakistani People's Party

Philippines

BMA Bangsa Moro Army ILF Islamic Liberation Front (PLO connected)

MNLF Moro National Liberation Front

NPA New People's Army

PRF People's Revolutionary Front

TNPLA The New People's Liberation Army

TPLA The Philippines Liberation Army

Sri Lanka

JVP People's Liberation Front

Taiwan

PLF People's Liberation Front

Thailand

PLF Pattani Liberation Front TPLF Thai People's Liberation Front

Anti-Castro Cuban Organizations

ABDALA April 17th Movement

Anti-Castro Commando B2506 Brigade

Bay of Pigs Veteran's Association

CAC Cuban Action Commando

CORU Coordination of the United Revolutionary Organization

CRD Cuban Revolutionary Directorate

EC El Condor

EPC *El Poder Cubano* (Cuban Power 76)

F-14 Organization

FIN National Integration Front/AKA Cuban National Front

FLNC Cuban National Liberation Front

ISRUC International Secret Revolutionary United Cells

JCN Joint Cuban Coordination Group M-7

Movement of the 7th

Omega 7

PLBC Pedro Luis Boitel Commando

PR *Pragmatistas*

SCG Secret Cuban Government

SFE Second Front of Escambray

SHO Secret Hand Organization (Crime connected)

JFACC United Front of Anti-Castro Cubans

YOS Youth of the Star

Puerto Rico

Puerto Rican Separatist Terrorist Organization

CAL Armed Liberation Commandos

COPAAN Anti-Annexation Patriotic Committee

CRIA Independent Armed Revolutionary Commandos

CRP People's Revolutionary Commandos

FALN *Fuerzas Armadas de Liberacion* (Armed Forces of National Liberation)

FARP Armed Forces of Popular Resistance

MAR *Movimiento de Accion Revolucionaria* (Revolutionary Action Movement)

MIRA Armed Revolutionary Independence Movement

NLN National Liberation Movement (Puerto Rican and Chicano)

MPR People's Revolutionary Movement—*Machateros*

OVPR Organization of Volunteers of the Puerto Rican Revolution

SSDAC Student Self-Defense Armed Commando (Cuban connections)

Transnational Terrorist Organizations

APRM Armenian Popular Revolutionary Movement

ARF Armenian Revolutionary Federation

ASLA Armenian Secret Liberation Army

AYF Armenian Youth Federation

CGIB Che Guevera International Brigade

CIS Croation Intelligence Service

EANJAF East Asia NATO-Japanese Armed Front

HRB Croation [R]evolutionary Brotherhood

IASF Iranian and Arab Student Federation

IIG Islamic International Guerrillas

ILO Islamic Liberation Organizations (Shiite)

IRF International Revolutionary Front

JCAG Justice Commando of the Armenian Genocide

JDL Jewish Defense League

JRA/UJRA Japanese Red Army/United Japanese Red Army

MB Moslem Brotherhood

MRC Mohammed Boudia Commando (Carlos)

Canada/United States

Canada

FLQ—*Front de Liberation du Canada*

United States

AIM—American Indian Movement

Alpha 66

A.M.E.R.I.C.A.N. Army

Army of God

Aryan Nations

Black Guerrilla Family

BLA—Black Liberation Army

Black Panthers

Croation Revolutionary Army

Cuban Nationalist Movement

FALN—*Fuerzas Armadas de Liberacion* (Armed Forces of National Liberation)

JDL—Jewish Defense League

JDA—Jewish Direct Action

KKK—Ku Klux Klan

M-19 Communist Organizations

>   Armed Resistance Unit

>   Guerrilla Resistance Movement

>   Red Guerrilla Resistance

Revolutionary Armed Task Force

United Freedom Front

Macheteros

NIRCA—Northern Ireland Civil Rights Association

NORIAD—Irish Northern Aid Committee (Money collected goes to IRA)

Republic of New Africa

Revolutionary Communist Party

SLA—Symbionese Liberation Army

TT—Tribal Thumb/Wells Spring Commune

Wolverines

WUO—Weather Underground Organization

PFOC—Prairie Fire Organizing Committee (Front Organization for WUO)

EZU—Emiliano Zapata Unit

International Groups Operating in the United States

ASALA—Armenian Secret Army for the Liberation of Armenia

FMLN—El Salvador Intelligence and Support Cells

FSLN—Nicaraguan Intelligence and Support Cells

IRA—Intelligence and Logistics Cells

Iranian bombing/Assassination Teams

JCAG—Justice Commandos of the Armenian Genocide

Libyan Assassination Teams

M-19—Columbia Support Cells

PFLP—Popular Front for the Liberation of Palestine Intelligence

CellsPLO—Popular Liberation Front Support Groups

OSAMA BIN LADEN AND OTHERS CALL FOR ATTACKS ON JEWS AND AMERICANS

This statement was signed by Osama bin Laden, as well as leaders of the Jihad Group in Egypt, the Islamic Group (IG), the *Jamiat-ul-Ulema-e-Pakistan*, and the Jihad Movement of Bangladesh.

INTERNATIONAL ISLAMIC FRONT FATWAH FOR JIHAD ON THE JEWS AND CRUSADERS

Praise be to God, who revealed the Book, controls the clouds, defeats factionalism, and says in His Book "But when the forbidden months are past, then fight and slay the pagans wherever ye find them, seize them, beleaguer them, and lie in wait for them in every stratagem (of war)"; and peace be upon our Prophet, Muhammad Bin-'Abdallah, who said "I have been sent with the sword between my hands to ensure that no one but God is worshipped, God who put my livelihood under the shadow of my spear and who inflicts humiliation and scorn on those who disobey my orders."

The Arabian Peninsula has never—since God made it flat, created its desert, and encircled it with seas—been stormed by any forces like the crusader armies now spreading in it like locusts, consuming its riches and destroying its plantations. All this is happening at a time when nations are attacking Muslims like people fighting over a plate of food. In the light of the grave situation and the lack of support, we and you are obliged to discuss current events, and we should all agree on how to settle the matter.

No one argues today about three facts that are known to everyone; we will list them, in order to remind everyone:

First, for over seven years the United States has been occupying the lands of Islam in the holiest of places, the Arabian Peninsula, plundering its riches, dictating to its rulers, humiliating its people, terrorizing its neighbors, and turning its bases in the Peninsula into a spearhead through which to fight the neighboring Muslim peoples.

If some people have formerly debated the fact of the occupation, all the people of the Peninsula have now acknowledged it.

The best proof of this is the Americans' continuing aggression against the Iraqi people using the Peninsula as a staging post, even though all its rulers are against their territories being used to that end, still they are helpless. Second, despite the great devastation inflicted on the Iraqi people by the crusader-Zionist alliance, and despite the huge number of those killed, in excess of 1 million . . . despite all this, the Americans are once against trying to repeat the horrific massacres, as though they are not content with the protracted blockade imposed after the ferocious war or the fragmentation and devastation.

So now they come to annihilate what is left of this people and to humiliate their Muslim neighbors.

Third, if the Americans' aims behind these wars are religious and economic, the aim is also to serve the Jews' petty state and divert attention from its occupation of Jerusalem and murder of Muslims there.

The best proof of this is their eagerness to destroy Iraq, the strongest neighboring Arab state, and their endeavor to fragment all the states of the region such as Iraq, Saudi Arabia, Egypt, and Sudan into paper statelets and through their disunion and weakness to guarantee Israel's survival and the continuation of the brutal crusade occupation of the Peninsula.

All these crimes and sins committed by the Americans are a clear declaration of war on God, his messenger, and Muslims. And ulema have throughout Islamic history unanimously agreed that the jihad is an individual duty if the enemy destroys the Muslim countries. This was revealed by Imam Bin-Qadamah in "Al- Mughni," Imam al-Kisa'i in "Al- Bada'i," al-Qurtubi in his interpretation, and the shaykh of al-Islam in his books, where he said "As for the militant struggle, it is aimed at defending sanctity and religion, and it is a duty as agreed. Nothing is more sacred than belief except repulsing an enemy who is attacking religion and life."

On that basis, and in compliance with God's order, we issue the following fatwa to all Muslims.

The ruling to kill the Americans and their allies—civilians and military—is an individual duty for every Muslim who can do it in any country in which it is possible to do it, in order to liberate the al-Aqsa Mosque and the holy mosque from their grip, and in order for their armies to move out of all the lands of Islam, defeated and unable to threaten any Muslim. This is in accordance with the words of Almighty God, "and fight the pagans all together as they fight you all together," and "fight them until there is no more tumult or oppression, and there prevail justice and faith in God."

This is in addition to the words of Almighty God "And why should ye not fight in the cause of God and of those who, being weak, are ill-treated and oppressed—women and children, whose cry is 'Our Lord, rescue us from this town, whose people are oppressors; and raise for us from thee one who will help!'"

We—with God's help—call on every Muslim who believes in God and wishes to be rewarded to comply with God's order to kill the Americans and plunder their money wherever and whenever they find it. We also call on Muslim ulema, leaders, youths, and soldiers to launch the raid on Satan's U.S. troops and the devil's supporters allying with them, and to displace those who are behind them so that they may learn a lesson.

Almighty God said "O ye who believe, give your response to God and His Apostle, when He calleth you to that which will give you life. And know that God cometh between a man and his heart, and that it is He to whom ye shall all be gathered."

Almighty God also says "O ye who believe, what is the matter with you, that when ye are asked to go forth in the cause of God, ye cling so heavily to the earth! Do ye prefer the life of this world to the hereafter? But little is the comfort of this life, as compared with the hereafter. Unless ye go forth, He will punish you with a grievous penalty, and put others in your place; but Him ye would not harm in the least. For God hath power over all things."

Almighty God also says "So lose no heart, nor fall into despair. For ye must gain mastery if ye are true in faith."

Source: As published in *Al-Quds al-'Arabi*, on February 23, 1998.

WHY THEY HATE US

In the wake of September 11, 2001, Americans kept asking themselves and one another the question, Why? Why do they hate us so much that they would attack us in such a horrible way? That question was answered in some detail by the following letter, allegedly written by Osama bin Laden, and released in Arabic over the Internet. The letter was later reprinted in full—and in English—in the Sunday edition of *The Observer* newspaper, on November 24, 2002.

BIN LADEN'S "LETTER TO AMERICA"

In the Name of Allah, the Most Gracious, the Most Merciful,

> "Permission to fight (against disbelievers) is given to those (believers) who are fought against, because they have been wronged and surely, Allah is Able to give them (believers) victory" [Quran 22:39]

> "Those who believe, fight in the Cause of Allah, and those who disbelieve, fight in the cause of Taghut (anything worshipped other than Allah e.g. Satan). So fight you against the friends of Satan; ever feeble is indeed the plot of Satan." [Quran 4:76]

Some American writers have published articles under the title 'On what basis are we fighting?' These articles have generated a number of responses, some of which adhered to the truth and were based on Islamic Law, and others which have not. Here we wanted to outline the truth—as an explanation and warning—hoping for Allah's reward, seeking success and support from Him.

While seeking Allah's help, we form our reply based on two questions directed at the Americans:

(Q1) Why are we fighting and opposing you?

(Q2) What are we calling you to, and what do we want from you?

As for the first question: Why are we fighting and opposing you? The answer is very simple:

(1) Because you attacked us and continue to attack us.

a) You attacked us in Palestine:

(i) Palestine, which has sunk under military occupation for more than 80 years. The British handed over Palestine, with your help and your support, to the Jews, who have occupied it for more than 50 years; years overflowing with oppression, tyranny, crimes, killing, expulsion, destruction and devastation. The creation and continuation of Israel is one of the greatest crimes, and you are the leaders of its criminals. And of course there is no need to explain and prove the degree of American support for Israel. The creation of Israel is a crime which must be erased. Each and every person whose hands have become polluted in the contribution towards this crime must pay its price, and pay for it heavily.

(ii) It brings us both laughter and tears to see that you have not yet tired of repeating your fabricated lies that the Jews have a historical right to Palestine, as it was promised to them in the Torah. Anyone who disputes with them on this alleged fact is accused of anti-semitism. This is one of the most fallacious, widely-circulated fabrications in history. The people of Palestine are pure Arabs and original Semites. It is the Muslims who are the inheritors of Moses (peace be upon him) and the inheritors of the real Torah that has not been changed. Muslims believe in all of the Prophets, including Abraham, Moses, Jesus and Muhammad, peace and blessings of Allah be upon them all. If the followers of Moses have been promised a right to Palestine in the Torah, then the Muslims are the most worthy nation of this.

When the Muslims conquered Palestine and drove out the Romans, Palestine and Jerusalem returned to Islaam [sic], the religion of all the Prophets peace be upon them. Therefore, the call to a historical right to Palestine cannot be raised against the Islamic Ummah that believes in all the Prophets of Allah (peace and blessings be upon them)—and we make no distinction between them.

(iii) The blood pouring out of Palestine must be equally revenged. You must know that the Palestinians do not cry alone; their women are not widowed alone; their sons are not orphaned alone.

b) You attacked us in Somalia; you supported the Russian atrocities against us in Chechnya, the Indian oppression against us in Kashmir, and the Jewish aggression against us in Lebanon.

c) Under your supervision, consent and orders, the governments of our countries which act as your agents, attack us on a daily basis;

(i) These governments prevent our people from establishing the Islamic Shariah, using violence and lies to do so.

(ii) These governments give us a taste of humiliation, and places us in a large prison of fear and subdual.

(iii) These governments steal our Ummah's wealth and sell them to you at a paltry price.

(iv) These governments have surrendered to the Jews, and handed them most of Palestine, acknowledging the existence of their state over the dismembered limbs of their own people.

(v) The removal of these governments is an obligation upon us, and a necessary step to free the Ummah, to make the Shariah the supreme law and to regain Palestine. And our fight against these governments is not separate from ou[r] fight against you.

d) You steal our wealth and oil at paltry prices because of your international influence and military threats. This theft is indeed the biggest theft ever witnessed by mankind in the history of the world.

e) Your forces occupy our countries; you spread your military bases throughout them; you corrupt our lands, and you besiege our sanctities, to protect the security of the Jews and to ensure the continuity of your pillage of our treasures.

f) You have starved the Muslims of Iraq, where children die every day. It is a wonder that more than 1.5 million Iraqi children have died as a result of your sanctions, and you did not show concern. Yet when 3,000 of your people died, the entire world rises and has not yet sat down.

g) You have supported the Jews in their idea that Jerusalem is their eternal capital, and agreed to move your embassy there. With your help and under your protection, the Israelis are planning to destroy the Al-Aqsa mosque. Under the protection of your weapons, Sharon entered the Al-Aqsa mosque, to pollute it as a preparation to capture and destroy it.

(2) These tragedies and calamities are only a few examples of your oppression and aggression against us. It is commanded by our religion and intellect that the oppressed have a right to return the aggression. Do not await anything from us but Jihad, resistance and revenge. Is it in any way rational to expect that after America has attacked us for more than half a century, that we will then leave her to live in security and peace?!!

(3) You may then dispute that all the above does not justify aggression against civilians, for crimes they did not commit and offenses in which they did not partake:

a) This argument contradicts your continuous repetition that America is the land of freedom, and its leaders in this world. [*sic*] Therefore, the American people are the ones who choose their government by way of their own free will; a choice which stems from their agreement to its policies. Thus the American people have chosen, consented to, and affirmed their support for the Israeli oppression of the Palestinians, the occupation and usurpation of their land, and its continuous killing, torture, punishment and expulsion of the Palestinians. The American people have the ability and choice to refuse the policies of their Government and even to change it if they want.

b) The American people are the ones who pay the taxes which fund the planes that bomb us in Afghanistan, the tanks that strike and destroy our homes in Palestine, the armies which occupy our lands in the Arabian Gulf, and the fleets which ensure the blockade of Iraq. These tax dollars are given to Israel for it to continue to attack us and penetrate our lands. So the American people are the ones who fund the attacks against us, and they are the ones who oversee the expenditure of these monies in the way they wish, through their elected candidates.

c) Also the American army is part of the American people. It is this very same people who are shamelessly helping the Jews fight against us.

d) The American people are the ones who employ both their men and their women in the American Forces which attack us.

e) This is why the American people cannot be not innocent of all the crimes committed by the Americans and Jews against us.

f) Allah, the Almighty, legislated the permission and the option to take revenge. Thus, if we are attacked, then we have the right to attack back. Whoever has destroyed our villages and towns, then we have the right to destroy their villages and towns. Whoever has stolen our wealth, then we have the right to destroy their economy. And whoever has killed our civilians, then we have the right to kill theirs.

The American Government and press still refuses to answer the question:
Why did they attack us in New York and Washington?
If Sharon is a man of peace in the eyes of Bush, then we are also men of peace!!! America does not understand the language of manners and principles, so we are addressing it using the language it understands.

(Q2) As for the second question that we want to answer: What are we calling you to, and what do we want from you?

(1) The first thing that we are calling you to is Islam.

    a) The religion of the Unification of God; of freedom from associating partners with Him, and rejection of this; of complete love of Him, the Exalted; of complete submission to His Laws; and of the discarding of all the opinions, orders, theories and religions which contradict with the religion He sent down to His Prophet Muhammad (peace be upon him). Islam is the religion of all the prophets, and makes no distinction between them—peace be upon them all.

    It is to this religion that we call you; the seal of all the previous religions. It is the religion of Unification of God, sincerity, the best of manners, righteousness, mercy, honour, purity, and piety. It is the religion of showing kindness to others, establishing justice between them, granting them their rights, and defending the oppressed and the persecuted. It is the religion of enjoining the good and forbidding the evil with the hand, tongue and heart. It is the religion of Jihad in the way of Allah so that Allah's Word and religion reign Supreme. And it is the religion of unity and agreement on the obedience to Allah, and total equality between all people, without regarding their colour, sex, or language.

    b) It is the religion whose book—the Quran—will remained preserved and unchanged, after the other Divine books and messages have been changed. The Quran is the miracle until the Day of Judgment. Allah has challenged anyone to bring a book like the Quran or even ten verses like it.

(2) The second thing we call you to, is to stop your oppression, lies, immorality and debauchery that has spread among you.

    (a) We call you to be a people of manners, principles, honour, and purity; to reject the immoral acts of fornication, homosexuality, intoxicants, gambling's [sic], and trading with interest.

    We call you to all of this that you may be freed from that which you have become caught up in; that you may be freed from the deceptive lies that you are a great nation, that your leaders spread amongst you to conceal from you the despicable state to which you have reached.

    (b) It is saddening to tell you that you are the worst civilization witnessed by the history of mankind:

      (i) You are the nation who, rather than ruling by the Shariah of Allah in its Constitution and Laws, choose to invent your own laws as you will and desire. You separate religion from your policies, contradicting the pure nature which affirms Absolute Authority to the Lord and your Creator. You flee from the embarrassing question posed to you: How is it possible for Allah the Almighty to create His creation, grant them power over all the creatures and land, grant them all the amenities of life, and then deny them that which they are most in need of: knowledge of the laws which govern their lives?

(ii) You are the nation that permits Usury, which has been forbidden by all the religions. Yet you build your economy and investments on Usury. As a result of this, in all its different forms and guises, the Jews have taken control of your economy, through which they have then taken control of your media, and now control all aspects of your life making you their servants and achieving their aims at your expense; precisely what Benjamin Franklin warned you against.

(iii) You are a nation that permits the production, trading and usage of intoxicants. You also permit drugs, and only forbid the trade of them, even though your nation is the largest consumer of them.

(iv) You are a nation that permits acts of immorality, and you consider them to be pillars of personal freedom. You have continued to sink down this abyss from level to level until incest has spread amongst you, in the face of which neither your sense of honour nor your laws object.

Who can forget your President Clinton's immoral acts committed in the official Oval office? After that you did not even bring him to account, other than that he 'made a mistake', after which everything passed with no punishment. Is there a worse kind of event for which your name will go down in history and remembered by nations?

(v) You are a nation that permits gambling in its all forms. The companies practice this as well, resulting in the investments becoming active and the criminals becoming rich.

(vi) You are a nation that exploits women like consumer products or advertising tools calling upon customers to purchase them. You use women to serve passengers, visitors, and strangers to increase your profit margins. You then rant that you support the liberation of women.

(vii) You are a nation that practices the trade of sex in all its forms, directly and indirectly. Giant corporations and establishments are established on this, under the name of art, entertainment, tourism and freedom, and other deceptive names you attribute to it.

(viii) And because of all this, you have been described in history as a nation that spreads diseases that were unknown to man in the past. Go ahead and boast to the nations of man, that you brought them AIDS as a Satanic American Invention.

(xi) You have destroyed nature with your industrial waste and gases more than any other nation in history. Despite this, you refuse to sign the Kyoto agreement so that you can secure the profit of your greedy companies and industries.

(x) Your law is the law of the rich and wealthy people, who hold sway in their political parties, and fund their election campaigns with their gifts. Behind them stand the Jews, who control your policies, media and economy.

(xi) That which you are singled out for in the history of mankind, is that you have used your force to destroy mankind more than any other nation in history; not to defend principles and values, but to hasten to secure your interests and profits. You who dropped a nuclear bomb on Japan, even though Japan was ready to negotiate an end to the war. How many acts of oppression, tyranny and injustice have you carried out, O callers to freedom?

(xii) Let us not forget one of your major characteristics: your duality in both manners and values; your hypocrisy in manners and principles. All manners, principles and values have two scales: one for you and one for the others.

a) The freedom and democracy that you call to is for yourselves and for white race only; as for the rest of the world, you impose upon them your monstrous, destructive policies and Governments, which you call the 'American friends'. Yet you prevent them from establishing democracies. When the Islamic party in Algeria wanted to practice democracy and they won the election, you unleashed your agents in the Algerian army onto them, and to attack them with tanks and guns, to imprison them and torture them—a new lesson from the 'American book of democracy'!!!

b) Your policy on prohibiting and forcibly removing weapons of mass destruction to ensure world peace: it only applies to those countries which you do not permit to possess such weapons. As for the countries you consent to, such as Israel, then they are allowed to keep and use such weapons to defend their security. Anyone else who you suspect might be manufacturing or keeping these kinds of weapons, you call them criminals and you take military action against them.

c) You are the last ones to respect the resolutions and policies of International Law, yet you claim to want to selectively punish anyone else who does the same. Israel has for more than 50 years been pushing UN resolutions and rules against the wall with the full support of America.

d) As for the war criminals which you censure and form criminal courts for—you shamelessly ask that your own are granted immunity!! However, history will not forget the war crimes that you committed against the Muslims and the rest of the world; those you have killed in Japan, Afghanistan, Somalia, Lebanon and Iraq will remain a shame that you will never be able to escape. It will suffice to remind you of your latest war crimes in Afghanistan, in which densely populated innocent civilian villages were destroyed, bombs were dropped on mosques causing the roof of the mosque to come crashing down on the heads of the Muslims praying inside. You are the ones who broke the agreement with the Mujahideen when they left Qunduz, bombing them in Jangi fort, and killing more than 1,000 of your prisoners through suffocation and thirst. Allah alone knows how many people have died by torture at the hands of you and your agents. Your planes remain in the Afghan skies, looking for anyone remotely suspicious.

(e) You have claimed to be the vanguards of Human Rights, and your Ministry of Foreign affairs issues annual reports containing statistics of those countries that violate any Human Rights. However, all these things vanished when the Mujahideen hit you, and you then implemented the methods of the same documented governments that you used to curse. In America, you captured thousands the Muslims and Arabs, took them into custody with neither reason, court trial, nor even disclosing their names. You issued newer, harsher laws.

What happens in Gua[n]tanamo is a historical embarrassment to America and its values, and it screams into your faces—you hypocrites, "What is the value of your signature on any agreement or treaty?"

(3) What we call you to thirdly is to take an honest stance with yourselves—and I doubt you will do so—to discover that you are a nation without principles or manners, and that the values and principles to you are something which you merely demand from others, not that which you yourself must adhere to.

(4) We also advise you to stop supporting Israel, and to end your support of the Indians in Kashmir, the Russians against the Chechens and to also cease supporting the Manila Government against the Muslims in Southern Philippines.

(5) We also advise you to pack your luggage and get out of our lands. We desire for your goodness, guidance, and righteousness, so do not force us to send you back as cargo in coffins.

(6) Sixthly, we call upon you to end your support of the corrupt leaders in our countries. Do not interfere in our politics and method of education. Leave us alone, or else expect us in New York and Washington.

(7) We also call you to deal with us and interact with us on the basis of mutual interests and benefits, rather than the policies of sub dual [sic], theft and occupation, and not to continue your policy of supporting the Jews because this will result in more disasters for you.

If you fail to respond to all these conditions, then prepare for fight with the Islamic Nation. The Nation of Monotheism, that puts complete trust on Allah and fears none other than Him. The Nation which is addressed by its Quran with the words: "Do you fear them? Allah has more right that you should fear Him if you are believers. Fight against them so that Allah will punish them by your hands and disgrace them and give you victory over them and heal the breasts of believing people. And remove the anger of their (believers') hearts. Allah accepts the repentance of whom He wills. Allah is All-Knowing, All-Wise." [Quran 9:13–1]

The Nation of honour and respect:

"But honour, power and glory belong to Allah, and to His Messenger (Muhammad- peace be upon him) and to the believers." [Quran 63:8]

"So do not become weak (against your enemy), nor be sad, and you will be superior (in victory)if you are indeed (true) believers" [Quran 3:139]

The Nation of Martyrdom; the Nation that desires death more than you desire life:

"Think not of those who are killed in the way of Allah as dead. Nay, they are alive with their Lord, and they are being provided for. They rejoice in what

Allah has bestowed upon them from His bounty and rejoice for the sake of those who have not yet joined them, but are left behind (not yet martyred) that on them no fear shall come, nor shall they grieve. They rejoice in a grace and a bounty from Allah, and that Allah will not waste the reward of the believers." [Quran 3:169–171]

The Nation of victory and success that Allah has promised:

"It is He Who has sent His Messenger (Muhammad peace be upon him) with guidance and the religion of truth (Islam), to make it victorious over all other religions even though the Polytheists hate it." [Quran 61:9]

"Allah has decreed that 'Verily it is I and My Messengers who shall be victorious.' Verily Allah is All-Powerful, All-Mighty." [Quran 58:21]

The Islamic Nation that was able to dismiss and destroy the previous evil Empires like yourself; the Nation that rejects your attacks, wishes to remove your evils, and is prepared to fight you. You are well aware that the Islamic Nation, from the very core of its soul, despises your haughtiness and arrogance.

If the Americans refuse to listen to our advice and the goodness, guidance and righteousness that we call them to, then be aware that you will lose this Crusade Bush began, just like the other previous Crusades in which you were humiliated by the hands of the Mujahideen, fleeing to your home in great silence and disgrace. If the Americans do not respond, then their fate will be that of the Soviets who fled from Afghanistan to deal with their military defeat, political breakup, ideological downfall, and economic bankruptcy.

This is our message to the Americans, as an answer to theirs. Do they now know why we fight them and over which form of ignorance, by the permission of Allah, we shall be victorious?

Source: © Guardian Newspapers Limited 2002

THE PERMANENT MEMBERS OF THE SECURITY COUNCIL CALL ON THE NATIONS OF THE WORLD TO ACT TOGETHER TO COMBAT TERRORISM

In 1999, following a decade in which international terrorism proliferated around the world, the Foreign Affairs Ministers of the five permanent members of the UN Security Council—China, France, the Russian Federation, the United Kingdom, and the United States—issued the following joint statement.

STATEMENT ON COMBATTING INTERNATIONAL TERRORISM

The growth in acts of international terrorism endangers the lives and well-being of ordinary people worldwide, as well as threatening the peace and security of all states. We consider it vital to strengthen, under the auspices of the United Nations, international cooperation to fight terrorism in all its forms. Such cooperation must be firmly based on the principles of the UN Charter and norms of international law, including respect for human rights.

In the context of such cooperation all states should take all appropriate steps to: protect their nationals against terrorist attacks;

cooperate with each other to prevent and suppress terrorist acts whenever and by whomsoever committed and to bring to justice the perpetrators of terrorist acts;

prevent and suppress in their territories the preparation and financing of any acts of terrorism;

deny terrorists safe havens; those who plan, finance or commit terrorist acts should be denied the night of asylum afforded to legitimate refugees;

exchange information in accordance with international and domestic law, and cooperate on administrative and judicial matters in order to prevent the commission of terrorist acts;

adhere to the international anti-terrorist conventions and continue to work to strengthen the international legal regime to combat terrorism.

Issued on 23 September 1999

By the Ministers for Foreign Affairs
of the Five Permanent Members of the Security Council

THE GENERAL ASSEMBLY OF THE UNITED NATIONS CALLS ON MEMBER STATES TO COMBAT TERRORIST BOMBINGS

Bombing has become the favored method of terrorism of groups throughout the world. Responding to the growing threat, the General Assembly of the United Nations passed the following resolution in 1993.

INTERNATIONAL CONVENTION FOR THE SUPPRESSION OF TERRORIST BOMBINGS

UNITED NATIONS GENERAL ASSEMBLY A/RES/52/164

09 January 1998
Fifty-second session
Agenda item 152

RESOLUTION ADOPTED BY THE GENERAL ASSEMBLY [on the report of the Sixth Committee (A/52/653)]

International Convention for the Suppression of Terrorist Bombings
The General Assembly,

Recalling its resolution 49/60 of 9 December 1994, by which it adopted the Declaration on Measures to Eliminate International Terrorism, and its resolution 51/210 of 17 December 1996,

Having considered the text of the draft convention for the suppression of terrorist bombings prepared by the Ad Hoc Committee established by General Assembly resolution 51/210 of 17 December 1996[1] and the Working Group of the Sixth Committee,[2]

1. Adopts the International Convention for the Suppression of Terrorist Bombings annexed to the present resolution, and decides to open it for signature at United Nations Headquarters in New York from 12 January 1998 until 31 December 1999;

2. Urges all States to sign and ratify, accept or approve or accede to the Convention.

72nd plenary meeting 15 December 1997
ANNEX International Convention for the Suppression of Terrorist Bombings
The States Parties to this Convention,

Having in mind the purposes and principles of the Charter of the United Nations concerning the maintenance of international peace and security and the promotion of good-neighbourliness and friendly relations and cooperation among States,

Deeply concerned about the worldwide escalation of acts of terrorism in all its forms and manifestations,

Recalling the Declaration on the Occasion of the Fiftieth Anniversary of the United Nations of 24 October 1995,[3]

Recalling also the Declaration on Measures to Eliminate International Terrorism, annexed to General Assembly resolution 49/60 of 9 December 1994, in which, inter alia, "the States Members of the United Nations solemnly reaffirm their unequivocal condemnation of all acts, methods and practices of terrorism as criminal and unjustifiable, wherever and by whomever committed, including those which jeopardize the friendly relations among States and peoples and threaten the territorial integrity and security of States",

Noting that the Declaration also encouraged States "to review urgently the scope of the existing international legal provisions on the prevention, repression and elimination of terrorism in all its forms and manifestations, with the aim of ensuring that there is a comprehensive legal framework covering all aspects of the matter",

Recalling General Assembly resolution 51/210 of 17 December 1996 and the Declaration to Supplement the 1994 Declaration on Measures to Eliminate International Terrorism annexed thereto,

Noting that terrorist attacks by means of explosives or other lethal devices have become increasingly widespread,

Noting also that existing multilateral legal provisions do not adequately address these attacks,

Being convinced of the urgent need to enhance international cooperation between States in devising and adopting effective and practical measures for the prevention of such acts of terrorism and for the prosecution and punishment of their perpetrators,

Considering that the occurrence of such acts is a matter of grave concern to the international community as a whole,

[2] A/C.6/52/L3, annex I.
[3] General Assembly resolution 50/6.

Noting that the activities of military forces of States are governed by rules of international law outside the framework of this Convention and that the exclusion of certain actions from the coverage of this Convention does not condone or make lawful otherwise unlawful acts, or preclude prosecution under other laws,

Have agreed as follows:

Article 1

For the purposes of this Convention:

1. "State or government facility" includes any permanent or temporary facility or conveyance that is used or occupied by representatives of a State, members of Government, the legislature or the judiciary or by officials or employees of a State or any other public authority or entity or by employees or officials of an intergovernmental organization in connection with their official duties.

2. "Infrastructure facility" means any publicly or privately owned facility providing or distributing services for the benefit of the public, such as water, sewage, energy, fuel or communications.

3. "Explosive or other lethal device" means:

   (a) An explosive or incendiary weapon or device that is designed, or has the capability, to cause death, serious bodily injury or substantial material damage; or

   (b) A weapon or device that is designed, or has the capability, to cause death, serious bodily injury or substantial material damage through the release, dissemination or impact of toxic chemicals, biological agents or toxins or similar substances or radiation or radioactive material.

4. "Military forces of a State" means the armed forces of a State which are organized, trained and equipped under its internal law for the primary purpose of national defence or security and persons acting in support of those armed forces who are under their formal command, control and responsibility.

5. "Place of public use" means those parts of any building, land, street, waterway or other location that are accessible or open to members of the public, whether continuously, periodically or occasionally, and encompasses any commercial, business, cultural, historical, educational, religious, governmental, entertainment, recreational or similar place that is so accessible or open to the public.

6. "Public transportation system" means all facilities, conveyances and instrumentalities, whether publicly or privately owned, that are used in or for publicly available services for the transportation of persons or cargo.

Article 2

1. Any person commits an offence within the meaning of this Convention if that person unlawfully and intentionally delivers, places, discharges or detonates an explosive or other lethal device in, into or against a place of public use, a State or government facility, a public transportation system or an infrastructure facility:

   (a) With the intent to cause death or serious bodily injury; or

(b) With the intent to cause extensive destruction of such a place, facility or system, where such destruction results in or is likely to result in major economic loss.

2. Any person also commits an offence if that person attempts to commit an offence as set forth in paragraph 1 of the present article.

3. Any person also commits an offence if that person:

(a) Participates as an accomplice in an offence as set forth in paragraph 1 or 2 of the present article; or

(b) Organizes or directs others to commit an offence as set forth in paragraph 1 or 2 of the present article; or

(c) In any other way contributes to the commission of one or more offences as set forth in paragraph 1 or 2 of the present article by a group of persons acting with a common purpose; such contribution shall be intentional and either be made with the aim of furthering the general criminal activity or purpose of the group or be made in the knowledge of the intention of the group to commit the offence or offences concerned.

Article 3

This Convention shall not apply where the offence is committed within a single State, the alleged offender and the victims are nationals of that State, the alleged offender is found in the territory of that State and no other State has a basis under article 6, paragraph 1 or paragraph 2, of this Convention to exercise jurisdiction, except that the provisions of articles 10 to 15 shall, as appropriate, apply in those cases.

Article 4

Each State Party shall adopt such measures as may be necessary:

(a) To establish as criminal offences under its domestic law the offences set forth in article 2 of this Convention;

(b) To make those offences punishable by appropriate penalties which take into account the grave nature of those offences.

Article 5

Each State Party shall adopt such measures as may be necessary, including, where appropriate, domestic legislation, to ensure that criminal acts within the scope of this Convention, in particular where they are intended or calculated to provoke a state of terror in the general public or in a group of persons or particular persons, are under no circumstances justifiable by considerations of a political, philosophical, ideological, racial, ethnic, religious or other similar nature and are punished by penalties consistent with their grave nature.

Article 6

1. Each State Party shall take such measures as may be necessary to establish its jurisdiction over the offences set forth in article 2 when:

    (a) The offence is committed in the territory of that State; or

    (b) The offence is committed on board a vessel flying the flag of that State or an aircraft which is registered under the laws of that State at the time the offence is committed; or

    (c) The offence is committed by a national of that State.

2. A State Party may also establish its jurisdiction over any of that when:

    (a) The offence is committed against a national of that State; or

    (b) The offence is committed against a State or government facility of that State abroad, including an embassy or other diplomatic or consular premises of that State; or

    (c) The offence is committed by a stateless person who has his or her habitual residence in the territory of that State; or

    (d) The offence is committed in an attempt to compel that State to do or abstain from doing any act; or

    (e) The offence is committed on board an aircraft which is operated by the Government of that State.

3. Upon ratifying, accepting, approving or acceding to this Convention, each State Party shall notify the Secretary-General of the United Nations of the jurisdiction it has established under its domestic law in accordance with paragraph 2 of the present article. Should any change take place, the State Party concerned shall immediately notify the Secretary-General.

4. Each State Party shall likewise take such measures as may be necessary to establish its jurisdiction over the offences set forth in article 2 in cases where the alleged offender is present in its territory and it does not extradite that person to any of the States Parties which have established their jurisdiction in accordance with paragraph 1 or 2 of the present article.

5. This Convention does not exclude the exercise of any criminal jurisdiction established by a State Party in accordance with its domestic law.

Article 7

1. Upon receiving information that a person who has committed or who is alleged to have committed an offence as set forth in article 2 may be present in its territory, the State Party concerned shall take such measures as may be necessary under its domestic law to investigate the facts contained in the information.

2. Upon being satisfied that the circumstances so warrant, the State Party in whose territory the offender or alleged offender is present shall take the appropriate measures under its domestic law so as to ensure that person's presence for the purpose of prosecution or extradition.

3. Any person regarding whom the measures referred to in paragraph 2 of the present article are being taken shall be entitled to:

   (a) Communicate without delay with the nearest appropriate representative of the State of which that person is a national or which is otherwise entitled to protect that person's rights or, if that person is a stateless person, the State in the territory of which that person habitually resides;

   (b) Be visited by a representative of that State;

   (c) Be informed of that person's rights under subparagraphs (a) and (b).

4. The rights referred to in paragraph 3 of the present article shall be exercised in conformity with the laws and regulations of the State in the territory of which the offender or alleged offender is present, subject to the provision that the said laws and regulations must enable full effect to be given to the purposes for which the rights accorded under paragraph 3 are intended.

5. The provisions of paragraphs 3 and 4 of the present article shall be without prejudice to the right of any State Party having a claim to jurisdiction in accordance with article 6, subparagraph 1 (c) or 2 (c),to invite the International Committee of the Red Cross to communicate with and visit the alleged offender.

6. When a State Party, pursuant to the present article, has taken a person into custody, it shall immediately notify, directly or through the Secretary-General of the United Nations, the States Parties which have established jurisdiction in accordance with article 6, paragraphs 1 and 2, and, if it considers it advisable, any other interested States Parties, of the fact that that person is in custody and of [t]he circumstances which warrant that person's detention. The State which makes the investigation contemplated in paragraph 1 of the present article shall promptly inform the said States Parties of its findings and shall indicate whether it intends to exercise jurisdiction.

Article 8

1. The State Party in the territory of which the alleged offender the [*sic*] is present shall, in cases to which article 6 applies, if it does not extradite that person, be obliged, without exception whatsoever and whether or not the offence was committed in its territory, to submit the case without undue delay to its competent authorities for the purpose of prosecution, through proceedings in accordance with the laws of the [State]. Those authorities shall take their decision in the same manner as in the case of any other offence of a grave nature under the law of that State.

2. Whenever a State Party is permitted under its domestic law to extradite or otherwise surrender one of its nationals only upon the condition that the person will be returned to that State to serve the sentence imposed as a result of the trial or proceeding for which the extradition or surrender of the person was sought, and this State and the State seeking the extradition of the person agree with this option and other terms they may deem appropriate, such a conditional extradition or surrender shall be sufficient to discharge the obligation set forth in paragraph 1 of the present article.

Article 9

1. The offences set forth in article 2 shall be deemed to be included as extraditable offences in any extradition treaty existing between any of the States Parties before the entry into force of this Convention. States Parties undertake to include such offences as extraditable offences in every extradition treaty to be subsequently concluded between them.

2. When a State Party which makes extradition conditional on the existence of a treaty receives a request for extradition from another State Party with which it has no extradition treaty, the requested State Party may, at its option, consider this Convention as a legal basis for extradition in respect of the offences set forth in article 2. Extradition shall be subject to the other conditions provided by the law of the requested State.

3. States Parties which do not make extradition conditional on the existence of a treaty shall recognize the offences set forth in article 2 as extraditable offences between themselves, subject to the conditions provided by the law of the requested State.

4. If necessary, the offences set forth in article 2 shall be treated, for the purposes of extradition between States Parties, as if they had been committed not only in the place in which they occurred but also in the territory of the States that have established jurisdiction in accordance with article 6, paragraphs 1 and 2.5. The provisions of all extradition treaties and arrangements between States Parties with regard to offences set forth in article 2 shall be deemed to be modified as between State Parties to the extent that they are incompatible with this Convention.

Article 10

1. States Parties shall afford one another the greatest measure of assistance in connection with investigations or criminal or extradition proceedings brought in respect of the offences set forth in article 2, including assistance in obtaining evidence at their disposal necessary for the proceedings.

2. States Parties shall carry out their obligations under paragraph 1 of the present article in conformity with any treaties or other arrangements on mutual legal assistance that may exist between them. In the absence of such treaties or arrangements, States Parties shall afford one another assistance in accordance with their domestic law.

Article 11

None of the offences set forth in article 2 shall be regarded, for the purposes of extradition or mutual legal assistance, as a political offence or as an offence connected with a political offence or as an offence inspired by political motives. Accordingly, a request for extradition or for mutual legal assistance based on such an offence may not be refused on the sole ground that it concerns a political offence or an offence connected with a political offence or an offence inspired by political motives.

Article 12

Nothing in this Convention shall be interpreted as imposing an obligation to extradite or to afford mutual legal assistance, if the requested State Party has substantial grounds for believing that the request for extradition for offences set forth in article 2 or for mutual legal assistance with respect to such offences has been made for the purpose of prosecuting or punishing a person on account of that person's race, religion, nationality, ethnic origin or political opinion or that compliance with the request would cause prejudice to that person's position for any of these reasons.

Article 13

1. A person who is being detained or is serving a sentence in the territory of one State Party whose presence in another State Party is requested for purposes of testimony, identification or otherwise providing assistance in obtaining evidence for the investigation or prosecution of offences under this Convention may be transferred if the following conditions are met:

   (a) The person freely gives his or her informed consent; and

   (b) The competent authorities of both States agree, subject to such conditions as those States may deem appropriate.

2. For the purposes of the present article:

   (a) The State to which the person is transferred shall have the authority and obligation to keep the person transferred in custody, unless otherwise requested or authorized by the State from which the person was transferred;

   (b) The State to which the person is transferred shall without delay implement its obligation to return the person to the custody of the State from which the person was transferred as agreed beforehand, or as otherwise agreed, by the competent authorities of both States;

   (c) The State to which the person is transferred shall not require the State from which the person was transferred to initiate extradition proceedings for the return of the person;

   (d) The person transferred shall receive credit for service of the sentence being served in the State from which he was transferred for time spent in the custody of the State to which he was transferred.

3. Unless the State Party from which a person is to be transferred in accordance with the present article so agrees, that person, whatever his or her nationality, shall not be prosecuted or detained or subjected to any other restriction of his or her personal liberty in the territory of the State to which that person is transferred in respect of acts or convictions anterior to his or her departure from the territory of the State from which such person was transferred.

Article 14

Any person who is taken into custody or regarding whom any other measures are taken or proceedings are carried out pursuant to this Convention shall be guaranteed fair treatment, including enjoyment of all rights and guarantees in conformity with the law of the State in the territory of which that person is present and applicable provisions of international law, including international law of human rights.

Article 15

States Parties shall cooperate in the prevention of the offences set forth in article 2, particularly:

(a) By taking all practicable measures, including, if necessary, adapting their domestic legislation, to prevent and counter preparations in their respective territories for the commission of those offences within or outside their territories, including measures to prohibit in their territories illegal activities of persons, groups and organizations that encourage, instigate, organize, knowingly finance or engage in the perpetration of offences as set forth in article 2;

(b) By exchanging accurate and verified information in accordance with their national law, and coordinating administrative and other measures taken as appropriate to prevent the commission of offences asset forth in article 2;

(c) Where appropriate, through research and development regarding methods of detection of explosives and other harmful substances that can cause death or bodily injury, consultations on the development of standards for marking explosives in order to identify their origin in post-blast investigations, exchange of information on preventive measures, cooperation and transfer of technology, equipment and related materials.

Article 16

The State Party where the alleged offender is prosecuted shall, in accordance with its domestic law or applicable procedures, communicate the final outcome of the proceedings to the Secretary-General of the United Nations, who shall transmit the information to the other States Parties.

Article 17

The States Parties shall carry out their obligations under this Convention in a manner consistent with the principles of sovereign equality and territorial integrity of States and that of non-intervention in the domestic affairs of other States.

Article 18

Nothing in this Convention entitles a State Party to undertake in the territory of another State Party the exercise of jurisdiction and performance of functions which are exclusively reserved for the authorities of that other State Party by its domestic law.

Article 19

1. Nothing in this Convention shall affect other rights, obligations and responsibilities of States and individuals under international law, in particular the pur-

poses and principles of the Charter of the United Nations and international humanitarian law.

2. The activities of armed forces during an armed conflict, as those terms are understood under international humanitarian law, which are governed by that law, are not governed by this Convention, and the activities undertaken by military forces of a State in the exercise of their official duties, inasmuch as they are governed by other rules of international law, are not governed by this Convention.

Article 20

1. Any dispute between two or more States Parties concerning the interpretation or application of this Convention which cannot be settled through negotiation within a reasonable time shall, at the request of one of them, be submitted to arbitration. If, within six months from the date of the request for arbitration, the parties are unable to agree on the organization of the arbitration, any one of those parties may refer the dispute to the International Court of Justice, by application, in conformity with the Statute of the Court.

2. Each State may at the time of signature, ratification, acceptance or approval of this Convention or accession thereto declare that it does not consider itself bound by paragraph 1 of the present article. The other States Parties shall not be bound by paragraph 1 with respect to any State Party which has made such a reservation.

3. Any State which has made a reservation in accordance with paragraph 2of the present article may at any time withdraw that reservation by notification to the Secretary-General of the United Nations.

. . .

1IN [*sic*] WITNESS WHEREOF, the undersigned, being duly authorized thereto by their respective Governments, have signed this Convention, opened for signature at United Nations Headquarters in New York on 12 January 1998.

Articles 21 through 24, which [have been] omitted here, relate to the procedures for States to follow in signing, ratifying, accepting, approving or denouncing the Convention.

Issued 1993
By the General Assembly of the United Nations

A CIA DIRECTOR REPORTS TO THE SENATE

Just seven months before the attacks of September 11 2001, the Director of the CIA, George Tenet, gave a Senate Committee his assessment of the terrorist threat.

WORLDWIDE THREAT 2001: NATIONAL SECURITY IN A CHANGING WORLD

As I reflect this year, Mr. Chairman, on the threats to American security, what strikes me most forcefully is the accelerating pace of change in so many arenas that affect our nation's interests. Numerous examples come to mind: new communications technology that enables the efforts of terrorists and narco-traffickers as surely as it aids law enforcement and intelligence, rapid global population growth that will create new strains in parts of the world least able to cope, the weakening internal bonds in a number of states whose cohesion can no longer be taken for granted, the breaking down of old barriers to change in places like the Koreas and Iran, the accelerating growth in missile capabilities in so many parts of the world—to name just a few.

Never in my experience, Mr. Chairman, has American intelligence had to deal with such a dynamic set of concerns affecting such a broad range of US interests. Never have we had to deal with such a high quotient of uncertainty. With so many things on our plate, it is important always to establish priorities. For me, the highest priority must invariably be on those things that threaten the lives of Americans or the physical security of the United States. With that in mind, let me turn first to the challenges posed by international terrorism.

Transnational Issues

We have made considerable progress on terrorism against US interests and facilities, Mr. Chairman, but it persists. The most dramatic and recent evidence, of course, is the loss of 17 of our men and women on the USS *Cole* at the hands of terrorists.

The threat from terrorism is real, it is immediate, and it is evolving. State sponsored terrorism appears to have declined over the past five years, but transnational groups—with decentralized leadership that makes them harder to identify and disrupt—are emerging. We are seeing fewer centrally controlled operations, and more acts initiated and executed at lower levels.

Terrorists are also becoming more operationally adept and more technically sophisticated in order to defeat counterterrorism measures. For example, as we have increased security around government and military facilities, terrorists are seeking out "softer" targets that provide opportunities for mass casualties. Employing increasingly advanced devices and using strategies such as simultaneous attacks, the number of people killed or injured in international terrorist attacks rose dramatically in the 1990s, despite a general decline in the number of incidents. Approximately one-third of these incidents involved US interests.

Usama bin Ladin and his global network of lieutenants and associates remain the most immediate and serious threat. Since 1998, Bin Ladin has declared all US citizens legitimate targets of attack. As shown by the bombing of our Embassies in Africa in 1998 and his Millennium plots last year, he is capable of planning multiple attacks with little or no warning.

His organization is continuing to place emphasis on developing surrogates to carry out attacks in an effort to avoid detection, blame, and retaliation. As a result it is often difficult to attribute terrorist incidents to his group, Al Qa'ida.

Beyond Bin Ladin, the terrorist threat to Israel and to participants in the Middle East peace negotiations has increased in the midst of continuing Palestinian-Israeli violence. Palestinian rejectionists—including HAMAS and the Palestine Islamic Jihad (PIJ)—have stepped up violent attacks against Israeli interests since October. The terrorist threat to US interests, because of our friendship with Israel has also increased.

At the same time, Islamic militancy is expanding, and the worldwide pool of potential recruits for terrorist networks is growing. In central Asia, the Middle East, and South Asia, Islamic terrorist organizations are trying to attract new recruits, including under the banner of anti-Americanism.

International terrorist networks have used the explosion in information technology to advance their capabilities. The same technologies that allow individual consumers in the United States to search out and buy books in Australia or India also enable terrorists to raise money, spread their dogma, find recruits, and plan operations far afield. Some groups are acquiring rudimentary cyberattack tools. Terrorist groups are actively searching the internet to acquire information and capabilities for chemical, biological, radiological, and even nuclear attacks. Many of the 29 officially designated terrorist organizations have an interest in unconventional weapons, and Usama bin Ladin in 1998 even declared their acquisition a "religious duty."

Nevertheless, we and our Allies have scored some important successes against terrorist groups and their plans, which I would like to discuss with you in closed session later today. Here, in an open session, let me assure you that the Intelligence Community has designed a robust counterterrorism program that has preempted, disrupted, and defeated international terrorists and their activities. In most instances, we have kept terrorists off-balance, forcing them to worry about their own security and degrading their ability to plan and conduct operations.

. . .

Mr. Chairman, drug traffickers are also making themselves more capable and efficient. The growing diversification of trafficking organizations—with smaller groups interacting with one another to transfer cocaine from source to market—and the diversification of routes and methods pose major challenges for our counterdrug programs. Changing production patterns and the development of new markets will make further headway against the drug trade difficult.

Colombia, Bolivia, and Peru continue to supply all of the cocaine consumed worldwide including in the United States. Colombia is the linchpin of the global cocaine industry as it is home to the largest coca-growing, coca-processing, and trafficking operations in the world. With regard to heroin, nearly all of the world's opium production is concentrated in Afghanistan and Burma. Production in Afghanistan has been exploding, accounting for 72 percent of illicit global opium production in 2000.

The drug threat is increasingly intertwined with other threats. For example, the Taliban regime in Afghanistan, which allows Bin Ladin and other terrorists to operate on its territory, encourages and profits from the drug trade. Some Islamic extremists view drug trafficking as a weapon against the West and a source of revenue to fund their operations.

. . .

Conclusion

Mr. Chairman, I have spoken at some length about the threats we face to our national security. It is inevitable given our position as the world's sole superpower that we would attract the opposition of those who do not share our vision or our goals, and those who feel intimidated by our strength. Many of the threats I've outlined are familiar to you. Many of the trends I've described are not new. The complexity, intricacy, and confluence of these threats, however, is necessitating a fundamental change in the way we, in the Intelligence Community, do our business. To keep pace with these challenges:

We must aggressively challenge our analytic assumptions, avoid old-think, and embrace alternate analysis and viewpoints.

We must constantly push the envelope on collection beyond the traditional to exploit new systems and operational opportunities to gain the intelligence needed by our senior policymakers.

And we must continue to stay ahead on the technology and information fronts by seeking new partnerships with private industry as demonstrated by our IN-Q-TEL initiative.

Our goal is simple. It is to ensure that our nation has the intelligence it needs to anticipate and counter threats I have discussed here today.

Thank you Mr. Chairman, I would welcome any questions you and your fellow Senators may have for me.

Statement by Director of Central Intelligence George J. Tenet before the Senate Select Committee on Intelligence (as prepared for delivery) 07 February 2001

U.S. PRESIDENT GEORGE W. BUSH RESPONDS TO "AN ACT OF WAR"

On September 20, 2001, less than two weeks after the attacks of September 11, President Bush addressed a joint session of Congress, the nation, and the world.

ADDRESS TO A JOINT SESSION OF CONGRESS AND THE AMERICAN PEOPLE

Mr. Speaker, Mr. President Pro Tempore, members of Congress, and fellow Americans:

In the normal course of events, Presidents come to this chamber to report on the state of the Union. Tonight, no such report is needed. It has already been delivered by the American people.

We have seen it in the courage of passengers, who rushed terrorists to save others on the ground—passengers like an exceptional man named Todd Beamer. And would you please help me to welcome his wife, Lisa Beamer, here tonight.

We have seen the state of our Union in the endurance of rescuers, working past exhaustion. We have seen the unfurling of flags, the lighting of candles, the giving of blood, the saying of prayers—in English, Hebrew, and Arabic. We have seen the decency of a loving and giving people who have made the grief of strangers their own.

My fellow citizens, for the last nine days, the entire world has seen for itself the state of our Union—and it is strong.

Tonight we are a country awakened to danger and called to defend freedom. Our grief has turned to anger, and anger to resolution. Whether we bring our enemies to justice, or bring justice to our enemies, justice will be done.

I thank the Congress for its leadership at such an important time. All of America was touched on the evening of the tragedy to see Republicans and Democrats joined together on the steps of this Capitol, singing "God Bless America." And you did more than sing; you acted, by delivering $40 billion to rebuild our communities and meet the needs of our military.

Speaker Hastert, Minority Leader Gephardt, Majority Leader Daschle and Senator Lott, I thank you for your friendship, for your leadership and for your service to our country.

And on behalf of the American people, I thank the world for its outpouring of support. America will never forget the sounds of our National Anthem playing at Buckingham Palace, on the streets of Paris, and at Berlin's Brandenburg Gate.

We will not forget South Korean children gathering to pray outside our embassy in Seoul, or the prayers of sympathy offered at a mosque in Cairo. We will not forget moments of silence and days of mourning in Australia and Africa and Latin America.

Nor will we forget the citizens of 80 other nations who died with our own: dozens of Pakistanis; more than 130 Israelis; more than 250 citizens of India; men and women from El Salvador, Iran, Mexico and Japan; and hundreds of British citizens. America has no truer friend than Great Britain.

Once again, we are joined together in a great cause—so honored the British Prime Minister has crossed an ocean to show his unity of purpose with America. Thank you for coming, friend.

On September the 11th, enemies of freedom committed an act of war against our country. Americans have known wars—but for the past 136 years, they have been wars on foreign soil, except for one Sunday in 1941. Americans have known the casualties of war—but not at the center of a great city on a peaceful morning. Americans have known surprise attacks—but never before on thousands of civilians. All of this was brought upon us in a single day—and night fell on a different world, a world where freedom itself is under attack.

Americans have many questions tonight. Americans are asking: Who attacked our country? The evidence we have gathered all points to a collection of loosely affiliated terrorist organizations known as Al Qaeda. They are the same murderers indicted for bombing American embassies in Tanzania and Kenya, and responsible for bombing the USS *Cole*.

Al Qaeda is to terror what the mafia is to crime. But its goal is not making money; its goal is remaking the world—and imposing its radical beliefs on people everywhere.

The terrorists practice a fringe form of Islamic extremism that has been rejected by Muslim scholars and the vast majority of Muslim clerics—a fringe movement that perverts the peaceful teachings of Islam. The terrorists' directive commands them to kill Christians and Jews, to kill all Americans, and make no distinction among military and civilians, including women and children.

This group and its leader—a person named Osama bin Laden—are linked to many other organizations in different countries, including the Egyptian Islamic Jihad and the Islamic Movement of Uzbekistan. There are thousands of these terrorists in more than 60 countries. They are recruited from their own nations and neighborhoods and brought to camps in places like Afghanistan, where they are trained in the tactics of terror. They are sent back to their homes or sent to hide in countries around the world to plot evil and destruction.

The leadership of Al Qaeda has great influence in Afghanistan and supports the Taliban regime in controlling most of that country. In Afghanis-tan, we see Al Qaeda's vision for the world.

Afghanistan's people have been brutalized—many are starving and many have fled. Women are not allowed to attend school. You can be jailed for owning a television. Religion can be practiced only as their leaders dictate. A man can be jailed in Afghanistan if his beard is not long enough.

The United States respects the people of Afghanistan—after all, we are currently its largest source of humanitarian aid—but we condemn the Taliban regime.

It is not only repressing its own people, it is threatening people everywhere by sponsoring and sheltering and supplying terrorists. By aiding and abetting murder, the Taliban regime is committing murder.

And tonight, the United States of America makes the following demands on the Taliban: Deliver to United States authorities all the leaders of al Qaeda who hide in your land. Release all foreign nationals, including American citizens, you have unjustly imprisoned. Protect foreign journalists, diplomats and aid workers in your country. Close immediately and permanently every terrorist training camp in Afghanistan, and hand over every terrorist, and every person in their support structure, to appropriate authorities. Give the United States full access to terrorist training camps, so we can make sure they are no longer operating.

These demands are not open to negotiation or discussion. The Taliban must act, and act immediately. They will hand over the terrorists, or they will share in their fate.

I also want to speak tonight directly to Muslims throughout the world. We respect your faith. It's practiced freely by many millions of Americans, and by millions more in countries that America counts as friends. Its teachings are good and peaceful, and those who commit evil in the name of Allah blaspheme the name of Allah.

The terrorists are traitors to their own faith, trying, in effect, to hijack Islam itself. The enemy of America is not our many Muslim friends; it is not our many Arab friends. Our enemy is a radical network of terrorists, and every government that supports them.

Our war on terror begins with al Qaeda, but it does not end there. It will not end until every terrorist group of global reach has been found, stopped and defeated.

Americans are asking, why do they hate us? They hate what we see right here in this chamber—a democratically elected government. Their leaders are self-appointed. They hate our freedoms—our freedom of religion, our freedom of speech, our freedom to vote and assemble and disagree with each other.

They want to overthrow existing governments in many Muslim countries, such as Egypt, Saudi Arabia, and Jordan. They want to drive Israel out of the Middle East. They want to drive Christians and Jews out of vast regions of Asia and Africa.

These terrorists kill not merely to end lives, but to disrupt and end a way of life. With every atrocity, they hope that America grows fearful, retreating from the world and forsaking our friends. They stand against us, because we stand in their way.

We are not deceived by their pretenses to piety. We have seen their kind before. They are the heirs of all the murderous ideologies of the 20th century. By sacrificing human life to serve their radical visions—by abandoning every value except the will to power—they follow in the path of fascism, and Nazism, and totalitarianism. And they will follow that path all the way, to where it ends: in history's unmarked grave of discarded lies.

Americans are asking: How will we fight and win this war? We will direct every resource at our command—every means of diplomacy, every tool of intelligence, every instrument of law enforcement, every financial influence, and every necessary weapon of war—to the disruption and to the defeat of the global terror network.

This war will not be like the war against Iraq a decade ago, with a decisive liberation of territory and a swift conclusion. It will not look like the air war above Kosovo two years ago, where no ground troops were used and not a single American was lost in combat.

Our response involves far more than instant retaliation and isolated strikes. Americans should not expect one battle, but a lengthy campaign, unlike any other we have ever seen. It may include dramatic strikes, visible on TV, and covert operations, secret even in success. We will starve terrorists of funding, turn them one against another, drive them from place to place, until there is no refuge or no rest. And we will pursue nations that provide aid or safe haven to terrorism. Every nation, in every region, now has a decision to make. Either you are with us, or you are with the terrorists.

From this day forward, any nation that continues to harbor or support terrorism will be regarded by the United States as a hostile regime.

Our nation has been put on notice: We are not immune from attack. We will take defensive measures against terrorism to protect Americans. Today, dozens of federal departments and agencies, as well as state and local governments, have responsibilities affecting homeland security. These efforts must be coordinated at the highest level. So tonight I announce the creation of a Cabinet-level position reporting directly to me—the Office of Homeland Security.

And tonight I also announce a distinguished American to lead this effort, to strengthen American security: a military veteran, an effective governor, a true patriot, a trusted friend—Pennsylvania's Tom Ridge. (Applause.) He will lead, oversee and coordinate a comprehensive national strategy to safeguard our country against terrorism, and respond to any attacks that may come.

These measures are essential. But the only way to defeat terrorism as a threat to our way of life is to stop it, eliminate it, and destroy it where it grows.

Many will be involved in this effort, from FBI agents to intelligence operatives to the reservists we have called to active duty. All deserve our thanks, and all have our prayers. And tonight, a few miles from the damaged Pentagon, I have a message for our military: Be ready. I've called the Armed Forces to alert, and there is a reason. The hour is coming when America will act, and you will make us proud.

This is not, however, just America's fight. And what is at stake is not just America's freedom. This is the world's fight. This is civilization's fight. This is the fight of all who believe in progress and pluralism, tolerance and freedom.

We ask every nation to join us. We will ask, and we will need, the help of police forces, intelligence services, and banking systems around the world. The United States is grateful that many nations and many international organizations have already responded—with sympathy and with support. Nations from Latin America, to Asia, to Africa, to Europe, to the Islamic world. Perhaps the NATO Charter reflects best the attitude of the world: An attack on one is an attack on all.

The civilized world is rallying to America's side. They understand that if this terror goes unpunished, their own cities, their own citizens may be next. Terror, unanswered, can not only bring down buildings, it can threaten the stability of legitimate governments. And you know what—we're not going to allow it.

Americans are asking: What is expected of us? I ask you to live your lives, and hug your children. I know many citizens have fears tonight, and I ask you to be calm and resolute, even in the face of a continuing threat.

I ask you to uphold the values of America, and remember why so many have come here. We are in a fight for our principles, and our first responsibility is to live by them. No one should be singled out for unfair treatment or unkind words because of their ethnic background or religious faith.

I ask you to continue to support the victims of this tragedy with your contributions. Those who want to give can go to a central source of information, libertyunites.org, to find the names of groups providing direct help in New York, Pennsylvania, and Virginia.

The thousands of FBI agents who are now at work in this investigation may need your cooperation, and I ask you to give it.

I ask for your patience, with the delays and inconveniences that may accompany tighter security; and for your patience in what will be a long struggle.

I ask your continued participation and confidence in the American economy. Terrorists attacked a symbol of American prosperity. They did not touch its source. America is successful because of the hard work, and creativity, and enterprise of our people. These were the true strengths of our economy before September 11th, and they are our strengths today.

And, finally, please continue praying for the victims of terror and their families, for those in uniform, and for our great country. Prayer has comforted us in sorrow, and will help strengthen us for the journey ahead.

Tonight I thank my fellow Americans for what you have already done and for what you will do. And ladies and gentlemen of the Congress, I thank you, their representatives, for what you have already done and for what we will do together.

Tonight, we face new and sudden national challenges. We will come together to improve air safety, to dramatically expand the number of air marshals on domestic flights, and take new measures to prevent hijacking.

We will come together to promote stability and keep our airlines flying, with direct assistance during this emergency.

We will come together to give law enforcement the additional tools it needs to track down terror here at home. We will come together to strengthen our intelligence capabilities to know the plans of terrorists before they act, and find them before they strike.

We will come together to take active steps that strengthen America's economy, and put our people back to work.

Tonight we welcome two leaders who embody the extraordinary spirit of all New Yorkers: Governor George Pataki, and Mayor Rudolph Giuliani. As a symbol of America's resolve, my administration will work with Congress, and these two leaders, to show the world that we will rebuild New York City.

After all that has just passed—all the lives taken, and all the possibilities and hopes that died with them—it is natural to wonder if America's future is one of fear. Some speak of an age of terror. I know there are struggles ahead, and dangers to face. But this country will define our times, not be defined by them. As long as the United States of America is determined and strong, this will not be an age of terror; this will be an age of liberty, here and across the world.

Great harm has been done to us. We have suffered great loss. And in our grief and anger we have found our mission and our moment. Freedom and fear are at war. The advance of human freedom—the great achievement of our time, and the great hope of every time—now depends on us. Our nation—this generation—will lift a dark threat of violence from our people and our future. We will rally the world to this cause by our efforts, by our courage. We will not tire, we will not falter, and we will not fail.

It is my hope that in the months and years ahead, life will return almost to normal. We'll go back to our lives and routines, and that is good. Even grief recedes with time and grace. But our resolve must not pass. Each of us will remember what happened that day, and to whom it happened. We'll remember the moment the news came—where we were and what we were doing. Some will remember an image of a fire, or a story of rescue. Some will carry memories of a face and a voice gone forever.

And I will carry this: It is the police shield of a man named George Howard, who died at the World Trade Center trying to save others. It was given to me by his mom, Arlene, as a proud memorial to her son. This is my reminder of lives that ended, and a task that does not end.

I will not forget this wound to our country or those who inflicted it. I will not yield; I will not rest; I will not relent in waging this struggle for freedom and security for the American people.

The course of this conflict is not known, yet its outcome is certain. Freedom and fear, justice and cruelty, have always been at war, and we know that God is not neutral between them.

Fellow citizens, we'll meet violence with patient justice—assured of the rightness of our cause, and confident of the victories to come. In all that lies before us, may God grant us wisdom, and may He watch over the United States of America.

Thank you.

Office of the Press Secretary, the White House, Washington, D.C.

PRESIDENT GEORGE W. BUSH DENOUNCES THE "AXIS OF EVIL"

The first State of the Union Address following the attacks of September 11, 2001 was entirely dominated by those events. The speech dramatically conveyed the extent to which terrorism had come to be the central concern of American public life.

2001 STATE OF THE UNION ADDRESS

January 30, 2001

As we gather tonight, our nation is at war, our economy is in recession and the civilized world faces unprecedented dangers. Yet the state of our union has never been stronger.

We last met in an hour of shock and suffering. In four short months, our nation has comforted the victims, begun to rebuild New York and the Pentagon, rallied a great coalition, captured, arrested and rid the world of thousands of terrorists, destroyed Afghanistan's terrorist training camps, saved a people from starvation and freed a country from brutal oppression.

The American flag flies again over our embassy in Kabul. Terrorists who once occupied Afghanistan now occupy cells at Guantánamo Bay. And terrorist leaders who urged followers to sacrifice their lives are running for their own.

America and Afghanistan are now allies against terror. We'll be partners in rebuilding that country, and this evening we welcomed the distinguished interim leader of a liberated Afghanistan, Chairman Hamid Karzai.

The last time we met in this chamber, the mothers and daughters of Afghanistan were captives in their own homes, forbidden from working or going to school. Today women are free, and are part of Afghanistan's new government, and we welcome the new minister of women's affairs, Dr. Sima Samar.

Our progress is a tribute to the spirit of the Afghan people, to the resolve of our coalition and to the might of the United States military.

When I called our troops into action, I did so with complete confidence in their courage and skill, and tonight, thanks to them, we are winning the war on terror. The men and women of our armed forces have delivered a message now clear to every enemy of the United States: Even 7,000 miles away, across oceans and continents, on mountaintops and in caves, you will not escape the justice of this nation.

For many Americans, these four months have brought sorrow and pain that will never completely go away. Every day a retired firefighter returns to Ground Zero, to feel closer to his two sons who died there. At a memorial in New York, a little boy left his football with a note for his lost father: "Dear Daddy, please take this to Heaven. I don't want to play football until I can play with you again someday." Last month, at the grave of her husband, Michael, C.I.A. officer and Marine who died in Mazar-i-Sharif, Shannon Spann said these words of farewell: "Semper Fi, my love." Shannon is with us tonight.

Shannon, I assure you and all who have lost a loved one that our cause is just and our country will never forget the debt we owe Michael and all who gave their lives for freedom.

Our cause is just, and it continues. Our discoveries in Afghanistan confirmed our worst fears and showed us the true scope of the task ahead. We have seen the depth of our enemies' hatred in videos where they laugh about the loss of innocent life. And the depth of their hatred is equaled by the madness of the destruction they design. We have found diagrams of American nuclear power plants and public water facilities, detailed instructions for making chemical weapons, surveillance maps of American cities and thorough descriptions of landmarks in America and throughout the world.

What we have found in Afghanistan confirms that, far from ending there, our war against terror is only beginning. Most of the 19 men who hijacked planes on Sept. 11 were trained in Afghanistan's camps, and so were tens of thousands of others. Thousands of dangerous killers, schooled in the methods of murder, often supported by outlaw regimes, are now spread throughout the world like ticking time bombs, set to go off without warning.

Thanks to the work of our law enforcement officials and coalition partners, hundreds of terrorists have been arrested, yet tens of thousands of trained terrorists are still at large. These enemies view the entire world as a battlefield, and we must pursue them wherever they are. So long as training camps operate, so long as nations harbor terrorists, freedom is at risk, and America and our allies must not, and will not, allow it.

Our nation will continue to be steadfast and patient and persistent in the pursuit of two great objectives. First, we will shut down terrorist camps, disrupt terrorist plans and bring terrorists to justice. And second, we must prevent the terrorists and regimes who seek chemical, biological, or nuclear weapons from threatening the United States and the world.

Our military has put the terror training camps of Afghanistan out of business, yet camps still exist in at least a dozen countries. A terrorist underworld, including groups like Hamas, Hezbollah, Islamic Jihad, Jaishe-Muhammad, operates in remote jungles and deserts, and hides in the centers of large cities.

While the most visible military action is in Afghanistan, America is acting elsewhere. We now have troops in the Philippines helping to train that country's armed forces to go after terrorist cells that have executed an American and still hold hostages. Our soldiers, working with the Bosnian government, seized terrorists who were plotting to bomb our embassy. Our Navy is patrolling the coast of Africa to block the shipment of weapons and the establishment of terrorist camps in Somalia.

My hope is that all nations will heed our call, and eliminate the terrorist parasites who threaten their countries, and our own. Many nations are acting forcefully. Pakistan is now cracking down on terror, and I admire the strong leadership of President Musharraf. But some governments will be timid in the face of terror. And make no mistake about it: If they do not act, America will.

Our second goal is to prevent regimes that sponsor terror from threatening America or our friends and allies with weapons of mass destruction.

Some of these regimes have been pretty quiet since Sept. 11. But we know their true nature. North Korea is a regime arming with missiles and weapons of mass destruction, while starving its citizens.

Iran aggressively pursues these weapons and exports terror, while an unelected few repress the Iranian people's hope for freedom.

Iraq continues to flaunt its hostility toward America and to support terror. The Iraqi regime has plotted to develop anthrax and nerve gas and nuclear weapons for over a decade. This is a regime that has already used poison gas to murder thousands of its own citizens, leaving the bodies of mothers huddled over their dead children. This is a regime that agreed to international inspections, then kicked out the inspectors. This is a regime that has something to hide from the civilized world.

States like these, and their terrorist allies, constitute an axis of evil, arming to threaten the peace of the world. By seeking weapons of mass destruction, these regimes pose a grave and growing danger. They could provide these arms to terrorists, giving them the means to match their hatred. They could attack our allies or attempt to blackmail the United States. In any of these cases, the price of indifference would be catastrophic.

We will work closely with our coalition to deny terrorists and their state sponsors the materials, technology, and expertise to make and deliver weapons of mass destruction. We will develop and deploy effective missile defenses to protect America and our allies from sudden attack. And all nations should know: America will do what is necessary to ensure our nation's security.

We'll be deliberate. Yet time is not on our side. I will not wait on events while dangers gather. I will not stand by as peril draws closer and closer. The United

States of America will not permit the world's most dangerous regimes to threaten us with the world's most destructive weapons.

Our war on terror is well begun, but it is only begun. This campaign may not be finished on our watch, yet it must be and it will be waged on our watch.

We can't stop short. If we stopped now, leaving terror camps intact and terror states unchecked, our sense of security would be false and temporary.

History has called America and our allies to action, and it is both our responsibility and our privilege to fight freedom's fight.

Our first priority must always be the security of our nation, and that will be reflected in the budget I send to Congress. My budget supports three great goals for America: We will win this war, we'll protect our homeland and we will revive our economy.

Sept. 11 brought out the best in America, and the best in this Congress, and I join the American people in applauding your unity and resolve.

Now Americans deserve to have this same spirit directed toward addressing problems here at home. I'm a proud member of my party. Yet as we act to win the war, protect our people and create jobs in America, we must act first and foremost not as Republicans, not as Democrats, but as Americans.

It costs a lot to fight this war. We have spent more than a billion dollars a month, over $30 million a day, and we must be prepared for future operations. Afghanistan proved that expensive precision weapons defeat the enemy and spare innocent lives, and we need more of them. We need to replace aging aircraft and make our military more agile to put our troops anywhere in the world quickly and safely. Our men and women in uniform deserve the best weapons, the best equipment, the best training, and they also deserve another pay raise. My budget includes the largest increase in defense spending in two decades, because while the price of freedom and security is high, it is never too high. Whatever it costs to defend our country, we will pay.

The next priority of my budget is to do everything possible to protect our citizens and strengthen our nation against the ongoing threat of another attack.

Time and distance from the events of Sept. 11 will not make us safer unless we act on its lessons. America is no longer protected by vast oceans. We are protected from attack only by vigorous action abroad, and increased vigilance at home.

My budget nearly doubles funding for a sustained strategy of homeland security, focused on four key areas: bioterrorism, emergency response, airport and border security, and improved intelligence. We will develop vaccines to fight anthrax and other deadly diseases. We'll increase funding to help states and communities train and equip our heroic police and firefighters. We will improve intelligence collection and sharing, expand patrols at our borders, strengthen the security of air travel and use technology to track the arrivals and departures of visitors to the United States.

Homeland security will make America not only stronger, but in many ways better. Knowledge gained from bioterrorism research will improve public health; stronger police and fire departments will mean safer neighborhoods; stricter border enforcement will help combat illegal drugs.

And as government works to better secure our homeland, America will continue to depend on the eyes and ears of alert citizens. A few days before Christmas, an airline flight attendant spotted a passenger lighting a match. The crew and passengers quickly subdued the man, who had been trained by Al Qaeda and was armed with explosives. The people on that plane were alert, and as a result likely saved nearly 200 lives, and tonight we welcome and thank flight attendants Hermis Moutardier and Cristina Jones.

Once we have funded our national security and our homeland security, the final great priority of my budget is economic security for the American people.

To achieve these great national objectives—to win the war, protect the homeland and revitalize our economy—our budget will run a deficit that will be small and short term so long as Congress restrains spending and acts in a fiscally responsible manner. We have clear priorities, and we must act at home with the same purpose and resolve we have shown overseas.

We will prevail in the war and we will defeat this recession.

Americans who've lost their jobs need our help. And I support extending unemployment benefits and direct assistance for health care coverage. Yet American workers want more than unemployment checks, they want a steady paycheck. When America works, America prospers, so my economic security plan can be summed up in one word: jobs.

Good jobs begin with good schools, and here we've made a fine start.

Republicans and Democrats worked together to achieve historic education reform so that no child is left behind. I was proud to work with members of both parties, Chairman John Boehner and Congressman George Miller, Senator Judd Gregg. And I was so proud of our work I even had nice things to say about my friend Ted Kennedy. I know the folks at the Crawford coffee shop couldn't believe I'd say such a thing. But our work on this bill shows what is possible if we set aside posturing and focus on results.

There is more to do. We need to prepare our children to read and succeed in school with improved Head Start and early childhood development programs. We must upgrade our teacher colleges and teacher training and launch a major recruiting drive with a great goal for America, a quality teacher in every classroom.

Good jobs also depend on reliable and affordable energy. This Congress must act to encourage conservation, promote technology, build infrastructure, and it must act to increase energy production at home so America is less dependent on foreign oil.

Good jobs depend on expanded trade. Selling into new markets creates new jobs, so I ask Congress to finally approve trade promotion authority. On these two key issues, trade and energy, the House of Representatives has acted to create jobs, and I urge the Senate to pass this legislation.

Good jobs depend on sound tax policy. Last year, some in this hall thought my tax relief plan was too small; some thought it was too big. But when the checks arrived in the mail, most Americans thought tax relief was just about right. Congress listened to the people and responded by reducing tax rates, doubling the child credit and ending the death tax. For the sake of long-term growth and to help Americans plan for the future, let's make these tax cuts permanent.

The way out of this recession, the way to create jobs, is to grow the economy by encouraging investment in factories and equipment, and by speeding up tax relief so people have more money to spend. For the sake of American workers, let's pass a stimulus package.

Good jobs must be the aim of welfare reform. As we reauthorize these important reforms, we must always remember the goal is to reduce dependency on government and offer every American the dignity of a job.

Americans know economic security can vanish in an instant without health security. I ask Congress to join me this year to enact a patients' bill of rights, to give uninsured workers credits to help buy health coverage, to approve an historic increase in the spending for veterans' health, and to give seniors a sound and modern Medicare system that includes coverage for prescription drugs.

A good job should lead to security in retirement. I ask Congress to enact new safeguards for 401(k) and pension plans. Employees who have worked hard and saved all their lives should not have to risk losing everything if their company fails. Through stricter accounting standards and tougher disclosure requirements, corporate America must be made more accountable to employees and shareholders and held to the highest standards of conduct.

Retirement security also depends upon keeping the commitments of Social Security, and we will. We must make Social Security financially stable and allow personal retirement accounts for younger workers who choose them.

Members, you and I will work together in the months ahead on other issues: productive farm policy, a cleaner environment, broader home ownership, especially among minorities, and ways to encourage the good work of charities and faith-based groups. I ask you to join me on these important domestic issues in the same spirit of cooperation we have applied to our war against terrorism.

During these last few months, I have been humbled and privileged to see the true character of this country in a time of testing. Our enemies believed America was weak and materialistic, that we would splinter in fear and selfishness. They were as wrong as they are evil.

The American people have responded magnificently, with courage and compassion, strength and resolve. As I have met the heroes, hugged the families, and looked into the tired faces of rescuers, I have stood in awe of the American people.

And I hope you will join me in expressing thanks to one American for the strength, and calm, and comfort she brings to our nation in crisis: our first lady, Laura Bush.

None of us would ever wish the evil that was done on Sept. 11, yet after America was attacked, it was as if our entire country looked into a mirror, and saw our better selves. We were reminded that we are citizens, with obligations to each other, to our country, and to history. We began to think less of the goods we can accumulate, and more about the good we can do. For too long our culture has said, "If it feels good, do it." Now America is embracing a new ethic and a new creed: "Let's roll." In the sacrifice of soldiers, the fierce brotherhood of firefighters and the bravery and generosity of ordinary citizens, we have glimpsed what a new culture of responsibility could look like. We want to be a nation that serves goals larger than self. We've been offered a unique opportunity, and we must not let this moment pass.

My call tonight is for every American to commit at least two years, four thousand hours over the rest of your lifetime, to the service of your neighbors and your nation.

Many are already serving and I thank you. If you aren't sure how to help, I've got a good place to start. To sustain and extend the best that has emerged in America, I invite you to join the new U.S.A. Freedom Corps. The Freedom Corps will focus on three areas of need: responding in case of crisis at home, rebuilding our communities and extending American compassion throughout the world.

One purpose of the U.S.A. Freedom Corps will be homeland security. America needs retired doctors and nurses who can be mobilized in major emergencies, volunteers to help police and fire departments, transportation and utility workers well-trained in spotting danger.

Our country also needs citizens working to rebuild our communities. We need mentors to love children, especially children whose parents are in prison, and we need more talented teachers in troubled schools. U.S.A. Freedom Corps will expand and improve the good efforts of AmeriCorps and Senior Corps to recruit more than 200,000 new volunteers.

And America needs citizens to extend the compassion of our country to every part of the world. So we will renew the promise of the Peace Corps, double its volunteers over the next five years and ask it to join a new effort to encourage development and education and opportunity in the Islamic world.

This time of adversity offers a unique moment of opportunity, a moment we must seize to change our culture. Through the gathering momentum of millions of acts of service and decency and kindness, I know we can overcome evil with greater good.

And we have a great opportunity during this time of war to lead the world toward the values that will bring lasting peace. All fathers and mothers, in all societies, want their children to be educated and live free from poverty and violence. No people on earth yearn to be oppressed or aspire to servitude or eagerly await the midnight knock of the secret police.

If anyone doubts this, let them look to Afghanistan, where the Islamic "street" greeted the fall of tyranny with song and celebration. Let the skeptics look to Islam's own rich history, with its centuries of learning and tolerance and progress.

America will lead by defending liberty and justice because they are right and true and unchanging for all people everywhere. No nation owns these aspirations and no nation is exempt from them. We have no intention of imposing our culture, but America will always stand firm for the non-negotiable demands of human dignity, the rule of law, limits on the power of the state, respect for women, private property, free speech, equal justice and religious tolerance.

America will take the side of brave men and women who advocate these values around the world, including the Islamic world, because we have a greater objective than eliminating threats and containing resentment. We seek a just and peaceful world beyond the war on terror.

In this moment of opportunity, a common danger is erasing old rivalries. America is working with Russia and China and India in ways we never have before to achieve peace and prosperity. In every region, free markets and free trade and free societies are proving their power to lift lives. Together with friends and allies, from Europe to Asia and Africa to Latin America, we will demonstrate that the forces of terror cannot stop the momentum of freedom.

The last time I spoke here, I expressed the hope that life would return to normal. In some ways, it has. In others, it never will. Those of us who have lived through these challenging times have been changed by them. We've come to know truths that we will never question: Evil is real, and it must be opposed.

Beyond all differences of race or creed, we are one country, mourning together and facing danger together. Deep in the American character, there is honor, and it is stronger than cynicism. And many have discovered again that even in tragedy, especially in tragedy, God is near.

In a single instant, we realized that this will be a decisive decade in the history of liberty, that we've been called to a unique role in human events.

Rarely has the world faced a choice more clear or consequential.

Our enemies send other people's children on missions of suicide and murder.

They embrace tyranny and death as a cause and a creed. We stand for a different choice, made long ago, on the day of our founding. We affirm it again today. We choose freedom and the dignity of every life.

Steadfast in our purpose, we now press on. We have known freedom's price.

We have shown freedom's power. And in this great conflict, my fellow Americans, we will see freedom's victory.

Thank you all. May God bless.

Office of the Press Secretary, the White House, Washington, D.C.

AN UNPRECEDENTED APOLOGY

On July 16, 2002, a few days before the 30th anniversary of its "Bloody Friday" bombing attack in Belfast, Northern Ireland, the Irish Republican Army issued a rare apology to the victims of its long campaign of terror against British rule over Northern Ireland.

IRA STATEMENT

Sunday, July 21 marks the 30th anniversary of an IRA operation in Belfast in 1972 which resulted in nine people being killed and many more injured. While it was not our intention to injure or kill noncombatants, the reality is that on this and on a number of other occasions, that was the consequence of our actions.

It is, therefore, appropriate on the anniversary of this tragic event, that we address all of the deaths and injuries of noncombatants caused by us.

We offer our sincere apologies and condolences to their families.

There have been fatalities amongst combatants on all sides. We also acknowledge the grief and pain of their relatives.

The future will not be found in denying collective failures and mistakes, or closing minds and hearts to the plight of those who have been hurt. That includes all of the victims of the conflict, combatants and noncombatants.

It will not be achieved by creating a hierarchy of victims in which some are deemed more or less worthy than others.

The process of conflict resolution requires the equal acknowledgement of the grief and loss of others. On this anniversary, we are endeavoring to fulfill this responsibility to those we have hurt.

The IRA is committed unequivocally to the search for freedom, justice and peace in Ireland. We remain totally committed to the peace process and to dealing with the challenges and difficulties which this presents. This includes the acceptance of past mistakes and of the hurt and pain we have caused to others.

As received by *An Phoblacht (Republican News)* Tuesday, July 16, 2002, and published on the Conflict Archive, available at http://cain.ulst.ac.uk/events/peace/docs/ira160702.htm.

THE U.S. GOVERNMENT'S CASE AGAINST AL QAEDA

In December, 2001, the U.S. Justice Department indicted Zacarias Moussaoui, the so-called "20th hijacker" on six counts. Included in that indictment was a summary of what the government then knew, or believed, about the al Qaeda organization to which Moussaoui belonged, and about the group's leader, Osama (Usama) bin Laden.

IN THE UNITED STATES DISTRICT COURT FOR THE EASTERN DISTRICT OF VIRGINIA

DECEMBER 2001 TERM—AT ALEXANDRIA

INDICTMENT

UNITED STATES OF AMERICA v. ZACARIAS MOUSSAOUI aka "Shaqil,"aka "Abu Khalid al Sahrawi"

THE GRAND JURY CHARGES THAT:

COUNT ONE (Conspiracy to Commit Acts of Terrorism Transcending National Boundaries)

Background: al Qaeda

1. At all relevant times from in or about 1989 until the date of the filing of this Indictment, an international terrorist group existed which was dedicated to opposing non-Islamic governments with force and violence. This organization grew out of the "mekhtab al khidemat" (the "Services Office") organization which had maintained offices in various parts of the world, including Afghanistan, Pakistan (particularly in Peshawar), and the United States. The group was founded by Usama Bin Laden and Muhammad Atef, a/k/a "Abu Hafs al Masry," together with "Abu Ubaidah al Banshiri," and others. From in or about 1989 until the present, the group called itself "al Qaeda" ("the Base"). From 1989 until in or about 1991, the group (hereafter referred to as "al Qaeda") was headquartered in Afghanistan and Peshawar, Pakistan. In or about 1991, the leadership of al Qaeda, including its "*emir*" (or prince) Usama Bin Laden, relocated to the Sudan. Al Qaeda was headquartered in the Sudan from approximately 1991 until approximately 1996 but still maintained offices in various parts of the world. In 1996, Usama Bin Laden and other members of al Qaeda relocated to Afghanistan. At all relevant times, al Qaeda was led by its *emir*, Usama Bin Laden. Members of al Qaeda pledged an oath of allegiance (called a "*bayat*") to Usama Bin Laden and al Qaeda. Those who were suspected of collaborating against al Qaeda were to be identified and killed.

2. Bin Laden and al Qaeda violently opposed the United States for several reasons. First, the United States was regarded as an "infidel" because it was not governed in a manner consistent with the group's extremist interpretation of Islam. Second, the United States was viewed as providing essential support for other "infidel" governments and institutions, particularly the governments of Saudi Arabia

and Egypt, the nation of Israel, and the United Nations organization, which were regarded as enemies of the group. Third, al Qaeda opposed the involvement of the United States armed forces in the Gulf War in 1991 and in Operation Restore Hope in Somalia in 1992 and 1993. In particular, al Qaeda opposed the continued presence of American military forces in Saudi Arabia (and elsewhere on the Saudi Arabian peninsula) following the Gulf War. Fourth, al Qaeda opposed the United States Government because of the arrest, conviction and imprisonment of persons belonging to al Qaeda or its affiliated terrorist groups or those with whom it worked. For these and other reasons, Bin Laden declared a jihad, or holy war, against the United States, which he has carried out through al Qaeda and its affiliated organizations.

3. One of the principal goals of al Qaeda was to drive the United States armed forces out of Saudi Arabia (and elsewhere on the Saudi Arabian peninsula) and Somalia by violence. Members of al Qaeda issued *fatwahs* (rulings on Islamic law) indicating that such attacks were both proper and necessary.

4. Al Qaeda functioned both on its own and through some of the terrorist organizations that operated under its umbrella, including: Egyptian Islamic Jihad, which was led by Ayman al-Zawahiri, and at times, the Islamic Group (also known as "el Gamaa Islamia" or simply "Gamaa't"), and a number of jihad groups in other countries, including the Sudan, Egypt, Saudi Arabia, Yemen, Somalia, Eritrea, Djibouti, Afghanistan, Pakistan, Bosnia, Croatia, Albania, Algeria, Tunisia, Lebanon, the Philippines, Tajikistan, Azerbaijan, and the Kashmiri region of India and the Chechnyan region of Russia. Al Qaeda also maintained cells and personnel in a number of countries to facilitate its activities, including in Kenya, Tanzania, the United Kingdom, Germany, Canada, Malaysia, and the United States.

5. Al Qaeda had a command and control structure which included a *majlis al shura* (or consultation council) which discussed and approved major undertakings, including terrorist operations. Al Qaeda also had a "military committee" which considered and approved "military" matters.

6. Usama Bin Laden and al Qaeda also forged alliances with the National Islamic Front in the Sudan and with representatives of the government of Iran, and its associated terrorist group Hizballah, for the purpose of working together against their perceived common enemies in the West, particularly the United States.

7. Since at least 1989, until the filing of this Indictment, Usama Bin Laden and the terrorist group al Qaeda sponsored, managed, and/or financially supported training camps in Afghanistan, which camps were used to instruct members and associates of al Qaeda and its affiliated terrorist groups in the use of firearms, explosives, chemical weapons, and other weapons of mass destruction. In addition to providing training in the use of various weapons, these camps were used to conduct operational planning against United States targets around the world and experiments in the use of chemical and biological weapons. These camps were also used to train others in security and counterintelligence methods, such as the use of codes and passwords, and to teach members and associates of al Qaeda about traveling to perform operations. For example, al Qaeda instructed its members and associates to dress in "Western" attire and to use other methods to avoid detection by security officials. The group also taught its members and associates to monitor media reporting of its operations to determine the effectiveness of their terrorist activities.

8. Since in or about 1996, Usama Bin Laden and others operated al Qaeda from their headquarters in Afghanistan. During this time, Bin Laden and others forged

close relations with the Taliban in Afghanistan. To that end, Bin Laden informed other al Qaeda members and associates outside Afghanistan of their support of, and alliance with, the Taliban. Bin Laden also endorsed a declaration of jihad (holy war) issued by the "Ulema Union of Afghanistan."

. . .

Overt Acts

In furtherance of the conspiracy, and to effect its objects, the defendant, and others known and unknown to the Grand Jury, committed the following overt acts:

The Provision of Guesthouses and Training Camps

1. At various times from at least as early as 1989, Usama Bin Laden, and others known and unknown, provided training camps and guesthouses in Afghanistan, including camps known as Khalden, Derunta, Khost, Siddiq, and Jihad Wal, for the use of al Qaeda and its affiliated groups.

The Training

2. At various times from at least as early as 1990, unindicted co-conspirators, known and unknown, provided military and intelligence training in various areas, including Afghanistan, Pakistan, and the Sudan, for the use of al Qaeda and its affiliated groups, including the Egyptian Islamic Jihad.

Financial and Business Dealings

3. At various times from at least as early as 1989 until the date of the filing of this Indictment, Usama Bin Laden, and others known and unknown, engaged in financial and business transactions on behalf of al Qaeda, including, but not limited to: purchasing land for training camps; purchasing warehouses for storage of items, including explosives; purchasing communications and electronics equipment; transferring funds between corporate accounts; and transporting currency and weapons to members of al Qaeda and its associated terrorist organizations in various countries throughout the world.

The Efforts to Obtain Nuclear Weapons and Their Components

4. At various times from at least as early as 1992, Usama Bin Laden, and others known and unknown, made efforts to obtain the components of nuclear weapons.

The *Fatwahs* Against American Troops in Saudi Arabia and Yemen

5. At various times from in or about 1992 until the date of the filing of this Indictment, Usama Bin Laden, working together with members of the *fatwah* committee of al Qaeda, disseminated *fatwahs* to other members and

associates of al Qaeda that the United States forces stationed on the Saudi Arabian peninsula, including both Saudi Arabia and Yemen, should be attacked.

The *Fatwah* Against American Troops in Somalia

6. At various times from in or about 1992 until in or about 1993, Usama Bin Laden, working together with members of the *fatwah* committee of al Qaeda, disseminated *fatwahs* to other members and associates of al Qaeda that the United States forces stationed in the Horn of Africa, including Somalia, should be attacked.

The *Fatwah* Regarding Deaths of Nonbelievers

7. On various occasions, an unindicted co-conspirator advised other members of al Qaeda that it was Islamically proper to engage in violent actions against "infidels" (nonbelievers), even if others might be killed by such actions, because if the others were "innocent," they would go to paradise, and if they were not "innocent," they deserved to die.

The August 1996 Declaration of War

8. On or about August 23, 1996, a Declaration of Jihad indicating that it was from the Hindu Kush mountains in Afghanistan entitled, "Message from Usamah Bin-Muhammad Bin-Laden to His Muslim Brothers in the Whole World and Especially in the Arabian Peninsula: Declaration of Jihad Against the Americans Occupying the Land of the Two Holy Mosques; Expel the Heretics from the Arabian Peninsula" was disseminated.

The February 1998 *Fatwah* Against American Civilians

9. In February 1998, Usama Bin Laden endorsed a *fatwah* under the banner of the "International Islamic Front for Jihad on the Jews and Crusaders." This *fatwah*, published in the publication *Al-Quds al-'Arabi* on February 23, 1998, stated that Muslims should kill Americans—including civilians—anywhere in the world where they can be found.
10. In an address in or about 1998, Usama Bin Laden cited American aggression against Islam and encouraged a jihad that would eliminate the Americans from the Arabian Peninsula.

Bin Laden Endorses the Nuclear Bomb of Islam

11. On or about May 29, 1998, Usama Bin Laden issued a statement entitled "The Nuclear Bomb of Islam," under the banner of the "International Islamic Front for Fighting the Jews and the Crusaders," in which he stated that "it is the duty of the Muslims to prepare as much force as possible to terrorize the enemies of God."

Usama Bin Laden Issues Further Threats in June 1999

12. In or about June 1999, in an interview with an Arabic-language television station, Usama Bin Laden issued a further threat indicating that all American males should be killed.

Usama Bin Laden Calls for "Jihad" to Free Imprisoned Terrorists

13. In or about September 2000, in an interview with an Arabic-language television station, Usama Bin Laden called for a "jihad" to release the "brothers" in jail "everywhere."

THE RISE AND FALL OF THE URBAN GUERILLAS

In the spring of 1998, the following communiqué was issued by what remained of the Red Army Faction, once one of the most notorious—and glamorous—revolutionary terrorist organizations in the Western world. The document describes, sometimes in excruciating detail, the development of the group's strategic and tactical thinking. It provides a unique and unrepentant insider's view of the aims and history of the revolutionary movement that grew up in the 1960s, flourished in the 1970s, flailed about in the 1980s, and finally collapsed altogether in the 1990s. The author, or authors, acknowledge the failure of their effort, but neither remorse nor guilt. They announce the end of the RAF, but do not renounce its methods. The text that is somewhat abridged here was translated by Arm the Spirit and is available on the This is Baader-Meinhof Web site.

COMMUNIQUÉ ANNOUNCING THE DISBANDING OF THE RED ARMY FACTION (EXCERPTS)

Almost 28 years ago, on May 14, 1970, the RAF was born from an act of liberation: Today we are ending this project. The urban guerrilla in the form of the RAF is now history.

We, that is all of us who were organized in the RAF until the end, are taking this step jointly. From now on, we, like all others from this association, are former RAF militants.

We stand by our history. The RAF was the revolutionary attempt by a minority of people to resist the tendencies in this society and contribute to the overthrow of capitalist conditions. We are proud to have been part of this attempt.

The end of this project shows that we were not able to succeed on this path. But this does not speak against the necessity and legitimacy of revolt. The RAF was our decision to stand on the side of those people struggling against domination and for liberation all across the world. For us, this was the right decision to make.

Hundreds of years in prison terms for RAF prisoners were not able to wipe us out, nor could all the attempts to eradicate the guerrilla. We wanted a confrontation with the ruling powers. We acted as subjects when we decided upon the RAF 27 years ago. We remain subjects today, as we consign ourselves to history.

The results are critical of us. But the RAF—like all of the left until now—was nothing more than a phase of transition on the path to liberation.

After fascism and war, the RAF brought something new into the society: The moment of a break with the system and the historic flash of decisive opposition to the conditions which structurally subject and exploit people and which brought about a society in which the people are forced to fight against one another. The struggle in the social cracks, which marked our opposition, pushed a genuine social liberation forward; this break with the system, a system in which profit is the subject and people are the objects, and the desire for a life without the lies and weight of this distorted society. Fed up with stooping down, functioning, kicking, and being kicked. From rejection to attack, to liberation.

The RAF Arose from the Hope for Liberation

Backed by the courage which emanated from the guerrillas from the South to the rich nations of the North, the RAF came about in the early 1970s in solidarity with liberation movements in order to take up a common struggle. Millions of people saw in the struggles of resistance and liberation around the globe a chance for themselves as well. The armed struggle was a hope for liberation in many parts of the world. In Germany, too, tens of thousands of people were in solidarity with the struggles of the militant organizations Second of June Movement, the Revolutionary Cells (RZ), the RAF, and later Rote Zora. The RAF came about as a result of the discussions of thousands of people in Germany who began to think about armed struggle as a means to liberation in the late 1960s and early 1970s. The RAF took up the struggle against the state, a state which had never broken with its national-socialist past following the liberation from Nazi fascism.

The armed struggle was a rebellion against an authoritarian form of society, against alienation and competition. It was a rebellion for a new social and cultural reality. In the euphoria of the global attempts at liberation, the time was right for a decisive struggle which seriously aimed at overturning and no longer accepting the pseudo-natural legitimacy of the system.

1975–77

With the 1975 occupation of the German embassy in Stockholm, the RAF launched a phase during which it did everything possible to liberate its prisoners from jail.

First came the "1977 Offensive", during which the RAF kidnapped [one of Germany's leading industrialists, Hanns-Martin] Schleyer. The RAF posed the question of power. This began a radical and decisive attempt to push through an offensive position for the revolutionary left against the state power. It was exactly this which the state wanted to prevent. The explosive escalation of the conflict, however, also came against the background of German history: The continuity of Nazism in the West German state, which the RAF attacked with its offensive.

Schleyer, a member of the SS during the Nazi regime, was, like many Nazis in all levels of society, back in office with all his honor intact. Nazis built careers in the West German state in government positions, the courts, the police apparatus, the armed forces, the media, and in major corporations. These anti-Semites, racists, and genocidal murderers were often times the same people responsible for crimes against humanity under the Nazis, and now they were back among the powerful elite.

Schleyer worked towards the ends of the Nazis and the capitalists to create a European economic region under German dominance. The Nazis had wanted a Europe in which there were neither struggles between industrial workers and capital nor any resistance whatsoever to their system. They wanted to end the class struggle by utilizing German workers or workers who could "be made like Germans" and incorporating them into their society. All others were to be enslaved to forced labor or systematically destroyed in concentration camps.

With the liberation from Nazi fascism came the end of the industrial destruction of people by the Nazis, but there was no liberation from capitalism. After 1945, Schleyer worked towards the same economic goals—in a more modernized form. The push towards modernization came with the social democratic model of the 1970s. As the chief of industry, Schleyer was continually building up a system to contain social resistance to the conditions of capital—for example, by locking out workers—and to integrate workers into the system by means of negotiated contracts for social security. This integration was meant to incorporate the German portion of the society most of all, meanwhile capital increasingly exploited immigrant workers and, at the global level, dominated and exploited the people of the southern hemisphere, which resulted in massive destruction from hunger. The continuity of the system which Schleyer embodied—in the 1970s during the period of the social democratic model—was a crucial moment in the building and development of the Federal Republic of Germany.

The Absolute Necessity to Approve of All Measures Enacted by the Crisis Staff and the Repression of All Critical Voices, Going So Far As to Try and Eliminate the Political Prisoners—These Were the Same Reactionary Techniques Utilized by the Nazis

The actions of the 1977 offensive made it clear that there were elements in the society which would in no way be integrated into or controlled by the system. After the Nazis had eliminated the resistance, the actions of the urban guerrilla groups after 1968 marked a return to a moment of class struggle, no longer integrated to the ruling powers, in post-fascist West Germany. The abduction of Schleyer heightened this aspect even more. The state did not by any means react with panic, as has often been said. The state reacted by suppressing all forms of expression which did not support the state of emergency measures. The state ordered all media to follow the line of the Crisis Staff, which [it] most willingly did. All who refused risked a confrontation with the system. Intellectuals, who everyone knew did not sympathize with the RAF, but who nonetheless contradicted the state of emergency, were no longer safe from smear campaigns and repression. The members of the government's Crisis Staff, some of whom had military backgrounds, reacted with the same means in 1977 as the Nazis had done—although the Nazis, of course, went to a far greater degree of barbarity—to prevent and wipe out anti-capitalist and anti-fascist struggles. Under Nazi fascism, and in 1977, the state's policies were aimed at eliminating any space between total loyalty to the state in an emergency situation on the one side and repression on the other.

When it became more clear that the state was prepared to abandon Schleyer [whom the RAF later killed], the RAF gave its approval for a civilian airliner to be hijacked [by the Popular Front for the Liberation of Palestine] in a guerrilla action as part of its own offensive, and this made it appear as though the RAF no longer differentiated between the top and bottom sectors of the society. Although the attempt to free the prisoners from torture was justified, the social-revolutionary dimension of the struggle was now no longer visible. From the break with the system and the rejection of the conditions in the society—the preconditions for any revolutionary movement—had come a break with the society as a whole.

From the 1970s to the 1980s

The RAF had gambled everything and suffered a huge defeat. In the process of struggle until the end of the 1970s, it became clear that the RAF was left with just a few people from the period of the 1968 upheavals. Many people from the '68 movement had given up on movement politics and used their chances to build careers. The RAF, as part of the global anti-imperialist struggle, had taken up the war of liberation within West Germany. The year 1977 had shown, however, that the RAF had neither the political nor the military strength to direct the situation after the subsequent reaction, the domestic war. It was right to make use of the historical situation at the beginning of the 1970s and open a new and previously unknown chapter of struggle in the metropoles in the fight between imperialism and liberation. The experiences of the defeat of 1977 revealed the limitations of the old urban guerrilla concept of the RAF. There needed to be a new concept of liberation.

The front concept of the 1980s was an attempt to achieve this. The RAF wanted new ties and a basis for a joint struggle with radical segments of the resistance movements which had arisen in the late 1970s. But the front concept held on to many of the basic notions of the old project from the 1970s. Armed actions remained the central focus and the decisive moment of the revolutionary process, which was seen as a war of liberation.

The Anti-Imperialist Front of the 1980s

In the early 1980s, there were several struggles directed against inhumane projects of the system, but which were also expressions of the search for free forms of living. A social revolt which sought a new social reality, now.

Thousands of people from these new movements went onto the streets in the 1980s to protest the same thing which the RAF sought to attack since 1979: The militarization policies of the NATO states, which would enable the West to wage "one and a half" wars simultaneously, the war against the Soviet Union and, at the same time, warlike interventions against liberation movements and revolutions, like in Nicaragua, where the first step towards liberation from Western dictatorship had been taken.

The RAF assumed that they would not be alone during this new phase. The concept was fueled by the hope that militant sectors of various movements would join a common front. But this concept failed to recognize that, in the given social situation, only very few people saw any purpose in a liberation struggle on the level of a war. The liberation struggle, whose central moment is that of war, only makes sense when there is a possibility that there are forces in the society who are willing to take it up and expand it—at the very least, the radical elements of the movements.

But even those who were in solidarity—and they were by no means few in number—did not take up the struggle with this in mind. A guerrilla war requires a perspective for expansion to a level of struggle. This is necessary for the existential development of the guerrilla, and we were not able to achieve this.

The RAF's notion of armed action at the focal point of the struggle placed less importance on the political and cultural processes outside of the political-military struggle. Overcoming this strategic direction, which had come from the fundamental structure of the concept in the 1970s, should have been a precondition for any new revolutionary project. The front could not become this new liberation project to remove the distinctions between the movements and the guerrilla.

In the 1980s, the RAF operated under the assumption that a social-revolutionary approach lay in the attacks on the central power structures of imperialism. With this approach, the RAF's politics became increasingly abstract. This led to a split of what should be united: anti-imperialism and social revolution. The social revolutionary outlook disappeared from the theory and praxis of the RAF. The orientation became reduced to the anti-imperialist line, and the result of this was the anti-imperialist front. The RAF was not a factor in social questions. This was a fundamental mistake.

Subsuming all social and political content under the anti-imperialist attack against the "entire system" produced false divisions instead of a process of unity; and it led to a lack of identity on concrete questions and the content of the struggle.

The resonance within the society remained limited, because the proposal to create consciousness in the society and to break the consensus between the state and the society—a central moment of any revolutionary process—disappeared. Instead, the RAF sought to destroy the state's dominance of control by increasing the intensity of its attacks. The priority shifted to the military dimension. This emphasis remained throughout the 1980s and it defined our struggle.

We carried out attacks against NATO projects as well as the military-industrial complex of capital, together with other guerrilla groups in Western Europe; an attempt was made to forge a West European Guerrilla Front comprised of the RAF, Action Directe in France, and the Red Brigades/ PCC in Italy.

. . .

There was a great discrepancy between the willingness of RAF militants to give everything in the confrontation and the ability, at the same time, to seek new ideas for the process of liberation. In this respect, very little was risked.

. . .

We, Most of Whom Became Organized in the RAF Very Late . . .

. . . joined in the hope that our struggle could contribute new impulses for global revolt in the changed conditions. We sought changes for the liberation struggle, for a new path on which we could join ourselves with others. And we wanted to give something back to those who had taken up the struggle before us, and who had died or been sent to prison. The struggle in illegality had a very attractive affect on us. We wanted to break though our borders and be free of everything which confined us within the system.

Armed struggle in illegality was, for us, nothing more than the only possible and necessary way for the liberation process. But also, especially considering the crisis of the left all around the world, we wanted to further develop the urban guerrilla as a possibility and keep illegality as a terrain for the liberation process. But we recognized then that that alone would not be enough. The guerrilla, too, would have to change.

Our hope was to create new ties between the guerrilla and other sectors of the resistance in the society.

. . .

It Was Important for Us, Following the Collapse of East Germany, to Bring Our Struggle in Tune with the New Existing Social Situation

We wanted to take steps to relate to all those people whose dreams had ended with the collapse of the DDR and its annexation into West Germany. Some had realized that "real existing socialism" was not liberation after all. Others, who were part of the opposition to real existing socialism in East Germany, had dreamed of something different from either capitalism or real existing socialism . . . We wanted to relate to all those people, during this historical situation which was unknown to everyone, who had struggled for liberation in confrontation with the West German state and also those who were fed up with the racist and completely reactionary developments unfolding in the now non-existent East Germany. We did not want to abandon these people to resignation, or to the right-wing.

. . .

The Attempt to Anchor the RAF in the 1990s Was an Unrealistic Proposal

We wanted to transform a concept which had arisen from the 1968 movement into a new, social revolutionary and internationalist concept in tune with the 1990s. This was a time when we sought for something new, but—weighed down by the dogmas of the past years—we did not go radically enough beyond the old concept. So we made the same mistakes which all of us made after 1977: We overestimated the support for this continuity of our conception of struggle. Fundamentally, the danger exists of discrediting armed struggle when it is maintained without explaining how it concretely advances the revolutionary process and leads to a strengthening of the liberation struggle. It is important to deal with this issue in a responsible manner, because otherwise the armed struggle becomes discredited— even for another situation, in which it is needed again.

The crisis, when the left reached its limits in the 1980s and began partially to disband, made our attempt to link the RAF into some new project an unrealistic proposal. We were much too late—even to transform the RAF after a period of reflection. Criticism and self-criticism do not aim at ending something, rather at further developing it. In short, the end of the RAF is not the result of our process of (self-)criticism and reflection, rather because it is necessary, because the concept of the RAF does not contain the necessary elements from which something new can arise.

. . .

Following our defeat in 1993, we knew that we couldn't just keep going on as we had since we began the break with our struggle in 1992. We were sure that we had set the correct goals for ourselves, but that we had made some serious tactical mistakes. We wanted to think things over one more time with those who were in prison, and take a new step together.

MORDVERSUCH
in Berlin
10.000 DM BELOHNUNG

Am Donnerstag, dem 14. Mai 1970, gegen
11.00 Uhr wurde anläßlich der Ausführung
des Strafgefangenen ANDREAS BAADER
in Berlin-Dahlem, Miquelstr. 83.
und seiner dabei durch mehrere bewaff-
nete Täter erfolgten Befreiung der
Institutsangestellte Georg Linke durch
mehrere Pistolenschüsse lebensgefährlich
verletzt. Auch zwei Justizvollzugsbeamte
erlitten Verletzungen.

Der Beteiligung an der Tat dringend
verdächtig is die am 7. Oktober 1934 in
Oldenburg geborene Journalisten

Ulrike Meinhof
geschiedene R O H L

Personenbeschreibung: 35 Jahre alt,
165 cm groß, schlank, längliches Ge-
sicht, langes mittelbraunes Haar,
braune Augen.

Die Gesuchte hat am Tattage ihren Wohn-
sitz in Berlin-Schöneberg, Kufsteiner Str. 12, verlassen und ist seitdem flüchtig.
Wer kann Hinweise auf ihren jetzigen Aufenthalt geben?
Für Hinweise, die Aufklärung des Verbrechens und zur Ergreifung der an der
Tat beteiligten Personen führen, hat der Polizeipräsident in Berlin eine
Belohnung von **10.000.-DM** ausgesetzt, Die Belohnung is ausschließlich für
Personen aus der Bevölkerung bestimmt und nicht für Beamte, zu deren Be-
rufspflichten die Verfolgung strafbarer Handlungen gehört, Ihre Zuerkennung
und Verteilung erfolgt unter Ausschluß des Rechtsweges.
Mitteilungen, die auf Wunsch vertraulich behandelt werden, nehmen die
Staatsanwaltschaft in Berlin, 1 Berlin 21, Turmstr. 91 (Telefon 350111) und
der Polizeipräsident in Berlin, 1 Berlin 42, Tempelhofer Damm 1 - 7
(Telefon 691091) sowie jede andere Polizeidienetstelle entgegen.

Berlin im Mai 1970

Der Generalstaatsanwalt
bei dem Landgericht Berlin

In the weeks following the armed freeing of Andreas Baader
from police custody, thousands of these posters featuring Ulrike
Meinhof were posted throughout West Berlin. The headline
reads "Attempted Murder in Berlin, 10,000 DM Reward"—a reference to the shooting of an elderly librarian during the operation. Now available for the first time in three decades,
an exact reproduction of the famous poster. Courtesy of Collection of Richard Huffman, www.baader-meinhof.com.

But in the end, the very hurtful split of one group of the prisoners from us, who
declared us to be enemies, completely erased the very conditions which had given
rise to the RAF in the first place—solidarity and the struggle for collectivity.

The Process of Our Own Liberation . . .

. . . was important to us, and yet we always seemed to become stagnant. We
desired collectivity just as we desired the joint overcoming of all forms of alienation. But the contradiction between war and liberation often got pushed off or
talked away by us. Revolutionary war also produces alienation and structures of
authority, which is in contradiction to liberation. . . .

It Was a Strategic Mistake Not to Build Up a Political-Social Organization Alongside the Illegal, Armed Organization

In no phase of our history was an outreaching, political organization realized in addition to the political-military struggle. The concept of the RAF knew only the armed struggle, with a focus on the political-military attack.

In the formative communiqués of the RAF up to the mid-1970s, this important question was never even posed, nor could it have been. In the metropoles in general, and especially in Germany, there was no previous experience with an urban guerilla. Many things had [to] be discovered and learned along the way, and shown to be true or false in practice. Nevertheless, there was never an orientation to the decisive question, whether the project of liberation can be fulfilled by an illegal organization and the armed struggle—or if the building up of the guerilla should go hand in hand with the expansion of political structures which can grow in the base processes. In January 1976, our imprisoned comrades wrote about this, stating that only an armed struggle from illegality could be a practical–critical opposition to imperialism. The concept in the May 1982 paper also maintained this position, despite all the contradictions and despite the fact that it was an attempt to find a new political association together with other people. Because this concept, too, did not break with the notion that the armed struggle should be central in the metropoles. The political activities which arose from the front process got bogged down in communicating the attacks within the structures of the radical left.

The lack of a political organization for more than 20 years resulted in the continual weakening of the political process. The over-estimation of the political-military actions in the metropoles of the last few decades was the precondition for this concept. The RAF based its strategy on armed struggle, in different ways during different phases, but at no point did it arrive at the point where militant actions aim at: The tactical option of a comprehensive liberation strategy. This weakness also led to the fact that our organization could not transform itself after two decades. The preconditions for placing the focus of the struggle on the political level—which is what we wanted to do in 1992—were not at hand. But, in the end, that was simply the result of fundamental strategic mistakes. The lack of a political-social organization was a decisive mistake by the RAF. It wasn't the only mistake, but it's one important reason why the RAF could not become a stronger liberation project, and in the end the necessary preconditions were lacking to build up a fighting counter-movement searching for liberation, one which could have a strong influence on social developments. The mistakes inherent in the concept, such as these, which accompanied the RAF throughout its entire history show that the concept of the RAF can no longer be relevant in the liberation processes of the future.

The End of the RAF Comes at a Time When the Whole World Is Confronted with the Effects of Neo-Liberalism—The International Struggle against Displacement, Alienation, and for a Just and Fundamentally Different Social Reality Is in Opposition to the Entire Development of Capitalism

Global and inner-societal relations are becoming heightened in the turbulence of the historical developments following the end of real existing socialism. Nevertheless, it is not a contradiction for us to end our project while still recognizing the necessity that everything which is useful and possible must be done so that a world without capitalism can come about, one in which the emancipation of humanity can be realized. Considering the devastating effects of the collapse of real existing socialism world wide, and the mass poverty of millions of people in the former Soviet Union, it's not enough to talk today of the chances which have been brought about by the end of real existing socialism. Nevertheless, we recognize that true liberation was not possible under the model of real existing socialism. It is possible to draw consequences from the anti-emancipatory experiences with the authoritarian and state bureaucratic concepts of real existing socialism and to recognize future paths to liberation.

With the collapse of real existing socialism, the competition between systems ended, meaning that the proponents of the capitalist system no longer feel the need to make their system appear to be "better". In the absence of an ideological check on capital, a process of global unleashing of capital has resulted: All of humanity are to be subjected to the needs of capital. Neo-liberalism is the ideological and economic foundation for a world wide push towards optimization and the evaluation of people and nature according to the demands of capital. Representatives of the system call this "reform" or "modernization".

It is more than clear that the present stage of the development of the system will bring an overwhelming majority of humanity further social and existential difficulty. For the majority of the people in the world, neo-liberalism adds a new dimension to the threats on their lives.

. . .

Paradoxically, the successful maximization of profits by capital and the process of social collapse called forth by it seems to be pushing capitalism to its limits. This development threatens, above all else, to result in further outbreaks of barbarity: From the independent dynamic of system development, this negative process will continue, until such time as there is a proposal for liberation which can call forth a new force to overturn the system. But today, there is not only the defeat of the historic left and the violence of the global social relations, there is also a wealth of rebel movements who can draw on the experiences of the global history of resistance.

In this global development, capitalism, in the metropoles as well, tries to buy social peace by means of "welfare systems". Instead, however, increasingly large segments of the society become marginalized when they are no longer needed in the production process. The "world power" and the "welfare state" can no longer exist together under one roof. In Europe, for example, the old "welfare states" are coming under the political and economic hegemony of Germany, with Germany serving as a racist frontline state in an entire continent which is turning into a police state.

The police and military are deployed against those fleeing from poverty, war, and oppression. A society full of prisons. Cops and security forces tossing the homeless out of the consumer shopping areas, as well as youths and anyone else who upsets the regular customers and the bourgeoisie. The re-introduction of closed facilities as prisons for kids. The attempt to exert total control over refugees in the near future by means of computer chip cards, with other social groups coming later on. Police batons and weapons against the foreseeable revolts by those pushed to the edges. Exclusion, repression, and displacement. Even the total perfection of humans by means of genetic engineering can no longer be considered unthinkable.

Exclusion and repression through a lack of social feeling within the society as well is normal both here and elsewhere. Racism from below threatens the lives of

Jewish prisoners paraded by the SS and local police through the streets of Baden-Baden, November 10, 1938. Courtesy of Yad Vashem Archives.

millions, which in Germany is the murderous mark of the historical continuity which this society carries with it. The exclusion of handicapped persons from above and aggression against them from below are expressions of the day to day brutality of the society. Only people who don't contradict the efficiency of the economic system are desired, as well as anything which can be capitalized. Anything else which is outside of the needs of the capitalist society are given no place. The great many people who can no longer live here, or who no longer want to—and there are many people who chose to end their lives every day—speak of the emptiness of the system and the hardness in the society.

The marketing of people and the violence in the home and on the streets, these are the violence of suppression, the social coldness against others, the violence against women—all of these are expressions of patriarchal and racist conditions.

The RAF always stood in contradiction to the conscious mentality of a large segment of this society. That is a necessary moment in the process of liberation, because it's not only the conditions which are reactionary, rather the conditions produce reactionary character in people, and this continually suppresses their ability to become liberated. Without a doubt, it is a matter of existence to resist and fight against racism and all forms of oppression. Future outlines for liberation must be measured according to this, and they must find a key to unlocking the closed, reactionary consciousness and awakening the desire for emancipation and liberation.

The Reality of the World Today Proves That It Would Have Been Better If the Global Wave of Revolt, Which the RAF Was a Part of, Had Been Successful

The global wave of revolt, which the RAF arose from as well, did not succeed, which does not mean that the destructive and unjust developments up until today can't still be turned around. The fact that we still don't see sufficient answers to these developments weighs more heavily upon us than the mistakes which we made. The RAF came from the revolts of the last decades, which did not exactly foresee how the system would develop, but which at least recognized the threat which it posed. We knew that this system would allow fewer and fewer people around the world to live their lives with dignity. And we also knew that this system seeks total access to people, so that they subjugate themselves to the values of the system and make them their own. Our radicalism sprung from these realizations. For us, we had nothing to lose with this system. Our struggle—the violence with which we resisted these relations—had a difficult, a heavy side. The liberation war has its shadows, too. Attacking people in their capacity as functionaries for the state is a contradiction to the thoughts and feelings of all revolutionaries in the world—it contradicts their notion of liberation. Even when there are phases in the liberation process when this is viewed as necessary, because there are people who desire injustice and oppression and who seek to defend their own power or the power of others. Revolutionaries desire a world in which no one has the right to decide who may live and who may not. Nevertheless, our violence upset some people in an irrational way. The real terror is the normality of the economic system.

The RAF Was Not the Answer for Liberation—It Was One Aspect of It

Although many questions remain open today, we are sure that from the liberation ideas of the future the seed of future relations can arise, if it truly does embrace the variety which is needed to overturn the conditions. It is useless to speak of "the correct line," the aspect of life outside of which everything else seems inefficient, just as it is to seek a revolutionary subject. The project of liberation in the future will know many subjects and a variety of aspects and content, and this had nothing to do with being random. We need a new proposal in which seemingly very different individuals or social groups can be subjects, and yet still be together. In this sense, the liberation project of the future will not contain the old concepts of the German left since 1968, not those of the RAF or other groups. The joy of building an encompassing, anti-authoritarian, and yet binding organizing project of liberation lies before us still, sadly too little attempted up until now. We see that there are people all over the world who are trying this, to finds ways out of the vacuum.

We draw hope from the fact that everywhere, even in the most remote corners of this country—where the cultural hegemony of the fascist right is no longer a seldom thing—there are people who have the courage to join together against racism and neo-nazism, to defend themselves and others and to struggle.

It is necessary to recognize that we are at a dead end and we need to find ways out. So it makes sense to abandon things which can only be carried forward in a theoretical sense. Our decision to end something is the expression of our search for new answers. We know that we are joined with many other people around the world in this search.

There will be many future discussions until all the experiences have been brought together and we have a realistic and reflective picture of history.

We want to be part of a joint liberation. We want to make some of our own processes recognizable, and we want to learn from others.

This excludes the notion of a vanguard which leads the struggle. Although the concept of being the "vanguard" had been dropped from our understanding of the struggle for years, the old concept of the RAF would not allow this to be actually done away with. That's another reason why we had to cut ourselves loose from this concept.

The Guerrillas in the Metropoles Brought the War Back into the Belly of the Beast, to the Imperialist States Which Waged Their Wars Outside Their Own Centers of Power

Despite everything which we could have done better, it was fundamentally correct to oppose the conditions in West Germany and to seek to wage resistance to the continuity of German history. We wanted to open up chances for revolutionary struggle in the metropoles as well.

The RAF took up its own social terrain of struggle and sought to develop it for more than two decades, a terrain which historically knew little resistance, lacked a movement against fascism, and which was characterized by a population loyal to fascism and barbarism. Unlike in other countries, in Germany, liberation from fascism had to come from the outside. There was no self-determined break with fascism "from below" here. There were very few people in this country who resisted fascism; too few with any trace of humanity. Those who struggled in the Jewish resistance, in the communist resistance—in whatever anti-fascist resistance—were right to struggle. And they will always be right. They were the few glimmers of light in the history of this country since 1933, when fascism began to kill off all that was social in this society.

In contrast to these people, the trend in this society was always more or less to accept what those in power said; authority determined what is legitimate. In the social destruction of this society, which was a precondition for the genocide by the Nazis, the indifference to any other essential moment remains today. The RAF broke with German tradition after Nazi fascism and refused to grant it any legitimacy. The RAF came from the revolt against it. It not only rejected this national and social continuity, it waged an internationalist struggle in place of this negation, a struggle whose praxis rejected the ruling conditions in the German state and attacked the military structures of its NATO allies. All over the world, this alliance, in whose hierarchy the USA was the driving force and the unquestioned leader, sought to defeat social rebellions and liberation movements by means of the military and war. The guerrillas in the metropoles brought the war, which the imperialists waged outside their centers of power, back into the belly of the beast.

We answered the violent conditions with the violence of revolt.

It is not possible for us to look back on a smooth and perfect history. But we tried to do something, and in doing so we overstepped many of the ruling powers' laws and the internalized boundaries of bourgeois society.

The RAF was not able to point out the path to liberation. But it contributed for two decades to the fact that there are still thoughts about liberation today. Putting the system in question was and still is legitimate, as long as there is dominance and oppression instead of freedom, emancipation, and dignity for everyone in the world.

There are nine former militants from the struggle of the RAF still in prison. Although the struggle for liberation is far from over, this conflict has become part of history. We support all efforts which seek to get the prisoners from this conflict out of prison upright.

At this time, we'd like to greet and thank all of those who offered us solidarity on our path for the past 28 years, who supported us in various ways, and who struggled together with us in the ways that they could. The RAF was determined to contribute to the struggle for liberation. This revolutionary intervention in this country and in this history would never have taken place if many people, not organized in the RAF themselves, hadn't given a part of themselves to this struggle. A common path lies behind all of us. We hope that we will all find ourselves together again on the unknown and winding paths of liberation.

Our thoughts are with all those around the world who lost their lives in the struggle against domination and for liberation. The goals which they strived for are the goals of today and tomorrow—until all relations have been overturned in which a person is but a lowly object, a downcast, abandoned, and contemptuous being. It is sad that so many gave their lives, but their deaths were not in vain. They live on in the struggles and the future liberation.

We will never forget the comrades of the Popular Front for the Liberation of Palestine (PFLP) who lost their lives in the fall of 1977 in an act of internationalist solidarity, seeking to liberate the political prisoners. Today we would especially like to remember all those who chose to give their all to the armed struggle here, and who lost their lives.

Our memories and all our respect goes out to those whose names we do not know, because we never knew them, and to

Petra Schelm

Georg von Rauch

Thomas Weissbecker

Holger Meins

Katharina Hammerschmidt

Ulrich Wessel

Siegfried Hausner

Werner Sauber

Brigitte Kuhlmann

Wilfried Bose

Ulrike Meinhof

Jan-Carl Raspe

Gudrun Ensslin

Andreas Baader

Ingrid Schubert

Willi-Peter Stoll

Michael Knoll

Elisabeth van Dyck

Juliane Plambeck

Wolfgang Beer

Sigurd Debus

Johannes Timme

Jurgen Peemoeller

Ina Siepmann

Gerd Albartus

Wolfgang Grams

    The revolution says:

I was

I am

I will be again

Red Army Faction
March 1998

Selected Bibliography

ARTICLES

Barich, Bill. 1988. "Ulster Spring." *The New Yorker,* 21 November.

Brenner, Marie. 2003. "France's Scarlet Letter." *Vanity Fair,* June.

Daraghmeh, Mohammed. 2003. "Training Female Suicide Bombers." *Salt Lake City Tribune*, 1 June.

Journal of the American Medical Association. 1997. 278(5)August 6 (special issue on biological warfare and terrorism).

Lugar, Richard G. 2002. "Redefining NATO's Mission: Preventing WMD Terrorism." *Washington Monthly,* Summer.

Newhouse, John. 1985. "A Freemasonry of Terrorism." *The New Yorker,* July 8.

Panich, Leo. "Violence as a Tool of Order and Change: The War on Terrorism and the Anti-Globalization Movement." 2002. *Monthly Review,* January 6.

BOOKS

Adams, James. 1986. *The Financing of Terror—Behind the PLO, IRA, Red Brigades & M-19 Stand the Paymasters*. New York: Simon & Schuster.

Asprey, Robert B. 1997. *War in the Shadows: The Guerilla in History*. New York: Harper Collins.

Atkins, Stephen E. 1992. *Terrorism: A Reference Handbook*. Santa Barbara, Calif.: ABC-CLIO.

Beck, Charles Aronson, Reggie Emilia, Lee Morris, and Ollie Patterson. 1986. *Strike One to Educate One Hundred: The Rise of the Red Brigades in Italy in the 1960–1970s*. Chicago: Seeds Beneath the Snow.

Becker, Julian. 1989. *Hitler's Children—The Story of the Baader-Meinhof Terrorist Gang*. London: Pickwick Books.

Begin, Menachem. 1978. *The Revolt*. New York: Dell.

Bodansky, Yosef. 1999. *bin Laden: The Man Who Declared War on America*. New York: Crown.

Collins, Larry and Dominique LaPierre. 1972. *O Jersualem!* New York: Simon and Schuster.

Coogan, Tim Pat. 1993. *The IRA: A History.* Niwat, Colo.: Roberts Rhinehart Publishers.

Corbin, Jane. 2002. *Al-Qaeda: In Search of the Terror Network that Threatens the World.* New York: Thunder's Mouth Press/Nation Books.

Corson, William R. 1977. *The Armies of Ignorance.* New York: Dial Press/James Wade.

Crenshw, Marsha, and John Pimlott, eds. 1996. *Encyclopedia of World Terrorism.* Armonk, NY: M. E. Sharpe.

Davies, Nicholas. 1999. *Ten Thirty Three—The Inside Story of Britain's Secret Killing Machine in Northern Ireland.* Edinburgh: Mainstream Publishing.

Emerson, Steven. 2002. *American Jihad: The Terrorists Living among Us.* New York: Free Press.

Follain, John. 1999. *Jackal—The Secret Wars of Carlos the Jackal.* London: Orion Books.

Hate Groups in America: A Record of Bigotry and Violence. 1988. New York: Anti-Defamation League of B'nai B'rith.

Hirst, David. 1976. *The Gun and the Olive Branch—The Roots of Violence in the Middle East.* London: Futura Publications.

Hoen, Alan.2002. *Terrorism and Modern Literature: From Joseph Conrad to Ciaran Carson.* New York: Oxford University Press.

Hoffman, Bruce. 1998. *Inside Terrorism.* London: Victor Gollancz.

Jenkins, Brian, and Paul Wilkinson. 2001. *Aviation Terrorism and Security.* London: Frank Cass Publishers.

Laqueur,Walter. 1977. *Terrorism.* Boston: Little Brown.

———, ed. 1978. *The Terrorism Reader: A Historical Anthology.* New York: New American Library.

———. 2001. *A History of Terrorism.* Somerset, N.J.: Transaction Publishers.

Leventhal, Paul, and Yonah Alexander, eds. 1987. *Preventing Nuclear Terrorism.* Lexington, Mass.: Lexington Books.

Long, David E. 1990. *Anatomy of Terrorism.* New York: The Free Press.

McKittrick, David, Seamus Kelters, Brian Feeny, and Chris Thornton. 1999. *Lost Lives—The Stories of the Men, Women, and Children Who Died as a Result of the Northern Ireland Troubles.* Edinburgh: Mainstream Publishing.

Medhurst, Paul. 2000. *Global Terrorism.* Denver, Colo.: United Nations Institute for Training and Research Programme of Correspondence Instruction.

Miller, Judith, Stephen Engelberg, and William Broad. 2001. *Germs: Biological Weapons and America's Secret War.* New York: Simon & Schuster.

Quandt, William B. 2001. *Peace Process: American Diplomacy and the Arab-Israeli Conflict since 1967.* Berkeley: University. of California Press.

Reeve, Simon. 1999. *New Jackals—Ramsi Yousef, Osama bin Laden and the Future of Terrorism.* London: Andrê Deutsch.

———. 2000. *One Day in September.* New York; Arcade.

Ruthven, Malise. 2002. *A Fury for God: The Islamist Attack on America.* New York: Granta.

Schweitzer, Glenn E., and Carole Dorsch Sweitzer. 2002. *A Faceless Enemy: The Origins of Modern Terrorism*. Cambridge, Mass.: Perseus Books.

Seale, Patrick. 1992. *Abu Nidal: A Gun for Hire*. New York: Random House.

Shanty, Frank G., Raymond Picquet, eds., and John Lalla, document ed. 1996. *Encyclopedia of World Terrorism, 1996–2002; Encyclopedia of World Terrorism: Documents*. 2 vols. Armonk, N.Y.: M. E. Sharpe.

Stepniak, Sergei. 1973. *Underground Russia: Revolutionary Profiles and Sketches from Life*. Westport, Conn.: Hyperion Press.

Stern, Jessica. 1999. *The Ultimate Terrorists*. Cambridge, Mass.: Harvard University Press.

Vanstrum, Glenn S., and James P. Sterba. 2003. *Terrorism and International Justice*. New York: Oxford University Press.

Wade, Wyn Craig. 1987. *The Fiery Cross*. New York: Simon & Schuster.

Whittaker, David J., ed. 2003. *Terrorism Reader*. New York: Routledge.

Williams, Paul L. 2002. *Al Qaeda: Brotherhood of Terror*. Indianapolis, Ind.: Alpha.

Wright, Robin. 1985. *Sacred Rage*. New York: Linden Press.

PAPERS AND REPORTS

Alexander, Yonah. 1994. "Middle East Terrorism: Selected Group Profiles." Jewish Institute for National Security Affairs, Washington, D.C., September.

Bell, Daniel. 2002. "Revolutionary Terrorism: Three Justifications." *Correspondence: And International Review of Culture and Society*, 9 (spring).

Braithwaite, John. 2003. Pre-Empting Terrorism.. Paper. Law Program, Research School of Social Sciences, Australian National University.

Epstein, Simon. 1993. "Patterns in Antisemitism: The Dynamics of Anti-Jewish Violence in Western Countries since the 1950s." Paper. Vidal Sassoon Center for the Study of Antisemitism..

Hudson, Rex A. 1999. "The Sociology and Psychology of Terrorism: Who Becomes a Terrorist and Why?" Report.: Federal Research Division, Library of Congress. Washington, D.C., September.

"Irish Nationalist Terrorism Outside Ireland: Out-of-Theatre Operations 1972–1993." 1994. Report. Canadian Security Intelligence Service, Ottawa. February.

Katzman, Kenneth. 2002. "Terrorism: Near Eastern Groups and State Sponsors, 2002." Report. Congressional Research Service, Library of Congress, Washington, D.C.

Lord, Alexandra M. 2002. "A Brief History of Biowarfare." Paper. Office of Public Health Service Historian, January.

Newsome, Jennifer L. 2001. "Nuclear Terrorism: A New Kind of War." Paper. University of Texas at Austin, December 5.

Purver, Ron. 1995. "Chemical and Biological Terrorism: The Threat according to the Open Literature." Canadian Security Intelligence Service, Ottawa, June.

Seger, Karl A.. 2001. "Left-Wing Extremism: The Current Threat." Paper prepared for U.S. Department of Energy. Oak Ridge Institute for Science and Education, April.

Smith, G. (Tim). 1991. "Terrorism and the Rule of Law: Dangerous Compromise in Colombia." Canadian Security Intelligence Service, Ottawa, October.

Tamimi, Azzam. 1998. "The Legitimacy of Palestinian Resistance: An Islamist Perspective." Paper presented at the 7th Annual Conference of the Centre for Policy Analysis on Palestine, in Washington, D.C., September 11.

Wilkinson, Paul. 1995. "Terrorism, Motivations and Causes." Ottawa: Canadian Security Intelligence.

Index

Page numbers that appear in bold indicate the terrorist group histories included in Chapter 6.

About the Author

MICHAEL KRONENWETTER is an independent author. He has written many books on U.S. history and social issues, including *Encylcopedia of Modern American Social Issues, Capital Punishment: A Reference Handbook, America in the 1960s,* and *How Democratic Is the United States?*